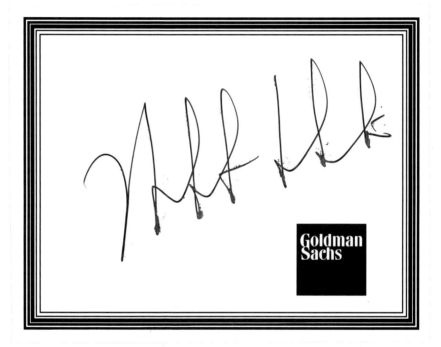

The Price of
Liberty

The Price of
Liberty

PAYING FOR AMERICA'S WARS

Robert D. Hormats

TIMES BOOKS
HENRY HOLT AND COMPANY
NEW YORK

TIMES BOOKS
HENRY HOLT AND COMPANY, LLC
PUBLISHERS SINCE 1866
175 FIFTH AVENUE
NEW YORK, NEW YORK 10010
WWW.HENRYHOLT.COM

LIBRARY OF CONGRESS CATALOGING-IN-PUBLICATION DATA

HORMATS, ROBERT D.
    THE PRICE OF LIBERTY : PAYING FOR AMERICA'S WARS / ROBERT D. HORMATS.—1ST ED.
    P. CM.
    INCLUDES BIBLIOGRAPHICAL REFERENCES AND INDEX.
    ISBN-13: 978-0-8050-8253-1
    ISBN-10: 0-8050-8253-0
    1. DEBTS, PUBLIC—UNITED STATES. 2. FINANCE, PUBLIC—UNITED STATES—HISTORY.
3. UNITED STATES. DEPT. OF DEFENSE—APPROPRIATIONS AND EXPENDITURES.
4. UNITED STATES—ARMED FORCES—APPROPRIATIONS AND EXPENDITURES.
5. WAR—ECONOMIC ASPECTS—UNITED STATES. 6. NATIONAL SECURITY—UNITED
STATES—FINANCE—HISTORY. I. TITLE.

HJ8101.H67 2007
336.3'40973—DC22   2006051416

HENRY HOLT BOOKS ARE AVAILABLE FOR SPECIAL PROMOTIONS AND PREMIUMS.
FOR DETAILS CONTACT: DIRECTOR, SPECIAL MARKETS.

FIRST EDITION 2007

DESIGNED BY MERYL SUSSMAN LEVAVI

PRINTED IN THE UNITED STATES OF AMERICA
2 4 6 8 10 9 7 5 3 1

To the memory of my parents,

Ruth and Saul Hormats,

in deep gratitude for their love and inspiration

While the observance of that good faith, which is the basis of public credit, is recommended by the strongest inducements of political expediency, it is enforced by considerations of still greater authority. There are arguments for it, which rest on the immutable principles of moral obligation. And in proportion as the mind is disposed to contemplate, in the order of Providence, an intimate connection between public virtue and public happiness, will be its repugnancy to a violation of those principles.

This reflection derives additional strength from the nature of the debt of the United States. It was the price of liberty. The faith of America has been repeatedly pledged for it, and with solemnities, that give peculiar force to the obligation.

—Alexander Hamilton, "Report on Public Credit,"

January 9, 1790

Contents

Introduction

A COUNTRY BORN OF WAR AND DEBT

American history offers many political and economic lessons. But looking back over this nation's more than two hundred years, one central, constant theme emerges: sound national finances have proved to be indispensable to the country's military strength. Without the former, it is difficult over an extended period of time to sustain the latter. Generations of leaders have come to recognize that if the country chronically lives beyond its means or misallocates its financial resources, it risks eroding its economic base and jeopardizes its ability to fund its national security requirements. These considerations are particularly vital today, when terrorists seek to create turmoil in American society and destroy the crucial economic infrastructure and the institutions that underpin U.S. prosperity and stability. Understanding our past can aid us today in putting America's finances on a more sustainable track.

As commander of the Revolutionary army, George Washington pleaded repeatedly with the Continental Congress for the funds to pay and supply his troops. But because that Congress had no taxing power, it was frequently unable to provide the money Washington needed, so the army was deprived of vital provisions and vulnerable to desertions. The desperate Congress turned to Benjamin Franklin and John Adams to seek loans from France and the Netherlands. After considerable coaxing, these nations furnished money critically needed by the army. But this frustrating experience convinced Washington and his young lieutenant Alexander Hamilton that the new American nation required a sound financial system, solidly based government credit, and a predictable flow of tax revenues if it was going to be able to marshal sufficient resources to defend itself in the future.

In January 1790, Hamilton, by then the country's first secretary of the Treasury, confronted the American people with a stark fact: the nation had run up a huge debt fighting the Revolutionary War. This debt, he wrote, was the "price of liberty," and the new government had to repay it. The future creditworthiness of the United States, and ultimately its security and ability to finance future wars, would depend on how successfully and faithfully this was done.

Over the course of the next two centuries, America's wartime leaders have faced challenges similar to those confronted by Washington and Hamilton. Most have recognized that it is not enough to have a large number of troops, sound military strategy, and able generals to fight a war; the country also needed a sound financial strategy and skillful leaders at the Treasury and in Congress to ensure that the money was available to meet extraordinary military expenses. The techniques American officials have employed to generate these funds under the duress of war have produced dramatic innovations in the nation's tax and borrowing policies, innovations that lasted long beyond the conflict during which they were introduced and many of which remain in effect today. America's wars have been fiscally as well as politically transforming events; changes that could not have gained public acceptance in quieter times won support when they answered the urgent requirements of war.

Presidents at War

Americans today tend to take for granted that when the country fights a war, sufficient resources will be forthcoming to provide the troops with pay, weaponry, supplies, and equipment. This was not always the case. After the Revolution, the government's ability to obtain needed financial resources was highly problematic. During the War of 1812, lack of money jeopardized the country's very survival. Prior to the Civil War, there was no national income tax; it was imposed during the war in a desperate attempt to obtain more revenue and demonstrate fiscal fairness, but was allowed to phase out afterward and was not revived for another half century.

As the nation's economic condition and financial institutions strengthened, so did its capacity to mobilize the immense sums necessary for war.

In the twentieth century, America's ability to generate colossal amounts of tax revenues, conduct massive bond drives, and produce great volumes of weaponry became critical to its military successes. Without these, the country would not have been able to field large numbers of well-equipped forces to fight the two world wars and to project power into far-flung parts of the globe during the Cold War that followed.

But the story of how the United States has paid for its wars is only partly about money and finance. It is also about the political skills and vision of America's leaders. From Hamilton's time onward, the politics of financing a war has been inextricably tied to the politics of the war itself. Leaders have had to confront fundamental questions about equity: who would pay, how they would pay, and how the needs of war would relate to other national economic priorities. While military battles were being fought between the United States and its enemies, financial battles were being fought among powerful interests and politicians at home.

Toward the end of World War I, President Woodrow Wilson urged Congress to set aside domestic politics in the midst of the hostilities. They never were, during that war or any other war. Methods of paying for a given war have been the subject of contentious debates, featuring vigorous and often acrimonious competition among egos, political parties, ideologies, classes, regional interests, and economic philosophies. In the charged environment that often accompanies war, presidents have found that fiscal policy cannot only be about raising large sums of money, as important as that is. It has also been about finding ways to resolve internal differences in order to unite the country behind the war effort and maximize the productive output of the economy. If the government raises large sums at the cost of dividing the country, the goals that the country is fighting for abroad would be undermined from within. If the methods political leaders employ to secure the funds for a war are seen by large portions of the population—and particularly by low-income groups who supply the majority of troops in a war—as unfair, support for the war effort would suffer. And if the methods chosen to raise money weaken the economy—the foundation of the nation's military power—that, too, would undercut the war effort.

Forging wartime fiscal policy in America has been far from simple. Presidents have frequently faced congressional resistance to their massive tax and borrowing requests, occasionally even from those in their own party. As the War of 1812 began, James Madison's request for appropriations was blocked by a faction within his own Jeffersonian Republican

Party; there was also aggressive resistance from the Federalists, who opposed the war and sought to undermine Madison's military strategy by preventing the government from borrowing the money it needed. Early in Abraham Lincoln's administration, influential congressional Republicans balked at creating a federal bureaucracy to collect the Civil War income tax. Woodrow Wilson's World War I tax requests were frequently opposed by congressional Republicans and significantly altered by congressional Democrats. At the height of World War II, legislators on both sides of the aisle combined to slash Franklin D. Roosevelt's revenue requests. During the Vietnam War, Lyndon B. Johnson was forced by a resolute coalition of Democrats and Republicans to alter his tax and spending proposals. During the mid-1980s military buildup, Ronald Reagan encountered opposition from both parties to his fiscal policies. And prior to the first Gulf War, George H. W. Bush was bitterly attacked by Republicans when he supported a budget-cutting compromise that included a tax increase. For the most part, however, all sides in these often bruising confrontations eventually were willing to put aside parochial interests to ensure that the military was well supplied and well armed. And in the heat of these battles, each generation of wartime leaders learned valuable lessons and developed innovative fund-raising techniques that were instructive for their successors.

The Tradition of Paying Down Wartime Debt

A central feature of U.S. fiscal policy for the first century and a half of its history was a bipartisan tradition of paying down wartime debt as rapidly as possible. For many decades, it was a national compulsion. The Founding Fathers established a principle of avoiding debt when there was no war or other national emergency and quickly reducing the debt that was accumulated during such times.

In his farewell address, President Washington emphasized the need for "vigorous exertion in time of peace to discharge the debts which unavoidable wars may have occasioned, not ungenerously throwing upon posterity the burdens we ourselves ought to bear." Posterity was a compelling preoccupation of the Founding Fathers. They spoke of it often, seeing themselves as representing the interests of future generations of Americans as well as their own. In his second inaugural address, Jefferson echoed Washington's sentiments, emphasizing the need to avoid "encroaching on the right of future generations by burdening them with the debts of the past." In later years, populists and progressives who shared the Jeffersonian philosophy sought to prevent the accumulation of large amounts of debt. They feared that the wealthy holders of government bonds would force Congress to impose high duties and excise taxes on the goods purchased by the working class to enable the Treasury to service the interest due on the bonds.

Over the next century and a half, the principle of paying down debt was almost religiously adhered to. During the War of 1812, the national debt nearly tripled but then was sharply reduced as military spending was cut and a booming economy produced increased customs and excise tax revenues. In eighteen of the twenty years that followed, the government recorded budget surpluses, and during the 1830s the national debt was eliminated during Andrew Jackson's administration. By the end of the Civil War, Union debt had exploded to roughly forty times its 1860 level. After the war, the nation recorded twenty-eight years of budget surpluses, reducing that debt by two-thirds. During World War I, the nation's debt increased over twentyfold, but surpluses during the next eleven years reduced it by more than a third before the Great Depression caused it to climb again. World War II saw the national debt rise sixfold, to a record 110 percent of the gross domestic product (GDP). However, from the war's end through 1960, the government recorded surpluses half the time, even though it faced the high cost of financing postwar reconstruction in Europe and countering the new Soviet threat. Prudent fiscal policy during that period, coupled with a thriving economy, brought the debt down to 60 percent of GDP at the end of the Eisenhower administration.

The Cold War, which began in the late 1940s and ended in the early 1990s, presented a new financial challenge for the United States. In the past, there had been a sharp line of demarcation between periods of war and periods of peace, between mobilization and demobilization. The nation did not have a tradition of a large peacetime military. In the post-Revolutionary period, Americans were deeply suspicious of the very notion of a peacetime standing army, fearing a powerful individual or cabal could potentially use it to seize power, and perhaps even restore a monarchy. The vast majority at the time believed that citizen militias should primarily be relied upon for the nation's security.

During the Cold War, however, a large standing army was needed because of the constant threat to American and Allied security posed by the Soviet Union and its client nations. That required consistently large defense budgets relative to past periods when the country was not engaged in a major shooting war. The Cold War was also punctuated by two "hot wars," in Korea and in Vietnam, during which mobilization and military expenses spiked. The costly nuclear arms race, along with enormous expenditures on conventional weapons, required the appropriation of trillions of dollars from the 1950s through the 1980s at a time when escalating social spending imposed heavy demands on the budget. A substantial portion of the cost of these defense and social programs was met through borrowing. In the face of these requirements, the historic commitment to avoid accumulating debt except in times of national threat faded away; Keynesians as well as advocates of supply-side economic policy, at varying times, used deficit spending as a technique for boosting economic growth.

The Challenge Ahead

In the early years of the twenty-first century, the United States is confronted with the challenge of financing a new type of war—the war on terrorism. In the words of a 2006 Pentagon report, it is likely to be a "Long War" and is being fought in parallel with prolonged ground wars in Iraq and Afghanistan. Moreover, the country faces additional security threats, including increased nuclear proliferation, a collapse of moderate governments in the Middle East, a broadening of military conflicts in that region, and instability among major oil suppliers.

The approach taken by the administration and Congress to financing the U.S. role in these conflicts has been a substantial departure from past practices. The terrorist attacks of 9/11 appropriately triggered big increases in military and homeland-security appropriations. These were accompanied, however, by a wave of nonsecurity-related spending, including billions of dollars for items of low national priority. Two years after 9/11, Congress also enacted a large tax cut to stimulate a sluggish economy, but it did so with relatively little consideration of its significant long-term revenue costs and whether it was appropriate during a period of elevated national security spending.

Past wartime administrations and Congresses had eliminated, postponed, or reduced funding for low-priority domestic projects in order to make room in the budget for additional high-priority military spending. They also raised taxes to generate more resources for their war effort. Congress had never before increased nonsecurity spending and cut taxes while also appropriating large sums to fight a war. By supporting and signing expensive spending and tax legislation, President George W. Bush broke with a tradition that had extended from Madison through Lincoln, Wilson, Franklin Roosevelt, Truman, and, eventually, Johnson and Reagan. All of them insisted on, or at least acquiesced in, wartime tax increases, cuts in civilian programs, and sometimes both, as they devoted more resources to the nation's military requirements.

The chapters that follow describe how past generations have marshalled the financial resources to meet the security needs of the nation during periods of war, tracing and describing how earlier administrations and Congresses have reconciled competing political agendas to assemble massive amounts of financial resources in support of the nation's armed forces. This tale is as much a part of the history of the nation as the conflicts themselves.

These issues take on a new urgency today. The war on terrorism—against enemies seeking nuclear, chemical, and biological weapons to kill large numbers of Americans and seriously damage the U.S. economy—poses a unique financial challenge. Like the Cold War, it will require constant and elevated military, intelligence, and foreign-policy-related spending and is likely to be punctuated by periods of high alert, dangerous threats, and perhaps severe crises. But the financial challenge of this war goes beyond that of the Cold War.

Osama Bin Laden has made clear his desire to disrupt and destabilize the American economy. He has boasted that the attacks of 9/11 struck the U.S. economy "in the heart"—claiming that Al Qaeda spent only $500,000 while the United States lost over $500 billion. Experts believe that in the future, Al Qaeda or other groups of global terrorists spawned or inspired by it intend to deploy weapons of mass economic disruption. The U.S. government will have to spend large sums on all facets of homeland security to prevent another attack. In addition, it will have to win the battle for the hearts and minds of large numbers of people who might be attracted to radical terrorist movements. And it must also be able to mobilize resources for recovery in the event another attack should occur—and the amounts required in that event would likely be far greater than after 9/11.

America's leaders have to find ways to meet these critical security needs while addressing another long-term financial challenge: the rapidly rising retirement and health-care costs of an aging population. Other generations have faced significant defense spending requirements, but none has confronted them along with such an imposing combination of nondefense budgetary demands. Social Security, Medicare, and Medicaid will place unprecedented financial burdens on the budget for decades to come. Ultimately, their costs and those of protecting America's national security will clash unless a long-term fiscal strategy can be found for meeting both priorities. It must include a more rigorous prioritization of resource allocation, curbs on nonessential spending, tax policy that avoids chronic deficits, and matching payouts under entitlement programs more closely to the money flowing in.

Further, America's heavy dependence on foreign capital exacerbates the financial threat facing the country. These early years of the twenty-first century mark the first time since the Revolutionary War period that the U.S. government has been so dependent on funds from abroad during wartime. In 2006, foreign private investors and governments bought over half of all newly issued Treasury securities, which means that foreigners financed over half of the U.S. budget deficit. Central banks abroad keep over 70 percent of their reserves in dollar assets. Another terrorist attack could precipitate a dramatic reduction of capital inflows or even an exodus of funds. With the country's high dependence on overseas capital, these developments could trigger a spike in U.S. interest rates and a collapse in the value of the dollar, further disrupting an already damaged economy.

The new century presents the country with new kinds of security threats, new demographic challenges, new health-care demands, and new external pressures from global trade and finance. An extensive reexamination of fiscal policy has taken place at the outset of most major wars in U.S. history. Yet today the United States is living in a post-9/11 world with a pre-9/11 fiscal policy. These new circumstances require a realignment of policies and priorities to meet the unique financial challenges posed by the global war on terrorism in the face of the equally unprecedented requirements posed by America's aging population and the rising heath-care needs of its society. Although U.S. leaders have warned that the war against terrorism could last for decades, the country lacks a multidecade financial strategy to address that challenge. With such large sums of money committed by past legislation and such large deficits on the horizon, the flexibility to respond to new dangers is badly constrained. The current long-term direction of U.S. fiscal policy is inconsistent with, and could ultimately undermine, America's national security. A heavily debt-laden, overobligated, revenue-squeezed government, highly dependent on foreign capital, creates major security vulnerabilities. The long war on terrorism requires a sound long-term financial strategy.

1

Hamilton's Vision

SECURING THE NATION'S FINANCES

VIGOROUS EXERTION IN TIME OF PEACE [IS REQUIRED] TO DIS-
CHARGE THE DEBTS WHICH UNAVOIDABLE WARS MAY HAVE OC-
CASIONED, NOT UNGENEROUSLY THROWING UPON POSTERITY
THE BURDENS WE OURSELVES OUGHT TO BEAR.

—GEORGE WASHINGTON

Few of the multitudes of bankers and lawyers hurrying past the forty-four-story office building that currently stands at 57 Maiden Lane, in New York's financial district, are likely to be aware that more than two hundred years earlier a defining moment in America's history occurred there. At a dinner on that spot, in the home of Thomas Jefferson, Alexander Hamilton and James Madison reached a compromise that resolved a bitter and divisive dispute about how to repay the debts incurred by the states during the American Revolution—a dispute that threatened the very unity of the newly formed United States.

The just-born nation was highly indebted and had no plan to repay its domestic or foreign Revolutionary War obligations. It faced a potential collapse of its creditworthiness that would have left it unable to borrow funds to pay for military mobilization in the event of a widely anticipated future war with Britain or France. It was a moment in America's history—one like many that have followed over the centuries—that underscored how decisions on financing the country's security have proven to be a catalyst for shaping its institutions and many of its core values.

In 1789, Hamilton and the Congress had agreed on a plan to restructure the debt incurred by the national government during the Revolution. The old debt would be replaced with more credible financial instruments backed by the federal collection of customs duties and taxes. The proposal enjoyed strong political support, and holders of the old wartime obligations welcomed these as replacements because of their federal government guarantee and the revenue streams to back them. However, the question of how to deal with the war debts incurred by the states proved to be highly controversial. In 1790, an estimated $25 million of state debt remained outstanding. Virginia and a few other Southern states had paid off much of their war obligations, but other states, including Massachusetts, still carried large amounts of unpaid liabilities. The issue was whether the federal government should step in. Hamilton believed that these unpaid state debts undermined the creditworthiness of the entire nation and insisted that the federal government assume responsibility.

The situation put creditors of some states at a disadvantage relative to others and to creditors of the federal government. Hamilton warned that this lack of equity would "operate injuriously, both for the creditors and the credit of the United States." He also worried that the states, whose main source of revenue in the past had been customs duties, the collection of which under the new Constitution was now reserved exclusively for the federal government, might challenge that provision if they remained responsible for repaying their war debts. Hamilton believed that if the federal government were to assume responsibility for paying off state obligations, such disruptive measures would be less likely. In addition, he thought that holders of federal bonds that replaced state debt would have a new reason to shift loyalties from their states to the national government. In particular, these bondholders would support the authority of the federal government to collect taxes and duties to ensure the bonds' repayment.

For months, legislation authorizing "assumption" of state debts had been blocked in Congress by James Madison, then a leading member of the House of Representatives from Virginia, and a Southern coalition that he headed. Southerners feared assumption would lead to an unhealthy concentration of financial power in the hands of the federal government at the expense of the states. On June 2, 1790, the House of Representatives, influenced heavily by Madison, voted down Hamilton's proposed bill providing for federal assumption of state debts.

Meanwhile, Hamilton and Madison were at odds on another issue—"Residency," the question of where to locate the permanent federal capital. Again regional issues played a major role in the debate. Southerners perceived a threat to their economic and political interests from Northern domination of the federal government, which they charged was an outgrowth of the current location of the capital in New York. Moreover, they were generally suspicious of urban life and culture, and believed the strength and stability of the new country lay in its rural roots. Supported by Thomas Jefferson, who was then the secretary of state in the Washington administration, Madison urged that the capital be relocated to a southern and more rural location, near Georgetown, on the banks of the Potomac River. Hamilton preferred that it stay in New York, his own political base.

To complicate the issue, the Pennsylvania congressional delegation lobbied for the capital to be moved to Philadelphia, where much of America's young history already had been made. For several weeks, work on a compromise had been under way but no agreement had been reached and tempers were beginning to fray. The final deal was struck over a dinner served up by Jefferson, who had cultivated his widely appreciated skills as a host during his years of entertaining in Monticello and a prolonged stay in Paris in the 1780s.

Jefferson was anxious to facilitate an accommodation. Influential Southerners were beginning to talk of taking up arms against the North and splitting the country. The prominent Virginia revolutionary hero Henry "Light Horse Harry" Lee (later to be the father of Robert E. Lee) wrote to Madison complaining of "a monopoly that will take place from the northern hives" and asserting, "[I would] rather myself submit to all the hazards of war and risk the loss of everything dear to me in life, than to live under the rule of a fixed insolent northern majority." He urged a "change of the seat of government to the territorial center . . . to effect a material change." In this tense atmosphere, Jefferson saw compromise as critical to avoid a breakup of the country. He realized that, even if this extreme outcome could be avoided, a continued impasse over state debt repayment would make "our credit . . . burst and vanish." He recognized the security implications of the matter. "The possession of a good credit," he observed, was "indispensable to the present system of carrying on war."

The final "deal" made at 57 Maiden Lane—the Compromise of 1790—secured Hamilton's goal of financial consolidation and Madison's desire for a southern capital. Hamilton agreed to encourage a few of his supporters to accept the Potomac site; Madison agreed to end his campaign against assumption and to free up a handful of his supporters to vote in its favor, although he would not do so himself. On July 16, the House passed the Residence Act, authorizing the construction of the permanent capital on the Potomac (the precise site was to be selected by President Washington); Philadelphia was designated as the temporary capital. Two weeks later, the House narrowly passed the Assumption Act. Together, these two pieces of legislation preserved the unity of the young nation. Jefferson later claimed that Hamilton had deceived him into supporting the agreement as it related to assumption but, nonetheless, took pleasure in the knowledge that he had brokered the "compromise which was to save the union."

Many times in America's history, financially transforming events have taken place in response to a threat to the country's security. This was the first, and in many ways the most significant, because it occurred at a moment when the very survival of the nation was on the line.

A Bold Treasury Secretary

As a key participant in this compromise and most other major political events of this era, Alexander Hamilton was the driving force in establishing both the fiscal policy of President George Washington's administration and the financial system of the United States. In approach and style of argument, he was far removed from the Virginians who were to be his adversaries throughout much of the post-Revolutionary period. Historian Joseph Ellis described the contrast: "While Madison and Jefferson had come through the Virginia school of politics, which put a premium on an understated style that emphasized indirection and stealth, Hamilton had come out of . . . impoverished origins in the Caribbean . . . which produced a dashing, out-of-my-way style that imposed itself ostentatiously much in the manner of the bayonet charge he had led at Yorktown."

Hamilton played the dominant role in American finances during this period in part because of his brilliance and in part because he had been named the country's first Treasury secretary, but not to be underestimated was the fact that he enjoyed the strong support of his president. Hamilton had the unique ability among his generation of leaders to understand and respond to the needs of George Washington. "As Washington's aide-de-camp during the war, Hamilton had occasionally shown himself to be a somewhat feisty and headstrong surrogate son," Ellis noted, "but his loyalty to his mentor was unquestioned, and his affinity for the way Washington thought was unequalled."

Beginning with Washington, U.S. presidents have placed primary responsibility for management of the nation's finances in the hands of their Treasury secretaries. They have especially done so in times of war, when the commander in chief has turned most of his attention to military matters. Hamilton's wartime successors have been instrumental in reshaping the government's borrowing techniques and the nation's tax system in order to mobilize massive sums to support military requirements. Each drew lessons from the experiences of his predecessors, yet each also recognized that the scope and character of the economic and political challenges he confronted demanded new and generally more ambitious methods for raising funds. This search for successively bolder techniques during wartime produced transformational changes in America's financial system.

And, like James Madison, influential legislators also have played decisive roles in shaping financial policy in response to threats to America's security. Senior members of Congress who followed in Madison's footsteps have made crucial contributions to the nation's wartime approach to taxation, borrowing, and resource allocation. On many occasions, they differed sharply with the president, even when they were members of his political party. These frequently colorful and often highly assertive men pushed through many of the most innovative and controversial changes in the nation's financial system, the first income tax and the creation of the "greenback" as the nation's currency being two prominent examples.

The battles often were waged at the most partisan level. As the historian Arthur Schlesinger Jr. reminds us, "presidents in wartime remained objects of criticism and dissent." Most presidents have avoided becoming personally involved in the day-to-day, month-to-month business of pressuring Congress to raise the large amounts of new resources necessary to finance a war. They have given major speeches urging Americans to pay higher taxes, buy bonds, and endure economic sacrifice during wartime, sent numerous messages to Congress in support of their proposed revenue and spending legislation, and twisted congressional arms. But as in the case of Hamilton, each Treasury secretary has generally been left more or less on his own to do the heavy lifting—to craft legislative initiatives, as well as to work with and at times confront Congress in order to obtain its support for increases in revenues and borrowing.

As he shaped the economic and financial policies of post-Revolutionary America, Hamilton studied the financial practices of major European nations, particularly Britain, and was impressed by their capacity to borrow large sums to wage major wars. He recognized, too, that the ability of the United States' first government, the Continental Congress, to obtain loans from France and the Netherlands had been central to its victory in the Revolution.

With these lessons in mind, Hamilton presented his *First Report on Public Credit* to Congress on January 9, 1790. It was as important a national security document as it was a financial one. At its very beginning, he noted, "Loans in times of public danger, especially from foreign war, are found an indispensable resource, even to the wealthiest" of nations. To obtain foreign loans, a country had to establish its creditworthiness—its capacity to assure potential lenders that wartime debt could and would be repaid. For the fledgling American nation, overseas creditworthiness was especially vital. The United States, Hamilton said, was "possessed of little active wealth, or, in other words, little moneyed capital." In a war, the need for such capital would escalate, but because so little was available at home, a large portion would have to come from abroad. "The necessity for that resource [foreign loans]," he wrote, "must in such emergencies, be proportionately urgent."

Hamilton felt sound credit was also essential for the nation to build a prosperous economy, which should be based on thriving manufacturing and commerce. He recommended a system of protective customs duties. The prosperous, strong America he envisaged also needed a strong central bank, modeled on the Bank of England. The new bank would be partially owned by the government but operate on private-market principles; it would ensure a stable currency, supervise other banks, and lend money to the Treasury.

The first step in establishing the nation's fiscal soundness under Hamilton's plan was to restructure and faithfully repay its Revolutionary War debt. With America's credit on the line, Hamilton devised a plan to "fund" the debt—which meant redeeming the old obligations with new long-term bonds and setting aside revenues each year to service and repay them. The new bonds were to bear the full faith and credit of the federal government. He considered the plan an integral part of a larger vision for America—a unified country, headed by a strong central government, capable of countering fractious regional and local loyalties, and able to mobilize the resources required to meet public needs in times of peace and to defend the country in times of war.

In 1790, the federal government had only minor domestic expenses, so peacetime expenditures did not present major financial challenges. But wars cost a lot of money, and the United States was still a minor power constantly under threat from the world's two superpowers, Britain and France. If it ever had to fight one of them, it would require foreign loans. Success in conducting such a future war required, as Hamilton wrote, that the government be able to "borrow, at pleasure, considerable sums on moderate terms" in order to distribute "over successive years, the extraordinary [financial] efforts, found indispensable" in wartime. Levying high taxes to pay for a war, as opposed to relying more heavily on borrowing, would mean "great disturbance and oppressiveness" for the people. For Hamilton, "war without credit would mean more than a great calamity—it would be ruin."

For the funding plan to succeed, the new and as yet untested U.S. government would have to assume responsibility for repaying all of the old Revolutionary War debts. To do so, it needed a steady stream of revenues. Those being asked to accept the new bonds had to be assured that the government's tax receipts would be sufficient to service the interest as it came due and—ultimately—to redeem the securities.

The Taxing Power

Hamilton had a special problem in raising the revenues to service and pay down the Revolutionary debt. British colonial rule had produced strong and widespread antipathy to taxes. Resistance to onerous and arbitrary taxes imposed by the British on the American colonies, after all, had been a driving force behind the Revolution.

A fervent populism had emerged in late-eighteenth-century America, particularly among agrarian interests—yeoman farmers, small-town craftsmen, and rural tradesmen. Unlike most European nations, America did not have a single center of political and economic power like London or Paris, and there was great suspicion of concentrating power in one place. To revolutionary-minded Americans, that spelled a threat to their newly won liberties. The colonies had been separate political entities; each had its own assembly, the members of which increasingly reflected their constituents' seething resentment of the abuses of the British Crown.

After the Revolution, distrust of and resistance to high taxes, a strong national government, and economic and political elites ran deep and continued to be widespread for many generations. An armed uprising of debtors in western Massachusetts, dubbed Shays's Rebellion, took place during 1786 and 1787 in reaction to the state's high taxes, a portion of which was earmarked to pay off its Revolutionary War borrowing. The taxes forced some farmers to sell their land and possessions; the punishment meted out to those who could not pay their obligations was severe. The rebellion was an alarming reminder of the intensity of antitax sentiment, of popular resistance to creditors, and of the profound resentment of government authority.

Small farmers, who comprised the vast portion of the nation's post-Revolutionary population, were deeply suspicious of Hamilton and other politicians who advocated giving substantial power, particularly taxing power, to the new federal government. They also feared the growing political strength of wealthy financiers, who were widely regarded as an alarmingly influential "financial aristocracy," and who happened to be Hamilton's allies. It was a first taste of how agrarian sentiment, rising to the level of passion, would exert itself as a powerful force in shaping America's financial system and its fiscal policy for decades to come. It was also a powerful signal to business and financial interests that the country needed a strong central government if property and credit were to be secure.

During the Revolutionary War, the Continental Congress had no authority to levy taxes of any sort, so the Continental army regularly lacked funds, as Hamilton vividly remembered from his war experience, during which lack of pay, supplies, and food for soldiers triggered desertions and attempted mutinies. Before the war, the colonies had used a mélange of currencies: colonial notes, British pounds, Spanish and Portuguese coins, and other foreign money. Commodities, such as tobacco and whiskey, were used regularly for barter, especially on the frontier, where more conventional currencies were often in short supply. During the war, the Continental Congress had few financial options. One was to print money, a technique called "currency finance." Seizing this option, it issued massive amounts of a rapidly invented new American currency, known as "Continentals."

Initially the Continental Congress agreed to print a limited number of Continentals and asked the individual colonies to back them with hard money, primarily gold coin. But the printing got out of hand, and backing by the colonies never materialized. Roughly a quarter-billion Continental dollars were printed. Produced in such staggering amounts, by the time of Britain's surrender they had lost nearly all of their value. For generations, the expression "not worth a Continental" was used to denote a nearly worthless object. The states had also printed currencies, but these fared much better because their governments had taxing powers to back up their currencies with gold or other hard money.

The ultragenerous issuance of paper currency had enabled the Continental Congress to avoid imposing a formal tax, which its members knew would meet with a hostile public reaction. Noah Webster, who chronicled the legislative proceeding of this period, reported that one member of that Congress quipped, "Do you think, gentlemen, that I will consent to load my constituents up with taxes, when we can send to our printer, and get a wagon-load of money?" Yet America's leaders also tacitly recognized that the sharp depreciation of the purchasing power of Continentals constituted a tax. The *Pennsylvania Packet* summed up the situation: "There is at present no absolute necessity for high government taxes. The natural unavoidable tax of depreciation is the most certain, expeditious, and equal tax that could be devised."

The Continental Congress also engaged in heavy borrowing, including the issuance of what were called loan certificates. When these did not generate sufficient resources, it was forced to go hat in hand to the states, but received limited help. Foreign loans eventually provided the nation with critically needed money—funds essential to the continuation and success of the war effort.

Immediately after the Revolution, the country was little more than a loose affiliation of states with virtually no central government, in keeping with the revolutionary temperament of the day. It was governed under the Articles of Confederation, which were passed by the Second Continental Congress in the fall of 1777, but it took more than three years, until early 1781, before all of the states ratified them. Ratification was delayed by a squabble over who would benefit from the sale of western lands, the territories extending beyond the Appalachians that were part of the United States but had not yet been incorporated into the existing thirteen states. The issue had been whether the national government or the states with claims on those territories would have the authority to sell the lands and keep the proceeds. The national government prevailed, providing it with an important early source of funds.

The Articles had denied the Confederation Congress, then the nation's governing body, the power to impose taxes, rendering it as financially impotent as the Continental Congress had been. The Confederation Congress could issue what were called "requisitions" to obtain funds from the states, but it could not compel the states to send the money. On several occasions, supporters of fiscal reform tried and failed to enact legislation imposing a uniform 5 percent "national impost," or tariff.

Following the dire experiences of the Continental and Confederation Congresses, America's leaders concluded that lack of a national taxing power condemned the country to permanent weakness and the government to a debilitating dependence on the states for revenues. As Hamilton wrote in "The Federalist Number 15," "There is scarcely anything that can wound the pride or degrade the character of an independent nation that we do not experience. . . . We owe debts to foreigners and to our own citizens. . . . These remain without any proper or satisfactory provision for their discharge. We have neither troops, nor treasury nor government. . . . Is the public credit an indispensable resource? We seem to have abandoned its cause."

When it came time to draft the Constitution, the framers sought to remedy the absence of reliable federal revenue. The Constitution vested in Congress exclusive authority to authorize federal borrowing and to "lay and collect Taxes, Duties, Excises and Imposts." The authority to tax was a bold advance compared to the fiscal impotence of the Continental and Confederation Congresses, but it did not guarantee that sufficient resources would be available when the president requested them. To obtain such resources, the president had to convince Congress to provide them. Congress held full power not only over revenues and borrowing, but also over how the money collected was to be spent: "No money shall be drawn from the Treasury," the Constitution reads, "but in consequence of appropriations made by law." And because Congress was formed as the only federal institution that could pass a law, it alone could determine what the Treasury could spend. So although the nation's commander in chief was given control over the military, he was completely dependent on the Congress to authorize taxes and borrowing, and appropriate the funds, to pay its bills.

The Taxing Limits

While the power to tax was vested in Congress, the framers of the Constitution, mindful of public opinion, imposed distinct limits on legislators' ability to exercise that power. They provided Congress with the broad authority to levy customs duties and excise taxes, commonly referred to as "indirect taxes" because they were assessed on individual commercial transactions and collected by intermediaries, who then transferred the money to the government. The tax authorities did not touch citizens individually. "Direct taxes," on the other hand, were to be assessed on the value of a person's assets and paid directly to the government—a distinction that seems arcane today but was very real in the post-Revolutionary ferment. Providing Congress with the authority to collect taxes and customs duties was resisted by some who wanted the states to retain this power. But even opponents conceded that the federal government would be rendered impotent without that ability. Americans were generally comfortable with the imposition of import duties, at the time referred to as "imposts," because they had been levied by the separate colonies before 1776 and later by the individual states under the Articles of Confederation. Moreover, they were considered to be fair; they were seen primarily as a tax on the rich, because the average American living on a farm or in a small village bought few imported goods. There also was an element of voluntarism regarding them, because people paid duties only if they chose to buy foreign-made goods.

Far more controversial was the power to collect direct taxes, and here the framers imposed stringent constraints on Congress. What precisely constituted a direct tax was not specified in the Constitution or made clear in the framers' debates. It was primarily considered to be a tax on "property," at the time primarily houses, buildings, land, and slaves. Some states already had legislated property taxes. But most Americans during the period were considerably more loyal to the government of the state in which they lived than to the federal government. They frequently referred to their native states as their "country." (The practice continued as late as the Civil War, and Lincoln himself often referred to Illinois that way.) Further, state legislatures were generally considered more responsive to the interests of their constituents than the federal government. Many Americans accepted the authority of state legislatures to levy direct taxes, but not of the federal government to do so.

To understand the nature and depth of these attitudes—and it is important to do so in order to understand the next hundred years of U.S. financial history—we must consider what the country was like in the years just after the Revolution. The vast majority of Americans lived in small, widely dispersed villages and family farms that lay between the Atlantic Coast and the Appalachians; most had very little contact with one another, much less with the federal government, then seated in New York. The federal government was a remote institution for most people, providing few tangible benefits. The only national official most Americans ever saw was the local postmaster. State and county officials handled most civic problems. The federal government was the object of suspicion, viewed by many as a potential threat to Americans' newly won liberties. Some feared the return of a monarchy, imposed not from London but by an American government dominated by powerful elites.

The Constitution contained a number of checks and balances to limit the potential abuse of power, but despite these embedded safeguards, significant numbers of Americans opposed its ratification. Many of those who did, known as the "anti-Federalists," objected to the extent of the new government's taxing power. They argued that the federal government's distance from, and lack of contact with, the large majority of the people meant that it could not be trusted to check its potential for tax abuse and should be denied any significant taxing authority. Patrick Henry made the case that "the oppression arising from [federal] taxation is not from the amount, but from the mode—a thorough acquaintance with the condition of people is necessary to a just distribution of taxes." Henry and his supporters asserted that the federal government did not possess such "acquaintance" and therefore taxing authority should stay largely or entirely in the hands of the states, as it was under the Articles of Confederation. Similar arguments were heard in Congress not only during the late eighteenth century but also during much of the nineteenth century.

After the Revolution, critics of allowing the federal government to impose direct taxes also worried that these levies would siphon potential revenues away from state treasuries. George Mason, one of the most prominent of the Founding Fathers, argued that the "assumption of this power of laying direct taxes" by the federal government was "calculated to annihilate entirely the state governments." Others feared that a dominant regional faction in Congress could misuse the direct taxing power; for example, opponents of slavery in the North might levy a pointed, direct tax on slaves in Southern states, or legislators under the influence of big-city merchants might do the same with respect to farms in rural states, or representatives of agrarian interests might impose a tax on business property in the more industrial New England. More broadly, a direct tax was seen as more coercive than import duties; everyone who owned property was compelled to pay the direct tax, whether they wanted to or not.

Hamilton attempted to assuage public concerns, noting that "it is evident from the state of the country, from the habits of the people, from the experience that we have had . . . that it is impractical to raise very considerable funds by direct taxation." For his part, Madison attempted to reassure opponents of the Constitution that when "direct taxes are not necessary they will not be recurred to. It can be of little advantage to those in power to raise money in a manner oppressive to the people. . . . They will be recurred to only for great purposes." To Madison, "great purposes" meant war. The Founding Fathers understood that the ability to raise large sums through taxes and borrowing was a prerequisite for defending the country in time of war. "How is it possible a war could be supported without money or credit?" Madison asked rhetorically. "Would it be possible for the government to have credit without having the power of raising money?" "No," he answered, "it would be impossible for any government, in such a case, to defend itself. Then I say, sir, that it is necessary to establish funds for extraordinary exigencies, and to give this power to the general government; for the utter inutility of previous requisitions on the states is too well known."

To be sure that a direct tax was used only in times of emergency, the framers tightly limited the ability of the Congress to impose one. Article 1, section 2, of the Constitution stipulated that "direct taxes shall be apportioned among the several states . . . according to their respective numbers." The numbers were to be determined by the latest census. If a property tax were designed to raise $20 million, a state that contained 10 percent of the population of the United States would be responsible for raising $2 million of that. Even if the "property" of all the people in, for instance, Virginia was worth ten times that in Maryland, each state's portion of the national property tax would correspond only to its portion of the national population, not the value of its collective property. Thus, members of Congress could not gang up to impose disproportionate burdens on slave states, farm states, or states with wealthy merchants. And unlike an import duty, Congress was required to indicate a precise purpose for the direct tax as well as the amount to be collected. The authorization for the tax would expire as soon as the designated amount was received.

The importance of this issue, which might otherwise have been considered constitutional trivia, is that Congress rarely enacted a property tax during the nineteenth century and, when it did appear, it was almost exclusively during wartime. The country had to rely on customs duties and excise taxes for the vast bulk of its revenues.

Swift Action

Despite the constitutional authority provided to Congress to impose taxes, Hamilton knew he would have to work hard to persuade legislators to actually authorize the collection of the revenue necessary to run the government and repay interest on the new bonds he intended to issue, a formidable task since the sums required were enormous by the standards of the time. The money, however, was crucial to his funding plan. The Treasury needed to assure holders of the old Revolutionary debt that the government would be able to service and repay its new securities.

Hamilton had to move quickly. He knew there would be resistance and that it would build the longer his plan languished before Congress. Robert Morris, who held the title of superintendent of finance (the equivalent of the Treasury secretary) under the Articles of Confederation, had proposed a similar plan to retire and restructure Revolutionary War debt through a new series of Confederation government bonds. He had argued that this arrangement was both sound financial practice and a means to strengthen the unity of the loosely knit new nation. "A public debt supported by public resources," Morris wrote, "will provide the strongest cement to keep our confederacy together." Unanimity was required to pass legislation in the Confederation Congress. The plan failed when only twelve of the thirteen states voted to give the Confederation Congress the power to levy taxes to service the new bonds. Once Rhode Island withheld its support and Virginia withdrew its vote, taxing power remained with the states. Without a national tax or an assurance of substantial voluntary payments from the states, the Confederation government could not hope to persuade holders of the old obligations that it would make timely interest payments on new ones.

Hamilton echoed Morris's arguments when he decided to seek revenues to back his new federal bonds. The federal government required a reliable and adequate source of revenue. Imposing a "direct" federal tax on real estate or slave owners was constrained by the Constitution and, in any case, Hamilton's plan would have been destroyed by the very suggestion that the government would impose such a deeply controversial tax to support it. Rural and Southern states already were profoundly suspicious of Hamilton and would have resisted fiercely. The government had to consider other options.

Hamilton and Madison, at the time working together although they would later become bitter adversaries, identified import duties—imposts—as the easiest of taxes to push through Congress. Madison regarded imposts as the most benign form of taxation, and the least harmful to the poor. Jefferson agreed, justifying his support on grounds that a "tax on importation . . . falls exclusively on the rich. . . . In fact, the poor man in this country who uses nothing but what is made within his own farm or family, or within the United States, pays not a farthing of the tax to the general government. . . . The farmer will see his government supported, his children educated, and the face of his country made a paradise by the contributions of the rich alone."

As it worked its way through Congress, the nation's first revenue bill—"An Act for laying a Duty on Goods, Wares and Merchandise Imported into the United States"—gathered a diverse alliance of advocates. In its preamble, it defined the varied objectives of its supporters; the money collected was "necessary for the support of government, for the discharge of the debts of the United States, and the encouragement and protection of manufactures." During the course of deliberations, representatives of the more industrialized states, especially Pennsylvania and Massachusetts, insisted on including certain duties that had been applied by those states to protect local manufacturing.

The final legislation imposed two types of duties: those of specified amounts (e.g., two cents on a pound of imported coffee) on a variety of items, including coffee, rum, wine, beer, cocoa, molasses, iron, and coal; and ad valorem duties ranging from 5 percent to 15 percent on other imported products. The highest levies were imposed on luxury goods: for example, 15 percent on carriages, 7 percent on hats and leather goods. A number of necessities were placed on a duty-free list, including cotton, wool, hides, and skins. These differentiations constituted a hint of the progressivity that later would emerge at the heart of American tax policy. Passed in 1789, the revenue act was the second law enacted under the new Constitution. (The first had established procedures for administering oaths.) A subsequent piece of legislation, the Tonnage Act, assessed modest duties on the registered tonnage of American-owned ships and considerably higher ones on foreign-built and -owned ships.

The Fight over "Discrimination"

Having secured legislation to raise revenues, Hamilton turned to the task of restructuring and redeeming the Revolutionary War debt. In 1782, the Confederation Congress had sent teams of commissioners around the country to verify claims against the Continental Congress and the Continental army. These claimholders were largely veterans, farmers, and merchants to whom the government incurred liabilities during the war. The commissioners issued them certificates verifying those claims considered legitimate. The Confederation Congress hoped to be able to redeem war obligations but had no revenues with which to do so. There was little controversy about the appropriateness of the new federal government assuming responsibility for these debts; that principle had been accepted by the framers. Article 6, clause 1, of the Constitution states, "All debts contracted and engagements entered into before the adoption of this Constitution, shall be as valid against the United States under this Constitution, as under the Confederation." Congress readily agreed that the Treasury could substitute new federal bonds for the old Continental Congress debt. It also agreed that interest on these bonds should be paid in gold and that they should be redeemed in gold when they came due. The terms on which the substitution was to take place, however, stoked bitter controversy.

Because the Confederation government was unable to pay interest on the Revolutionary War debt, its value had dropped significantly. Speculators had then bought many of these debt certificates at bargain prices—often ten to thirty cents on the dollar—from holders who were in immediate need of cash and uncertain as to whether the government would or could make good on its promise to redeem them. Some enterprising people had acquired obligations by rushing out to small towns and rural areas to buy them at a deep discount after Hamilton's plan was announced but before news of it was widely disseminated throughout the country. Hamilton insisted that in redeeming the old debt there be no "discrimination" between those who originally owned Revolutionary War obligations and those who subsequently purchased them.

Madison supported the original owners' claims and fiercely opposed Hamilton's plan. He considered it an enormous injustice against patriotic soldiers and army suppliers in favor of speculators. Madison pointed out that many speculators stood to realize enormous gains if the debt they had purchased was redeemed with new bonds at or close to the face value of the original debt. He could not stomach that. He and his allies insisted that the government provide secondary holders of the old debt with new bonds equal only to the amount they had paid, plus interest. The original creditor would receive a new bond equivalent to the difference between the low price at which he or she had sold the debt and its original face value. A veteran who had sold a one-hundred-dollar certificate to a speculator for thirty dollars would receive a new bond worth seventy dollars, while the purchaser would receive a bond worth thirty dollars plus interest.

Hamilton contended that Madison's scheme "would be ruinous to public credit." His determination to oppose such discrimination was based in part on his understanding of a warning by Montesquieu, one of the many European writers and philosophers whose works he had read, that "a breach in the public faith cannot be made on a certain number of subjects without seeming to be made on all." Hamilton's stance was unequivocal: "discrimination between the different classes of creditors of the United States cannot, with propriety, be made." In practical terms, determining who was an original debt holder and who had bought an obligation from an original owner—and, if so, at what price—would be virtually impossible, he argued. But there was an even more fundamental consideration. If the government were to make a "distinction" between the "transferee" and the "original proprietor," Hamilton declared, it would "operate a diminution of the value of the stock [debt certificate] in the hands of the first, as well as of every other holder." In other words, if the government established the practice of denying second- or third-round buyers the profits they might make on the sale of the obligations they held, the value of any original bond issued in the future would be compromised. Original investors would have difficulty selling government securities to other potential buyers if the buyers felt they could not profit from the securities' later appreciation. Keeping faith with all creditors—"original holders" as well as "present possessors"—was essential to maintaining the value of, and public faith in, all government and private securities in the future. Hamilton's argument against discrimination prevailed. Congress ultimately accepted his position that discrimination was impractical and would permanently undermine the government's creditworthiness.

Hamilton was adamant on another funding issue as well: for reasons of national security the young republic needed to be scrupulous in keeping faith with overseas creditors, who were primarily French and Dutch. If the United States were forced to fight another war, it would have to borrow abroad again and for it to be able to do so foreigners must regard the U.S. government as impeccably creditworthy. There was "no time, no state of things, in which credit is not essential to the nation," Hamilton wrote, "especially so long as nations in general continue to use it as a resource for war." Under Hamilton's funding plan, the foreign-held debt was "to be provided for according to the precise terms of the contracts relating to it." Overseas creditors would receive new bonds that carried exactly the same terms as the old loans. It was not a small decision as they were owed nearly $11.7 million, including interest in arrears.

The status of the United States as a large debtor nation, dependent on foreign capital, played a major role in Hamilton's thinking—indeed, in the thinking of most American leaders at the time. And, as historian Walter Russell Mead wrote, it remained "one of the great determining factors of [U.S.] existence during the late eighteenth and through the nineteenth centuries. Virtually every American business and household was kept constantly aware of its connection to and dependence on the international financial system." In this respect, the situation the nation faced in the 1790s bears an uncanny similarity to that faced in the early twenty-first century, with a heavy U.S. dependence on foreign capital affecting all aspects of the economy and requiring the country to maintain the confidence of foreign creditors.

The fact that Hamilton succeeded in establishing America's financial credibility abroad can be seen in the numbers. At the time Hamilton launched his funding plan, foreigners held roughly 30 percent of the federal debt. A decade later, in 1801, the first year of Thomas Jefferson's administration, foreign holdings of government debt had tripled, to nearly $50 million—half of all federal outstanding debt.

At the time of the funding debate, outstanding domestic debt issued by the Continental Congress amounted to just over $42 million, including arrears; under Hamilton's plan, holders would be provided with new bonds valued at par (face value), but would receive a slightly lower interest rate than on the old obligations. The lower rate was justified on the grounds that the quality of the new bonds was greater than that of the original debt and reflected the lower risk. Holders of outstanding state-issued debt— estimated at the time to total $25 million including arrears (although the figure finally turned out to be around $18 million)—would receive new bonds at par, but with lower and deferred interest payments. Holders of Continentals were able to redeem their notes for new federal bonds at a rate of a hundred to one.

Assumption of State Debt

The second highly controversial issue with which Hamilton had to contend involved the question of assumption. Hamilton's stance that the federal government should assume responsibility for the states' debts pitted him against the Jeffersonians, who represented agrarian interests and were suspicious of concentrated economic power, urban commerce, and big banks. To them, assumption was one more step in what they saw as a dangerous and calculated set of strategic moves, masterminded by the "devious" Hamilton, to "consolidate" political and economic power in the hands of the national government and the "financial elites." The more extreme anti-Federalists in Jefferson's crowd considered "consolidation" the first step toward a return to monarchy. Virginia's governor, Beverley Randolph, a staunch critic of Hamilton's funding scheme, warned President Washington that "in an Agricultural Country like this, to erect and concentrate and perpetuate a large insured interest . . . must in the course of human events, produce one or other of two evils—the Prostration of Agriculture at the feet of Commerce, or a change in the present form of Federal Government, fatal to the existence of American liberty."

Madison, who led the Jeffersonian faction in the House, shared Randolph's concerns. He fought to retain maximum political and financial power, including the responsibility for repaying state debt and the capacity to tax that went with it, in the hands of the states. Representatives of the states that already had paid down most of their debt, primarily Virginia, resented, as Randolph did, the proposal that the federal government would foot the bill for the states that were delinquent. The opposition was fueled by two concerns: assumption would disproportionately benefit Northern bond speculators and would consolidate taxing power in the hands of the federal government, undermining the financial strength of the states.

Yet Hamilton would not back down. He was adamant that a strong central government was essential for the stability and unity of the republic. Perceiving that Americans who held state-issued debt obligations from the war would have an additional reason to support the national government if the responsibility for repaying them were shifted to the federal Treasury, he believed that assumption was an integral part of a broader, more sweeping concept of an effective American government. By tying the interests of wealthy Americans and of the states to the national government, a well-funded public debt would be a "national blessing." Jefferson disagreed. To him, assumption meant a centralized federal financial power that would undermine state power.

In the end, Congress's support for assumption was primarily based not on Jefferson's or Madison's acceptance of Hamilton's financial logic but on their willingness to give up opposition to it in exchange for Hamilton's support for a permanent Southern capital. The Funding Act of August 4, 1790, which incorporated Hamilton's controversial assumption plan, helped pull together the fledgling nation's diverse interests and allegiances. It also put America's post-Revolutionary credit on a sound basis and reduced the prospect of state challenges to the primacy of the federal government's taxing role. In this respect, it greatly strengthened the financial foundation of the federal government and its capacity to raise money for the defense of the nation. The total amount of debt taken on by the new government amounted to around 40 percent of the nation's gross national product (GNP). Roughly half of federal revenues in the 1790s were devoted to servicing the nation's debt—a figure not matched or exceeded since.

Jefferson called the fight over assumption "the most bitter and angry contest ever known in Congress, before or since the Union of the States." It was an extraordinary statement, given that enormous rancor also surrounded Hamilton's embattled proposal to establish a Bank of the United States. Jefferson personally had urged the president to veto the legislation establishing the bank. Jefferson's perception that the assumption debate was even more heated was largely due to the way it pitted regional interests against one another and because it was destined to determine the size and scope of the federal government's taxing power.

That Hamilton prevailed over Southern resistance was as important strategically as it was economically. It provided assurance that during wartime the government would not have to depend on the states for funds. Early in the nineteenth century, individual states disputed the federal government's foreign and military policies and, if the states had held preeminent taxing authority, they could have withheld funds, too. The 1790 deal also satisfied one of Jefferson's security concerns: it permanently separated America's financial center from its political center, which in his eyes reduced the likelihood that the country would go to war under the influence of powerful financial interests.

Hamilton's decision to issue long-term bonds to effect his re-funding plan added yet another element of stability. He chose to issue bonds that would mature decades later rather than those with shorter-term maturities so that the government would not have to constantly engage in new financing to repay its debt. The combination of sound creditworthiness and long-term financing distinguished the United States in Hamilton's era from many emerging nations in more recent times, whose less rigorous financial policies and vulnerabilities to the markets have riddled their histories with frequent breaches of creditworthiness.

New Revenues

With the federal government's taxing authority established and the Revolutionary War debts consolidated, Hamilton headed to Congress to get the additional revenues he needed to service and repay the debt. He persuaded legislators to enact a new sales tax—the Excise or Duties on Distilled Spirits Act. As he had with imposts, Hamilton was able to rally Madison's support for the legislation, since Madison regarded excise taxes as preferable to the "still more generally obnoxious" direct taxes. It also helped Hamilton's cause that Madison thought that the tax on whiskey would increase "sobriety" and "prevent disease and ultimately deaths." At Hamilton's recommendation, in March 1792 Congress also voted to increase the average tariff rate to give additional protection to America's fledgling manufacturing sector.

While Hamilton considered the excise taxes and imposts necessary, Washington was concerned about their political ramifications. In a letter to Hamilton, he observed that he had heard criticisms that "we are already obliged to strain the impost till it produces clamor, and will produce evasion, and war on our citizens to collect it, and even to resort to an Excise law, of odious character with the people." To make excises more palatable, Hamilton and his Federalist allies in Congress, joined by a number of sympathetic Jeffersonians, structured them, as they had imposts, to impose the highest burden on items generally purchased by wealthy consumers. The Revenue Act of 1794 taxed luxuries such as carriages, snuff, and refined sugar.

Despite the agreement in Congress to impose new taxes, the public's reaction was not always measured. The levy on distilled spirits was a particularly seductive one for the government because whiskey was produced in great volume in many parts of the country—Washington himself was a major distiller of rye whiskey at Mount Vernon—and the tax could quickly pump up federal revenues. However, it proved to be highly unpopular. The tax was levied at the stills to pick up revenues from those who produced for home use and barter, and that required direct collection by revenue agents. In 1794, moonshiners in western Pennsylvania—a group of fiercely independent Scots-Irish settlers who produced homemade whiskey for merriment, for sale, and for barter in a cash-short environment—rebelled against the new levy. Many protested, with some justification, that they did not have much actual money to pay the tax. In their barter economy, whiskey was their primary currency.

To put down the insurrection and to demonstrate in convincing fashion the government's determination to enforce its power to tax, Washington personally traveled to the region at the head of a thirteen-thousand-man force composed of troops from the Pennsylvania, Maryland, Virginia, and New Jersey militias. The force was large compared to the size of the insurrection because, in an early version of what has been called the Powell Doctrine of overwhelming force, Hamilton advised Washington, "Whenever the government appears in arms, it ought to appear like Hercules." The Whiskey Rebellion fizzled after a few arrests. When the threat faded, the president returned to the capital, leaving Hamilton in charge of the troops along with General Henry Lee, who had earlier warned Madison about Southerners' unhappiness with the North's dominance. This particular moment in the annals of tax collection is unique in American economic history. Hamilton was the first, last, and only Treasury secretary to lead an army to enforce U.S. tax law.

Repaying the Revolution

Although Hamilton saw a properly funded debt as a blessing, he did not see a big debt as one. He warned that transferring heavy financial obligations to coming generations threatened the nation's future creditworthiness. In his view, debts incurred during wartime should be paid down during periods of peace. In his *First Report on Public Credit*, Hamilton wrote that he wished "to see it incorporated as a fundamental maxim in the system of public credit of the United States that the creation of debt should always be accompanied with the means of extinguishment." In December 1791, he further pointed out that "as the vicissitudes of nations beget a perpetual tendency to the accumulation of debt, there ought to be a perpetual, anxious, and unceasing effort to reduce that which at any time exists, as fast as should be practicable, consistent with integrity and good faith." The need to pay down wartime debt was a recurrent political theme during this period. Three years later, Hamilton called on Congress to "extinguish" the federal debt within thirty years, by making some old taxes permanent and creating new ones, and urged it to "prevent that progressive accumulation of debt which must ultimately endanger all Government."

Most American leaders recognized that carrying too much debt would be a source of financial vulnerability. In the August 1790 Funding Act, Congress authorized the use of surplus revenues from the collection of imposts and tonnage duties, as well as extra borrowing of up to $2 million, to establish a "sinking fund" to buy back government bonds that were selling at a discount. To ensure that the buy-back procedure was not skewed to favor any one economic interest group or region of the country, Congress set up a high-profile commission, composed of the chief justice, the secretary of the Treasury, the attorney general, the president of the Senate (the vice president), and the secretary of state, to oversee its operations. The commission could authorize the purchase of government securities in the open market if they fell below par value. Hamilton advocated establishing the new facility because it would stabilize demand for government securities and help to sustain their value, strengthening investor confidence and better positioning the government to borrow in the event of another war. Government purchase of securities in the open market to stabilize their value was a remarkably innovative approach; widespread use of this technique would not take place again until the twentieth century, when it was done by the Federal Reserve.

In March 1792, encouraged by Hamilton, Congress passed legislation setting up a permanent sinking fund to buy Treasury securities on a regular basis. It was governed by the same high-level commissioners and financed by interest paid on the public debt that had been "purchased, redeemed or paid into the Treasury in satisfaction of any debt or demand." It also received any money appropriated to the Treasury to pay interest on the public debt that was not used for that purpose.

Revenues increased significantly through the later part of the 1790s. However, Washington and John Adams after him incurred significant expenses: building the new national capital, financing the army and the navy during what came to be known as the Quasi-War with France, fighting Indians, and paying tributes to the Barbary pirates. These expenditures thwarted their administrations' ability to reduce the federal debt despite their intentions. Government debt rose from $77 million in 1790 to $83 million in 1801, although it was offset in part by cash balances in the Treasury and the value of the stock the government held in the newly chartered Bank of the United States.

The United States enjoyed rapid economic growth during the 1790s. On a per capita basis, its wealth rivaled that of Great Britain. Because the economy grew more rapidly than borrowing, debt declined as a portion of GNP from 40 percent at the very end of the Revolution to 18 percent in 1795. Robust revenues enabled the government to service all of Hamilton's bonds on time, and U.S. government securities came to enjoy a high degree of investor acceptance in Europe. By 1795, the United States was able to borrow $8 million in Dutch florins from private bankers in the Netherlands, a strong testament to the financial credibility the nation had achieved in its brief history. It was the last time the federal government borrowed in a foreign currency until the late twentieth century.

★

Within the remarkably short period of less than a decade, Alexander Hamilton almost single-handedly created a sound financial foundation for the United States and established its international creditworthiness. But his success still required a top-level political compromise—in fact, a last-minute miracle. In the end, the nation's most influential leaders recognized that the bitter disputes over funding, assumption, and discrimination in 1789 and 1790 placed the country's credit and even its survival in jeopardy. They then produced a series of remarkable agreements that effectively restructured America's formidable war debt and, at least temporarily, reconciled the interests of North and South.

In post-Revolutionary America, the compromises and negotiations were over how to pay the debts incurred during a past war. Over the next two hundred years, U.S. leaders regularly would struggle with the requirement to pay the high cost of the wars of their own times. But in all cases, the underlying requirement for success would prove to be the same: the willingness of leaders to reconcile their competing regional loyalties, economic philosophies, and political aspirations to produce breakthrough legislation and assemble the financial resources required. Throughout history, wars have transformed America's finances, because the urgent need to mobilize resources in a time of threat impelled leaders to champion reforms that would have been unnecessary, or politically unacceptable, otherwise.

After the Revolution, there were no guarantees that the United States would hold together. It faced external threats from Britain and France, and internal threats from those who valued loyalty to their states and regions more highly than to the fledgling nation. The highly charged debate over how to service and pay off debts accumulated during the war was the crucible within which the fundamental principles of a sound U.S. financial system were established. As such, the outcome of this debate also was vital to the nation's security. Hamilton and many of his adversaries had seen the Revolution nearly collapse for want of funds and had observed that Britain and France borrowed with relative ease to finance their military efforts and confront threats to their security. They understood that unless the United States had a sound financial system, it would be condemned to be a weak and ineffective military power.

Hamilton succeeded due to his intellectual power, political courage, and financial sophistication, but it is doubtful that he could have been as effective as he was without strong support from his president, who gave him sweeping authority to make deals on behalf of the administration and backed him when he was under attack. As his successors ultimately would, Hamilton recognized that however skillful he was, accomplishing his objectives would be impossible without that backing, which was particularly critical to his ability to effectively bargain with congressional leaders.

Congress's power over borrowing and taxation has made extensive bargaining and compromise between legislators and the executive branch an integral part of America's fiscal process. During the early years of the Washington administration, the process for negotiating fiscal legislation was ad hoc; various congressional interest groups, more often than not led by Madison, would deal with Hamilton directly. That was because no organized committee structures yet existed with respect to taxes and borrowing. In the summer of 1789, the House established a Committee on Ways and Means to advise it on these questions, but the committee was disbanded shortly after Hamilton assumed the job as Treasury secretary. His Federalist supporters, who held the majority in Congress at the time, felt there was no need for the committee since Hamilton was their principal adviser and source of information on financial matters. After Hamilton resigned in 1795, the House strengthened its hand vis-à-vis the Treasury—and asserted its legislative autonomy—by reestablishing the Committee on Ways and Means. It was made a standing committee in 1802. The House also ended the practice it had adopted during Hamilton's tenure of allowing the Treasury secretary to write revenue bills. From 1795 on, such bills would be drafted by the Ways and Means Committee.

The key financial arrangements Hamilton forged would not have been possible without recognition from the major protagonists, including his adversaries, that the country was under threat from European powers and in danger of internal disintegration. Hamilton harnessed that sense of danger to push through compromises between Northern and Southern, urban and rural, and mercantile and agrarian interests, compromises that could have been made only in the face of a threat to the nation's security and unity. Even those who were more focused on their own regional, political, and economic interests understood that the country's collapse would lay it open to intervention from Britain, France, or both.

But these compromises did not eliminate an underlying bitterness that had been stirred up during the rancorous debates of the period. The 1790 Compromise notwithstanding, rural Americans, particularly in the South, as well as veterans and others who had sold their wartime debt obligations at deep discounts, were intensely resentful that well-connected speculators, many from the burgeoning financial centers of Boston, New York, and Philadelphia, had made big profits. This added to regional frictions and grievances already simmering because the Southern states believed they were shouldering an inordinate portion of repaying the Revolutionary War debts of the northern states. The excise taxes of the period—especially the whiskey tax—were also deeply resented in rural America as yet another perceived discrimination. Walter Russell Mead summed it up: "Anger at these and similar measures brought Jefferson to power as an anti-centralizing, anti-debt candidate, and the lasting disenchantment of the people with Hamiltonian financial shenanigans is one of the keys to understanding the politics of the nineteenth century."

In his farewell address, George Washington enjoined Congress and future generations to "discharge the debts which unavoidable wars may have occasioned, not ungenerously throwing upon posterity the burdens we ourselves ought to bear." While Washington's famous phrase cautioning the country to avoid "entangling alliances" is well known, his warning on debt has been nearly forgotten, although it has become highly relevant in recent decades as the nation's fiscal discipline has deteriorated. The Founding Fathers displayed a strong commitment to avoid burdening coming generations with large amounts of debt that would hamstring governance and impose prolonged and crippling tax burdens.

As former Federal Reserve chairman Alan Greenspan observed in a speech praising Hamilton's legacy, "In those simpler times, before we became too sophisticated for our own good, deficit financing was prompted solely by peril, not as a tool of active demand management or as an excuse to put off hard decisions."

2

The First Great Test

FINANCIAL SABOTAGE AND THE WAR OF 1812

GO TO WAR WHEN YOU HAVE NOT THE COURAGE, WHILE YOUR
LIPS UTTER "WAR," TO LAY NEW TAXES.

—JOHN RANDOLPH

In early 1813, John Randolph, who customarily wore riding attire to affect the appearance of the English aristocracy, led one of his hunting dogs onto the floor of the House of Representatives. It was a stunning act of defiance. A senior Republican, onetime majority leader, and deposed chairman of the Ways and Means Committee, Randolph was a foe of the recently declared War of 1812. The Speaker of the House, Henry Clay, a Republican whom Randolph had derided as a "war hawk," ordered the sergeant at arms to remove the animal. Randolph, who had recently berated his colleagues for going to war without having the courage to raise taxes to pay for it, assaulted his pro-war colleagues with insults. It was just one of many confrontations between the two bitter rivals; Randolph and Clay later fought a duel, which ended in a draw when Clay grazed Randolph's coat and Randolph spared Clay's life, shooting over his head.

Emotions over the war, and wartime finance, ran high. Throughout 1812, 1813, and 1814, the Madison administration struggled to raise funds. Jefferson had won the presidency and the Jeffersonian Republicans had gained control of Congress in the elections of 1800 largely because they had opposed the taxes introduced by the Federalists during the Washington and Adams administrations. James Madison, then Jefferson's secretary of state, had been one of the most prominent opponents. But when war broke out in June 1812, the administration urged Congress to reinstitute such taxes. Madison, now president, found that he was unable to persuade his fellow Republicans to do so.

The antiwar Federalists seized on this unwillingness. They attempted to discourage investors from buying government bonds to finance the war, arguing that the interest on these securities would never be paid because the antitax Republican Congress "meant to abandon creditors once the government had secured the funds it needed." The Federalists believed that Madison would be forced to end the war if the government was unable to borrow.

It was the first great test of the financial strength and unity of the new nation—and the country came close to failing and disintegrating in the process. In his book *America on the Brink*, the historian Richard Buel describes how fighting among powerful political and financial factions "almost destroyed the young Republic." Representing one Republican faction, Madison and his Treasury secretary, Albert Gallatin, struggled to obtain funds to prosecute the war. Randolph and his antiwar colleagues formed another faction, a splinter group of Republicans who opposed the war effort and taxes to pay for it. The bulk of the Federalist Party comprised yet another faction. After John Adams had retired to Massachusetts following his defeat by Jefferson, and Hamilton fell mortally wounded in a duel with Aaron Burr, the party was largely left in the hands of extremists, including Timothy Pickering of Massachusetts, who sought determinedly to block government fund-raising. Financing the War of 1812 under such strained partisan conditions proved enormously difficult. The unified financial system that Hamilton had installed to hold the country together came very close to falling apart, and the country along with it.

A Public Curse

Thomas Jefferson won the closely contested presidential election of 1800 during which the American party system came into existence. The Jefferson administration considered the national debt they inherited on assuming office anything but Hamilton's "blessing." Jefferson was determined to pay it down, even though the departing Federalists had failed to do so. Earlier he had written that if he could "add a single amendment" to the Constitution, it would be one "taking from the federal government the power of borrowing." Madison had called the public debt a "public curse."

The philosophical and political dispute between Hamiltonians and Jeffersonians over the matter of debt was part of a broader disagreement over the proper role of the federal government, and the relationship between capitalism and democracy, that would reoccur throughout the nineteenth and much of the twentieth centuries. Those who considered a well-funded public debt a curse or a blessing based their arguments on the same premise—that a large national debt created a strong interest group of bondholders in favor of enhanced federal taxing power and established a robust alliance between the financial community and the government. Debt reinforced the powerful centralized national government that Hamilton wanted and Jefferson abhorred.

Early nineteenth-century concerns about the benefits and risks of accumulating large federal deficits and debt differed from those expressed today. The modern focus tends to be on the impact of increased borrowing on inflation, interest rates, dependence on foreign capital, and thrusting a heavy financial burden on future generations. Jefferson and his colleagues shared the last of these, yet saw something much more dangerous. They believed that debt posed a " 'danger to democracy' because it divided . . . citizens into two classes—taxpayers and interest collectors." They feared that "the creditor class would use its wealth to gain control of an ever more powerful federal government. . . . The deeper into debt the federal government went, the larger and stronger would be this class of creditors, insisting that the government use its monopoly of force and its taxing authority to extract resources from the mass of the people to pay off the creditor class."

Jefferson believed that wars, deficits, and taxes were closely linked. Because future wars would cost large sums of money, he reasoned, they would require the government to incur vast amounts of debt. That would increase the power of the "monied classes," who would likely be the major financiers of the war and afterward use their leverage to force legislation that placed a heavy tax burden for repaying the debt on the working-class. As the historian Walter Russell Mead described the nature of these concerns, "Wars cost money, piling up debts that concentrated power in the central government and forced most of the population to support the minority that owned the government bonds issued to cover the debt; wars built up concentrated economic and political machinery dependent on government funds. . . . The more the government spent the larger and stronger the class of military contractors and other dependents would be." A remarkably similar view was expressed in the 1950s by none other than Dwight D. Eisenhower in his denunciation of the "military industrial complex." Although the Jeffersonians' stance softened later, particularly after the War of 1812 began, the concern that war would benefit capitalists to the disadvantage of workers and small farmers was prominent for generations to come.

In the early 1800s, nearly a third of the budget was committed to interest on the federal debt. Jefferson's goal was to pay the debt down quickly. Between a booming economy and government spending cuts, his administration managed to reduce the $83 million debt it had inherited to $57 million (less than 10 percent of GNP) within six years. America's growing trade boosted duty collections, and Jefferson targeted the military, especially the navy, for budget tightening. The magnitude of the debt reduction was particularly impressive considering Jefferson had borrowed over $11 million from European banks to finance the Louisiana Purchase.

Of course, Jefferson would not have been able to obtain European loans for his western expansion if Hamilton's funding plan had not established the country's credit. Jefferson was Hamilton's archrival on most political matters, but he agreed with his adversary on one critical financial issue: for reasons of national security, the nation's ability to borrow had to be maintained. "Though I am an enemy of the system of borrowing," Jefferson wrote, "I feel strongly the necessity of preserving the power to borrow. Without that, we may be overwhelmed by another nation merely by the force of its power to borrow." While he may not have wanted to extend, or even maintain, the federal government's power to borrow in peacetime, Jefferson's realistic side recognized that in times of war, money and creditworthiness were indispensable to the nation's security.

During the early 1800s, this uncommon agreement between Jefferson and Hamilton preempted any serious challenges to Hamilton's plan to fund and service the Revolutionary War debt. But other factors were at play as well. Hamilton had encouraged his fellow Federalists to vote for Jefferson as part of the deal that enabled Jefferson to defeat Aaron Burr's presidential bid in 1800. The two had tied in the electoral college and the contest was thrown into the House of Representatives. Although Jefferson was his rival, Hamilton detested Burr and was determined to block him. To win Hamilton's support, Jefferson agreed to make a number of concessions, including a promise to faithfully implement Hamilton's funding arrangements.

The strategy was well orchestrated. James Bayard, Delaware's lone congressman and a Hamilton ally, was a key actor. Once he had sufficient assurances that Jefferson was indeed committed to preserving Hamilton's plan, he withdrew his earlier support for Burr and submitted a blank ballot; three other Federalist state delegations voted similarly, handing Jefferson the presidency.

The implementation of Hamilton's plan to maintain the high quality of public credit also was driven by Jefferson's Treasury secretary, Albert Gallatin, the leading figure in U.S. fiscal policy in the early nineteenth century. Gallatin had emigrated from Geneva in the 1780s, initially settling in Massachusetts before taking up residence on the frontier of western Pennsylvania. There he briefly participated in the Whiskey Rebellion, but stood down and urged moderation among his colleagues to avoid a confrontation with the forces of President Washington, including Alexander Hamilton.

A fervent anti-Federalist, Gallatin opposed the Constitution because he believed it provided for an excessively strong national government. He had been a member of the Pennsylvania Constitutional Convention and then the state assembly. In 1793, he was elected to the U.S. Senate, but the Federalists claimed he had not been a citizen long enough to meet constitutional residency requirements and he was disqualified from taking his seat. However, just two years later he was elected to the House, where he gained standing as the Republican Party's chief financial spokesman. In that role, he forcefully advocated reducing the federal debt and hounded Hamilton relentlessly for a meticulous accounting of the sources and the uses of federal revenues.

When Jefferson named him Treasury secretary, Gallatin held to his principles. He urged Congress to slash the cost of government and reduce the nation's debt. However, although Gallatin was a sharp critic of Hamilton, when Jefferson asked him to search the records for mistakes or scandals during Hamilton's tenure at the Treasury, he reported that he had found none, much to Jefferson's disappointment. Moreover, he enthused, Hamilton had created "the most perfect system ever formed. Any change that should be made in it would injure it."

On Gallatin's advice, and in keeping with Jefferson's recognition that the country's good credit was essential for its security, the administration faithfully implemented the deal the president had reached with Hamilton's camp in 1800 and made no attempt to reopen the issues of discrimination and assumption. Jefferson and his Republican successors continued to service government bonds on the terms Hamilton had set. In so doing, they en-shrined what Hamilton had established—the sanctity of the government's credit as the bedrock of the American financial system. National security and sound financial practice had trumped partisan politics in cementing support for faithful payment of the federal debt.

Down with Taxes

An important reason for the electoral success of Republican congressional candidates in 1800 was their opposition to the internal taxes imposed by the Federalists. In order to service the nation's Revolutionary War debt, the Federalists had sought to augment revenues by introducing a wide range of excise taxes, which George Washington himself had acknowledged were seen by many as "odious." Even more unpopular was the $2 million "direct property tax" on the owners of houses, land, and slaves signed into law by John Adams in order to raise money during the Quasi-War with France that lasted from 1798 to 1800. Adams's direct tax was to be collected from property owners by the individual states, based on their portion of the overall U.S. population. To ensure that the administration of this contro-versial levy was consistent with local practices, each state was authorized to form a board of commissioners to determine how to assess its portion of the tax. As with earlier tariffs and excise taxes, there was an element of progressivity; the most expensive homes were taxed at a higher rate than the least expensive ones. But these measures did not temper adverse pub-lic opinion.

After Jefferson entered office and the Republicans had taken control of the House and Senate, the Federalist minority in Congress argued that the government needed to continue to maintain at least some excise taxes in case another war broke out. In the event one did, they pointed out, shipping would be interrupted and consequently duty collections would dry up; the war could be paid for only with internal taxes. Although no fan of such taxes, Gallatin favored maintaining them—at least until sufficient revenues had been collected to pay off the nation's debt. He aimed to accomplish this over sixteen years by ensuring that revenues exceeded spending by $7.3 mil-lion annually, but that depended on collections from current taxes. Jefferson, however, wanted to completely and immediately eliminate all Federalist-era excise taxes.

Jefferson was deeply mistrustful of the Federalists' desire to retain high excise taxes because he linked them with a desire on their part to prepare for a war with France, a country he admired. In his mind, high taxes generated large amounts of revenue, which made it easier for the country to engage in a new war, while lower taxes would impose a restraint on war advocates, an argument strikingly similar to one used by modern-day conservatives, who claim that depriving the government of revenues would "starve the beast." In recent times, it has been the "welfare beast" that was to be starved; in the early nineteenth century, it was the "warfare beast."

A deal was brokered by John Randolph, then chairman of the Ways and Means Committee. The twenty-eight-year-old Randolph persuaded the secretaries of war and the navy to cut expenditures for their departments by "an amount sufficient to offset the repeal" of the excise taxes—giving Gallatin his $7.3 million. As a result, the army, which had achieved a peak level of about 4,000 men during the Quasi-War, was reduced to 3,220 and the navy was also pared down significantly. To provide the nation with additional military forces without having to pay for them, and to avoid a powerful national army that was offensive to the Republicans, the federal government planned to rely heavily on militias that were funded by the states, a strategy that would later have serious military consequences owing to the militias' lack of preparedness and often inept leadership.

In defying his fellow Republicans' exhortations about excise taxes and in other controversial areas, Randolph was targeted for criticism. Congressman William Plumer, a Republican from New Hampshire, was derisive: "Mr. Randolph goes to the House booted and spurred with his whip in his hand, in imitation, it is said, of members of the British Parliament. . . . As a popular speaker, he is not inferior to any man in the House . . . but I dislike his politics."

Randolph's deal eliminated the need to continue using excise tax revenues to pay down the debt, and Gallatin came on board for eliminating the taxes altogether. He wrote to Jefferson that a frontal assault on the Federalist excise taxes was necessary in order "to strike at the root of the evil and arrest the danger of encroaching taxes, encroaching government, temptations to offensive wars, etc." Even if the level of these taxes were to be reduced, Gallatin reasoned, the legislative authority to apply even minimal levels of internal levies made it easier for Congress to raise them significantly in the future. Thus, he argued, "nothing can be more effectual than a repeal of *all* internal taxes, but let them all go, and not one remain on which sinister taxes may heretofore be grafted." For him, it was as much a strategic as an economic matter, because "Treasury preparations and army preparations against contingent wars tend only to encourage wars."

To fund the government, Jefferson, Gallatin, and their congressional allies relied on imposts. Because of the abundance of revenues they generated, in his second annual message to Congress Jefferson was in a position to proudly announce, "We are able, without a direct tax, without internal taxes, and without borrowing, to make large and effectual payments toward the discharge of our public debt and the emancipation of our posterity from that moral cancer."

Then, in 1803, Congress was forced to find an extra $750,000 for the navy and for a blockade of the four Barbary states of North Africa. Privateers from these states frequently raided U.S. merchant ships, and the administration wanted to protect American commerce and subdue the rulers who permitted the practice to continue. To prepare the navy to confront the Barbary pirates, imposts were raised and the extra revenues dedicated to a new "Mediterranean Fund," set up specifically to pay for the campaign and scheduled to lapse once hostilities had ended. Yet the higher imposts were retained for several years after the confrontation ended, and America's robust trade caused collections to grow rapidly. In 1806, Gallatin faced the dilemma of what to do with large budget surpluses, well in excess of the amounts required to retire the outstanding Revolutionary debt when it came due. By the time James Madison entered the White House in 1809, the federal debt had fallen to just 8 percent of GNP.

This demonstrated capacity of the government to generate substantial budget surpluses during peacetime and to use the funds to pay down much of its war debt shaped Gallatin's philosophy that borrowing was the best way to pay for any future conflict. Even though increasing the national debt was "an evil" that would strengthen the leverage the financial elites held over the government, he was confident that such leverage would be short-lived. After any new war, Gallatin said, "the return to peace would, without any effort, afford ample resources for reimbursing whatever may have been borrowed." Because peacetime revenues from imposts would enable the Treasury to pay down war debt relatively quickly, any untoward influence powerful financial interests might exert by holding federal debt would be fleeting. Gallatin also believed that financing with debt was preferable to a sharp increase in taxes; in his view, the "losses and privations caused by war should not be aggravated by taxes beyond what is strictly necessary." He was also wary that any new wartime taxes passed by Congress might become difficult to repeal afterward. Extreme vigilance was required.

Maintaining the Peace

Throughout the Jefferson and first Madison administrations, France and Britain were embroiled in the Napoleonic Wars, and each country sought to disrupt the other's shipping. The British Orders in Council of 1807 and the French "Continental System" imposed harsh restrictions on American trade with the opposing nation. Although the United States remained neutral during the Jefferson administration, American-flagged vessels were frequently captured by one side or the other on the grounds that they were trading with the enemy. The Royal Navy also impressed some six thousand American seamen to supply manpower for its fleet, claiming that the U.S. citizenship papers of Americans born in Britain were not legitimate and that they were still subjects of the Crown.

The Jefferson administration responded with diplomatic protests, attempts at negotiations, and threats. A frustrated Jefferson then, in 1806, sought congressional approval for the Non-Importation Act that banned the import of most British goods and imposed embargoes on non-American ships. When that failed to achieve redress, at Jefferson's behest Congress passed the sweeping Embargo Act of 1807, which prohibited all exports from American ports to any foreign destination and aimed to compel both belligerents to respect the neutrality of American ships by denying them the benefits of the lucrative trade with the United States. Jefferson called the embargo "peaceable coercion," an attempt to avoid war and its financial consequences based on his premise that Europe needed American cotton and food more than America needed European manufactures. He hoped that by restricting their access to American goods, the embargo would deter Britain and France from taking hostile actions against U.S. merchant ships.

The legislation received support from southern and western states, but was opposed by northeastern Federalists, who maintained that it damaged the budding New England shipping industry. New England merchants evaded the embargo, smuggling goods across the Canadian border. Then, in 1808, Britain's big grain crop further undermined it. It was repealed in

March 1809, just as Jefferson left office. In its place, Congress enacted the Non-Intercourse Act, which narrowed the embargo, retaining it only on direct exports to Britain and France. But that too was largely ineffective and was repealed the following year. The failure of these acts moved the United States closer to war, as the government was left with few other ways to assert its rights of neutrality and to stop attacks on American vessels and citizens.

When British violations intensified in late 1811 and early 1812, Congress increased the size of the army to over thirty-five thousand troops, raised military pay, and provided generous incentives to those who enlisted. But it appropriated no additional funds to meet the expenses of these measures. The challenge of devising a plan to obtain the money fell to Gallatin, who had been asked by Madison to continue as Treasury secretary.

Gallatin initially opposed the war. A fiscal hawk, long committed to reducing the nation's debt, he feared that the cost of hostilities would erode all his work to eradicate the federal debt. He "believed that eliminating the public debt was the nation's first priority," and, at a minimum, "was determined as far as possible to resist its increase." Gallatin's concerns about bolstering the power of the financial elite also were a factor in his antidebt philosophy. He was convinced that "unrestrained borrowing" for a war could lead to the "oppression of the people to satisfy claims of public creditors." War-minded Republicans attacked him for his fixation on money. William Duane, the fiery editor of the influential *Philadelphia Aurora,* wrote that "The Genevan Secretary" had unpatriotically counseled "base submission" to Britain's "outrageous violations of American maritime rights to ensure that the Treasury would continue to fatten its customs receipts." But Gallatin was not the only Republican with such reservations. In 1808, when a conflict also appeared possible, Jefferson had told James Monroe, a close confidant who had just left his post as the U.S. minister in London, "If we go to war now, I fear we may renounce forever the hope of seeing an end to our national debt. If we can keep at peace eight years longer, our income, liberated from debt, will be adequate for any war, without taxes or loans, and our position and increasing strength put us 'hors d'insulte' from any nation."

Once Madison had resolved himself to the need to go to war, he directed Gallatin to devise a strategy to meet its substantial financial requirements. Consistent with his view that duty collections would be sufficient to quickly retire wartime debt, Gallatin proposed a plan that relied primarily on borrowing, but he recognized that he could not escape asking Congress for higher taxes. Just as Hamilton had needed to impose new taxes to support the bonds in his funding plan, Gallatin would need them to back up the bonds he would have to issue to finance the war. Gallatin aimed to sell bonds sufficient to cover the government's additional wartime expenditures and to levy new taxes only to pay interest on those bonds and to establish a pool of funds to help repay the debt after hostilities had ceased. On the eve of war, he wrote to Jefferson, now retired at Monticello, that the administration faced the challenge of conducting the war without succumbing to "the evils inseparable from it . . . debt, perpetual taxation, military establishments, and the corrupting or anti-republican habits of institutions."

On January 10, 1812, Gallatin tallied up the amounts required in a report to the new chairman of the House Ways and Means Committee, Ezekiel Bacon, Randolph having been replaced in 1807 because of his eccentric conduct and opposition to Jefferson's plan to acquire Florida from Spain. The Treasury secretary's proposed package included a request for $5 million in excise taxes on salt and a variety of other products. Explaining to his fellow Republicans that he would be unable to persuade investors to buy large amounts of new bonds if tax revenues were insufficient to make the required interest payments and repay the bonds, Gallatin urged them to drop their antitax stance. The new taxes were especially urgent, he argued, because, as the Federalists had earlier warned, hostilities were certain to lead to a collapse in trade with Britain—and thus to a plunge in duty collections. The Royal Navy was also likely to blockade American ports, cutting off trade with other countries. His forecast turned out to be correct, and customs revenues fell by half during the war.

The legislators resisted. The "war hawk Congress," as Randolph dubbed it, was long on support for the war, but short on fiscal responsibility. Many members, particularly Jeffersonian Republicans from the West and South, led by the young Speaker of the House, Henry Clay of Kentucky, and South Carolinians John C. Calhoun and Langdon Cheves, were enthusiastic about taking on Britain again, but many of their colleagues were unwilling to raise taxes to pay the costs. One member accused Gallatin of trying to "chill the war spirit" by calling for higher taxes. The Republicans had taken advantage of the popular resentment of taxes—especially the still-smoldering aversion to the direct tax of 1798—to defeat the Federalists in 1800 and to sustain anti-Federalist feelings afterward, so they were reluctant to embrace higher taxes now, even with a president and Treasury secretary of their own party urging them to do so. One way Congress attempted to hold down the cost of the war to the federal government was to empower President Madison to call up fifty thousand militia men—whom the states would have to pay.

The split over taxation presented the party's leadership with a dilemma. Ideological and practical objections to increasing taxes inhibited the Republicans' ability to form the consensus needed to go to war with Britain. Many Republicans cited concerns, voiced earlier by Jefferson and Gallatin, that war would strengthen the financial aristocracy. A more pragmatic worry related to domestic political consequences. The Federalists had financed the Quasi-War with France using high excise and direct taxes, and the American people had voted them out of office. Enacting Federalist-type taxes now, some Republicans feared, could spell the same fate for them.

Yet the Republicans were also desperate to avoid a reprise of the humiliation they had suffered when the various embargo acts had failed, making them appear impotent. In early 1812, they scraped together a majority to support going to war by sidestepping a clash over taxes. In March, Congress authorized many of the internal taxes that Gallatin wanted—but with the stipulation that they would not come into effect until war was actually declared. The war hawks hoped that once the nation was engaged in conflict, an outpouring of patriotism would eliminate the public's—and their colleagues'—opposition to taxes.

Republicans who opposed the war seized on their colleagues' unwillingness to finance preparations for it. Randolph had a deep affection for Britain and was also convinced that a war would dangerously strengthen the power of the federal government vis-à-vis the states. In caustic criticism of pro-war Republicans, he lambasted them for hypocrisy, accusing them of lacking the courage to give the government the financial tools to conduct the war that they supported: "Go to war without money, without a military, without a navy!" To him it was a total contradiction. He then attacked his colleagues' inconsistency, arguing that "passing resolutions to lay taxes by overwhelming majorities, and letting them lie on the table . . . prove that you have no system."

The Republican administration and the congressional leadership were also subject to intense pressure from advocates of a war with Britain. They argued that the British Orders in Council not only adversely affected American shipping but also insulted American sovereignty. Further, the British had reneged on their promise in the Treaty of Paris to vacate a number of forts located on the western border of the United States, and were arming Indians who were attacking American settlers from them—engaging in the nineteenth-century equivalent of state-sponsored terrorism. Most also believed that an invasion of Lower Canada (now the province of Quebec) would be quick and easy because many of its citizens would see American troops as liberators and rise up against their colonial masters. Jefferson had predicted a quick success, stating that victory was merely "a matter of marching." The pro-war *Niles' Weekly Register* attacked Republicans who resisted the war because they were reluctant to raise taxes, editorializing, "People will pay the proposed taxes to defend their lives from the tomahawks, their persons from the press gang, their government from treason, and their property from theft."

In June 1812, due to a drop in duty collections, federal revenues were insufficient even to cover the nation's peacetime spending requirements. Yet that month, without voting through a tax increase, Congress formally declared war on Britain. The vote reflected deep divisions in the country; four-fifths of Republicans voted in favor, but every Federalist member opposed it.

With war under way, Congress doubled existing customs duties and imposed several new tariffs. It also added a 10 percent duty on goods imported on foreign ships and a new levy on the foreign ships themselves when they delivered goods to the United States. However, the House chose, by a wide margin, not to consider action on new excise taxes until the following session of Congress. The internal taxes that Gallatin had said were essential, and that Congress had promised to enact when war began, were now postponed indefinitely. To fill the gap, Congress authorized the Treasury to issue long-term bonds.

Borrowing without the Bank

The nation's financial situation deteriorated quickly once hostilities began. Gallatin had few places to turn to borrow the needed money. A year before the outbreak of the war, Congress had failed to renew the charter of the Bank of the United States.

The bank had been chartered in Philadelphia by Congress early in the Washington administration over the objections of Jefferson and the attorney general, Edmund Randolph, who contended that it was unconstitutional. Washington had been prepared to veto the bank legislation based on Jefferson's and Randolph's counsel, but had given Hamilton the opportunity to persuade him otherwise. Within a week, Hamilton had prepared a masterful document arguing that the authority of Congress to create such a bank was "implied" in the clause of the Constitution that empowered that body to make all laws "necessary and proper" to carry out its delegated powers. The president was convinced and signed the bill in February 1791.

Operating much like other private commercial banks chartered by individual states around the same time, the Bank of the United States issued a form of currency, called notes, which it lent to borrowers at set rates of interest. However, it enjoyed a unique position: 20 percent of its shares were held by the federal government, and the bank served as the government's fiscal agent, its repository for tax revenues, and its bill payer. It also had a mandate to facilitate the government's ability to borrow by buying Treasury bonds. The bank was in an excellent position to play all these roles because, unlike a state-chartered bank (which could operate only within the confines of the state and whose notes were generally accepted only within that state), it set up branches in the major commercial centers around the country and thus enjoyed a broad deposit base. And because the bank's notes were accepted throughout the country, they circulated widely, constituting about one-third of the nation's money supply. The Bank of the United States could also facilitate the flow of cash and credit throughout the country in response to the needs of various regions. On occasion, it also shifted funds to state-chartered banks that were grappling with shortfalls.

Consistent with their philosophy of agrarian populism, Jeffersonian Republicans reviled the very concept of such a large and powerful bank, established by the federal government (in effect, by the Federalists). For them, it exemplified excessive government complicity with financial elites and would inexorably lead to a consolidation of wealth and economic power in the hands of big-city financiers and merchants. That, they concluded, was antithetical to the interests of farmers and small shopkeepers, the fundamental pillars of the new republic. The state-chartered banks, which were favored by the Jeffersonians, also resented the bank's power and lobbied against it. The Republicans also criticized the large number of British shareholders who benefited from the bank's profits.

Still, despite the Republican domination of Congress, the 1811 vote against renewing the bank's charter was razor thin; in the Senate, the vice president was called upon to break the tie. Defenders had rallied support by insisting that the bank was essential for the federal government's ability to efficiently raise funds in the event of another war, because it could use its deposits to buy large amounts of Treasury bonds and also market them to its customers. Republicans countered that the state-chartered banks could mobilize the necessary funds. Many state legislatures, at the instigation of these banks, instructed their senators and representatives to vote against renewing the bank's charter.

In eliminating the bank, the Republicans came dangerously close to undermining the government's ability to finance—and thus win—a war to which most of them were committed. The state-chartered banks faltered when pressed for funds. Further, foreign investors in the Bank of the United States had to be paid off when it was dissolved. They had originally contributed their funds in gold and $7 million worth of that precious metal was returned to them and shipped to Europe just as the country was preparing for war. In assessing the financial problems that beset the Madison administration, the historian Henry Adams, great-grandson of John Adams and grandson of John Quincy Adams, called the vote against the bank "the first and fatal blow to the Treasury" during the war.

Without the Bank of the United States, the Treasury was left in an extremely precarious position. Foreign funds were generally unavailable to it in 1812. Although British citizens had invested large sums in America after the Revolution, they were of no mind to continue sending money across the Atlantic with a war threatening, let alone once one had been declared. Nor were other foreign lenders eager to provide funds to the United States, as the superior military strength of the British was universally acknowledged. It was with relief, then, that Congress heard Gallatin report that, assuming his proposed revenue package was passed, the funds required to fight the war could be raised with relative ease from within the country. He estimated that domestic sources of capital would be "fully adequate to the support of the national forces that could be usefully and effectively employed."

He was wrong. Of the $11 million in bonds issued early in 1812 to pay for war preparations, only about $8 million were sold. In mid-1812, Congress authorized an issue of $5 million in short-term interest-bearing Treasury notes; these could be used for private transactions and would be accepted for payment of duties, taxes, and debts to the government. The printing of these notes, a form of government-issued currency, was a wartime innovation justified by the lack of availability of other forms of financing.

In early 1813, Congress authorized yet another bond issue, this time for $16 million—an amount far greater than any borrowing since the Revolution, and more than the total revenue of the entire federal government the year before. Seeking to broaden support for the sale, Gallatin appealed to patriotic sentiment, offered bonds in relatively small denominations, as low as a hundred dollars, and permitted individuals to pay for them in installments. However, he overestimated public enthusiasm, and the bonds encountered a poor reception among investors. A hundred dollars was a lot of money for most Americans at the time.

One reason for investors' reluctance to buy these bonds was the failure of Congress to enact the taxes Gallatin had requested. Leaders of the House Ways and Means Committee scolded other members of Congress about the severe fiscal consequences of their inaction. The committee reported that the lack of sufficient revenues to service the bonds would "sap the foundations of [the nation's] credit . . . leading to that general state of public discredit which attended the national finances during the War of Revolution."

Without a guarantee that the government would be able to service or repay its bonds, the Treasury's $16 million issue was on the verge of failure. With less than $6 million of securities sold, as John Steele Gordon observes in his book *An Empire of Wealth*, "the government was broke and the war effort was likely to sputter out not because of military defeat but because of financial collapse." More than six months after the war began, most Republicans "were still unwilling to risk their popularity by confronting the need for additional tax revenues to finance the war." On March 5, 1813, Gallatin told Madison that "we have hardly enough money left to last to the end of the month."

Fortunately for Gallatin, and the war effort, a few wealthy financiers had the resources and the will to support the government. Chief among them was Stephen Girard. At the time, Girard, a Philadelphia banker and merchant who was born in France, was America's richest man. He had recently purchased the building and much of the stock of the former Bank of the United States. Girard agreed to underwrite a large share of the unsubscribed portion of the loan—an amount far greater than his own considerable net worth. John Jacob Astor, who had emigrated from Heidelberg in the 1780s and made a fortune in furs and finance, also took a significant portion, at a hefty discount. David Parish, an agent for Baring Brothers, bought a large share as well. Together they prevented the collapse of the bond issue. Owing to their high standing in the financial community, they were able to sell many of their bonds to others. Buyers reasoned that if Girard, Astor, and Parish had been willing to underwrite the securities, the government must be a good credit. Girard was able to sell around half of his bonds, but this still left him holding a hefty portion of the government's debt.

By mid-1813, Gallatin had been appointed to a commission charged with negotiating a treaty to end the war. His successor, George W. Campbell, bluntly told Congress that its unwillingness to pass new taxes, forcing the government to rely almost exclusively on tariffs during a duty-starving war, was placing the nation in jeopardy. He urged Congress to impose new internal taxes, pointing out that compared to tariffs, they were "more stable and less liable to be weakened or cut off by the natural effect of war upon external commerce." If the legislators passed these new taxes, he predicted, "Capitalists will advance with greater readiness and at a low rate of interest, the funds necessary for the prosecution of the war." As long as the government had to rely so heavily on tariff collections, it would be unable to borrow significant amounts of funds, and what was available could only be obtained on unfavorable terms.

Under pressure from Madison and Campbell, and facing alarmingly weak investor support for the government's bond issues, Congress relented and finally levied internal taxes. In the words of one Federalist, however, the Republicans "approached the subject with fear and trembling." Accepting the key elements of Gallatin's earlier proposals, legislators voted to impose excise taxes on a wide range of items, including retailers' licenses, carriages, refined sugar, and (once again) whiskey. They also enacted a $3 million direct tax—a property tax on homes, slaves, and land, apportioned among the states on the basis of the 1810 census. States were given a 15 percent discount for paying the tax promptly, so desperate was the government's need for funds. To qualify for the discount, many states borrowed money from local banks, paid it to the government immediately, and then began the task of collecting the tax from their citizens. To minimize public criticism, the legislation stated explicitly that the taxes were extraordinary measures, required by the war, and would be eliminated within a year of the end of hostilities.

It was not a perfect solution. Without a universally usable currency, taxes were paid primarily in the form of notes issued by the state-chartered banks. Many of these were not accepted as payment for goods bought in other states. When the revenues from a state were lower than the federal government's purchasing requirements in that state, the Treasury had difficulty buying supplies and was often in arrears.

In early 1814, the Treasury again faced enormous revenue shortages. In February, John W. Eppes, Jefferson's nephew and son-in-law, now chairman of the House Ways and Means Committee, proposed covering the projected deficit by floating a loan of $25 million and issuing $5 million in short-term bills of credit. Eppes acknowledged that "the sum to be borrowed is much larger than any loan heretofore authorized in this country," but echoed Gallatin's argument after the Quasi-War: "Funds . . . in time of peace will enable us to pay [it] off, within a reasonable period." Daniel Sheffey, a Federalist representing the Shenandoah Valley area of Virginia, opposed this borrowing, contending that the lack of funds gave opponents "the best moment to arrest" the war. The legislation passed over Federalist objections.

The dangers to the country mounted in the middle of the year. After the abdication of Napoleon, the British army was "freed from having to sustain operations on the continent of Europe" and the British government then "decided to redeploy substantial forces in North America to teach the United States a lesson." With British military triumphs in Maine and Connecticut that summer, a number of antiwar Federalists had a change of heart and urged their colleagues to vote more funds to support the war effort. Among them was New York senator Rufus King, who "pleaded for unity in meeting the common threat." He implored his fellow Federalists to support a new proposal from Campbell to enact a $6 million direct tax, because it "promised to revive and support the public credit."

Congress fled Washington in August as the city was sacked, and the White House, Capitol building, and Treasury were torched. British forces then laid siege to Baltimore. Bond sales froze and investors withdrew their gold and silver from U.S. banks, believing that an American defeat was imminent. Many state banks nearly ran out of specie, forcing them to suspend redemption of their notes in gold or silver, which was tantamount to a default. The U.S. financial system was close to collapse.

By mid-September, the federal government had regained control of Baltimore and Washington, and American naval ships had defeated a small British squadron off the coast of New York and achieved another victory in the Battle of Plattsburgh on Lake Champlain. On September 19, Congress reconvened in Blodgett's Hotel, one of the few large buildings still standing in Washington. One of its urgent agenda items was to consider a letter from Madison urging that the "inadequacy of the existing provisions for the wants of the Treasury might be supplied." Explaining that "the situation of our country calls for the greatest of efforts," he pleaded that Congress "take up without delay . . . the subject of pecuniary supplies . . . on a scale commensurate with the extent and the character which the war has assumed." Federal expenditures had escalated from $10 million in 1812 to $35 million in 1814, producing a deficit of over $23 million that year.

The Federalist Resistance

In light of Congress's reluctance to raise taxes throughout much of the war, the revenue-deprived Madison administration constantly lacked credibility among potential lenders. Its ability to borrow was undermined further by partisan fissures. Many of the major lenders in the country, including most northeastern state-chartered banks, were aligned with the Federalists, who refused to support the "offensive war." To them, it was a war of choice rather than a war of necessity. Ironically, that point was made even more salient when the country learned that two days before the United States declared war, the British government had agreed to suspend the offensive Orders in Council. Word of the repeal did not reach America's shores until mid-August, by which time hostilities were well under way.

Federalists in New England opposed the war for a variety of reasons. A major consideration was that the livelihoods of many of them depended on trade with Britain and Canada. In addition, New England ports were extremely vulnerable to attacks from the British navy. As the Treasury was attempting to borrow large sums of money, a Boston paper asked rhetorically, "Will Federalists . . . lend money to our national rulers? It is impossible. . . . If they lend money now, they make themselves parties to violation of the Constitution. . . . Any federalist who lends money to the government will be infamous." To cast doubt on the willingness of the government to repay the bonds, the writer went on to query, "Who can tell whether future rulers may think the debt contracted under such circumstances . . . ought to be repaid?"

Banks in the financial hub of Boston put pressure on those in regions that supported the war not to subscribe to the government's bonds or lend to individuals or corporations who wanted to purchase them. Denying the administration adequate funds, they reasoned, would force a quick end to the war. Until 1814, Boston was excluded by Britain from its naval blockade of American ports. That gave Boston's merchants wartime advantages: when they sold goods imported from Britain to merchants in other parts of the country, they were paid in notes (debt obligations) denominated in gold or silver, drawn on local, state-chartered banks. The Boston middlemen sold these notes to their state-chartered banks, owned mostly by Federalist supporters. The banks then had the option of holding the notes to draw interest, or presenting them to the issuing banks for collection in specie. The possibility that the New England banks might take the latter course in wholesale fashion provided them with leverage to dissuade other regions' banks from buying government bonds.

Boston banks frequently threatened to present these notes for payment—and often did, draining many non-Federalist banks of their holdings of gold and silver and leaving them unable to meet their pledges to buy Treasury securities. Federalist-owned banks also arranged for the sale of short-term British bonds in major East Coast cities. Given the frequent defeats suffered by the U.S. military during the war, these were considered by some American investors more secure than Treasury securities, and they found a receptive market in New York and New England. The bonds had to be paid for with gold, which was then transferred to British authorities in Canada, thereby drawing down American resources.

Federalist members of Congress further undermined the Treasury's borrowing effort. Early in the war, one prominent Federalist, Senator Timothy Pickering of Massachusetts, "warned potential investors that war loans might never be repaid," because the antitax Republicans would repeal the wartime levies, leaving the government with insufficient revenues to redeem its bonds. He sought to fuel the doubts of potential creditors by stating his intention to "oppose any measures for honoring debts contracted during hostilities," whatever course of action the Republicans might follow. Other Federalists made similar statements, believing that Madison would be forced to end the war if the government was unable to borrow. A passionate Federalist who had served as secretary of state under John Adams and earned notoriety by promoting arrests and prosecutions under the Sedition Act of 1798, Pickering had attempted to damage the credibility of his opponents by charging that "Napoleon Bonaparte himself had bribed the Congressional majority [to declare war]."

The Federalists created even more uncertainty by holding a secret convention in Hartford, Connecticut, in December 1814. Rumors circulated that they were plotting secession. They were not; but to show their discontent they issued a report aimed at preventing a recurrence of Jefferson's Embargo Act. It called for amendments to the Constitution that would deny Congress the authority to impose new export restrictions lasting more than two months and would require a two-thirds vote to pass measures restricting trade. To prevent the establishment of a "Virginia dynasty" in the White House, they also sought to limit the presidency to one term and require the president to come from a different state than his immediate predecessor. Congress, though, was dominated by Madison's allies, so such proposals had no chance of being enacted. By the time they were presented, the war was over.

In late 1814, with the commission charged with forging a peace treaty struggling to reach agreement with British authorities and American troops under General Andrew Jackson and Captain Thomas Macdonough winning stunning victories, "most Federalists in Congress, despite disclaimers to the contrary, continued to do everything they could to deny the government the resources it needed." The *Independent Chronicle* of Boston, a critic of efforts to deny the administration such funds, complained about the "pains [the Federalists had] taken to excite every suspicion against our fiscal resources . . . and to persuade many well disposed persons, that the loan of money was an immoral act."

In October 1814, Campbell was replaced as Treasury secretary by Alexander Dallas. Born in Jamaica and educated in Edinburgh and Westminster, the highly talented Dallas had served as secretary of the Commonwealth of Pennsylvania for ten years and was an early supporter of Jeffersonian principles of governance and finance. Nevertheless, faced with the enormity of the Treasury's problems, he proposed doubling excise taxes and other measures aimed at generating $7 million in additional revenues. He also recommended rechartering a national bank as "the only efficient remedy for the disorderly conditions of our circulating medium." As the administration struggled to resolve the crisis created by the war, Dallas confronted the antiwar Federalists and the antitax Republicans much more aggressively than his predecessors had done, insisting on far bolder legislative action from Congress.

With the nation in danger, Congress accepted most of Dallas's recommendations, doubling the direct tax, and increasing and expanding existing excise taxes. Tax receipts surged: in the following year, internal revenues exceeded tariff revenues for the first time since the Washington administration, a situation that would not occur again until the Civil War. Tax payments covered nearly half of government expenditures.

On December 24, 1814, John Quincy Adams, Henry Clay, and Albert Gallatin signed the Treaty of Ghent on behalf of the United States, ending the war. Word of the treaty did not reach all of the American forces until early 1815 and, before it did, Jackson defeated the British at the Battle of New Orleans on January 8.

In the midterm elections of November 1814, held in the midst of an unpopular war in which taxes had been increased significantly, the Republicans maintained roughly a two-to-one majority in both chambers. When Congress reconvened in Washington in early 1815, the Capitol building was still under reconstruction. The new Congress took two major actions to strengthen the nation's security. First, it authorized the creation of a standing army of ten thousand men, roughly a third of its peak strength during the war, but about ten times the size of the small force that the nation had maintained during the early 1800s. It decided that it would be ruinous to continue to rely on state militias to fight a war, as it had attempted to do in 1812. While more than 450,000 militia men had been called up, many did not see action or leave their home states. Later, Congress voted to strengthen the nation's coastal defenses and to expand the facilities at West Point to enable more officers to be trained.

Second, on the recommendation of Dallas, and with Madison's support, Congress chartered the Second Bank of the United States in 1816. The difficulties faced by the government in borrowing funds for the war without the First Bank of the United States, the instability that had resulted from the deterioration of the financial conditions of state-chartered banks, and what Madison referred to as the "embarrassment arising from the want of a uniform national currency," finally convinced Republicans to set aside their fears of a "monstrous" federal financial power. Chartered for twenty years, the second bank was authorized to issue notes backed by specie, receive government deposits, pay government bills, and lend to the Treasury. The federal government would subscribe to one-fifth of its capital. Dallas also proposed an income tax, arguing that it was an indirect tax and therefore did not have to be apportioned among the states. But Congress would not accede to this request, and the idea was abandoned.

The organized effort by the opposition party in Congress and its supporters in the financial community to undermine federal borrowing in order to force the administration to end the war stands as a singular event in U.S. history. There were, to be sure, many valid reasons for opposing the war and for bringing it to a swift conclusion after it was learned that the Orders in Council had been repealed and that the predicted spontaneous uprising in Canada did not occur. But the tactics used by the Federalists to deny the government financing undermined rather than enhanced their credibility and effectiveness as an antiwar party. In the future, there would be partisan efforts to shift the burden of borrowing and taxes from one group to another, or to cut back appropriations requests to limit wartime spending, but the Federalists' organized sabotage of the government's effort to borrow funds to finance the War of 1812 was unique in American history. By deliberately undermining the federal government's creditworthiness, the Federalists also undermined the nation's security.

Although the Federalists succeeded in damaging the government's finances, ultimately they failed to achieve their goals. They gained no political credit and were subject to a great deal of criticism for denying the government funds to prosecute the war. Many Americans had reservations about the war with Britain, but the Federalists' actions were widely seen as unpatriotic and hastened the decline of their party, narrowing its support to a few pockets, primarily in New England. Sean Wilentz, in his book *The Rise of American Democracy*, describes the post-1812 demise of the Federalist Party: "In their own mind the Federalists were bravely defending the political spirit and substance of 1776 against southern planters and the deluded democratic hordes. . . . Yet with their antiwar activities they turned their political movement . . . into a pro-British American Tory party. The sons of New Englanders who had once defied the British Empire now seemed, at best, equivocal in the face of British coercion. The confident, nationalistic party of Washington, Hamilton and Adams had shriveled into the phobic sectional party . . . of Pickering." The Federalists had dealt their own party its coup de grâce.

War Taxes Repealed

While the Republican Congress instituted many of Alexander Dallas's financial plans in 1815, after the war it returned to form and repealed the direct tax and various excise taxes. Still, it determinedly reduced the national debt, which by the end of the conflict had shot up to $127 million—roughly 15 percent of GNP. In his first postwar State of the Union message to Congress, Madison proposed higher tariffs both to produce more revenues for the Treasury and to protect American industry, which had grown dramatically during the war, when British goods were scarce or unavailable. In December 1816, in his final State of the Union, Madison predicted that robust customs revenues would lead to the "early extinguishment of the public debt."

In the elections of 1816, Madison's secretary of state, James Monroe, won the presidency handily. In his 1820 State of the Union message, he noted that in the five years following the war, the government debt had been reduced to just under $92 million. Leaner military spending, a strong economy, and booming trade that produced a flood of import duties, along with the sale of public lands to families moving west, then enabled the government to generate surpluses for nearly two decades. A large portion of these surpluses was to service and then retire wartime bonds, lowering the amount of federal debt dramatically until it was ultimately paid off in the 1830s during Andrew Jackson's administration.

After the War of 1812, legislators in the industrial states feared that the large federal surpluses would give free-trade Southerners ammunition to obtain congressional support for duty reductions. Around this time, the term "impost" receded in the American lexicon, and "tariff" came into common use. In 1816, a protective tariff was imposed, placing an average duty of 25 percent on imports that competed with goods made in the United States. In response, John C. Calhoun of South Carolina, former vice president under John Quincy Adams and Andrew Jackson and one of the giants in Congress during the period, spoke for Southern interests in denouncing this legislation as "an immense tax on one portion of the community [the rural South] to put money into the pockets of another [the manufacturing North]."

In 1818, Northern legislators engineered the passage of legislation to provide generous pensions to Revolutionary War veterans and their families. They did so in part to justify the continuation of protectionist duties, contending that the revenues these levies generated were now needed to fund those newly created pensions. (The final payment was made in 1906— 123 years after the Revolution had ended.) In the years that followed, growing numbers of factories were built throughout the country, broadening the number of workers and businesses that supported higher tariffs—and the number of congressmen and senators committed to sustaining them. Politicians who championed high duties claimed they enabled the country to establish a strong industrial sector by restricting the importation of goods made with cheap European labor. In addition, American citizens demanded more internal improvements, such as roads, canals, harbors, and bridges funded by the federal government. Henry Clay, Abraham Lincoln, and other prominent members of the Whig Party supported high tariffs in part to provide revenues for precisely this purpose. Pressures for more protection for manufacturing and for added customs collections to fund pensions and internal improvements solidified support for higher duties in much of the North and Midwest. Lingering resentment at Britain for dumping large amounts of manufactured goods onto the American market after the war added to demands for higher tariffs that would limit British imports. A growing sense of economic nationalism had taken hold.

Congress further ratcheted up tariffs in 1818, 1824, 1828—the so-called tariff of abominations—and 1832. In 1828, Calhoun derided these Northern-sponsored measures and voiced the South's emerging bitterness—a bitterness that would influence American fiscal policy for generations:

> We cultivate certain great staples for the supply of the general market of the world: They manufacture almost exclusively for the home market. Their object in the Tariff is to keep down foreign competition, in order to obtain a monopoly in the domestic market. The effect on us is to compel us to purchase at a higher price, both what we obtain from them and from others, without receiving a correspondent increase in the price of what we sell.

Pitched battles ensued between Northern and Southern legislators over the level, incidence, and impact of customs duties. Aside from slavery, tariff-related disputes sparked the most divisive confrontations in the nation in the first half of the nineteenth century. Attempts by Southern legislatures to nullify the federal government's tariff legislation as it applied to their states triggered the passage of the 1833 Tariff Act, which gradually reduced duties over the subsequent ten years.

In the 1830s, the population was expanding rapidly and cities were growing. An increasing share of the goods purchased by Americans was either imported, and thus subject to high tariffs, or made by domestic manufacturers whose goods were protected by those tariffs. In either case, they had a sizable impact on American pocketbooks and disproportionately hit low- and middle-income families, who devoted a large portion of their incomes to consumption. This amplified the class tensions surrounding future wartime financing, since government bonds issued during wars were generally bought by wealthy financiers and merchants who had surplus funds to invest, and a substantial portion of the money the government needed to pay interest on those bonds, and ultimately redeem them, was generated by tariffs and excise taxes.

★

The War of 1812 brought the United States, a small power caught between Britain and France, to the brink of disaster. Fraught with partisan and regional divisions, the country was especially vulnerable to foreign threats. The Jeffersonian Republicans did not have a well-thought-out plan to pay for the war and for two years refused to stand down from their populist antitax platform. The Federalists, on the other hand, understood the link between sound finances and the capacity of the government to sustain the war and accordingly sought to undermine America's finances to compel the government to conclude an early peace. This financial discord seriously jeopardized the nation's capacity to defend itself.

That both the president's own party and the opposition refused to give the government financial support during the early part of the war exposed one of the peculiar characteristics of the United States' system of governance: the president's ability to conduct a war as the nation's commander in chief is extensive, but it is also heavily dependent on the willingness of Congress to pay the bills. During the War of 1812, when the government was desperate for funds, the Republican-controlled Congress exercised—or failed to exercise—its financial powers by regularly refusing to vote for critically needed taxes even when the nation was in dire peril. It also added to the country's financial insecurity by abolishing the Bank of the United States just before the war.

For their part, influential Federalists engaged in a conscious effort to cast doubt on the Treasury's ability to pay its debts and to undercut banks that supported the government's attempts to borrow money. Ironically, the circumstances they faced as the party opposed to the war were uncannily similar to opponents of the Iraq War. After the United States declared war, the American people learned that the Orders in Council that had been used to justify the action had been repealed, and, instead of being greeted as liberators in Canada, American troops encountered stiff resistance from local militias. Yet, despite the unpopularity of the war, there was little support for those who sought to deny funding for the troops—a common thread in American history.

The combination of mismanagement, political stubbornness, and financial sabotage pushed the country close to bankruptcy, increasing the possibility of defeat at the hands of the British. At a minimum, it risked forcing the Madison administration into humiliating concessions. The nation's precarious financial situation along with the initial weakness of its regular forces and the excessive dependence on unreliable militias were major vulnerabilities.

In this first challenge to Alexander Hamilton's principles, the country's leaders gained a heightened consciousness of the importance of sound finances to national security. The threat of a financial collapse bore out a point that Hamilton had made two decades earlier—that a weak financial system, and an inability to borrow, would jeopardize the survival of the nation. The failure of the various congressional factions to reach an accommodation to strengthen the country's financial position—as Hamilton and Madison had done in the 1790s—jeopardized the nation's security.

Republican fears of a treacherous consolidation of financial power in the hands of the federal government during the war dissipated between 1812 and 1815. As Jeffersonians including Madison, Gallatin, and Dallas accepted the need for increased federal taxation and borrowing to pay for the war, they realized such measures would not endanger republican liberties but rather protect them. Following the war, the same Republicans who had weakened the ability of the government to finance the war by destroying the First Bank of the United States had a change of heart. The once implacable foes of the bank supported chartering a Second Bank of the United States. The Republicans also repealed most wartime excise taxes and the direct tax, setting at least a temporary precedent for high taxation only in times of war. High tariffs were retained and, in fact, increased after 1815. However, this was less the legacy of the war itself and more the product of the growing pressure for protection of the burgeoning industrial sector.

After the war, Presidents Madison and Monroe pressed Congress to reduce the nation's debt and meticulously reported on their progress, which became a regular feature in their State of the Union messages. In his first message after the war, Madison encouraged Congress to produce the "improved conditions of the public revenue" that "will not only afford the means of maintaining the faith of the Government with its creditors inviolate . . . but will also justify an immediate alleviation of the [debt] burdens imposed by the necessities of war." The next year, he announced with pride that "even within a short period which has elapsed since the return of peace the revenue has far exceeded all current demands on the Treasury." By 1824, President Monroe expressed the "well-founded hope . . . that, should no unexpected event occur, the whole of the public debt may be discharged in the course of ten years."

Within two decades of the war's end, the federal debt had been eliminated, though not without high costs to the nation's political harmony. The devices used—high tariffs, in particular—were to become a significant issue of contention between the North and the South in the decades leading up to the Civil War.

3

The Fiery Trial

A TAX TO SAVE THE UNION

CHASE HAS NO MONEY AND TELLS ME HE CAN RAISE NO MORE.

—ABRAHAM LINCOLN

In his Annual Message to Congress in 1862, President Abraham Lincoln described the traumatic military confrontation of the Civil War as "the fiery trial through which we pass," yet he just as easily could have been referring to the Union's frenetic search for money to pay for the war. There is a tendency today to see the North's success in obtaining that money as inevitable, or at least as foreordained. To Lincoln and the Congress, however, there was nothing inevitable or foreordained about it.

In 1860, the country had recorded a modest budget deficit. But by July 1861, just three months after the start of the war, the deficit had climbed, tracking the rapid increase in military expenditures. When Lincoln's Treasury secretary, Salmon P. Chase, sent Congress an urgent plea for $80 million to pay the government's mounting bills, among the methods he suggested for raising revenues was a new property tax designed to yield $20 million. There had been no such tax since the War of 1812, and it had been extremely unpopular then. Chase, though, praised the levy's "manifest equity" because it would affect only those who had accumulated enough wealth to buy a house or farm, sparing most people with low incomes.

Despite Chase's efforts to sell the idea, strong protests erupted from Republican leaders in Congress, primarily those representing agricultural regions. A property tax, Congressman Owen Lovejoy of Illinois charged, would fall heavily on farmers, but would not touch the earnings of "wealthy capitalists" who owned large amounts of stocks and bonds. Schuyler Colfax, the Speaker of the House, from Indiana, declared, "I cannot go home, and tell my constituents that I voted for a bill" that would tax a farmer while exempting "a millionaire, who has put his entire property into stock." In a heated debate, Thaddeus Stevens of Pennsylvania, chairman of the Ways and Means Committee, countered that for the Treasury's future wartime bond issues to succeed, prospective buyers would have to see "that we have laid taxes which we can enforce, and which we must pledge to them in payment of interest on their loans." The levy on property, in his view, was such a tax.

Opponents in Congress blocked consideration of the proposal and sought an alternate source of revenue that would be acceptable to rural Americans. Colfax proposed legislation to impose "internal duties or direct taxation upon personal income or wealth." Members from other rural constituencies advanced similar proposals. By August 1861, Congress had reached agreement on the nation's first income tax. Considered at the time a radical move, this was only one of many remarkable fiscal policy innovations introduced by the Union during the Civil War.

The challenge for Lincoln, Chase, and their colleagues in Congress was to raise enormous sums in a nation that, since the War of 1812, had relied on tariff collections for most of its revenues and was almost pathologically resistant to any other form of taxation. Moreover, Americans had become accustomed to their leaders reducing—not dramatically increasing—the country's debt. Except for periods of depression or recession, the government had run substantial surpluses since the War of 1812. The administration was further handicapped because the country had few credible financial institutions: no central bank, no national currency, no capacity to collect internal taxes, and no national banking system. And the Union's financial challenges had to be confronted during a war that many in the North opposed and that was marked by frequent military setbacks and horrible human carnage.

A second major challenge during the war was the loss of foreign capital. Inflows had nearly doubled between 1850 and 1860 but dropped sharply as European investors, who had been big buyers of railway stocks and bonds, bank stocks, and state and federal bonds, became increasingly concerned that the country would fragment. Chase recognized the futility of seeking funds abroad. While some foreign investors purchased Union bonds at big discounts, betting on the North's ultimate success, most shied away, believing that the Union's rapidly growing debt could never be repaid even if its troops prevailed in the war. Moreover, foreign investors feared that the North's decision to print large amounts of currency would trigger a collapse in the value of the dollar against gold. Thus, the vast majority of the resources to fund the war had to be mobilized at home.

Lincoln and many Republicans shared Hamilton's view that sound national finances and robust financial institutions were essential to a strong economy and to the government's ability to obtain the extraordinary resources to prosecute the war. During the conflict, they dramatically enlarged the federal government's taxing authority, created a uniform currency, and established a national banking system. These measures enabled them to mobilize massive sums and in the process strengthen the North's economic, political, and social cohesion. Accomplishing those changes proved to be a formidable undertaking. Yet the very wartime upheavals that necessitated such bold tax, banking, and currency reforms also made them possible. The urgent requirements of the period legitimized in the public mind dramatic changes in the nation's financial institutions and an unprecedented expansion of the federal government's fiscal role. At that time, such a dramatic augmentation of government financial power would have been politically impossible without the urgent fiscal requirements of war.

Critical to the Union's financial and political success was Lincoln's emphasis on promoting equity of economic sacrifice. Initially, Union leaders had expected the war to be short and inexpensive, enabling them to avoid levying high taxes, but as the conflict intensified the costs soared. As casualties mounted and victory seemed elusive, discontent grew. It became essential to raise the vast sums required in a way that avoided exacerbating the underlying regional and class divisions. Lincoln and congressional leaders understood this. Just as Hamilton had to forge compromises to fund Revolutionary War debt, Lincoln, Chase, and Congress had to soothe competing factions in order to meet urgent Civil War financial requirements and strengthen Northern political unity.

Financing the Civil War posed a unique, complex, and massive challenge. The scope and savagery of the conflict on the battlefield would leave a permanent mark on the country's social and political fabric, but the war would leave its mark on its financing as well. It was too big and its demands too great for the fiscal structures that preceded it. From small towns and villages throughout the North, men, mostly inexperienced in finance, came together in Washington to confront the task of mobilizing resources on an unprecedented scale in the deadly serious struggle for the Union's survival. The debates they engaged in, the policies they pursued to cope with this crisis, and the innovations they produced left an indelible imprint on the financial system of the United States.

The New Republicans

In the 1850s, the country settled into a business-as-usual mode following the brief Mexican War of 1846–48. Few Americans had any inkling of the intensity or duration of the storm that was about to break upon it or of the severe strain it would place upon the nation's financial resources.

After the Mexican War, members of the newly re-formed Republican Party, an amalgamation of antislavery Whigs, anti-immigration Know-Nothings, Free Soil Party renegades, and antislavery Democrats, regularly pressed to increase the low tariff rates of the 1846 Walker Act. The Walker Tariff reduced the Whigs' "Black Tariff " of 1842 and was crafted by former Democratic senator Robert J. Walker of Mississippi, President James K. Polk's secretary of the Treasury, to smooth over smoldering tensions with Britain over the Oregon boundary and to encourage other countries to open their markets to American grains and other goods. Northern manufacturers opposed it, but a coalition of Southerners and Westerners saw it as a way to boost their agricultural exports and pushed through its passage. Trade increased and, despite the reduction in tariff rates, duty collections rose from roughly $30 million in 1845 to $45 million in 1850. These additional revenues were a key reason that Polk did not have to raise taxes to pay for the Mexican War.

Congressmen from New England and Pennsylvania sought to repeal this tariff legislation to provide protection to their regions' manufacturing base. These efforts were blocked by Southern Democrats, who feared foreign retaliation against their region's agricultural exports, and whose constituents resented having to pay high prices for imported goods, as well as for New England and Mid-Atlantic manufactured products protected by steep import duties. They had sufficient votes to lower tariffs again in 1857.

However, the Panic of 1857—which was precipitated by the failure of the New York City branch of the Ohio Life Insurance and Trust company and a fall in American wheat prices—led to railroad bankruptcies, a collapse in land values, a sharp drop in imports and duty collections, and a depression. Budget deficits were recorded in 1858, 1859, and 1860. Supporters of higher tariffs now pressed their case again, using a new argument—that higher duties were necessary to generate sufficient revenues to reduce the big deficit. But Southerners again blocked their efforts.

The promise of higher tariffs was a central feature in the Republican platform in the 1858 midterm elections. "We demand," the party's platform declared, "that American laborers should be protected against the pauper labor of Europe." A higher tariff, they argued, would "give employment to thousands of mechanics, artisans, and laborers, who have languished for months in unwilling idleness." Voters in manufacturing states, especially in steel- and iron-producing Pennsylvania, rallied around the issue in the 1860 presidential election. Republican support for higher tariffs helped catapult a one-term former Whig congressman from downstate Illinois to the presidency.

At the time of Lincoln's election, the government was faced with a debt of nearly $75 million. With the Civil War looming, the chairman of the House Ways and Means Committee, John Sherman, an Ohio Republican and the brother of General William Tecumseh Sherman, worried that "the problem was not whether we could muster men, but whether we could raise money."

Republicans seized the opportunity to push for higher tariffs. Secession, which began soon after Lincoln's election, led most Southern Democrats to withdraw from Congress by early 1861. Just before Lincoln's victory in November 1860, Republicans held 26 seats in the Senate to the Democrats' 38; 113 seats in the House were occupied by Republicans and 101 by Democrats, with 23 from splinter parties. In the late winter of 1861, after the secession of the eleven states that soon banded together to form the Confederacy, Republicans enjoyed a two-to-one majority in the Senate and held roughly three out of five seats in the House. Capitalizing on these enormous majorities, they enacted legislation to substantially increase customs duties, even before Lincoln's inauguration in March. The champion of this legislation was Representative Justin Morrill of Strafford, Vermont, chairman of the House Ways and Means Subcommittee on Taxation. The son of a rural blacksmith, Morrill had been proprietor of a general store for twenty years and relished his deep small-town roots. Improving education was his passion and, having prospered in business, he founded the town's lending library and established a local lyceum.

In large measure because he had a great many sheep farmers in his district, Morrill was a strong advocate of high tariffs on wool and other textiles. To obtain support for tariffs to protect his constituents, he went along with higher duties to protect products made in the constituencies of other representatives. The war offered Morrill and his allies a new opportunity to pursue their agenda. In early 1861, they argued that increasing tariffs was necessary to generate additional revenues to pay for the war. As military costs increased, so did tariff rates; Congress raised average duties from roughly 20 percent in 1860 to more than 47 percent by 1864, producing around $300 million in customs revenues during the war.

But President Lincoln and most of his Republican colleagues in Congress, while convinced protectionists, also were mindful of who was fighting the war—primarily men from low- and middle-income families. These were precisely the families hurt most by tariffs, which raised the price of many basic consumer goods. To dampen class tensions, Congress structured duties following the model used immediately after the Revolution, "lowest for necessities like food and highest for luxuries like jewelry."

It soon became clear, however, that tariffs could provide only a small fraction of the Union's enormous financial requirements and the search was on for other revenue-raising devices. The prime responsibility fell to Lincoln's Treasury secretary, Salmon Chase, a devout abolitionist from Ohio who had been known as the "Attorney General for Fugitive Slaves." Formerly a Whig, like Lincoln, he had joined two upstart parties, first the Liberty Party and then the Free Soil Party, which opposed extending slavery to "western territories" such as Kansas and Nebraska. Soon, however, he defected to the newly created Republican Party, becoming the first from that party to be elected governor of a major state. When Chase lost the 1860 Republican presidential nomination to Lincoln, the Ohio legislature elected him to the Senate.

Although Lincoln tapped him as Treasury secretary, Chase had little financial experience. Lincoln believed that "his ability, firmness, and purity of character produce[d] the propriety" needed for the job. Moreover, the president-elect was looking for a salve for the merchant class in New York, longtime adversaries of William Seward, who had just been picked to be secretary of state. At first Chase played coy, indicating a reluctance to accept the job. But, as Lincoln had assumed, Chase's consuming ambition led him finally to agree to take charge of the finances of the country under circumstances that he termed "most unpropitious and forbidding." Within the administration, Chase and Secretary of War Edwin M. Stanton were the two most prominent Radical Republicans, pressing the president for immediate abolition and uncompromising toughness in the prosecution of the war.

When it came to fiscal matters, Chase had few strong convictions, other than a belief that a significant level of gold reserves was essential to ensure the government's creditworthiness. Chase was intrepid, if virtually alone, in constantly pressing the president and his advisers to exercise restraint in spending, scolding them for being "heedless of the abyss of bankruptcy and ruin which yawn before us." His stance on trade was shaped in part by his father's experiences during the War of 1812. Ithamar Chase, believing that the cessation of British glass imports offered a significant business opportunity, had invested in a glass factory in Keene, New Hampshire. When the war ended, glass imports resumed and the factory was forced into bankruptcy. The family's finances collapsed and Ithamar suffered a stroke and soon died.

In his early years as a Whig, Chase, perhaps to protect businessmen such as his father, supported the party's stance in favor of high tariffs, but he was not a blind advocate. Political pragmatism led him to seek compromises. When he moved to the Liberty Party and sought to make a political deal with the pro-free-trade Democrats, he compromised on the issue. Still later, reflecting the concerns of his predominantly rural constituents that high tariffs invited European retaliation against U.S. farm exports and disproportionately benefited New England manufacturers, he became a strong free trader. It was enough to make Lincoln hesitate in offering him the Treasury due to the "danger that the protectionists of Pennsylvania will be dissatisfied." Yet Lincoln felt that Chase was the right man for the job. During the war, with little time to devote to financial matters, he left them almost entirely to his Treasury secretary. When asked about such issues, the president reportedly responded, "Go to Secretary Chase; he is managing the finances."

A Tax to Borrow

In considering how best to finance the war, Chase closely studied the techniques employed by Albert Gallatin during the War of 1812. Following a strategy envisaged by his prominent predecessor, Chase stated that he planned to "finance . . . war costs on borrowed funds, and increase . . . taxes only for the purpose of covering service on the newly incurred debt."

Chase saw, as had Gallatin and Hamilton before him, that massive federal borrowing would be possible only if there were a large and reliable stream of revenues coming to the government to service and repay the debt. "Public credit can only be supported by public faith," he informed Congress, and that required "the prompt and punctual fulfillment of every public obligation." Quite simply, the Treasury could not borrow the necessary funds unless new taxes were introduced. In July 1861, Chase estimated that government spending would amount to $318 million through the middle of the following year. He concluded that if he could raise $80 million in taxes, he would have the financial credibility to go to the markets to borrow the remaining $240 million.

Chase found a staunch ally in Thaddeus Stevens. Stevens was by far the most powerful member of the House at the time and, as a child of poverty, a powerful voice for the underprivileged. But Stevens was also a tough legislator, the "despotic ruler of the House," as one observer wrote, and a formidable protagonist. "No Republican was permitted by 'Old Thad' to oppose his imperious will without suffering a tongue-lashing that terrified others if it did not bring the refractory representative back to harness." As a deeply committed abolitionist and Radical Republican, Stevens often criticized Lincoln for not being tough enough in his prosecution of the war. Yet his strong commitment to the preservation and success of the Union led him to vigorously defend the administration's requests for increased revenues. In a debate on fiscal policy early in the war, he warned his colleagues on the committee, "The capitalists must be assured that we have laid taxes which we can enforce, and which we must pledge to them in payment of interest on their loans, or we shall get no money."

The Union army's defeat at Bull Run in July 1861 cooled the desire of banks to lend to the government. Chase and congressional Republicans decided that they must raise taxes aggressively to produce more revenues to reassure investors. They first considered a property tax, a method last used during the War of 1812. Chase and his supporters estimated it could produce $20 million and Chase argued that it would be fairer to the average American than increasing tariffs or excise taxes, as it was based on accumulated wealth in the form of houses, buildings, or farms.

The suggestion evoked a sharp reaction from populist and agrarian interests and triggered a fierce debate over the issue of social equity.

Congressmen from prairie states, border states, and the less-affluent farming states in the East objected strenuously. Under the Constitution, this tax had to be apportioned among the states based on the relative size of their populations rather than on the value of their property, so if New Jersey and New York had precisely the same populations, they would pay the same proportion of the property tax even if the value of the land and buildings in New York were three times that in New Jersey. Representatives from these less affluent regions argued that the tax burden on their constituents as a percentage of their wealth would be greater than on inhabitants of the richer, industrialized northeastern states. Opponents also protested the unfairness of taxing the owners of homes and farms while not taxing the wealth derived from stocks and bonds. Indicative of the criticism of the property tax was the reaction of House Speaker Schuyler Colfax. A former Whig and Know-Nothing, a member of his state's constitutional convention and a Radical Republican, he strongly supported Lincoln throughout the war. Yet, when faced with Chase's property tax proposal, Colfax demurred. The property tax, proclaimed Colfax, is "the most odious tax we can levy."

Intense congressional opposition led to a search for a tax that would be considered fairer by rural constituencies. Legislators were aware of the various features of the British income tax, which had been first proposed by William Pitt the Younger in 1798 to pay for weapons and supplies in preparation for the Napoleonic Wars with France. Implemented in 1799, the tax featured graduated payment rates, with the lowest set below 1 percent and the highest at 10 percent. The tax was suspended in 1802 during a temporary peace, and then reinstated in 1803, when war broke out again. Abolished in 1816 after the Battle of Waterloo, it was restored again in 1842 to meet the government's growing revenue requirements and then increased substantially to pay for the Crimean War.

Members of Congress also were familiar with Adam Smith's classic book *The Wealth of Nations*, in which Smith had written, "The subjects of every state ought to contribute towards the support of the state, as nearly as possible, in proportion to their respective abilities; that is in proportion to the revenue they enjoy under the protection of the state." This argument was distilled into what came to be known as the "ability to pay" principle.

Smith, however, recognized the difficulty of raising taxes in time of war, when governments were "unwilling [to] increase their revenues in proportion to the increase of their expense . . . for fear of offending their people, who, by so great and so sudden an increase of taxes, would soon be disgusted with the war." He also noted that governments often are reluctant to impose new or higher taxes early in a war because of an "inability" to determine the war's future costs. "The facility of borrowing," he wrote, "delivers them from the embarrassment which this fear and inability would otherwise occasion." With these few words, Smith had articulated the central issues in the debate in the United States and other nations over whether and how much to borrow and tax during wartime.

The idea of a federal income tax was widely regarded as radical and nearly inconceivable. Those suspicious of any increase in federal financial power considered it to be another attempt by the federal government to undermine the power of the states. Wealthy Americans deplored it as an unjust and heavy-handed federal intrusion. Other critics derided it as a "burdensome impost" and "inquisitorial." Some denounced it as being antidemocratic on grounds that it "punished men because they are rich." Opponents also argued against it on constitutional grounds, declaring that it was a "direct tax" that failed the test of "apportionment."

Schuyler Colfax dismissed all the criticism. The Speaker of the House insisted that an income tax would be much fairer than the "odious" property tax. He proposed that Congress enact a tax on "stocks, bonds, mortgages, money and interest—and income earned from them." The idea of an income tax also received support from some high-tariff stalwarts, including Morrill of Vermont. The tax appealed to his populist leanings. Further, many of his low-income constituents had been hurt by the higher cost of consumer goods resulting from tariff increases. Though he had once regarded the proposed income tax as the "least defensible" of taxes, he understood its political viability, noting, "It will, in the end, be adopted and it would be the most just, and undoubtedly the most popular, if any tax can be popular."

There were semantic battles as well. Supporters of the income tax countered the charge that it was a direct tax, and therefore had to be apportioned among the states on the basis of population, claiming that the levy did not actually tax property "directly"—only the earnings from property—and should thus be considered an "indirect" tax.

In need of revenues and anxious to offset grumblings that low-income farmers and workers were bearing the brunt of the war's costs due to high tariffs, the House passed legislation levying a 3 percent tax on annual incomes above $600. The measure then went to the Senate, where its strongest supporter, the highly regarded chairman of the Finance Committee, William Pitt Fessenden of Maine, drew upon his reputation as a skilled debater and expert on financial matters. A former Whig who had served four terms in the House, Fessenden was a prominent founder of the Republican Party and an ardent abolitionist. His three sons had joined the Union army when the war began. Two rose to the rank of general and one was killed in the Second Battle of Bull Run. "I am inclined very much to favor the idea of a tax upon incomes," Fessenden declared, "for the reason that, taking both measures together [the income tax and a tariff bill being considered at the same time] the burdens will be more equalized on all classes of the community, especially on those who will be able to bear them." He proposed a higher, but more targeted, levy than that passed by the House: a 5 percent tax on incomes over $1,000. It was passed by the full Senate. The bills then went into a negotiation between the two bodies.

The outcome was the nation's first federal income tax, a "flat" 3 percent levy on incomes above $800 signed into law by President Lincoln on August 5, 1861. Most Americans made far less than $800—the average annual income that year was only $150—so the vast majority did not have to pay the tax. It was a victory for the populists and advocates for the working class and family farmers, who were largely untouched by the levy. The *New York Herald* announced that "millionaires like Mr. W. B. Astor, Commodore Vanderbilt . . . and others will henceforth contribute a fair proportion of their wealth to the support of the national government." The more understated *New York Times* editorialized that the income tax was "one of the most equitable and bearable taxes that can be proposed." Congress skirted the constitutionality issue by labeling the income tax an "income duty."

Yet the 1861 legislation had one big flaw: it did not create machinery to collect the levy, and, as Sidney Ratner observed in his book *American Taxation*, Secretary Chase "seized every excuse to avoid use of the income tax." He questioned whether it would raise much money, citing "the lack of statistics for estimating the probable yield [and] the large number of incomes exempted . . . by the provisions taxing incomes above $800 a year." Chase refused to establish a new collection vehicle, arguing that doing so would impose excessive administrative costs on the Treasury while producing little revenue. He essentially boycotted the tax; as a result, no income tax was collected under the 1861 act. The legislation also included a property tax designed to raise $20 million, allocated among the remaining states according to their percentage of the population, with the state governments responsible for collection. It was not to be assessed until April 1862, by which time most officials expected the war would be over, so a portion was also made applicable to the seceded states, which would then have to pay the tax when they rejoined the Union. As it turned out, even the states remaining in the Union did not pay cash; they fulfilled their obligations by supplying troops and supplies instead.

A Year of Despair

With steady news of the Union's defeats in 1861, public confidence fell sharply. Uncertain over the outcome of the war, nervous investors withdrew large amounts of gold from Northern banks to the point that in December most of them suspended specie payment and stopped purchasing government bonds. With the Treasury having lost a large amount of its gold reserves and facing resistance from the banks to its efforts to borrow more, it also suspended specie payments. Lincoln despaired that "Chase has no money and tells me he can raise no more." Adding to Lincoln's concerns, the Treasury secretary reported that he had underestimated the cost of the war for 1861–62. Rather than $318 million, Chase now put the figure at $532 million. And only $55 million in taxes and tariffs was expected.

Chase now did a complete about-face on the income tax, urging Congress to enact a new one quickly, with the aim of producing $10 million in additional revenues. While he still was concerned about the cost of establishing a bureaucracy for collection, he had become less skeptical about the tax's revenue-raising potential, concluding that it could generate significant sums and was "just in its principle, inasmuch as it requires largest contributions from largest means." Chase also requested enactment of a new direct tax on property aimed at generating another $20 million in revenues, along with excise taxes adding up to $30 million and higher duties on such staples as coffee, tea, and sugar. He capped the plan off with an innovative recommendation to create a national banking system that would establish a uniform national currency and enhance the sale of government bonds.

Urged on by Chase, in early 1862, Congress set about writing a new revenue bill. Justin Morrill, as chairman of the Taxation Subcommittee, introduced the legislation, lamenting that a "generation must be annually taxed for this parricidal attempt to destroy the government of our fathers."

Morrill advocated continuation of a flat income tax rather than enactment of a graduated one that imposed higher rates on the wealthy. The House accepted Morrill's recommendation to maintain the current uniform 3 percent tax rate, but in order to broaden the tax base and generate additional revenue it favored lowering the personal exemption to $600 from $800. Even with the lower exemption, House leaders comforted themselves with the assurance that only the rich would be subject to the tax. Since $600 was still a very high income, less than 3 percent of the population would have to pay the levy. Supporters also noted that equity was being served because "the modest tax on those above the $600 exemption . . . ensured that well-to-do Americans offered something extra to the national coffers."

The Senate agreed to the lower personal exemption, but powerful members from farm states insisted on rescinding the property tax, which was highly unpopular among their constituents. To make up for the lost revenues, Fessenden, who admitted that Congress was struggling "to find our way in the comparative dark," and his colleagues added new "brackets" in order to impose higher taxes on and obtain more funds from the most affluent. Their bill maintained the 3 percent tax rate on incomes between $600 and $10,000 but raised the rate to 5 percent on incomes between $10,000 and $50,000 and to 7.5 percent on incomes above $50,000. In the final House-Senate compromise, the Senate's top tax bracket was eliminated so everyone earning over $10,000 paid the same 5 percent rate.

To bring various interest groups on board, the legislation contained a host of deductions. Interest on mortgages was made deductible (to satisfy middle-class home owners) as were state and local tax payments (to satisfy state governments). Some indirect taxes paid to the government, such as customs duties, were also made deductible to avoid double taxation. In order to ease the Treasury's ability to borrow, interest on Union bonds would be taxed at a low 1.5 percent. Congress suspended the much resented property tax for two years, after which it was allowed to die. And this time, legislators established an institution to collect the income tax—the Bureau of Internal Revenue (BIR), located in the Treasury.

Congress attempted to increase tax fairness further, as well as to obtain additional revenues, by including in the bill an inheritance tax—the first in U.S. history—on estates in excess of $1,000. To avoid a constitutional conflict over the question of whether this was a direct tax and therefore had to be apportioned among the states, it was labeled an "excise tax." Large inheritances were taxed on a graduated scale, with rates ranging from 0.75 percent to 5 percent, depending on the size of the estate and an heir's relationship to the deceased. And for the first time since the War of 1812, Congress imposed excise taxes, assessing them on a wide range of items, including liquor, tobacco, commodities, jewelry, playing cards, telegrams, leather, licenses, and other legal documents. It also levied taxes on utilities, banks, insurance companies, railroads, and ferry boats.

As in the case of tariffs, legislators minimized the impact of these measures on low-income households. Thaddeus Stevens noted that Congress had placed "no burdens on those who have but small means . . . so that the poor man's tenement shall not be disturbed by the tax gatherer" and it had raised "the largest sums from articles of luxury, and from the large profits of wealthy men." No levies were imposed on farm produce in order to avoid a tax on "the food of the poor"; the legislation also eschewed levies on raw materials in order to avoid burdening manufacturers. It was a clever interregional compromise.

To improve tax collection, Congress adopted another practice from Britain called "collection of revenues at the source." The British Parliament had introduced the concept in 1803. Because of its success, William Gladstone had referred to his nation's income tax system as a "colossal engine of finance." The 1862 act, signed into law on July 1, grafted this practice onto U.S. tax law. It required federal agencies to withhold taxes from the pay of civilian and military employees and railroads and financial institutions to withhold taxes before distributing dividend and interest payments to investors.

The Battle over the Bureau

The decision to create the Bureau of Internal Revenue was highly controversial and ultimately reflected the distance the country had traveled since its early days. The old Hamiltonian-Jeffersonian debate over whether fiscal powers should be placed in the hands of the federal government or retained by the states reemerged. Some members of Congress wanted the states to collect the new income tax. In the 1861 debate on the direct property tax, Representative Roscoe Conkling of New York had insisted that "one of the most obnoxious . . . of all its features is that which creates an army of officials whose business it is to collect this tax." Conkling believed that such a bureaucracy could be avoided if the states were given authority to collect the tax on behalf of the federal government, as had been the case during the War of 1812.

Urging that the federal government assume responsibility for collecting all of its taxes, Thaddeus Stevens turned Conkling's "army" metaphor on him. "I know," he asserted, "that the army of collectors are odious everywhere; but I know, also, that they are not quite so dangerous to my constituents, and I hope they are not to the members of this House, as the army of rebels that renders this other army necessary; for the one must be raised or the other will be triumphant."

In 1861, Congress, imagining a short war and a short-term financial need, ultimately accepted Conkling's argument against setting up a new bureaucracy to collect the property tax and gave that responsibility to the individual states. In 1862, however, the outcome was different. This time, Conkling sought to have the states also collect the income tax. He echoed Jefferson's concern that giving national authorities the responsibility of revenue collection would lead to a dangerous "concentration and consolidation of power" in the hands of the federal government. But Stevens was able to rally other congressmen to his position that the federal government should collect this tax. Representative John Hutchins, a Republican from Ohio, noted that in the past leaders had been "carried away with the idea of state rights," but in view of the need to raise enormous amounts of revenue for the war, "Congress should not shrink from exercising those powers enshrined in the Constitution, including the right to impose and collect taxes."

Majorities in both houses of Congress agreed with his reasoning. They were no longer willing to leave the collection of federal income taxes to the states. For many, such dependence conjured up visions of the terrible financial situation the young country had faced under the Articles of Confederation. In the Hamiltonian tradition, Lincoln and his supporters in Congress insisted that the goal of the nation's financial system should be not simply to collect ample amounts of revenue but to do so in a way that also strengthened the financial role of the central government and pulled competing regional and economic interests into a more unified national economy.

Morrill gave voice to this sentiment: "In this emergency we cannot afford to return to the pusillanimity of the old Confederation, and request the states to make their contributions, and shiver in the wind if any should fail to do so. . . . It is indispensable that the [federal] government shall have within its own control . . . the means of meeting all its vast engagements." The necessities of war proved to be the decisive factor in the creation of the new Bureau of Internal Revenue.

Lincoln signed the new tax bill into law on July 1, 1862—making it the first operational income tax in U.S. history. It was the first of a series of measures, taken in the crucible of war, that radically changed the nation's fiscal structure. War, and in this case war to maintain the very unity of the nation, meant Congress was willing to greatly strengthen the federal government's financial powers, which would have been highly unlikely in more tranquil times.

Despite this revolutionary change, some familiar refrains emerged. Led by Morrill, supporters of protectionist tariffs considered this legislation to be a reason, or excuse, to raise duties again, arguing that higher customs levies would serve as a "reparation" for American manufacturing, which would suffer a loss in competitiveness compared to the manufacturers of other countries that did not have to pay such stiff internal taxes. "If we bleed manufacturers," Morrill argued, "we must see to it that the proper tonic is administered at the same time." Otherwise, he cautioned, "we shall destroy the goose that laid the golden egg." Higher tariffs did, in fact, strengthen domestic industry but were hardly needed, as surging wartime demand boosted the profits of most companies.

The Sacrifice of the Wealthy

As the war continued, the Treasury was under pressure to generate larger and larger sums to meet the Union's growing military expenditures. Lincoln, Chase, and Republican congressional leaders at the time hoped to avoid imposing higher income taxes to pay for the war. They worried that doing so might damage the North's private sector, which they saw as giving the Union a great advantage over the Confederacy. The North possessed far more steel foundries, food-growing farms, railway capacity, and manufacturing plants than the South, and these enabled it to turn out and quickly transport far greater amounts of food, supplies, and munitions than the Confederacy.

At the same time, Union leaders had to be mindful of the need to sustain popular support in light of already enormous military sacrifices and the growing economic hardship faced by many Northerners due to inflation and the prolonged service of their breadwinners in the military. The administration and Congress were determined to demonstrate to a broad section of the population that the wealthy, some of whom were making fortunes supplying the Union army and were often sheltered from the human cost of the war by paying others to fight for them, were doing their part to ensure victory.

In early 1864, Chase attempted to persuade congressional leaders to raise the income tax rate on the nation's most affluent citizens. Morrill resisted, declaring that "this inequality is in fact no less than a confiscation of property," and introduced the objection—which opponents of high taxes on the wealthy continue to make—that "people who are taxed unequally on their incomes regard themselves as unjustly treated, and seek all manner of ways and means to avoid it." He pressed for a return of a flat tax, of 5 percent on all incomes above $600. Resistance also came from the Senate; invoking more than a little hyperbole, New York Republican Ira Harris complained, "The very best men in New York by hundreds, nay by thousands, have been crushed and overthrown" by the income tax.

However, he was challenged by another New Yorker, a director of the Buffalo and New York Railway Company, Representative Augustus Frank. Frank countered that a highly graduated tax schedule was the best means available for adding money to the war coffers and adding credibility to the government's bonds. "It is just, right and proper" he said, "that those having a larger amount of income shall pay a larger amount of tax. . . . The larger the tax we pay at this time the safer we are and the better will be the securities of the government." Supporters of a sharply graduated rate structure prevailed. The government simply needed more money and majorities in the Senate and House recognized that a higher tax on the wealthy was one way to get it, with the added advantage that this made the system appear more just in the eyes of most of their constituents.

The Revenue Act of 1864, passed in June, increased the marginal tax rate on incomes between $600 and $5,000 from 3 percent to 5 percent; incomes above $5,000 but below $10,000 were to be taxed at a 7.5 percent rate; incomes above $10,000 were to be taxed at 10 percent. The tax rate on dividends and interest paid by railroads and financial institutions was increased and the practice of withholding was extended to dividends and interest paid by canal and turnpike companies. Congress also increased the inheritance tax rate, along with a host of excise, license, and business taxes.

In July, Congress passed another bill to generate extra funds to boost flagging army enlistment. That legislation imposed, retroactively, a "surcharge" of 5 percent on all taxable income earned in 1863, so that individuals who had expected to pay taxes at the 3 percent rate under the 1862 act suddenly found themselves facing an 8 percent rate, and those who had expected to pay 5 percent were now in the 10 percent bracket. Although the principle behind the legislation, which imposed greater burdens on those with the highest incomes than on those with lower incomes, was inconsistent with the one that had motivated Morrill to advocate a "flat tax," he defended the new tax's justice, noting that it would be "paid by those who are able to pay it and who have the most at stake in sustaining the credit of the country." However, James Brooks of New York, one of the remaining Democrats in Congress and the owner of the antiabolitionist, anti-Lincoln *New York Express,* denounced the legislation as "an exclusive burden on industry, enterprise, and labor and as failing to touch the farming class because their support was desired in the coming presidential election."

In early 1865, Congress was forced to raise taxes again. Once more, Morrill took the lead, introducing legislation to increase revenues "at the same time [that] we are adding to our forces in the field." He asserted that this was necessary to maintain the creditworthiness of the government, which was in the process of borrowing large additional sums of money. Returning to his earlier tax philosophy, Morrill proposed a single rate of 10 percent on incomes above $3,000, but the majority in the House supported a reduced levy on lower incomes along with a 10 percent rate on incomes above $5,000.

The issue of the rising federal debt played a prominent role in the Senate's debate over the bill. As during the early part of the nineteenth century, high debt was viewed by many Americans as a threat to the nation's working classes. John Sherman, now in the Senate, having been elected to fill the seat vacated when Chase went to the Treasury, summoned up the old Jefferson-Jackson argument that a massive sale of government bonds would produce significant economic benefits for those who owned them at the expense of workers and farmers who would pay high taxes after the war to service them. He predicted that the spiraling wartime debt would lead "in the dim future of our country [to] the same uneasy struggle between capital and labor, between the rich and the poor, between fund-holders and property-owners that has marked the history of Great Britain for the last fifty years."

Based on these concerns, the Senate countered the House legislation with a proposal to decrease the threshold for payment of the 10 percent tax in order to broaden the tax base and thus produce more revenues. In the House-Senate Conference Committee, supporters of a more steeply graduated rate structure prevailed. Congress ultimately enacted legislation that included a 5 percent tax on incomes between $600 and $5,000 and a 10 percent tax on incomes above $10,000. Roughly 10 percent of Northern households were subject to the income tax under the 1865 act.

Around the same time, Lincoln was considering yet another tax increase, aimed at financing an initiative to end the war later that spring. He hoped to raise $400 million to give compensation to states of the Confederacy—on a state-by-state basis—if they freed their slaves and agreed to end the war. A state would receive the first half of its funds when it had ceased "all resistance to the national authority" and the second half if it ratified the Thirteenth Amendment, freeing all slaves, by July 1, 1865. Lincoln's cabinet unanimously objected to the proposition, although the president pointed out that the amount requested was roughly equivalent to the likely cost of continuing the war for another one or two hundred days, and that an early peace would save countless lives and a great deal of property. The president never submitted the plan to Congress.

The various taxes imposed during the Civil War produced revenues unprecedented in American history to that point and ultimately paid for a quarter of the Union's enormous wartime expenses. (In contrast, the Confederacy's taxes covered only 5 percent of its war costs.) The income tax initially had been instituted primarily to improve the perception of fairness in the system, but once its revenue-raising potential was recognized, fairness became a secondary consideration, and income taxes became increasingly graduated. In the last year of the war, the income tax provided one-fifth of the Union's revenues.

The Birth of Greenbacks

To support the war effort, Union leaders also resorted to a device utilized liberally during the Revolution: the printing press.

Before the outbreak of the Civil War, federally issued money consisted of gold, silver, and copper coins. The government itself had not printed paper money since the Revolution; the only national currency had been notes issued by the now defunct First and Second Banks of the United States. Hamilton had been clear in warning that "the stamping of paper is an operation so much easier than the laying of taxes that a government in the practice of such paper emissions would rarely fail in any such emergency to indulge itself too far." His fear, of course, was that the overzealous printing of money would lead to inflation, whereas notes issued by an independent, nationally chartered bank, backed by gold, would be a credible national currency.

But there was no central bank in 1861. The Second Bank of the United States had been shut down by President Andrew Jackson. No national currency existed, and gold, silver, and copper were scarce, so only a limited number of coins could be minted. The existing supply of money was grossly inadequate to provide the enormous amount of funds the wartime government required.

To make matters worse, the banking system was in chaos. In the years immediately before the Civil War, roughly sixteen hundred state-chartered banks dotted the American landscape, each issuing its own notes. Roughly seven thousand varieties of banknotes were in circulation. Some were issued by legitimate state-chartered banks, but many were of dubious quality or simply counterfeit. Notes issued by banks that had been closed for years or were in default, as well as those bearing the names of fictional banks, were all part of the bewildering currency mélange of the 1850s. Even notes of legitimate banks tended to lose a significant portion of their value when they were presented at a great distance from the issuing bank. The banking system was haphazard and virtually unregulated.

Because the notes of state-chartered banks were generally accepted only in the state of the issuing bank, the government had difficulty in procuring goods and services for the military, just as it did during the War of 1812. Taxes paid in notes issued by a bank in one state generally could not be used to purchase supplies in another state, constraining the War Department's procurement flexibility. With the advent of war, most Northern workers and businesses essentially were mobilized in support of the war effort and came into the direct or indirect employ of the government, as soldiers, suppliers, or in other supporting roles. As a result, procurement inflexibility escalated into a serious military obstacle. The Union government "needed to establish a currency [that would be] uniformly acceptable."

In December 1861, the Ways and Means Subcommittee on Taxation and Loans, chaired by Elbridge G. Spaulding, a Republican representative from Buffalo, New York, drafted a bill to create a new currency that would enjoy the status of "legal money and legal tender in payment of all debts, public and private, within the United States." Spaulding's currency would be issued directly by the government and its value would be drawn solely from a federal requirement that it be accepted for all private, and most government, transactions. It would not be redeemable on demand for specie. Chase, who believed the financial system should be rooted in gold, registered his profound objections. Like Hamilton, he favored a currency consisting of notes issued by nationally chartered banks that were backed by government bonds, which were in turn backed by gold.

Spaulding's proposal initially was denounced as too radical by many of his committee colleagues, but wartime necessitated more federal resources and a less chaotic currency system. A majority of the Ways and Means Committee overcame their reservations, accepted Spaulding's proposal, and urged the full House to authorize the Treasury to print "legal tender."

The idea immediately drew fire on the House floor. The horrible precedent of the Continentals was frequently cited. Congressman George Pendleton of Ohio, a Democrat, observed that "the wit of man has never discovered a means by which paper currency can be kept at par value, except by its speedy, cheap certain convertibility into gold or silver." His passions rising, he went on to warn, "If this bill is passed, prices will be inflated . . . incomes will depreciate; the savings of the poor will vanish; the hoardings of the widow will melt away; bonds, mortgages, and notes—everything of fixed value—will lose their value." Chase threatened to resign if the legislation was enacted. An observer wrote, "I learn (but not from Governor C) that he has declared that if Congress persists in such a course, and fails to carry out his policy, bank bill included—he will no longer be responsible for the national finances by remaining in the Treasury." Morrill also opposed the legislation, prophesying that the creation of the currency would "be of greater advantage to the enemy . . . it will injure creditors; it will increase prices; it will increase many-fold the costs of war." Opponents also argued that the Constitution gave Congress the power only to "coin money" and "regulate the value thereof "—not to print money. The collapse in value of the Continentals had been much on the minds of the framers when this provision was written.

On February 3, 1862, desperate for cash, Chase changed his tune. "Immediate action is of great importance," the secretary informed Congress; "The Treasury is nearly empty." In view of the government's urgent resource requirements, Chase had come "with reluctance to the conclusion that the legal tender clause is a necessity."

Congressional leaders also realized that the financial demands of the war called for extraordinary measures. Although Thaddeus Stevens had reservations about the constitutionality of the bill, he supported it on grounds reminiscent of Hamilton's invocation of the doctrine of "implied powers" in defense of the First Bank of the United States. "If nothing could be done by Congress except what is enumerated in the Constitution, government would not last a week," Stevens said. Fessenden took a similar view. Although he considered legal tender "of doubtful constitutionality" and admitted that it "shocks all my notions of political, moral and national honor," he reconciled himself to it because "to leave the government without resources in such a crisis is not to be thought of."

Late in February, Congress passed the Legal Tender Act, authorizing an initial issue of $150 million of the new federal currency. Denominations ranged from five to one thousand dollars. Two additional issues followed; one, in August 1862, was composed only of one-dollar and two-dollar notes, and another, in 1863, included a wider range of denominations. The new notes could be used for virtually all transactions except for payment of customs duties and interest on federal bonds. Both had to be paid in gold coin. The inflow of gold through customs duties was essential because the sale of some categories of Union bonds depended on the government's credible promise to make the interest payments on them in gold. The new "legal tender" was printed with green ink on one side, and the notes were quickly nicknamed "greenbacks." (Confederate currency, printed with blue-gray ink, was known as "blue backs.") Chase, who was planning to challenge Lincoln for the Republican presidential nomination in 1864, had his portrait featured on the widely circulated one-dollar bill.

Despite supporting the printing of greenbacks and having his picture placed on them, Chase later had second thoughts. After failing to dislodge Lincoln as the Republican nominee, and then being fired by him, Chase was appointed by the president to be chief justice of the United States, following the death of Roger Taney. In 1870, Chase wrote the Court's majority opinion striking down the Legal Tender Act, holding that it was a violation of the Fifth Amendment's prohibition against taking property without due process because it forced Americans to accept greenbacks in repayment of private debts that originally had been contracted to be settled in gold. This decision was reversed in 1871, after President Ulysses

S. Grant deliberately appointed two justices who disagreed with the 1870 decision.

The $450 million worth of greenbacks that were issued covered nearly 15 percent of the cost of the war. The value of greenbacks fluctuated as the fortunes of the Union army ebbed and flowed. Originally, a one-dollar note was worth roughly one gold dollar. Its value hovered around that level in early 1862, but declined as the volume of greenbacks in circulation increased. When a series of Union military defeats increased fears of a Confederate victory, nearly three greenback dollars were required to buy a gold dollar or the equivalent amount of goods.

Many Northerners had taken to hoarding coins in case the Union lost. Some exported coins because the value of the metal contained in them when sold abroad fetched more than the value of the money itself in the United States. To make up for the decline in the number of coins in circulation, the Treasury allowed postage stamps to be used as cash and then printed currency in denominations as low as three, five, and ten cents, known as "fractional currency," "paper coins," or—as they lost value—"shinplasters." Fractional currency issues eventually totaled $50 million.

As Hamilton had predicted, overly enthusiastic use of the federal printing press proved to be a significant contributor to inflation. The Civil War required a large number of manufacturers to shift from civilian to military production and Northern factories embarked on a massive effort to turn out guns, munitions, uniforms, wagons, and other items. In later wars, taxes and bond drives would curb civilian purchasing power and avoid steep price increases. During the Civil War era, however, neither the fledgling economics professionals nor government financial officials understood the potential use of borrowing and taxation to control inflation. As a result, Union fiscal policy did little to stifle growing nonmilitary spending, which competed with rapidly increasing government purchases to push up prices. Printing greenbacks added further to civilian spending power, and prices rose by nearly 25 percent annually. This hit workers and soldiers on fixed salaries especially hard, contributing to social unrest.

The Confederacy fared much worse. Its economy was devastated by a 9,000 percent inflation rate, caused primarily by far greater resort to the printing press due to a weak tax base and an inability to raise outside funds. It had only small amounts of gold and silver at the outset of the war. Moreover, its once booming cotton exports, a potential source of revenue, were dramatically curtailed by the Union's naval blockade. Import duties and export tax revenues virtually disappeared and bond sales in Britain backed by future cotton exports produced poor results. Printing currency was the South's last option; by 1863, $900 million worth of Confederate currency was in circulation, and the amounts increased from there. The final figure is sheer guesswork. Even as many Northerners came to regard greenbacks as an unreliable store of value, Southerners increasingly hoarded the North's money, which inspired more confidence.

To improve financial regulation, better integrate the nation's banking system, boost bond sales, and enhance the country's liquidity, Congress acted on Secretary Chase's innovative proposal to create a national banking system. The National Bank Act of 1863 authorized the establishment of federally chartered banks. To qualify for a federal charter, a bank was required to purchase Treasury bonds in an amount equal to one-third of its capital, thus creating extra demand. The Treasury then authorized these banks to issue national banknotes in amounts equivalent to 90 percent of the value of the federal bonds. These notes bore the names of the individual issuing bank on their face, but were printed in a uniform size and design at the same facility that printed greenbacks. The notes collectively served as a de facto second national currency.

Initially, only a few state-chartered banks shifted to national charters, as most preferred the generally lax state regulations to more stringent federal oversight. To push the matter, in 1864, Congress levied a 2 percent tax on state-chartered banknotes, but with only modest results. So in the following year, Congress administered what it hoped would be the coup de grâce—a 10 percent tax on state banknotes, forcing all but the most recalcitrant or robust of these banks to seek federal charters. Fewer than one-fifth of the state-chartered banks survived the war, and by the end of 1865 a network of sixteen hundred nationally chartered banks had been established in the North.

Borrowing—and More Borrowing

The Civil War was the most expensive conflict the country had experienced. Its costs far outpaced the Union's rapidly growing collection of taxes and duties as well as the enormous volume of currency creation, forcing Chase to dramatically increase borrowing.

In the summer of 1861, a number of state-chartered banks had expressed a willingness to buy government-issued interest-bearing notes. Transactions were to be in gold coin. The banks initially pledged to purchase $50 million worth of notes at a 7.30 percent interest rate (these were commonly known as "seven-thirties"), with an option to buy $100 million more in two equal installments later in the year. The subscribing banks had expected to resell the notes quickly, but they soon encountered difficulties finding buyers. By the end of the year, they were facing serious financial problems of their own, and further bank subscriptions ceased.

Chase inadvertently complicated the banks' financial problems. Bank officials had assumed that the Treasury would keep the gold it had borrowed on deposit in the same banks that bought the notes and then draw down their deposits by use of checks when the money was needed. They also expected that contractors and others receiving the Treasury's checks would simply redeposit the money they earned in the banking system. Instead, Chase, ever focused on gold, insisted that the banks that had purchased the notes transfer the funds directly to the Treasury in the form of gold. This depleted the banks' already scarce specie reserves.

At the same time that it was selling the seven-thirties, the Treasury also issued one-year noninterest-bearing "demand notes" to pay the salaries of government employees. The notes carried a requirement to "pay to the bearer . . . [gold] dollars on demand," an option holders of greenbacks did not have. For a time, the notes served as yet another form of Union currency. However, declining fortunes on the battlefield, along with concerns about higher inflation, spurred many holders of these notes to present them to state banks for redemption. In time, these banks, ever shorter on gold, could no longer provide help in the Union's fund-raising.

In response, the Treasury embarked on a major drive to sell bonds directly to the public. The largest issue, authorized in 1862, was the so-called five-twenties—bonds yielding 6 percent interest that were redeemable in not less than five years and not more than twenty years. These were followed in 1863 by an issue of "ten-forties," bonds redeemable in not less than ten years and not more than forty years, paying 6 percent interest. More ten-forties, paying a lower 5 percent rate, were sold in 1864, followed by two more issues of five-twenties. In 1864 and 1865, a large amount of new seven-thirties were marketed as well.

Because interest on several categories of bonds was to be paid in gold, and because they were given preferred tax treatment, investors initially considered them an extremely attractive investment vehicle. To make them even more desirable, investors initially were permitted to purchase the bonds with greenbacks at par—even if the greenback declined 20 percent, it would still be deemed to be worth its original face value for the purpose of buying the bonds. The government could then reissue the greenbacks to finance additional procurements. The privilege of converting greenbacks into bonds at par was halted in 1863.

To facilitate the sale of five-twenties to middle-income households—and therefore broaden the Treasury's borrowing base—Philadelphia banker Jay Cooke suggested offering them in denominations as low as fifty dollars. As during the War of 1812, purchasers were permitted to buy on an installment plan. Hired as the Treasury's marketing agent for the five-twenties, Cooke advertised the bonds in local and national newspapers, including foreign-language journals that were widely read in growing immigrant communities. He also established a cross-country marketing force of some twenty-five hundred bankers, insurance salesmen, and real estate agents, linking them through the recently installed national telegraph network. Most Americans had never owned bonds, so Cooke and his team first focused on educating people about the basics of bond investing. Cooke's highly orchestrated sales campaign appealed to patriotism as well as to desires for a secure investment. One of his appeals to national pride read: "What our Revolutionary Fathers are to us, WE will be to *coming* generations, if we fail not in our plain and simple duty." In another advertisement, he promoted the bonds as "The Working Men's Savings Bank—an investment securely protected by the government."

Before the Civil War, many Americans shared Jefferson and Jackson's view of the evils of a large national debt. Jefferson had made a major effort to rid the country of debt; Jackson actually had done so, in order "to prevent a monied aristocracy from growing up around our administration that must bend to its views, and ultimately destroy the liberty of our country." An agrarian populist in the Jeffersonian tradition, Jackson feared that the federal government might end up owing so much money to this "aristocracy" that it would exert undue policy influence on the nation's leaders, forcing them to impose high tariffs or excise taxes that would have a disproportionate impact on farmers and workers.

Lincoln, who had spent his formative years in the prairie lands of southern Illinois, understood such concerns. But he did not accept the notion that federal borrowing must inevitably be a source of national division, pitting rich against poor or big cities against rural villages. Like Hamilton, who saw a well-funded debt as a "national blessing" because it would strengthen national unity, Lincoln regarded borrowing during the Civil War not only as a technique for raising large sums of money but also as a way to tie large numbers of Northerners to the Union's cause. For him, the broader the participation in war bond offerings the greater the number of individuals and families with a financial stake in the Union's success. Accordingly, Lincoln urged the purchase of Union bonds by "every person of small means who might be able to save enough for this purpose." Also, if large numbers of people "of small means" bought bonds, the government would be inoculated against the charge that its wartime borrowing was benefiting the rich, who could then use their leverage to force the government to bend to their will. "The great advantage of citizens being creditors as well as debtors with relation to the public debt," Lincoln pointed out, is that "men readily perceive that they can not be much oppressed by a debt which they owe to themselves."

Lincoln also encouraged small investors to buy bonds because he worried that the big banks would take undue advantage of the government's desperate need for money. His suspicions were illustrated in an exchange with one of his later Treasury secretaries, Hugh McCulloch. As McCulloch was preparing to introduce Lincoln to a group of bankers who had agreed to subscribe to a new issue of Union bonds, he informed the president that "these gentlemen from New York have come to see the Secretary of the Treasury about our new loan. . . . I can vouch for their patriotism and loyalty, for as the Good Book says, 'Where the treasure is, there will the heart be also.'" Lincoln mischievously asked whether McCulloch was not also familiar with another, less flattering, portion of the text: "Where the carcass is, there will the eagles be gathered together."

Ultimately, one in twenty Union families bought war bonds. Purchases picked up as government tax revenues rose (thus improving chances of repayment), and the Union army won important victories. Nonetheless, Cooke's campaign had a lot to do with the robust sales. Cooke was particularly proud that "out of the three million subscribers to our various public loans, over nine-tenths are of the class called the *people*." Many of the buyers lived in rural America, precisely the men and women Lincoln had hoped would purchase the bonds. "Only a few years earlier," historian James Macdonald noted, "such yeoman farmers, the very core of the old

Jeffersonian vision of America, would have been the natural opponents of public debt." Now they were significant holders of it.

Borrowing dramatically exceeded the collection of tax revenues early in the war, but the ratio fell as income taxes, wartime excise taxes, and tariff payments climbed. The ratio of borrowing to tax revenues, nearly nine to one in 1861, declined to approximately six to one in 1862, and to three to one in the last two years of the war. All told, money raised from bond issues covered more than 60 percent of Union wartime costs. In contrast, bond sales covered only 35 percent of the costs of the Confederacy, with much of the remainder paid through currency issues. The Union's greater creditworthiness, bolstered in substantial measure by its capacity to raise vastly greater amounts of tax revenues, provided it with an enormous advantage over the Confederacy, undergirding its ability to prevail in the war.

The Politics of War Money

The colossal costs of the war—in terms of men and money—would have been unimaginable to Americans when the conflict began in April 1861. After secession, the army, which had numbered 16,000 officers and enlisted men at the time, was augmented by the prompt arrival of 100,000 militia men. The navy expanded quickly from fewer than 10,000 men before the war to nearly 60,000. Massive military recruiting drives continued throughout the period. At its peak strength, the North could count a million men under arms; all told, roughly 2.1 million men served in Union forces during the war. (Confederate figures were 600,000 and 900,000, respectively.)

As troop levels and their requirements for provisions and munitions increased, federal spending ballooned from less than 2 percent of gross national product in early 1861 to a high of 25 percent at the time of General Robert E. Lee's surrender in the spring of 1865. Before the war the largest budget in U.S. history had been $74 million, the largest deficit had been $27 million, and the national debt had never risen above $127 million. The war made those figures appear quaint. The federal government's expenditures over the course of the war totaled $3.4 billion, and in 1865 it recorded its first annual budget of more than $1 billion. The unprecedented spending and borrowing produced a corresponding increase in debt, from an easily manageable $75 million in early 1861 to roughly $2.75 billion at the war's end.

As the war intensified, popular support eroded in areas of the North. Draft riots broke out in New York, Chicago, Detroit, and other Northern cities. The violence reflected deep underlying racial and class resentments and was a constant and troubling reminder to Lincoln and his colleagues that social issues could not be neglected if the Union was to sustain the public's support and obtain the manpower required. So, as the Union imposed stiff excise taxes and raised tariffs, Lincoln and Congress made a major effort to ensure that the average citizen regarded the financing of the war as equitable, which mitigated the feeling that the poor were fighting for the benefit of the rich. As Representative Morrill put it, "Ought not men . . . with large incomes, to pay more in proportion to what they have than those with limited means, who live by the work of their own hands, or that of their families?" Most Northerners readily agreed that they should; most believed that the government's policies were aimed at ensuring that they did. Middle-income Americans also benefited from the Homestead Act, which opened up Western regions to immigrants and urban families looking for land to farm; the Land Grant College Act, sponsored by Congressman Morrill, which provided educational opportunities to large numbers of young people; and tariff protection for manufacturing jobs, which sheltered workers from European competition. The rhetoric of economic justice, and the measures taken to promote it, were politically persuasive to many.

Chase Goes

By the middle of 1864, a prolonged period of tension between Lincoln and Chase reached a head. The final break occurred not over financial matters but over the conduct of the war and Chase's political ambitions. Chase constantly had pushed Lincoln for a more vigorous prosecution of the war, and in the lead-up to his challenge for the presidential nomination he was, as described by Doris Kearns Goodwin in her book *Team of Rivals*, "filling all the customs house positions with his own partisans"—former Democrats who had become Radical Republicans and were supporting Chase's presidential hopes.

On three previous occasions, Chase had submitted letters of resignation to Lincoln; the president had turned down all of them. In June 1864, however, Chase selected a crony who had little financial skill to replace the departing and highly respected John Cisco, who headed the Treasury's New York branch. In so doing, Chase defied an order from Lincoln to find someone acceptable to New York's key political factions and financial leaders. Although Cisco was convinced to stay on, which could have put the matter to rest, Lincoln was so incensed by Chase's flagrant disregard of his orders that he readily accepted the secretary's fourth letter of resignation, writing to Chase that "you and I have reached a point of mutual embarrassment in our official relation which it seems to me cannot be overcome, or longer sustained, consistently with the public service." Lincoln had concluded that "Chase has two bad habits. . . . He thinks he has become indispensable to the country. . . . He also thinks he ought to be President."

At first, the reaction to Chase's dismissal was highly negative. A senior Treasury official told Lincoln that the loss was "worse than another Bull Run defeat." The *Chicago Tribune* celebrated Chase as "the great magician of the treasury [whose] name will be handed down to history as the greatest financier of the century," implying that the country would stagger financially in his absence.

Lincoln first offered the position to former Ohio governor David Tod, who was widely regarded as not up to the job, though politically convenient. Tod turned it down for health reasons. The president then decided that Senate Finance Committee chairman William Pitt Fessenden would be the ideal choice. By coincidence, Fessenden had a prearranged appointment with Lincoln that very day. While Fessenden waited outside the president's office, Lincoln dispatched an assistant to convey his nomination to the Senate. In their meeting, Fessenden declined the position, also claiming his health prevented him from doing so, but by the time he returned to his office his selection had been unanimously confirmed by the Senate, and he reluctantly accepted the post.

Fessenden was a popular choice. The *Chicago Tribune*, which had just lamented the departure of Chase, labeled him a "man of undoubted financial ability." His appointment was also warmly welcomed by the business and financial communities, which had worked with him closely during his tenure on the Finance Committee.

Fessenden served for less than a year before resigning because of his ill health. While he did not pursue bold initiatives, he restructured part of the federal debt, redeeming some short-term bonds carrying a 5 percent interest rate, which were seen as unattractive by investors, with others that paid 6 percent and carried a longer-term maturity. He also moved "to clean up the corruption and inefficiency that had plagued the Treasury during the regime of Secretary Chase" and eventually left behind him both a cadre of more competent personnel and a department of significantly improved procedures.

Full Faith Restored

With the military outlook turning more positive in late 1864, particularly after Sherman's march through the South, Lincoln, running under the slogan, "Don't change horses in the middle of a stream," handily won reelection over General George McClellan. The war was now entering its final stage; spirits in the North were high and confidence in Union bonds was growing.

Despite the government's huge postwar debt, and the enormous political uncertainty that followed Lincoln's assassination in April 1865, within months of the South's surrender, hundreds of millions of dollars' worth of federal bonds were snapped up by European investors. They believed that the government would faithfully repay its debts, a belief inspired in part by the experiences of investors following the Revolution and the War of 1812.

The financial credibility of the federal government was reinforced by an extraordinary clause incorporated in the new Fourteenth Amendment to the Constitution. In addition to the due process clause, the equal protection clause, and a clause providing full citizenship to former slaves, the amendment stipulated that "the validity of the public debt of the United States, authorized in law, including debts incurred for payment of pensions and bounties for services in suppressing insurrection or rebellion, shall not be questioned." The language was reminiscent of a clause included by the framers seven decades earlier in Article 6 of the Constitution: "All debts contracted and engagements entered into, before the adoption of this Constitution, shall be as valid against the United States under this Constitution, as under the Confederation."

Reaffirming the validity of the public debt in the Constitution itself was deemed necessary because the Union's financial obligations had grown to an unprecedented level—far above what Americans would have thought manageable a few years earlier. Doubts had arisen about the government's

ability and willingness to repay these obligations. And, lest there had been any expectations in the South that federal money would be used to pay off Confederate debt or compensate slave owners, the amendment disabused those who harbored such hopes. "Neither the United States, nor any State," it read, "shall assume or pay any debt or any obligation incurred in the insurrection or rebellion against the United States, or any claim for the loss or emancipation of any slave; but all such debts, obligations and claims shall be held illegal and void."

In 1866, the government's interest payments alone were twice the size of its entire budget in the year before the war. But in that year tax collections from all sources hit $558 million, the peak level in the nineteenth century. Because of booming revenues and an end to wartime spending, the government generated large surpluses. Soon, pressures grew to sharply cut taxes, with the basic issue being which ones to cut. In March 1865, Congress authorized McCullough to appoint a commission to suggest changes in the tax system. It was headed by the noted New England investor and publisher David Wells. Because the war ended before the commission began its work, its emphasis shifted to the postwar tax system. Wells argued for "the rapid reduction of taxation, rather than a rapid reduction of the principal of the public debt." He recommended retaining the income tax as the least "detrimental to the country," counseled caution in raising tariffs, and called for removing excise taxes on manufactured goods but retaining them on luxuries such as liquor and tobacco.

While there was general agreement to reduce or eliminate most of the wartimes excise taxes as Wells had recommended, beyond that no consensus existed. The divisive issues surrounded whether to cut the income tax or tariffs. The public attention given to arguments in favor of abolishing the income tax, and their ultimate success, was remarkable in view of the small number of people who paid it. At its height, only a fraction of Northerners paid the tax, whereas virtually everyone bore the brunt of the high tariffs.

Congressmen and senators representing agricultural regions generally favored reducing tariffs while maintaining a high income tax; those representing manufacturing regions generally favored repealing the income tax but keeping tariffs high. The former came primarily from the Midwest and South, regions comprised mostly of low- and middle-income rural families who felt the impact of high tariffs on the price of consumer goods; most of them did not pay the income tax because they earned less than $600. The latter came primarily from industrial states, where a larger portion of the population paid the tax, and manufacturers and workers benefited from protection from foreign goods.

Supporters of the protective tariff declared that it was logical to abolish the income tax because the original authorizing legislation had stipulated that it should remain in place only for five years. Now that the five years had elapsed, they argued, so should the income tax. Representative Dennis McCarthy, a Republican from New York, asserted that the income tax "was only considered and passed as a war tax. . . . The five years are up; the war is over; our revenues will bear the reduction; and we can afford to let it die." Senator Henry Corbett of Oregon, also a Republican, cautioned, "If you want to make this tax so odious so that during another war you can never levy such a tax, you had better renew it and then I assure you, you will never be able, even in that crisis, to establish or levy it again."

Defending the tax, Senator John Sherman offered a different interpretation. He said the five-year period in the original law served as a "guarantee to bondholders that for that time at least they should have the security of the income tax." He suggested extending the tax to enable the government to generate more easily the revenues needed to repay bonds sold during the war. Other supporters of retaining the income tax and cutting tariffs argued that during the war increased duties had been enacted to compensate manufacturers for their higher internal tax payments. With the reduction in excise taxes, elevated tariffs were no longer needed for this purpose.

Sherman would not be as victorious as his sibling. In the following years, attempts to modify and then eliminate the income tax succeeded; attempts to reduce tariffs did not. Vermont's Justin Morrill, who had favored the wartime income tax but had opposed a graduated rate structure, saw in the postwar brawling an opportunity to reinstitute his pet flat tax. "In a republican form of government," he asserted, "the theory is to make no distinctions as to persons in the rates of taxation. Recognizing no class for special favors, we ought not to create a class for special burdens." In 1867, Morrill successfully led an effort in Congress to enact a 5 percent levy on all incomes above $1,000.

As millions of dollars' worth of debt were retired and federal revenues remained high over the next few years, the tide turned further against the income tax. Northern legislators, led by Roscoe Conkling (who was now in the Senate) and supported by Senator Charles Sumner of Massachusetts and Representative William "Pig-Iron" Kelley of Pennsylvania—who represented states whose citizens had paid over 60 percent of the income tax during the war—demanded its complete eradication. The main voices championing tariff cuts were the intrepid John Sherman, his agricultural-state allies, and Southern Democrats, who had begun to repopulate Congress at the end of the decade, but at the time held little sway.

In 1870, the income tax rate was further reduced, to 2.5 percent, and the inheritance tax was eliminated. The income tax was phased out in 1872. Nevertheless, the Bureau of Internal Revenue was retained to collect the handful of taxes that remained after the war: mainly tariffs, and the surviving excise taxes, the most important of which were levied on alcohol and tobacco. Retention of the bureau frustrated the states' efforts to regain their role as the intermediary between taxpayers and the federal government.

The Wells Commission reported to the Congress that the nation's "aggregate destruction of wealth" totaled $9 billion, "three times as much as the slave property of the country was ever worth." Yet the war also produced enormous benefits for the North. The issue of greenbacks, the creation of national banknotes, and increased wartime wages, followed by postwar tax cuts, put enormous spending power in the hands of millions of consumers and led to rapid growth. But this was not purely a demand-side boom; the country enjoyed a boom on the supply side, too. The capacity of the economy in the North, Midwest, and West to meet this expanded demand had exploded due to the construction of new factories and new rail lines to supply wartime needs as well as the introduction of new farming technologies and an increase in the number of farms. The war unleashed a boom in industry, which reaped significant profits from producing arms and supplies for the Union army. The Transcontinental Railway had been built. Large numbers of homesteads and new farms had been established. With the help of the expanded railway network, Western farmers increased shipments to the country's Eastern cities, now teeming with new immigrants, and to Atlantic ports for export to Europe.

Expanding internal commerce and trade produced a quarter century of rapid economic growth, high annual tax revenues, and uninterrupted budget surpluses. The abundance of tax receipts enabled the government to finance many internal improvements, such as river and harbor projects, pay retirement and disability benefits for Union soldiers and their dependents, and service the large federal debt. But such expenditures were modest compared to the size of postwar tariff and excise tax collections. As a consequence, large sums were available to retire outstanding government bonds. In the five years following the war, more than $300 million in federal debt was paid down, and by 1893, just before another panic and depression pushed the Treasury back into deficit, the nation's debt had been reduced by nearly two-thirds, to $961 million.

The importance of U.S. creditworthiness continued to loom large in American politics. In his March 1869 inaugural address, President Grant confronted those who wanted the government to repay wartime debt in depreciated greenbacks rather than in gold, as originally promised. In phrases reminiscent of Hamilton's declaration that Revolutionary War debt was the "price of liberty," Grant stated that the Civil War debt was the price of saving the Union. He insisted that "to protect the national honor, every dollar of Government indebtedness should be paid in gold, unless otherwise stipulated in contract." That, he asserted, would "go far towards strengthening a credit which ought to be the best in the world."

Markets responded. Investors were impressed by the proven commitment of American leaders to run big budget surpluses despite the costs of Reconstruction, debt servicing, military pensions, and veterans' disability payments. As a consequence, they bid up the price of federal bonds. They also welcomed the Grant administration's decision to use these surpluses to retire government bonds and to stop printing greenbacks, as well as the passage in 1875 of the Resumption Act, which required the Treasury to begin redeeming the currency for gold coin in 1879, until the amount outstanding was reduced to $300 million. In that year, remarkably, holders of the once greatly depreciated greenbacks could exchange their currency at parity—one gold coin dollar for one green paper dollar.

★

The Civil War swept away many of the apprehensions expressed by Jefferson and Jackson about the dangers posed by strengthening the federal government's financial powers. Lincoln and his allies in Congress recognized that in order to end the Southern rebellion, they needed to create a financial system capable of sustaining Northern unity and mobilizing enormous sums of money behind the war effort. The policies they pursued and the institutions they established resulted in a vastly more integrated and prosperous national economy than had existed before the war.

The postsecession departure of most Southern senators and congressmen enabled protectionist-minded Republicans to enact a series of previously blocked tariff increases. Moreover, because many of those who left Congress favored retaining maximum financial power in the hands of state governments and were suspicious of the consolidation of such powers in the national government, their departure eased the way to transform the country's tax, currency, and banking systems in ways that strengthened the federal role in each area. Government leaders with virtually no financial experience were remarkably successful in producing bold and innovative measures to meet the North's urgent and enormous resource requirements. Salmon Chase and legislators hailing from small farming towns in Maine and Vermont, Indiana and Pennsylvania, worked together—in the most frenetic of environments—to transform the American financial landscape. Virtually every possible source of funds was tapped, producing a remarkably creative, and in many ways very modern, financial and monetary system, which featured the historical antecedents of taxation and borrowing methods used during World War I, World War II, and today.

Most essentially, the commitment to honor federal financial obligations held firm. The Fourteenth Amendment reinforced that point. And Grant, no less than Hamilton, Jefferson, Madison, and Monroe, comprehended the need to service government bonds on the originally agreed terms. With the benefit of hindsight, the Union could have raised more money and curbed inflation more aggressively had it collected the income tax in 1861, increased rates more quickly, and reduced the exemption level earlier to put more middle-income earners on the tax rolls during the first part of the war. Contemporary critics of Chase's initial skepticism about the revenue-raising possibilities of the income tax have pointed to British prime minister William Gladstone's move to double that country's income tax in 1856, at the start of the Crimean War, as an example that Chase could have drawn on to take a bolder approach. But the income tax was a novel technique for raising federal revenues in the United States, whereas Britain had had one, on and off, for half a century. Still, Chase can be faulted for refusing to make arrangements to collect the tax after it was first enacted in 1861; he could have looked to Britain's experience to find evidence that the income tax could—as it ultimately did—produce a substantial amount of revenue.

It is difficult to see how Chase, Fessenden, Morrill, and the others who spearheaded the financial response to the war could have held inflation much lower. Neither politicians nor scholars of the time saw the potential

for using the income tax as an anti-inflationary device, as it would be during the next great military test, World War I. And for the income tax to have
significantly curbed civilian consumption, it would have to have been
structured to draw large sums of money from middle- and low-income
workers. But they were already paying high prices for their daily necessities
because of increased excise taxes and tariffs; burdening them with an income tax would have weakened Northerners' frequently tenuous support
for the war.

One helpful measure would have been to take a more aggressive approach to the coverage of "stoppage at source" in the Revenue Act of 1862,
by requiring large businesses, rather than just government agencies and the
military, to withhold taxes on wages; it would also have been useful at the
time to require all companies, not just railways and financial institutions,
to withhold taxes on the interest and dividends. Both measures would have
permitted more timely and greater revenue collection and thus helped to
contain inflation. But it took until World War II for the government to understand the inflation-fighting potential of this technique.

Because the vast portion of Union bonds, in dollar terms, was purchased by roughly the same affluent part of the population that paid taxes,
notwithstanding Lincoln's and Jay Cooke's stalwart efforts to sell them to
the average citizen, these securities did not absorb much civilian purchasing power either. They were bought mainly out of surplus savings, rather
than with money that otherwise would have been used for consumption.
Moreover, once the decision was made to issue greenbacks and to encourage their use in the purchase of Union bonds, any possibility that bond sales
might curb inflation evaporated.

After the war, the nation's debt once again emerged as a divisive social
issue. From the early days of the nation, Jefferson had warned that a large
federal debt would pit the investor classes against the farming and working
classes. Albert Gallatin and other Jeffersonian Republicans had sought to
avoid the War of 1812 in order to prevent an accumulation of such debt because they didn't want to saddle low-income Americans with the burden of
repaying it. Their concerns were borne out after the War of 1812, when
Congress enacted a series of high protectionist tariffs that raised the price
of consumer goods, thereby imposing a disproportionate share of the cost
of debt service and repayment on low- and middle-income consumers.

To meet the challenge of financing the Civil War, tariffs were increased
and extended to virtually all imported items, taking a large bite out of the

average worker's salary. However, political resentment was reduced because the wealthy had to pay an income tax and an inheritance tax. After the war, Congress eliminated the income and inheritance taxes and retained the high tariff. As historian Sidney Ratner observed, it shifted "the burden of taxes to the shoulders of the laboring and farming classes" and away from the "business classes," just as it had done after the War of 1812. "The debt," as Ratner pointed out, "had been accumulated in the process of preserving the Union in the name of all the people. But the cost of paying off the debt and paying the interest . . . was thrust upon the farmers and working classes by northern industrialists and financiers when they secured through Congress the maintenance of the protective tariff and the abolition of the income and inheritance taxes." With the continuation of high tariffs, Northern industrialists "increased their margin of profits by elimination of competition from European manufacturers through the high protective tariff." The unifying fiscal policy that had held the North together during the war was now replaced by a highly divisive one that pitted powerful business interests against workers and farmers.

The South felt particularly aggrieved. Southerners had to pay more than they otherwise would for imported goods because of very high tariffs and more for Northern manufactured goods that were protected by those tariffs. As a result, the nation's fiscal battles for the next half century took on an intensely regional character. Representatives from Southern states pressed for reductions in what they considered regressive and antiagrarian tariffs and for a reintroduction of the income tax on the nation's wealthiest citizens, most of whom were in the North. Post-Reconstruction Southerners waited for the moment when the seniority system in the Congress would catapult their senators and representatives—many of whom they constantly and loyally reelected, decade after decade—to powerful committee chairmanships. Their patience would pay off years later, when Southern legislators would play the decisive role in shaping fiscal policy during World War I.

4

Capitalizing Patriotism

PROGRESSIVE FINANCE DURING WORLD WAR I

WE WENT DIRECT TO THE PEOPLE. . . . WE CAPITALIZED ON THE
PROFOUND IMPULSE CALLED PATRIOTISM.

—WILLIAM GIBBS MCADOO

The outbreak of the Spanish-American War in 1898 unleashed intense
pressures for tax reform. The government had depended on highly regressive tariffs and excise taxes for much of its revenues since the end of the
Civil War. Supporters of reform wanted to ensure that the costs of the
conflict were not paid in the same way. Members of Congress representing
the South and poorer areas of the North, concerned that their citizens
would suffer disproportionately by increases in tariffs and excise taxes,
called for resurrecting the Civil War income tax, arguing it was a more equitable way to produce wartime revenues. They were thwarted by conservatives who regarded the tax as a threat to the affluent and to business.

Early in the twentieth century, however, the public mood had shifted
decisively toward reform and by the beginning of World War I important
changes—particularly the levying of the income tax and stiff taxes on
business—had taken place. The war dramatically accelerated these tax reforms, and, when it was over, American fiscal policy had been fundamentally and indelibly transformed.

The sums of money required to pay for the Great War dwarfed those that had been necessary during the brief Spanish-American War or even the Civil War. The massive mobilization of men and weaponry forced President Woodrow Wilson and the Democratic Congress to mobilize an equally massive amount of money. To do so, they had to confront three central issues: how much should be borrowed, how much should be obtained through taxation, and how much of the portion raised through taxes should be paid by the most affluent citizens and by businesses.

Populist Southern Democrats, who considered themselves heirs to the Jeffersonian tradition, and Northern Democratic progressives, who saw themselves as a new breed of reformers, opposed large-scale borrowing. They preferred a "pay-as-we-go" approach, emphasizing high taxes on the wealthiest Americans and on businesses, as part of a larger campaign to "redistribute wealth" and reduce corporate power. They were also deeply troubled that Civil War debt had been repaid primarily through regressive tariffs and excise taxes and assumed that unless they rallied a broad-based movement to find an alternative, any debt from World War I would be repaid in much the same way, with future generations of low-income Americans shouldering the burden for servicing the enormous volume of war bonds purchased largely by the wealthy. Their cause was championed in the House by the outspoken Claude Kitchin of North Carolina, who pushed for a stiff wartime "excess profits tax" over the objections of President Wilson. Similar pressures came from Senator Benjamin "Pitchfork Ben" Tillman of South Carolina, who warned Wilson that "the poor people throughout this country who have the votes are watching to see if the [Democratic] Party is going to call on . . . millionaires to pay for . . . the defense of the country, or even just a share of it."

Wilson agreed to most of the congressional Democrats' demands because the war required increased revenues. To do otherwise would have split the party. He also attempted, with only limited success, to restrain the most extreme populist and progressive positions to avoid alienating or weakening the corporate sector, which was producing massive amounts of arms and matériel vital to the war effort. In addition, Wilson was cognizant of the disastrous effect of inflation during the Civil War, and he attempted to use taxation to limit price increases by siphoning off civilian spending power. However, congressional Democrats, in keeping with their populist and progressive principles, resisted the administration's attempts to dampen inflationary pressures by imposing taxes on the working class to curb their consumption. The alternating episodes of cooperation, conflict, and competition between Wilson and the Congress during the war resulted in a series of revenue bills that transformed the country's nineteenth-century tax system into the one we are familiar with today.

Populist Fever

In the history of U.S. wartime financing, the four-month-long Spanish-American War plays only a minor role, but it foreshadowed many of the debates over fiscal policy that would emerge two decades later during World War I. The 1896 Republican platform had committed President William McKinley to "use America's . . . influence and good offices to restore peace and give independence" to Cuba, whose people were in rebellion against authoritarian Spanish rule. Although McKinley was under intense domestic pressure to intervene—by some groups for humanitarian reasons, by others to expand America's territorial influence—he tried to find a diplomatic solution that would bring an end to Spanish repression while avoiding a war. But when the battleship USS *Maine* exploded and sank in Havana Harbor in February 1898, and 260 of its sailors were lost, war fever rose. Although later evidence raised doubts that Spain was to blame, the United States declared war in late April. The president ordered a naval blockade of Cuba and an invasion of that beleaguered island; he also dispatched Commodore George Dewey, at the head of the Asiatic Squadron, to destroy the Spanish fleet in the Philippines, another colony of Spain. Americans mobilized quickly. The navy, which had begun a modernization and construction program in the 1880s, did not require a major expansion of men or of equipment for these campaigns, but the army required both; its troop level stood at twenty-six thousand just before the war and would rise to sixty thousand by its end in August. More than two hundred thousand volunteers also were authorized by Congress to serve in supplementary units.

During the depression that followed the Panic of 1893—which began when the bankruptcy of the Philadelphia and Reading Rail Road triggered frenzied selling on Wall Street, a surge in bank failures, massive unemployment, and widespread foreclosures on homes, businesses, and farms—the nation's debt had grown. In his 1897 inaugural address, McKinley had called for a hike in tariffs to provide additional protection to American industry and to pay this debt down. Representative Nelson Dingley Jr., a Republican from Maine, ardent protectionist, and chairman of the Ways and Means Committee, took up the president's charge. The Dingley Tariff of 1897 raised duties on a wide range of consumer and industrial goods to an average rate of 57 percent, higher than the peak reached during the Civil War. It sharply increased the price of raw sugar, fabrics, apparel, and goods made with steel. Revenues, however, did not increase as planned. Duty collections actually fell in 1898 because the tariff had a chilling effect on trade.

The McKinley administration and congressional Republicans wanted to avoid significant wartime borrowing and debt accumulation. Another plank in the party's 1896 platform had criticized Democratic president Grover Cleveland for "piling up the public debt . . . in time of peace." The Republicans did not want to pile it up in time of war either. But their major preoccupation was to block a revival of the income tax, which some were advocating to boost flagging revenues and pay for the war. To obtain more funds, Dingley decided on an increase in excise taxes. Recognizing that the government would still require additional money, he also sought authority for the Treasury to borrow up to $500 million.

To sell these initiatives, the Republicans tried invoking patriotism. John Dalzell, a congressman representing steel-producing Pittsburgh, asked Democrats to support Dingley's initiative on the grounds that during war, "we are brethren, and the cause of all is the sacred cause of each. One cause, one country, one flag." Democratic congressmen from the South and the West, however, did not buy this line. Issues of fairness and class figured prominently in the debate. Employing Jeffersonian rhetoric, Edward W. Carmack of Tennessee declared, "You count upon the heat of battle and the enthusiasm of patriotism to fasten fetters upon our people. . . . It is in time of war and under the cloak of patriotism that the most vicious schemes of legislation obtain a foothold upon our statute books and the most infamous conspiracies of public plunder are carried into execution." As Ratner, in his book *American Taxation,* wrote, Democrats were particularly troubled by the suggestion that the Treasury undertake a large debt offering. They charged that "the rich would receive the great benefits of the interest-bearing bonds as a safe and most desirable investment [while] the poorer classes, after fighting to free the Cubans, would return home to discover that they would be taxed for generations to pay the hundreds of millions of dollars of interest on these bonds." Aware of the groundswell among their constituents, they proposed a 3 percent tax on all incomes over $2,000—those taxpayers having an "ability to pay"—and the issue of

$42 million in silver coinage and $150 million in new greenbacks, along with a reduction in tariffs.

In the years before the Spanish-American War, rural America had become increasingly disenchanted with regressive taxation, especially high protective tariffs. After the Civil War, an angry peace had settled over the South. Agricultural communities were bitter about high tariffs; they viewed them as unjustified subsidies, paid out of Southern agrarian pockets, to wealthy northeastern industrialists. They and advocates of reform throughout the country saw the tax structure of the 1870s and 1880, which placed most of the revenue burden on consumer goods, as hostile to the interests of low-income Americans. There was considerable evidence to back up their claims. In late 1889, Thomas G. Shearman, a tax reformer and founding partner of the prominent Wall Street law firm Shearman and Sterling, commented in a widely circulated *Forum* magazine interview that the tax system "took from the rich only 3 to 10 percent of their annual savings while taking from the poor 75 to 90 percent."

In the early 1890s, the recently formed Populist Party, which vocally supported a revival of a graduated income tax, was successful in a number of state and local elections, primarily in the Midwest. In the 1892 presidential election, its candidate, James Weaver, received over a million votes. By 1896, many former Populists had joined the Democrats. Although the party itself ceased to be a major political factor before the turn of the century, grassroots populist sentiment remained strong. Organizations such as the Grangers, formed in the Midwest after the Civil War to defend the interests of farmers, and the Knights of Labor, formed in Philadelphia around the same time to defend worker interests, were forceful advocates of a graduated income tax. From 1874 to 1894, sixty-eight bills were introduced in the House and Senate attempting to impose an income tax; all were voted down. Finally, in 1894, Congress enacted income tax legislation as part of the Wilson-Gorman Tariff Act, but the tax was subsequently ruled unconstitutional by the Supreme Court in the case of *Pollock v. Farmers Loan and Trust Company*. The decision galvanized both sides.

A new group of urban activists, the progressives, who were to become a major political factor, added its calls for reform. Their movement was composed largely of middle-class professionals and even some of the country's most affluent citizens, many of whom lived in the Northeast; groups such as the National Woman Suffrage Association, the American Bar Association, and the National Municipal League embraced the progressive cause. As described by Benjamin Friedman in *The Moral Consequences of Economic Growth*, the progressives "eschewed the easy urban versus rural and regional divides that had sparked much of the political dialogue of the nineteenth century, instead targeting the gap between the rich and the poor." They argued passionately in the Jeffersonian-Jacksonian tradition for revamping the tax system to weaken the hold of the powerful corporate and financial forces that, they charged, exerted excessive influence on politicians and on the economy. They were not, said Friedman, like the Populists, who "sought to turn back to an earlier, simpler America," and were "weighed down by the pervasive symptoms of a stagnant economy and frustrated by continually unsuccessful efforts at personal advancement." The progressives were "invigorated and emboldened by the signs of economic growth and technical progress all around them," and "sought instead to go ahead and shape the future to their liking."

The tariff versus income tax debate was one of the defining political battles of the 1880s and 1890s. As tax historian W. Elliott Brownlee noted, "The two competing political parties came to base their economic appeals on sharply conflicting ideological views of the tariff and of taxation in general." When the Spanish-American War broke out, Republican leaders expressed concerns that it would give the Democrats the wedge they needed to revive the income tax at the expense of the tariff. If the income tax passed, they worried, the Supreme Court might cite the Civil War precedent and uphold it on the grounds that it was an appropriate way to raise revenue during times of war. Their next fear was that it might "open the door" to those who also wanted to make it a peacetime tax.

Indirect Inheritance

For the time being, Nelson Dingley and the protectionists prevailed. Instead of an income tax, Congress enacted new excise taxes reminiscent of those imposed during the Civil War. The excises on beer, liquor, and tobacco were doubled and new levies were imposed on recreational facilities, legal documents, cosmetics, drugs, and chewing gum. They accounted for much of the increase in government revenues during 1898 and 1899. To spread the burden between consumers and business, Congress also enacted a new tax on the gross receipts of sugar and oil refineries and slapped a levy on the recently introduced hot technology of the era, the telephone. On the theory that they were mostly placed by the wealthy and by businesses, it imposed a penny tax on long-distance calls costing over fifteen cents. (The tax still exists today.)

The Supreme Court had ruled in the Pollock case that because the income tax was a direct tax not apportioned among the states on the basis of population, it was unconstitutional. But the Court was silent on the question of inheritance taxes. Here was another way to increase the share of taxes the wealthy paid. Strong support for the inheritance tax came from Andrew Carnegie. In 1889, he had published "The Gospel of Wealth" in the *North American Review* in which he called for a progressive federal inheritance tax "beginning at nothing upon moderate sums to dependents, and increasing rapidly as the amounts swell." The last time the inheritance tax had been levied was during the Civil War, and since that time a significant number of Americans had accumulated extraordinary wealth. A self-made millionaire, Carnegie argued that allowing individuals to inherit large sums increased the concentration of wealth and was inconsistent with the American system of equality and democracy. Carnegie's proposal elicited a strong popular response. Large numbers of Americans saw the tax as a way to make the rich provide a greater share of the nation's revenues and reduce the Treasury's dependence on regressive tariffs and excise taxes. Many wealthy Americans also supported Carnegie on the grounds that such a levy was preferable to the dreaded income tax.

Motivated by both the public's enthusiasm and the need for revenue, in 1898 Congress imposed an inheritance tax. Republican leaders believed it was an "unpleasant but necessary" concession. The tax applied only to estates over $10,000, and, like the 1862 version, it was assessed on a graduated scale, up to a rate of 15 percent. After the Spanish-American War, the tax was extended because of a series of extraordinary revenue demands. The country needed to pay for the deployment of American forces to the Philippines to put down a rebellion against the American occupation and to China during the Boxer Rebellion of 1900. The Boxer Rebellion marked the first time since the Revolution that American forces had joined with forces of other nations in a military alliance—and the first time they had ever done so abroad.

Following the examples of the financing of the War of 1812 and the Civil War, Congress also authorized wartime borrowing: $400 million in small-denomination bonds, which was $100 million less than the original authorization because of more optimistic revenue projections. Had all of the bonds been issued, the federal debt, which was just under $850 million before the war, would have grown by nearly half. But because the war was both short and relatively inexpensive, only $200 million of the authorized bonds were offered, and the nation's debt inched up to just over $1 billion in 1899. As the economy recovered from the lingering effects of the Panic of 1893, excise taxes and tariffs imposed during the war generated enormous revenue growth. In 1901, the Treasury registered a substantial surplus that enabled it to retire much of the additional debt.

Support for the inheritance tax remained high among Democrats at the start of the twentieth century. They had no immediate expectation of passing an income tax and saw maintaining the inheritance tax as the only way to draw revenues from the wealthy and create a more progressive economy. But there were too few votes in Congress to retain the tax and, along with most other war levies, it was repealed.

The Return of the Income Tax

Tariffs had accounted for 80 to 90 percent of annual federal revenues immediately after the Civil War, but by 1900 the chief generator of government revenue was excise taxes. Conservative northeastern and mid-Atlantic Republicans consistently lobbied to increase tariffs to offer more protection for their regions' manufacturing plants. Senators and congressmen from industrialized states agreed to vote for import duties on wool, animal hides, and agricultural products in a successful attempt to obtain support from representatives of western and farm states for high tariffs on manufactured products. Over time, however, the politics of tariffs shifted. Middle- and lower-income Americans came to associate elevated tariffs with the high price of goods on store shelves, and increasing numbers of them viewed protective duties as a device that propped up the much-despised monopolies, enabling powerful corporations and financiers to accumulate massive wealth. Leading Southern Democrats denounced high tariffs as "the mother of trusts."

In early 1909, Senator Joseph Bailey, a conservative Democrat from Texas, introduced a bill to resurrect the income tax that had been levied during the Civil War but phased out in 1872. Bailey, described by one observer as "intellectually keen, physically impressive through his height and powerful build [and] gifted with melodious voice," was a powerful force in the Senate. The government, he said, was spending large sums of money protecting private property and maintaining law and order. Bailey argued that these expenditures primarily benefited the wealthy so the wealthy should pay their fair share of the cost. Bailey's other motive in introducing his bill was to embarrass the Republican-controlled Congress. He expected it to kill the legislation, handing the Democrats an issue that would appeal to their bread-and-butter constituencies of populists and progressives. The Supreme Court had declared an income tax passed in 1894 to be unconstitutional, but these groups were eager to try again. He initially envisaged an income tax similar to the one Morrill had supported during the Civil War: a straight 3 percent on all incomes above $5,000.

At first there appeared little chance of success, but when a group of reform-minded Republican "insurgents," led by Senator Albert B. Cummins, joined the fight on his side, the odds improved. As governor of Iowa, Cummins had led the effort to reduce the influence of railroad companies in local politics. In the Senate he took on a group of "Old Guard" Republican senators, including the former chairman of the board of directors of the New York Central Railroad, Chauncey Depew of New York, and Nelson Aldrich of Rhode Island, and proposed a graduated tax that would range from 2 percent to 6 percent on incomes above $5,000.

As the fight progressed, President Taft stepped in. The Supreme Court's 1894 ruling against the income tax was still fresh, in legal terms, and he argued that passing a new law would "produce a serious division" in the Court. The Court's reputation was at stake. "Nothing," Taft declared, "had ever injured the prestige of the Supreme Court more than the [1894] decision." But rather than oppose an income tax outright, and divide their party, Taft and Republican leaders in Congress collaborated to submit a constitutional amendment for ratification by the states. It was a cynical move; they expected most state legislatures to vote against ratification. At the same time, Taft engineered passage of legislation that would impose a small corporate profits tax. He believed this would satisfy the public's appetite for increased taxes on the wealthy, further reducing the amendment's chances of ratification. By the time it was passed, however, the political pendulum had clearly swung against the anti-income tax conservatives. Reformist passions ran deep in a country relentlessly exposed to such best sellers as Ida Tarbell's *History of the Standard Oil Company* and Gustavus Myers's *History of the Great American Fortunes* as well as newspaper accounts of extraordinary wealth, abusive trusts, and financial scandal.

The distribution of wealth and income had changed a great deal since passage of the 1894 income tax bill. Then, the richest 2 percent of the population earned roughly 10 percent of the national income, but by 1910 the richest 2 percent accounted for 20 percent. And powerful demographic forces were at work. Large numbers of families were moving westward. The nation's cities were bursting with energetic new immigrants. Farmers and workers were finding their political voices and the populist and progressive movements had risen into significant forces.

The income tax amendment resolution passed the Senate by a vote of 77 to 0 and the House by 318 to 14. Many legislators voted for it expecting ratification to fail and were astonished to discover the great support it enjoyed throughout the country. In less than a month, Alabama became the first state to ratify the amendment, and in February 1913 Massachusetts became the thirty-sixth and deciding state. In March, just before President Woodrow Wilson's inauguration, the Sixteenth Amendment, empowering the Congress to "lay and collect taxes on incomes, from whatever source derived without apportionment among the several states and without regard to any census or enumeration" became part of the Constitution.

Now advocates of an income tax moved quickly to pass legislation to enact one. The Democratic Party had won a majority in the House in the 1910 elections. In the 1912 elections that brought Wilson to power, they gained control of the Senate as well. A key figure in drafting the income tax bill in the new Congress was Cordell Hull, a veteran of the Spanish-American War and a Democratic representative from Pickett County, Tennessee. As a Southerner, he was resentful of the burden the post–Civil War revenue system had placed on his section of the country and was committed to undoing America's heavy dependence on tariffs. Hull had been born in a log cabin and lived in poverty during his youth, so the income tax appealed to him because he believed it would "advance economic justice." With eighteen years of seniority on the House Ways and Means Committee, he had considerable power, and he pressed hard for enactment of income tax legislation that would provide an alternative to regressive tariffs. Like the Federalists who sought to retain internal taxes during the Jefferson administration, he worried that tariff collections would fall during wartime because ocean commerce would be interrupted. Lacking that source of revenue, Hull declared, "The country would be helpless to prosecute that war or any other war of great magnitude," and it would have to tax "the wealth of the country in the form of incomes."

The modern income tax became law on a modest note in October 1913. It did not even warrant a bill of its own, but was included as a section of a tariff bill that was working its way through Congress to fulfill Wilson's campaign promise to slash customs duties. Its most powerful supporter in the House was Oscar Underwood of Alabama, the Democratic floor leader, chairman of the Ways and Means Committee, leading tax authority in that chamber, and a passionate populist. He was a key member of a group of legislators from the states of the former Confederacy who had single-mindedly risen to leadership positions by being reelected to Congress repeatedly. Underwood was a strong opponent of protective tariffs, and he used his enormous authority to cut them, believing, like Hull, that they imposed inordinate burdens on the South and propped up powerful Northern business interests. Underwood steered the bill through the House with little resistance.

When the bill came to the Senate it was taken up by the Finance Committee, chaired by North Carolinian Furnifold Simmons, a conservative Democrat who represented tobacco- and cotton-growing interests. Simmons was a white supremacist who supported Jim Crow laws and opposed women's suffrage and immigration. He was also aggressively probusiness. He initially resisted the legislation and it appeared destined to go down to defeat. But President Wilson launched a major public campaign across the country, charging that special interests inimical to the well-being of working Americans were thwarting his antitariff policies. That began to change sentiment in the Senate. To emphasize his commitment to lower duties and demonstrate that he was standing up to business interests, Wilson appeared before a joint session of Congress early in 1913 to urge passage of the tariff bill. He was the first president to appear before Congress since John Adams a hundred years earlier. And because the president had helped Simmons get the appointment as Finance chairman, Simmons felt beholden to him and ultimately supported the legislation.

The Underwood-Simmons Tariff Act of 1913 established what was called a "normal," or base, personal income tax at a rate of 1 percent. Individuals with incomes under $3,000 and married couples with a combined income of under $4,000 were exempt. The progressive feature was a graduated "surtax," which increased from 1 percent on incomes from $20,000 to $50,000 to 6 percent on incomes above $500,000. Because average annual personal income was just over $600 at the time, only a small portion of Americans, roughly 2 percent, paid the tax in the two years following its passage.

The act also lowered the Republican-era tariffs of the 1890s, with the biggest reductions on goods consumed by those with modest incomes. In its first full year, the income tax accounted for less than 10 percent of overall government revenues. Three-quarters of revenues still came from tariffs and excise taxes, the latter mainly "sin taxes" on liquor and tobacco products.

The passage of the 1913 act and the ratification of the Sixteenth Amendment were the result of political shifts in the country that fundamentally altered the way the government would raise funds to pay for the upcoming war. Hull wrote later, "The income tax law had been enacted in the nick of time for the demands of the war." Raising the enormous sums that were required to pay for World War I, and doing so in a way acceptable to large numbers of low- and moderate-income Americans, would have been immensely more difficult without it. As Congress and the administration sought broad-based public support for wartime mobilization, they were forced to respond sympathetically to demands from powerful agrarian and labor movements for increasingly stiff taxes on the wealthy and businesses.

A Tax System for a War

In the years just after the Spanish-American War, U.S. forces, aptly called by military historian Graham Cosmas "America's Army for Empire," were deployed in various parts of the world to protect and reinforce the country's rapidly growing commercial interests. Although U.S. armed forces did not participate in any major overseas conflicts between the Spanish-American War and World War I, they were posted as far away as the Philippines and China. In Asia, the Caribbean, and Latin America, the army and navy "were frequently called upon to assist with administration of newly acquired overseas possessions" and to protect "investments abroad threatened by native insurrections, revolutions, and other internal disturbances." In 1902, largely for these purposes, Congress authorized the army to increase its force strength to 100,000 men. Yet, during the first decade of the twentieth century, it averaged only 75,000, less than one-twentieth the size of the 2-million-man German army. The U.S. Navy, in contrast, had become a formidable force, the third largest in the world, just behind Britain's and Germany's navies.

The Great War broke out in Europe in September 1914, set in motion by the assassination of Archduke Franz Ferdinand, the heir to throne of the

Austro-Hungarian Empire. The war pitted the Allied powers—France, Britain, Italy, and Russia (until it dropped out after the Communist revolution)—against the Central powers—Austria-Hungary, Germany, Bulgaria, and the Ottoman Empire. Many Americans initially saw the war as a contest among aristocrats and the result of the excessive influence of the military in Germany and Austria; they felt it had little to do with the United States and wanted no part of it. But there also were powerful figures, such as former president Theodore Roosevelt, who foresaw a time when American intervention would be required.

The outbreak of war in Europe triggered a contentious public debate in the United States over the "preparedness question." Roosevelt and former army chief of staff Leonard Wood argued in favor of a major initiative to ready the country for war, primarily through military training. Anti-interventionist and pacifist groups protested that extensive preparedness measures would increase the chances that the country would eventually enter what was then seen as an exclusively European conflict. It took two years for Congress to pass the National Defense Act, which authorized an increase in the peacetime size of the regular army to 175,000 men, and, if needed, a wartime strength of 300,000, as well as a more than fourfold increase in the size of the National Guard.

President Wilson insisted that both Germany and Britain respect the neutrality of American merchant shipping. Despite American protests, the German government, intent on undermining the economies of Britain and its allies by cutting off their ocean commerce, continued its unrestricted attacks. In May 1915, a German submarine sunk the British passenger liner *Lusitania*, carrying 128 Americans on board. Wilson demanded that the attacks on nonbelligerent ships immediately cease, and the Germans complied.

Woodrow Wilson's Treasury secretary was William Gibbs McAdoo. McAdoo had grown up in poverty in the South and then established himself as a successful lawyer. After closing his practice in Tennessee, the highly energetic and entrepreneurial McAdoo had moved to New York, where he founded a company that developed and ran a system of train tunnels under the Hudson River between New York City and New Jersey known as "McAdoo's Tunnels," the precursor to today's PATH trains. Drawing on this experience, he also served as director general of railroads during the war. A widower, McAdoo had married Wilson's daughter Eleanor in the early days of the administration.

As the war intensified and America's entrance appeared likely, McAdoo began to plan for funding. He vowed to keep inflation from rising to the disruptive levels reached during the Civil War and reviewed the techniques Secretary Salmon P. Chase had used. As he later wrote, "I did not get much in the way of inspiration or suggestions from a study of the Civil War, except a pretty clear idea of what not to do. The fiscal part of it was a hodge-podge of unrelated expedients." He concluded, however, that Chase "did as well as anyone could have done in the circumstances. . . . When he came into office he found an empty Treasury and a wholly inadequate system of taxation; and, moreover, the currency was in a state of indescribable confusion. The country was not prepared for large-scale financing of any kind." McAdoo neglected to mention, however, that although Chase resorted to "expedients," they turned out to be reasonably successful and, in the final analysis, McAdoo copied a number of them.

McAdoo had major advantages over Chase. He did not confront an "empty Treasury," an "inadequate system of taxation," or a "currency in confusion." In the more than half century between the two wars, the nation's potential tax base had expanded dramatically, its currency had become sound, and its financial system had grown more sophisticated. Moreover, there were fewer economic dislocations during World War I than during the Civil War because the fighting was, in the words of George M. Cohan's popular patriotic song of the time, "Over There."

In part because World War I was an ocean away, its financial cost would dwarf that of the Civil War. While America's direct involvement in the war lasted only nineteen months, its weaponry was more sophisticated and costly. The Civil War had been fought primarily with cannons and rifles and a few ships; World War I was fought with expensive artillery, tanks, large ships, and airplanes. The size of the armed forces was much larger, and transatlantic deployment of troops and equipment was more expensive and complicated. In the end, the federal government spent ten times more paying for World War I than it had for the Civil War.

Of course, McAdoo was not alone in pondering how the United States might pay for the war. Woodrow Wilson was no financial expert, but he had been governor of New Jersey and understood government budgets. He believed strongly in fiscal discipline. Prior to the U.S. entrance into the war, Wilson had proclaimed before Congress that he did "not believe that the people of this country are prone to postponing the payment of their bills.

Borrowing money is shortsighted finance. It can be justified only where permanent things are to be accomplished which many generations will certainly benefit by." Accordingly, he insisted, "We should pay as we go. . . . The industry of this generation should pay the bills of this generation." In addition, Wilson was concerned about too much dependence on borrowing, fearing that it would empower the big financiers, who were fighting the political and tax reforms he was pursuing.

The major focus of Wilson's presidency until the country entered the war had been domestic reforms. Specifically he was trying to stand up to and limit what he believed to be the excessive power of large corporations and wealthy individuals. Wilson called his reforms the "New Freedom," and confided to friends, "Every reform we have won will be lost if we go into this war. We have been making a fight on special privilege. We have got new tariff and currency and trust legislation. . . . They are not thoroughly set." In language reminiscent of Jefferson, he disclosed his worry that "war means autocracy. The people we have unhorsed will inevitably come into the control of the country for we shall be dependent upon the steel, oil and financial magnates." Although he could not avoid a wartime dependence on steel and oil, he was determined to minimize dependence on borrowing from the "financial magnates" by paying for as much of the war as possible with taxes.

Most top congressional Democrats shared Wilson's view that there should be a minimum use of debt and a maximum reliance on taxes, with the richest Americans shouldering the greatest possible share of the burden. Conservatives, primarily in the Republican Party, pushed for a greater reliance on borrowing and cautioned that some of the more extreme Democratic tax proposals would deprive the "investor class" of resources needed to finance the productive enterprises that supplied the troops with munitions and other matériel. They argued further that if there were to be additional reliance on taxes, it should be on a broad-based consumption tax. In many ways, this was a rehash of the debate that had taken place during the Spanish-American War, only this time the Democrats were in power and progressive and populist views dominated the political process.

As the United States edged closer to war, populists and progressives pressed harder for an increase in the income tax on the wealthy. Wilson and McAdoo agreed with this position, but only up to a point. They favored a higher income tax, especially on the most affluent Americans and on big business, primarily to raise large amounts of revenue and secondarily to demonstrate to the average American that the tax system was fair, that the wealthy were not escaping their responsibility while the masses were being taxed. But neither man wanted to use the income tax to "redistribute wealth," recognizing that such a strategy would mean a direct confrontation with many of the businesses that were key to war production. However, most congressional Democrats emphatically did want a higher income tax to redistribute wealth and were eager for a confrontation. They regarded the prospect of war as an opportunity to "break the hold of corporate privilege" by levying harsh taxes on business.

Mobilizing the Treasury

In 1914, a sharp fall in imports from Europe led to a drop in one of the Treasury's most important sources of funds: customs revenues. Wilson asked Congress to raise $100 million in additional revenue through "internal" taxes to make up for these losses as well as to pay for the evacuation of Americans from Europe and provide war risk insurance for U.S. businesses. In response, in October Congress passed the Emergency Revenue Act of 1914, which revived a number of the excise taxes utilized during the Spanish-American War. It was set to expire at the end of 1915. In early 1915, in a move to implement his policy of "armed neutrality," the president sought and received increased appropriations for the army and navy, including $100 million annually for a five-year naval and merchant shipbuilding program.

To pay for the accelerating defense buildup, in December 1915 McAdoo asked Congress to enact another revenue bill, one that would reduce the exemption from $4,000 to $3,000 for married couples and from $3,000 to $2,000 for individuals. The change would increase the number of middle-income citizens on the tax rolls, and thus produce more revenues. McAdoo also proposed lowering the threshold for the surtax from $20,000 to $10,000 and slapping excise taxes on cars, gas, bank checks, iron, and steel. He was particularly eager to see these measures passed expeditiously because he feared that preparedness spending would rise rapidly and he wanted to avoid a large deficit. He warned Congress, "A nation cannot go constantly into debt for current expenditures without eventually impairing credit." Impaired credit was the last thing the Treasury secretary wanted. He was already anticipating a huge boost in borrowing if American forces actually became engaged in Europe. Democrats, especially those in the

House, considered McAdoo's approach too regressive; yet rather than embark on a bold, new tax initiative to produce more funds, they merely agreed to extend the 1914 Emergency Revenue Act to the end of 1916.

While the war raged in Europe, Wilson made a series of impassioned speeches in late January and early February 1916 calling for greater American preparedness and for higher taxes to pay for it. The Democratically controlled Congress, with its eyes on the 1916 elections, was reluctant to act. But by the summer congressional leaders recognized that elections or no, they would have to provide the administration with additional resources. However, they insisted on doing so in a way that would not adversely affect their core constituency of low- and middle-income families. This meant neither the House nor the Senate was willing to lower the personal exemption, as McAdoo had recommended. Instead, the House voted to increase the rate on existing taxpayers and hike the normal rate and the surtax to levels considerably above those the administration wanted. When it considered the bill, the Senate raised the surtax still further, even though Treasury officials expressed concern that this was placing too great a burden on affluent taxpayers.

Two months before the elections, the House and Senate came together to pass the Revenue Act of 1916. The bill raised the "normal" tax rate from 1 to 2 percent; it also increased the surcharge to 6 percent on incomes above $20,000, going up to 13 percent on incomes above $2 million, producing a maximum marginal tax rate of 15 percent. A sharply graduated inheritance tax, ranging from 1 to 10 percent, was imposed on estates above $50,000. The act broke new ground by including an "excess profits tax" of 12.5 percent on munitions manufacturers and an excise tax of fifty cents on each $1,000 of corporate capital stock, but earnings below $99,000 were exempt, so many small businesses were spared from having to pay. A number of unpopular excise taxes were also repealed and an earlier tax exemption for dividends was eliminated. With patriotism and populism running high, the bill passed by wide majorities.

Despite his reservations, Wilson signed the bill. W. Elliot Brownlee has noted that the administration might have secured a less progressive outcome, with a greater portion of the tax paid by middle-income citizens. But Wilson and McAdoo worried that working with a coalition of moderate Democrats and Republicans, as they would have had to do in order to achieve such a result, would have divided the Democratic Party and cost it the votes of farmers and workers in the coming elections.

Still, Wilson harbored serious misgivings about the fiscal zealotry of the populists and progressives. Rallying around the slogan that "conscription of wealth" to pay for the war should go hand in hand with "conscription of men" to fight it, these groups had pushed the Wilson administration further than it wished to go on the 1916 revenue act. In the end, writes Steven Weisman in his book *The Great Tax Wars*, the legislation represented a "clear triumph for the progressive and agrarian Democrats over the misgivings of the President and McAdoo." Just how much of a triumph can be seen in the tax collection figures. Roughly 95 percent of the revenues produced by the tax came from those with incomes over $20,000, a group that had accounted for less than half of the income tax revenues collected under the 1913 legislation. Many conservative Republicans who had supported the 1916 act in a climate of patriotic exuberance would look at those numbers and oppose any further tax bills that included aggressively progressive principles. The bipartisan consensus that enabled the Revenue Act of 1916 to pass easily soon broke down.

The New Tax Debate

In November 1916, Wilson was reelected by a thin margin of only twenty-three electoral votes and six hundred thousand popular votes over former Supreme Court justice Charles Evans Hughes. Democrats suffered significant losses in the House and Senate, yet narrowly retained control in both bodies. The close election reinforced the influence of the Democrats' base constituencies: labor groups, Southern agrarians, small business interests, and big-city political machines.

One of the key planks in Wilson's reelection platform was that he had kept the country out of war, but soon after his victory he was forced to confront the growing prospect of war and turned to the Congress to provide more money to meet the soaring costs of military preparedness. Democrats began talking about raising the income tax again. The *New York Times* editorialized that a tax hike would "bring home to the minds of . . . voters the fact that the defense of this nation is going to cost them something." Republicans, led by Old Guard conservatives in the Senate, stoutly resisted, but their minority status limited their effectiveness in blocking an increase.

Regional and class issues played a major role in the debate. Southern Democrats, the direct heirs to the Jeffersonian populist tradition, objected to accelerated preparedness for the same reasons Albert Gallatin initially had opposed the War of 1812—because it would empower powerful financial interests at the expense of working-class citizens. Among the most domineering and colorful legislators in this group was the chairman of the House Ways and Means Committee, Representative Claude Kitchin of North Carolina, a populist who had resolutely opposed U.S. participation in the war. A "large, kind and affable man with a remarkable memory for statistics, which he used to his advantage," Kitchin believed that industrialists and bankers were whipping up public support for military preparedness and U.S. intervention to boost their profits. He inveighed against the "sudden, rapid and stupendous move for war preparations," warning that the Democratic Party might "fall victim to the wiles of the patriots for profit," who supported the large buildup. In a similar vein, Senator George W. Norris, a Nebraska Republican with an independent streak, charged that "belligerency would benefit only the class of people who will be made prosperous . . . who have already made millions and who will make millions more . . . should we become entangled in the present war." He warned, "We are going to pile up debt that the toiling masses that shall come many generations after us will have to pay. Unborn millions will bend their backs in toil in order to pay for the terrible step we are now about to take." The Jeffersonian concern that wars inexorably lead to a dangerous increase in the influence of big business and powerful financial interests, who would then use this influence to inflict high tax burdens on the least affluent, was a central feature in the financing debate.

Chairman Kitchin emphasized repeatedly, as had Wilson earlier, that U.S. fiscal policy should follow the pay-as-we-go principle, relying to a maximum degree on taxation. He had a clear approach to preparedness financing: "graduated taxes upon income, inheritances, and especially upon the excess profits of corporations due to the war." Kitchin regularly pointed out to his colleagues that corporations stood to make inordinately large wartime profits and should accordingly be made to shoulder most of the costs. He took the lead in shaping the last revenue act passed before the United States entered the war, the Revenue Act of March 1917. At his insistence, the 1917 act included a significant increase in the estate tax, and, more controversially, a hefty excess profits tax: 8 percent on business profits that exceeded 8 percent of invested capital, after a deduction of $5,000. The tax, which embodied an approach Republicans derisively labeled "Kitchinism," was particularly appealing to the nation's large rural constituencies.

The way the law was written, the tax would be paid largely by big businesses, most of which were located in the North, and would cost rural America, particularly the agrarian South, very little. "You can tell your people," Kitchin stressed to his Southern and Western colleagues in the House, "that practically all of this will go north of the Mason-Dixon Line. . . . The preparedness agitation has its hotbed in such cities as New York." Recognizing that it would take time to collect the new taxes, Congress authorized the Treasury immediately to issue up to $300 million in certificates of indebtedness, short-term financial instruments that could be sold quickly to meet the government's urgent needs. These certificates were similar to the short-term securities used during the War of 1812 and the Civil War, and like those they were to be retired with proceeds from the new taxes or subsequent long-term bond issues.

All of this work, however, was for naught. The tax legislation never went into effect. In January 1917, the German government announced the resumption of unrestricted submarine warfare and unleashed a series of attacks that resulted in the sinking of three American vessels. Around the same time, U.S. authorities were made aware of the Zimmermann Note, which revealed a surreptitious German plot to induce Mexico, which was still seething from American interference in its recent revolution, to declare war on the United States. On April 2, 1917, one month after the bill was passed, in an emotionally charged address to a joint session of Congress, Wilson laid out the case for a declaration of war. In doing so, he warned that upcoming hostilities would "involve the granting of adequate credits to the government," that is, more borrowing, but he also insisted that the war's costs should be "sustained . . . as far as they can equitably be sustained by the present generation, by well conceived taxation."

Six weeks after declaring war, Congress passed the Selective Service Act authorizing a draft. In the months before the United States entered the conflict, the army had grown to just over 200,000 officers and enlisted men. The draft initially increased the force to 286,000. The National Guard was called on for roughly 450,000 troops, and a National Army (formerly called the Volunteer Army) provided additional soldiers throughout the conflict. The marines began the war with 13,000 men and were quickly enlarged to more than 72,000. The navy started with 48,000 men and expanded to ten times that figure. All told, 4.7 million soldiers, sailors, and marines were mobilized. The first units of the American Expeditionary Force—America's Doughboys—under the command of General John J. Pershing, arrived in France in June 1917.

A War for the Generations

Wilson reconciled himself to massive borrowing. Because this was to be a "war to end all wars," he believed that future generations of Americans would benefit from an American victory; therefore, in Wilson's mind, borrowing large sums that they would have to repay could be justified. However, he wanted both to avoid transferring an excessively heavy debt to coming generations and to minimize dependence on the "financial magnates" for money. He was also under pressure from progressives and populists. In an attempt to obtain additional support for their antiborrowing crusade, they argued that incurring a large war debt would place an enormous future tax burden on the nation's veterans. These men, they cautioned, having risked their lives in combat, should not return home to face high taxes to repay bonds held by wealthy investors who had not served in the military. Claude Kitchin dramatically illustrated the point, declaring, "I want the man who comes home with an empty sleeve to feel that the Congress which sent him away has not favored the profit-taker who stayed at home."

Although Wilson and McAdoo agreed that the wealthy should pay a large portion of wartime taxes, they recognized that there were limits to the financial burden the rich could be asked to bear, and they wanted middle-income Americans to assume a meaningful share as well. By expanding the number of families subject to the income tax, they believed, the government could finance a considerably greater portion of its wartime expenses with taxes than the Union had in the 1860s, when the income tax was brand-new and narrowly based. They also saw the need to drain large amounts of middle-class spending power to avoid reliving a Civil War–type inflation.

The question of inflation and how to avert it had played little role in the discussions about how to finance the Civil War. But sharp price increases during that conflict had posed such significant social and economic hardships, especially for soldiers and workers on fixed incomes, that the issue of runaway prices was very much on the minds of policymakers during World War I. As American manufacturers shifted their plants from civilian to war production, the availability of consumer goods dropped dramatically. At the same time, all-out defense production boosted employment, hours worked, and take-home pay for millions. The government's challenge now was to find a way to absorb large amounts of potential civilian spending in order to bring consumption in line with the limited availability of consumer goods.

Using the tax system to curb inflation presented a policy dilemma. Taxing the wealthy would produce lots of revenue, but only a limited reduction in civilian spending, because most people in the highest brackets had sufficient surplus funds to pay their taxes with little reduction in their everyday spending. In contrast, low-income wage earners, who had little surplus cash, would have less money to spend on consumption as their taxes rose, so imposing higher levies on them would put a major dent in inflation. But taxing them also ran counter to the deeply held populist and progressive concepts of fairness, which held that burdens on low- and moderate-income families should be avoided.

McAdoo had originally hoped to meet half of the government's spending needs during the war through taxation, but banking kingpin J. P. Morgan, whom he asked for advice, recommended that aiming for not more than 20 percent was more realistic. Morgan believed that taxes on the wealthy—including himself of course—needed to be kept low to avoid discouraging investors "by a scale of taxation which is felt by them to bear unjustly on the investing class of this country." Conservative legislators, particularly Senate Republicans, shared Morgan's view. In time, McAdoo concluded that 50 percent would "perhaps be destructive to some extent of the capitalized energy which keeps the wheels running" and decided that raising one-third was more realistic. He later wrote that he "realized that a policy of raising even one-third of the expenditure of government during the war [through taxes] would lay a heavy burden on the people; yet it was the better choice of two evils. The emission of greater quantities of government borrowing and short-term obligations would necessarily create a tremendous inflation. . . . The only possible way to restrain inflation, to some extent at least, was by the imposition of heavy taxation."

Like most Americans in 1917, McAdoo greatly underestimated the duration of the war and the cost of the U.S. involvement. He initially anticipated spending roughly $8.5 billion in 1918 and assumed he would have little difficulty raising the necessary resources. On April 5, 1917, the day before Congress formally declared war, he requested that it promptly appropriate $3.5 billion for the military, of which $3.4 billion would be for the army and navy. These funds would "place the United States on a wartime basis . . . and finance the war for one year." He also sought $3 billion to assist America's struggling European allies.

The protax Democrats in the House and the proborrowing Republicans in the Senate were left to hash it out. After receiving McAdoo's proposal, the

House Ways and Means Committee convened a series of hearings to listen to the views of eminent academicians. Professors O. M. W. Sprague of Harvard and Irving Fischer of Yale warned that "government reliance on loans would lead to an inflation of credit, a general and rapid rise in prices, an increase in the money costs of war, a reduction in real incomes and discriminatory profits." Professors E. R. A. Seligman and R. M. Haig of Columbia, while accepting the need for additional taxation, stressed the "depressing effects of high taxes on productivity and competition."

The debate among the academicians revealed the same divisions that had existed for decades. Congress confronted two sets of issues: the first was how much to tax; the second, what kind of tax was appropriate. Now that war had been declared, Kitchin, giving voice to the position of the Southern populists, strongly argued for high levies to pay for it. He remained faithful to his Jeffersonian-Jacksonian aversion to debt, insisting that "your children and mine had nothing to do with bringing on this war" and it would be "unjust and cruel and cowardly to shift upon them the burden." A similar position was taken by Senator Hiram Johnson, a California Republican, who railed against "the skin-deep dollar patriotism of some of those who [do not want to pay taxes but] have been loudest in declamations on war in their demands for blood." Speaking for the opposing view, Senator Porter McCumber of North Dakota contested McAdoo's desire to limit borrowing and Kitchin's pay-as-we-go approach. He argued that "the current generation will supply the men and supplies, the future generations should pay the greater part of the cost." He failed to grasp Kitchin's point that young workers and soldiers contributing to the war effort were precisely those who later would have to pay off bonds issued during this period.

The question of who should pay higher taxes led to another heated battle over the excess profits tax. Kitchin again insisted that tax legislation include a stiff excess profits tax similar to that contained in the bill he had pushed through Congress in March. But, as Weisman wrote, "The concept of taxing a business's capitalization—with the government effectively deciding what should constitute an appropriate profit—seemed to many businessmen . . . and to Wilson and McAdoo, as antithetical to the tenets of capitalism." The administration instead favored, as a compromise, a tax on "war profits," which would be based on the difference between prewar and wartime profits, without judgment on whether these returns were "excessive" or not. In a letter to Kitchin, Wilson maintained that the suggested compromise was "manifestly equitable." But Kitchin, whom Wilson once referred to as "that distinguished stubborn North Carolinian who when he made up his mind would never open it," stayed true to his inclinations and resisted. Ironically, Wilson had written his Ph.D. thesis at Johns Hopkins on "Congressional Governance," calling it "government by the chairmen of the standing Committees of Congress," and describing the "selfish and warring elements" that jockeyed for power on Capitol Hill. Little did he realize when he wrote those words in the 1880s that he would have to confront such powerful and often fractious chairmen four decades later. For their part, House Republicans were also unsympathetic to Wilson's war profits tax proposal. Joseph W. Fordney, an influential representative from Missouri who had made a fortune in the lumber business, argued against all corporate taxes.

Rebuffed by both sides in the House, McAdoo appealed to the more conservative Senate Finance Committee. Again, he met with little success. Senator Thomas Hardwick, a Georgia Democrat who, like Kitchin, had opposed President Wilson's war preparedness efforts, argued against a war profits tax on the grounds that it would "seriously affect the cotton milling industry in the South." Many Southern Democratic senators shared his concern noting that the tax would have a particularly adverse effect on their constituents' textile and apparel businesses, which had not been particularly profitable before the war but were now making huge profits by selling uniforms to the military. Recently elected senator Oscar Underwood, who while in the House had been instrumental in the passage of the first income tax bill, also fought against a war profits tax, advocating instead a tax on profits in excess of 18 percent of invested capital.

While the Senate was debating the bill, McAdoo raised his estimate of wartime spending for 1917–18 to $15 billion, including loans to allies. In October 1917, six months after the United States declared war, Congress reached a consensus on new legislation, the 1917 War Revenue Act. The act dramatically raised the "normal" income tax rate and imposed a new and higher surtax on those in the top income bracket who now faced a marginal tax rate of 67 percent, compared to the previous rate of 15 percent. It also lowered the personal exemption levels. Now the tax began at an income level of $1,000 for individuals and $2,000 for couples, with the result that roughly 5 million more Americans became subject to the income tax. The act also increased the corporate income and estate taxes and included an assortment of new and increased excise taxes. Wilson and his Democratic colleagues in Congress successfully opposed a Republican initiative to enact a broad "consumption tax" instead of raising the income and corporate taxes—although advocates of consumption-based taxation would persist in their efforts throughout the war and for the next forty years. Perhaps the most eloquent compromise in the act was the new graduated war excess profits tax imposed on profits that exceeded a certain percentage of invested capital with an adjustment for prewar returns. The details of the war excess profits taxes were so complicated that McAdoo appointed a group of businessmen to help companies and accountants interpret it.

The pay-as-we-go camp was displeased. The legislation raised only $2.5 billion; they had hoped for more, in part to accelerate the redistribution of wealth and in part to hold down borrowing, which was ballooning as war costs grew considerably faster than revenues. Yet the act was, as Brownlee wrote, "without a doubt" a victory for the adherents of progressive taxation. Eighty percent of those who paid this new version of income tax in its first year earned between $1,000 and $3,000 but their taxes accounted for less than 4 percent of all income tax receipts. Professor Seligman lauded the legislation for embracing "democratic principles hitherto unrealized in fiscal history." To improve compliance, the Treasury launched a major public relations campaign utilizing movies, cartoons, and newspaper editorials; it also encouraged the clergy to preach the patriotic duty to pay taxes in their sermons.

Shipping Out

By the end of 1917, hundreds of thousands of American doughboys were departing for France every month and the costs of the war were mounting steadily. At that rate, over a million American troops would be on the continent by the summer of 1918, 2 million by the fall. McAdoo realized that he had vastly underestimated the government's wartime financing needs. He anticipated now that the year's cost would be over $18 billion, including $6 billion in loans to America's European allies. Yet he "did not advise further tax increases, fearing that they would deter war production and interfere with efforts to borrow at low cost." The country, he wrote, "should be permitted to readjust itself to the new revenue laws before consideration should be given to the imposition of additional tax burdens."

In the spring of 1918, McAdoo reestimated wartime costs and calculated that the government would likely spend $24 billion in the following fiscal

year. Sticking to his goal of meeting no more than two-thirds of wartime
spending requirements through borrowing, the Treasury secretary calculated
that taxes would have to generate $8 billion in revenues. Accordingly,
he urged the Finance chairmen, probusiness Furnifold Simmons in the Senate and the irascible Claude Kitchin in the House, to increase the personal
income and business taxes. When they and other members of the president's
party in Congress balked, McAdoo urged Wilson to intervene, informing
him that "Congress is anxious to avoid new revenue legislation at this
time . . . but it is inescapable. Unless this matter is dealt with now firmly and
satisfactorily, we shall invite disaster." Wilson also was concerned with the
revenue outlook. On May 27, 1918, when news of a more intense German
offensive on the Western Front—the so-called Spring Offensive designed to
split British and French forces at the small French rail junction of Amiens before the bulk of American forces could be deployed—reached Washington,
he appeared before a packed and apprehensive joint session of Congress to
deliver what came to be known as the "politics is adjourned" speech. He attempted to reassure the legislators that Americans were willing to "bear any
burden and undergo any sacrifice" to win the war. He emphasized the importance of tax fairness. "We need not be afraid to tax them," he said, "if we
lay taxes justly. They know that the war must be paid for and that it is they
who must pay for it, and if the burden is justly distributed and the sacrifice
made the common sacrifice they will carry it . . . with a solemn pride."

A few days later, McAdoo appeared before the Ways and Means Committee to provide the specifics, which included higher and more graduated
taxes on incomes and an increase in the levy on business profits, including
a hike in the war excess profits tax. The committee accepted a number of
his proposals and then went considerably beyond them, deciding on an
even more aggressive approach, including a sharp increase in the normal
income tax and the surcharge. It also introduced a tougher version of the
war excess profits tax. The conservative *Globe-Democrat* newspaper editorialized that the bill threw "practically the whole of the burden on the rich
and well-to-do classes" and concluded that "in view of the contents of this
tax bill, we shall no more hear the nonsense that this is a 'capitalist' war,
waged for the benefit of men of capital. It . . . is waged at the expense of
capital, and its collateral effects will be to diffuse wealth."

The Senate Finance Committee voted to retain the House's new war
excess profits tax, but at McAdoo's suggestion agreed to reduce the rate
for small companies. Senator Reed Smoot, a prominent Utah Republican

businessman and banker, criticized the bill as a "piece of bungling absurdity," designed to reach "as few voters as possible" and to place a "prohibitive tax on American industry." Smoot's alternative, a 1 percent national sales tax estimated to raise roughly $1 billion, was rejected in committee. Although McAdoo urged Simmons to pass the legislation speedily, the chairman refused, informing the secretary that he would delay until after the 1918 midterm elections. As the political campaigning swung into full gear, the United States and its allies were launching the Hundred Days Offensive to breach the German barrier called the Hindenburg Line, a vast defensive system in northwest France. More than a quarter of a million American soldiers joined in the series of battles, which began to break German resistance.

In the November elections, the GOP ran on a platform attacking Wilson's taxes as too high and the administration's spending as bloated. It swept both houses of Congress, winning a majority of two seats in the Senate and forty in the House. A few days later, an armistice was declared, ending the war.

The new Congress was not scheduled to take office until March 4, 1919. In the meantime, the lame-duck Democratic Congress resumed work on the carry-over tax bill. In December, McAdoo reduced his revenue request from $8 billion to $6 billion. Senate and House Democrats used their last days in the majority to enact the Revenue Act of 1918 (notwithstanding the fact that it was passed in February 1919, three months after the armistice). It provided funds to pay the remaining bills from the war and for massive demobilization.

The act raised the "normal" income tax rate and the surtax. Marginal rates for the highest-income earners were increased to 77 percent; the corporate income tax rate, which had been 1 percent at the start of the war, was raised to 12 percent. The legislation also included a modified version of the 1917 excess profits tax, with a top rate of 65 percent on the amount of net income earned in excess of 20 percent of invested capital and a separate war excess profits tax of 80 percent on net income in excess of a portion of prewar profits. A business had to prepare both calculations and pay whichever yielded the higher amount. The *Journal of Political Economy* called it "the greatest measure of taxation in the financial history of the United States and probably of the history of the world."

The result of the higher normal tax and lower exemption levels instituted during the war was that a greater portion of the burden of the income tax was shifted from upper-income to middle-income taxpayers from 1917 to 1920. By the end of the war, about 15 percent of American households, many with only modest incomes, were paying the personal income tax. In 1920, the lowest-income group, which had accounted for less than 4 percent of income tax revenues in 1917, was paying 8 percent, the middle-income group 33 percent, compared to just under 21 percent in 1917, and the upper-income group 60 percent, compared to 75 percent in 1917. But the income tax was far from the biggest producer of revenues. The major focus of the Democrats in Congress had been to impose stiff taxes on businesses and they did. The various versions of the excess profits tax accounted for more revenue than all other wartime taxes combined.

By 1919, nearly 75 percent of federal revenues was derived from income, excess profits, and estate taxes. Federal tax revenues had gone from under $1 billion in fiscal year 1916 to more than $5 billion in fiscal year 1920. Much of this increase occurred because Congress imposed very high taxes on the wealthy and on business owners, but all Americans directly or indirectly paid large sums to cover the staggering cost of the war. As the *New York Times* wryly put it, "These burdens would have been thought incredible, unendurable, but for the education through which the world has passed under German compulsion."

The wartime graduated tax system and excess profits taxes, argued tax historian John F. Witte, had served "to make the larger public aware that something was being done about war profiteers and the few who were profiting from the hardship of the many." That perception helped sustain support, or at least tolerance, among middle-class Americans for the higher taxes they had to pay.

Borrowing for Liberty

While taxes did not produce a third of total government financial requirements during the war, as McAdoo had hoped, they did cover roughly a third of the actual war costs. The rest had to be borrowed, and to accomplish that McAdoo drew on techniques applied during the Civil War. Using Jay Cooke's template, he launched a massive effort to sell war bonds. But unlike bonds issued during the Civil War, with such pedestrian names as seven-thirties and five-twenties describing their yields and maturities, World War I bonds were named to appeal to patriots. Liberty Bonds were marketed heavily.

As part of his patriotic approach, McAdoo also changed the Civil War model of employing a private firm as the government's sales agent. His study of Civil War financing had convinced him that "Chase was evidently afraid that the public would not support him if he went directly to the people for money, so he turned the selling problem in its entirety over to private bankers." In McAdoo's opinion, this was a "fundamental error." He felt that "any great war must necessarily be a popular movement. . . . Chase did not attempt to capitalize on the emotions of the people. . . . You may be sure that men and women who send their sons and husbands to battlefields will not hesitate about sending their dollars after them if the need for money is properly presented."

Pursuing a policy that he called "capitalizing patriotism," McAdoo organized bond drives to sell the war and to consolidate patriotic unity. He insisted that Boy Scouts, small-town insurance agents, Wall Street bankers, and prominent entertainers all donate their services to bond drives. Rallies were held in cities and towns throughout the country. Every American was urged to buy bonds, not "on a commercial basis" but as an "expression of a fundamental patriotism." Ads read: "ARE YOU 100% AMERICAN? PROVE IT! BUY U.S. GOVERNMENT BONDS" or "FIGHT OR BUY BONDS."

McAdoo saw the massive bond drives, like income taxes, as a way of curbing civilian consumption and thus reducing inflation. "The great financial operations of the government," he wrote, "cannot be carried forward successfully unless the people . . . save their money and lend it to the government. . . . The lender is supposed to deny himself something which releases, in turn, a demand on the vital supplies of the country." The day after war was declared, he submitted legislation seeking congressional authorization for an issue of $5 billion in bonds and $2 billion in short-term notes. The House Ways and Means Committee quickly approved the bill. Distinguishing himself from earlier, and later, wartime Treasury secretaries, McAdoo asked for a very large sum at the outset. A prominent House Democrat trumpeted the legislation as the "largest authorization of bond issues ever contained in any bill presented to any legislative body in the history of the world." McAdoo did not intend to borrow all of the money right away. Writing about it later, he explained that he sought such a large initial authorization to make a point. "We knew that it was not going to be a cheap war, and that our position in respect to financing would be more flexible if we prepared the public mind as soon as possible for a huge expenditure." Preparing the public for a costly war, rather than downplaying the expected cost, proved essential to the administration's efforts to obtain the unprecedented sums that would ultimately be required—amounts far greater than even McAdoo had anticipated.

The bond drives were billed as the "financial front" in the war. A "man who could not serve in the trenches of France," McAdoo explained, "might nevertheless serve in the financial trenches at home." Like Lincoln, McAdoo believed that the sale of small-denomination bonds was especially important from a political perspective. The greater the number of middle-income citizens who bought Liberty Bonds, the less vulnerable the administration would be to the old populist charge that elites would be receiving interest on wartime bonds paid with the taxes of Americans of modest means or, as Claude Kitchin warned, of returning veterans. To appeal to those with modest incomes, McAdoo offered Liberty Bonds with a face value as low as fifty dollars. Large-denomination bonds, which were also issued in abundance, were urged on financial institutions.

The recently created Federal Reserve played a significant role in enabling the Treasury to sell and hold down interest rates on the enormous volume of government bonds issued to pay for the war. The Fed had been created as an independent entity in 1913 to improve bank supervision and provide an "elastic currency." At the outset of the war, the Treasury requested that the Fed ensure that bank reserves were adequate to finance a large increase in government borrowing. The Fed then established a special "preferential" interest rate to enable commercial banks to borrow from regional Fed banks at a rate below that offered to investors on Treasury securities. Thus, commercial banks would make money on the interest rate differential either by purchasing bonds themselves or by lending low-cost money to their customers, enabling them to buy bonds profitably. Throughout the war, as Milton Friedman and Anna Schwartz wrote in their monumental work, *A Monetary History of the United States,* "Member banks made loans to their customers, who used them to purchase government securities, and banks in need of reserves in turn rediscounted at a Federal Reserve Bank their customer loans or their own collateralized notes secured by war obligations." Large numbers of Americans borrowed from banks in order to purchase Treasury bonds, in what came to be known as a "borrow and buy" strategy.

But the real value of the securities eroded as the prices of goods and services rose during, and especially after, the war. The process of Federal Reserve lending that permitted low interest rates also created a dramatic increase in the nation's money supply, thereby contributing to inflationary pressures. While the government did not increase the money supply by issuing its own currency the way it had during the Civil War, the Fed became, according to Friedman and Schwartz, "to all intents and purposes the bond selling window of the Treasury, using its monetary powers almost exclusively to that end. Although no 'greenbacks' were printed, the same result was achieved by indirect methods." Notwithstanding the inflationary impact of the Fed's creation of large amounts of credit, its role in financing World War I was vital. The economic writer Eliott Janeway observed that if the Federal Reserve had not existed to be "drafted into a role for which it was not intended . . . the war could not have been financed at all."

Each of McAdoo's Liberty Bond issues was oversubscribed. The first Liberty Loan carried an interest rate of 3.5 percent and a thirty-year maturity. To make the securities more attractive, interest was made exempt from income tax and virtually all other forms of taxation. McAdoo soon recognized that such tax advantages were overly generous to upper-bracket investors but offered no benefit to those whose earnings were below the income-tax exemption level. "We cannot," he conceded, "sell bonds in billions on the basis of what they may be worth to the very rich."

In the next couple of bond issues, he eliminated some of the tax benefits. The Second Liberty Loan, launched in the fall of 1917, exempted interest from taxation for those who paid only the normal income tax rate, but made it subject to the surtax and excess profits tax for those who were paying them. The bonds carried an interest rate of 4 percent; that higher interest rate compensated wealthy investors for the less favorable tax treatment while the reduced tax benefits made the issue appear fairer to low-income Americans. To McAdoo's disappointment, however, the Second Liberty Loan issue "drew a smaller portion of the savings of the low-income groups than did the first loan." He was forced to admit that "bonds could be sold on a large scale only to those persons of more than average means." By the time the third Liberty Loan was offered in the spring of 1918, inflationary pressures had increased and the interest rate was set at 4.25 percent to compensate investors.

As the war's costs soared, McAdoo realized that he had to ratchet up bond sales and that to do so he needed to make the next Liberty Loan more attractive. His considered two alternatives: raising the interest rate on the bonds still further or improving their tax benefits. He chose the latter. The fourth issue exempted from virtually all taxes the interest on income earned by investors on their collective Liberty Bond holdings of up to

$30,000 until two years after the war. McAdoo expected that the change would increase the number and broaden the range of subscribers by appealing to those in the middle class who paid an income tax but had not bought bonds during earlier drives. He was correct. There was a substantial pickup in sales of small-denomination bonds. Over 13 million people bought $50 bonds, and nearly 6 million people bought $100 bonds. Together they constituted 75 percent of bond buyers for this issue. But sales of $10,000 bonds, purchased almost entirely by wealthy individuals and financial institutions, provided nearly half of the funds generated. Although disappointed by the modest sums of money collected from middle-income Americans, McAdoo did not consider the bond drives a failure. His goal was to sell the issues out, which he did. "Suppose hundreds of millions of bonds were left on our hands?" he queried. "The moral effect of such a failure would be equal to a crushing military disaster. It would not only dishearten our own people, but also the nations across the sea whose fortunes are joined to ours, and it would give our enemies new confidence and courage."

In December 1917, McAdoo decided to try a fresh approach to tap directly into the savings of low-income Americans. He crafted a program to sell War Savings Certificates and Stamps, to give "every man, woman and child, however small their means . . . an opportunity to assist the government in the financing of the War." These inexpensive savings devices were designed to both raise funds and contain inflationary pressures by siphoning off an added portion of potential consumer spending. The Treasury sold Thrift Certificates with five-year maturities in denominations as low as $5 and as high as $1,000, as well as twenty-five-cent Thrift Stamps that could be collected, pasted in books, and, when twenty stamps had been accumulated, exchanged for the $5 certificates. Between December 1917 and October 1919, the War Savings Certificates generated nearly $1.8 billion, a small amount in economic terms—less than one-tenth of the sales of Liberty Bonds—but a large amount politically. McAdoo predicted that these bond campaigns would have a long-term impact because they taught "the humblest person in the land . . . to save all that he can [and would show] the people of the United States on a nationwide scale . . . the value of saving." He expected that these beneficial effects would "survive the war and have a permanent influence upon the future economy of the country."

The four series of Liberty Bonds and a fifth Victory Loan to redeem short-term war debt raised $21.5 billion. Roughly half of all American families bought bonds, a third of them purchased by those with incomes below

$2,000. McAdoo later described his strategy: "We went direct to the people . . . we capitalized on the profound impulse called patriotism. It is the quality of coherence that holds a nation together. It is one of the deepest and most powerful of human motives." Successful pursuit of the "quality of co-herence"—a goal that animated Alexander Hamilton's efforts to shape his funding policy to strengthen the allegiance of former state bondholders to the federal government as well as Lincoln's effort to sell bonds to Northern fami-lies of modest means to solidify their support for the Union—constitutes an important test of the effectiveness of wartime fiscal policy. Although fiscal policy must, of course, set as the primary goal the raising of large sums of money, if conducted correctly it also can strengthen national unity in support of the war effort. McAdoo's borrowing program achieved both objectives.

But the country also paid a price for his success. In order to keep interest rates on federal securities low, the government had to provide generous tax concessions. Whether it saved more because of the lower-than-market inter-est rate than it gave up in forgone revenues is difficult to measure. And ulti-mately a large percentage of the funds came from bond sales to the most affluent, who bought their securities largely out of surplus funds or with bank loans, and thus were not forced to forgo normal spending. Thus, a sub-stantial portion of the sales did little or nothing to curb inflation. Moreover, the Fed's extension of credit to facilitate purchases through the "borrow-and-buy" approach, although a powerful stimulus to bond sales, significantly in-creased the money supply and inflationary pressures.

When the credit bubble, created by this large increase in the money supply, burst after the war, the economy suffered a sharp downturn. Eliot Janeway summed up the situation: "Banks held for their own accounts large amounts of recently floated government war loans whose market val-ues provided the basis for inflated loan portfolios. At the same time they were also carrying customers who had borrowed against government bonds and were therefore vulnerable—as was the entire credit bubble—to any snapping of the string."

The Return to "Normalcy"

After the armistice, inflation hit America hard. Millions of people who had bought and held Liberty Bonds, Victory Bonds, and War Savings Certifi-cates saw the purchasing power of their interest and principal shrink and their bonds decline in value, although the bonds would regain their values later as inflation subsided and interest rates declined. Among those adversely affected by the fall in bond prices was a struggling young politician from Independence, Missouri. Harry S. Truman was to remember this painful experience and attempt to avoid a recurrence when he was president during the Korean War.

Although World War I inflation was uncomfortably high and especially painful for those who had not enjoyed an increase in wartime earnings, McAdoo succeeded in his goal of keeping it below the levels of the Civil War. The annual rate of wholesale price inflation from 1914, when foreign war procurement in the United States began, until 1920, when demobilization was completed, was 15 percent compared to the Civil War average of 25 percent. Still, price increases could have been better contained. The administration and Congress could have moved more quickly to draw funds from working-class wage earners by reducing the income tax exemption level and increasing the normal tax rate. But the populist and progressive Democrats, many holding powerful congressional positions, insisted at the outset of the war on placing the maximum tax burden on the wealthy and business and the minimum on workers and family farmers. In addition, wartime price and wage controls generally were not imposed on nondefense goods. Most controls were aimed at limiting price rises on goods and services bought by the government for the war effort and not those bought by civilians. The Treasury and the Federal Reserve chose to accept the inflation risk of their bond-supporting monetary policy.

The Federal Reserve's *Annual Report* for 1919 warned that "the purchasing power of the public growing out of high wages and large profits is greater than it has ever been before; and this purchasing power, competing with export demands arising out of the necessities of Europe, has raised prices to a point that takes no account of prudence." It was a recipe for severe economic contraction. In 1920 and 1921, the nation suffered a sharp although brief recession. The major cause was the bursting of the credit bubble created by easy monetary policy during the war, although heavy taxes on businesses were largely blamed.

After the war, the public began demanding that Congress cut taxes. As one newspaper succinctly observed, "War-taxes should cease with the war." Many of them did. The business community was the prime driver. As Brownlee wrote, "No other single issue aroused as much corporate hostility to the Wilson administration as did the financing of the war. . . . The conflict between advocates of democratic, statist, soak-the-rich taxation on one hand and business leaders on the other hand would rage for more than two decades." What the critics objected to was more the work of the Democratic Congress than of Wilson, but the president had gone along with Congress and received the brunt of the criticism.

The fall of 1920 witnessed one of the "Big Wave" elections that led to sweeping changes in Washington. In the presidential race, the Republican senator from Ohio, Warren G. Harding, won a landslide victory over James M. Cox and his running mate, Franklin D. Roosevelt. Republicans also scored resounding victories in congressional contests, regaining control of both the House and Senate with wide majorities. Harding and his colleagues enjoyed especially strong support from big business, which immediately pressed them to repeal wartime taxes and regulations. And business interests also insisted that the Republicans enact significantly higher customs duties. World War I had been the first American war in which tariffs had not been increased, and in fact had been cut beforehand. Manufacturers wanted to be sure that the new Congress rectified the free trade, antibusiness polices of the Wilson administration.

In 1920, an exhausted Claude Kitchin, one of the chief architects of the wartime tax structure, suffered a fatal stroke after an impassioned speech in the House. A colleague eulogized, "He fell as truly a casualty of the war as if he had died leading the charge upon the crimson fields of France." But Kitchin's time was over. Probusiness Republicans held most of the power in Washington during the decade after the war and took the opportunity to reverse most of the wartime fiscal policies of the Democrats, especially high taxes on business, in their campaign to return to "normalcy." Even McAdoo's successor in the Wilson administration, Carter Glass, adopted this stance when, in November 1919, he argued against continuing the excess profits tax. He noted that it "encourages wasteful expenditures, puts a premium on over-capitalization and a penalty on brains, energy and enterprise."

Despite the political power shift, the income tax was retained and survived to become a central feature of the U.S. fiscal system. As after the Civil War, strong voices were heard in favor of abolishing the tax. Senator Smoot again pressed for a comprehensive national sales tax as an alternative, and was joined by Senator George Moses, a New Hampshire Republican, the editor in chief of the Concord *Evening Monitor*, who supported such a tax because it would "strike down the vicious principle of graduated taxation which . . . is but a modern legislative adaptation of the communist Doctrine of Karl Marx." But these had become the views of a distinct minority. Although the Republican Congress repealed the war and excess profits taxes in 1921, it rejected the sales tax proposal and kept the income tax. "The principle of income tax," Cordell Hull would write several decades later, "was now permanently established."

Yet the income tax did not escape untouched. The financial stalwart of the 1920s was Treasury Secretary Andrew Mellon. A formidable banking mogul, who dominated fiscal policymaking in Washington throughout the Harding and Coolidge administrations and at the beginning of the Hoover administration, Mellon spearheaded Republican efforts to cut deficits, spending, and especially taxes. His approach, which foreshadowed and to a degree inspired modern supply-side policy, called for across-the-board tax cuts, including a 50 percent decrease in the surtax. He advanced the proposition, to many almost incomprehensively radical at the time, that "the Government, when the full extent of the reduction is felt, will receive more revenue from the owners of large incomes at the lower rate of tax than it would have received at the higher rate."

Following Mellon's lead, Congress reduced taxes and halved spending. The surtax and the normal tax rate were cut dramatically. Middle-income Americans enjoyed significant tax reductions and many of them fell from the tax rolls altogether. Congress repealed the war profits and excess profits taxes. The excise tax on tobacco products was retained, as was a similar tax on alcoholic products, although this produced little revenue during Prohibition. The estate tax, which had become popular during the war, was left in place but significantly lowered.

Although a number of conservative Republicans sought to replace the graduated income tax with a flat national sales tax, Mellon resisted. By basing taxation to some degree on the "ability to pay," he argued, his fellow Republicans in Congress would "demonstrate their civic responsibility and diffuse attacks on capital by recognizing the popular support that soak-the-rich taxation had gathered." Mellon also advocated greater tax reductions for "earned" than for "unearned" income. With the economy in hyperdrive during much of the Roaring Twenties, and some Americans earning fortunes playing the stock market, "the fairness of taxing more lightly incomes from wages and salaries," compared to investment income, Mellon wrote, "is beyond question."

Largely due to Mellon's prestige and financial credibility earned over the years as an eminent banker, the Republican Congress gave enormous weight to his views. So while dramatically cutting taxes, it retained in more modest form a number of the progressive taxes enacted during the Wilson era. In one area, however, the Republicans deviated dramatically from their professed goal of lowering America's tax burden: tariff policy. Here they reverted to the policies of William McKinley's administration. Between 1920 and 1930, they reversed the Wilson-era tariff reductions and passed three protectionist tariff bills, culminating in the infamous Smoot-Hawley Tariff of 1930. These tariff increases, coupled with a decline in the income tax, shifted a portion of the burden for servicing and repaying the war debt onto the consumer exactly as Democratic legislators who had supported pay-as-we-go financing had feared. However, because of the retention of the graduated income tax and other legacies of the progressive movement, the shift to a regressive system of taxation was not nearly as great as the ones that occurred after the War of 1812 or the Civil War.

World War I also changed America's international financial position. As Janeway wrote, the government's wartime financing "catapulted the nation into a new era. The effect of the economic revolution precipitated by the accidents of wartime finance was to speed up the reversal of the historic process which had made American reactions dependent on European actions." In the short span of three years, the United States was transformed from a large international debtor to an even larger international creditor.

Except for a few periods during the nineteenth century, notably during the War of 1812 and the Civil War, America had been the recipient of enormous foreign investment. After the Civil War, foreign capital had poured in to finance the railroads and other infrastructure projects that opened the West as well as to snap up attractive government bonds. Inflows persisted throughout the remainder of the century, exceeding the growing American investment flowing overseas. In 1914, total U.S. investment abroad totaled $5 billion, while the total amount of investment held by foreigners in the U.S. amounted to over $7 billion. At the end of World War I, those figures stood at $10 billion and $3 billion, respectively. To generate funds to buy American supplies and weapons and to satisfy wartime debts to the United States, European corporations and governments had sold billions of dollars' worth of gold and U.S. financial assets to Americans. In addition, foreign governments, principally France and Britain, owed the United States billions in war loans. By 1929, U.S. investment abroad totaled over $20 billion, while foreign investment in America amounted to less than half of that figure.

In the early 1920s, despite McAdoo's and the Fed's efforts to hold down the cost of borrowing, interest payments accounted for 40 percent of all federal outlays, making it a priority of the Harding administration to reduce wartime debt. One way of accomplishing this was to reduce defense spending. In any case, the nation, eager for "normalcy," did not regard a large or heavily equipped military as necessary. After the armistice, the War Department asked Congress to authorize a standing regular army of 600,000, but Congress rejected the request as too high. Instead the troop level was reduced to fewer than 250,000 officers and enlisted men, the draft was canceled, and the force was again based on volunteers. No longer "an army for empire," the post–World War I military was designed primarily for the defense of the Western Hemisphere. In the 1920s, that meant a small land force with a modestly sized air force (still a part of the army) and a relatively large navy. Strategists reasoned that as long as U.S. forces could protect American interests close to home, the country did not have to maintain forces to fight a war an ocean away. If a war broke out abroad, they reasoned, foreign forces could hold off an enemy long enough for the United States to mobilize, as it had in World War I. The United States devoted only 1 percent of its GNP annually to defense in the twenties. During the same period, largely because money had been freed up by defense cuts, nearly $8 billion in bonds was retired. This left the Treasury with a debt of $17.6 billion on the eve of the Great Depression, which caused revenues to plunge, thus again increasing borrowing.

★

During the period from 1898 through 1919 America emerged as a major military, political, and economic power on the world stage. In that same period U.S. financial policy shifted from being based primarily on the tariff and excise taxes to being based heavily on income and corporate taxes. Massive wartime revenue requirements had produced both a broadening of the tax base and a highly progressive system. The borrowing had spawned huge patriotic bond drives. If the debate over how to fund the public debt after the Revolution was the crucible within which the fundamental principles of the U.S. financial system were forged, the debate over how to pay for World War I was the political battlefield from which the modern U.S. tax and borrowing systems emerged.

World War I cost so much more than its predecessors that unprecedented taxation and borrowing were required. Federal spending rose from just under $750 million in 1915 to more than $18 billion in 1919. At the height of the war, military appropriations comprised nearly 75 percent of the government's budget, compared to 40 percent before the war. Total government outlays as a portion of GNP had been below 2 percent in 1915; by the war's end, they were nearly 25 percent. Massive borrowing sent the federal debt skyrocketing, from $1.2 billion in 1916 to over $25 billion in 1919. The need to mobilize such large sums reshaped the American tax system. In the first years of the twentieth century, as during the century before, revenues had mostly been drawn from levies that raised the cost of consumer goods. At the war's end, by far the largest proportion of revenues was derived from taxes on personal income and profits. These have remained the major sources of federal proceeds (later joined by the payroll tax to fund Social Security) ever since.

Moreover, the U.S. government not only paid America's own war costs, it also financed a large portion of the military expenditures of its European allies, roughly $10 billion in war loans. The country's ability to mobilize enormous sums of money so quickly represented an important source of military strength. Justin Morrill, William Pitt Fessenden, and Salmon P. Chase would have recognized the World War I revenue system as an offspring of the one they had crafted, but they would have been flabbergasted at how high their successors had managed to jack up rates, how significantly they had broadened coverage, and how much revenue the income tax had generated.

But the administration's fiscal policy goals went well beyond raising huge sums of money. To control inflation it prodded Congress to add millions of middle-income Americans to the tax rolls, conducted mass bond drives, and issued over a billion dollars' worth of savings certificates. These devices were only modestly successful in containing prices because political pressures prevented the government from pursuing a consistent and sustained policy that could contain civilian spending power.

The most striking aspect of wartime financing was the degree to which the government was able at the outset to successfully call on Americans to make economic sacrifices. In virtually all of America's wars, the public's willingness to accept economic sacrifice has been closely correlated with the popularity of the war. Usually, a war has legitimized dramatic changes in the U.S. financial system and staggering increases in government taxation and borrowing. During World War I, high levels of patriotism at the outset, combined with populist and progressive support, enabled the government to transform the country's tax system and sharply increase revenues. This was no easy task in a country that a few short years earlier had had no income tax, no inheritance tax, and no tax on business. Fiscal policy was structured to strengthen support for the war effort by demonstrating that it was being financed fairly, and by using bond drives as devices for encouraging large numbers of people to demonstrate their patriotism. But by the time the elections of November 1918 came around, much of the earlier patriotic zeal had vanished, as had the nation's tolerance for high taxes.

The next generation of leaders to face war learned their lessons from Wilson and McAdoo. The losing vice presidential candidate Franklin D. Roosevelt and the struggling Missourian Harry S. Truman had watched their financial victories and experienced, quite personally, the results of their financial mistakes.

5

A Righteous Might

SHARED SACRIFICE DURING WORLD WAR II

BATTLES ARE NOT WON BY SOLDIERS OR SAILORS WHO THINK
FIRST OF THEIR OWN SAFETY. AND WARS ARE NOT WON BY
PEOPLE WHO ARE CONCERNED PRIMARILY WITH THEIR OWN
COMFORT, THEIR OWN CONVENIENCE, AND THEIR OWN POCKET-
BOOKS.

—FRANKLIN DELANO ROOSEVELT

On the day after Japan's attack on Pearl Harbor, President Franklin Roosevelt proclaimed his confidence that the American people, "in their righteous might," would prevail over their enemies. One manifestation of that might was America's financial and economic muscle—its ability to mobilize massive amounts of resources in the form of taxes and bonds to fund Roosevelt's call for a "crushing superiority" in weapons and supplies in support of the nation's armed forces and its allies. But for the president the process of obtaining money from Congress to achieve this superiority would rarely prove smooth—and often turned confrontational.

The confrontations in part were over issues of principle: who would be asked to pay for this new conflict, how they would pay, and how much would be left for future generations to pay. In 1941 and early 1942, relations between the president and Congress were tense, but the financial requirements of war impelled both ends of Pennsylvania Avenue to work together. Congress essentially accepted FDR's approach to raising revenue. Although many members had disagreed with the president, the two branches resolved their differences amicably. Congress enacted bills that raised levies

on business and the wealthy, while also adding more low- and middle-income Americans to the tax rolls.

The midterm elections of 1942 changed the political landscape. Popular dissatisfaction with a number of the president's policies produced enormous Democratic losses; Republicans gained ten seats in the Senate and forty-seven seats in the House, tilting future legislation steeply in favor of a more conservative approach. Democratic committee chairmen, many of whom were Southerners who embraced a more conservative fiscal philosophy than the president, found new allies. Many had unpleasant memories of the weak economy of the early 1920s, which had been blamed on high business taxes—especially wartime excess profits taxes—during the Wilson administration. There was also resentment over FDR's strong-arm tactics on tax policy, which members from both parties considered their constitutional prerogative.

Roosevelt insisted that taxes should pay for a larger share of the cost of World War II than of World War I. Based on his observations about the financing of the earlier war, he believed the government had depended too much on borrowing and too little on taxation, which led to an unacceptably high rate of inflation. He was determined to avoid repeating that mistake. FDR was equally determined to ensure that the higher tax burden was allocated equitably. He accepted the need to increase taxes on virtually all Americans, but insisted that the wealthy and large businesses bear the primary burden and that the system be purged of loopholes enabling "special interests" to avoid paying their fair share. In his fireside chats and messages to the Congress, he repeatedly preached the need for shared sacrifice.

Through clashes and (often grudging) compromises among contending economic philosophies, class interests, regional power blocs, bureaucracies, and egos, the two branches eventually managed to mobilize tens of billions of dollars to pay for the most expensive war in American history. But none of it was easy.

A New Deal on Taxes

The confrontations between FDR and Congress in fact were a continuation of a pattern of the ebb and flow of power between the White House and the Congress in the decade leading up to the war. During the 1920s, conservative Republicans, often with Democratic support, radically scaled back the progressive tax system that had helped fund World War I. But during the Great Depression, which began in 1929, Congress gradually increased taxes to offset the fall in revenues caused by the collapse of the economy. In the Revenue Act of 1932—the last full year of the ill-fated Hoover administration—Congress passed the largest peacetime tax increase in U.S. history in an attempt to reduce the large Depression-induced budget deficit. Personal and corporate income tax rates rose to levels close to those of World War I and stiff sales taxes were imposed on a wide range of consumer products, such as gasoline. Nonetheless, with revenues only trickling in, the deficit remained extremely large. Reflecting the Democrats' fiscal orthodoxy at the time, Roosevelt campaigned for the presidency in the summer and fall of 1932 on a platform promising a reduction in government spending as well as a balanced budget. He harshly criticized Republicans for their "loose fiscal policy."

When Democrats resoundingly regained control of the White House and Congress in the 1932 elections, with the Depression raging and the electorate blaming the Republicans, the tax debate resurfaced. The question was whether to restore significant progressivity to the system, and, if so, how far to go. FDR was a strong advocate of balanced budgets in the early years of his administration. He recognized that the public wanted "bold, persistent experimentation"and that after three Republican administrations many Americans were in favor of slapping a greater share of the tax burden on the wealthy. But he also realized that there was little support in Congress for wholesale changes in the tax system. Soon after Roosevelt's inauguration, Speaker of the House Henry T. Rainey paid a visit to the Oval Office to inform him that increasing taxes "would be inviting revolution." Heeding this warning, Roosevelt proposed only limited tax measures in 1933. Despite his campaign promises of fiscal responsibility, he did not believe he had a mandate to generate more revenues by pressing for aggressive tax increases on businesses or the rich. Much of his and the Democratic Party's reformist zeal had evaporated after their string of electoral losses in the post-Wilson period. A large portion of the business community had opposed FDR's election, and he worried that sharply increasing the corporate tax or the income tax on the wealthy would set off powerful resistance to his New Deal social initiatives.

Roosevelt also feared he would be blamed if he raised income or business taxes too high and the economy weakened. He remembered too well his unsuccessful bid for the vice presidency in 1920, when anger at Wilson's

and the Democratic Congress's tax policies had been stirred up by the business community. To fund the initiatives of the early New Deal years, he relied only on modest tax increases on the top income brackets, dividends, and excess profits; the lion's share of federal revenue still came from taxes on consumer goods such as tobacco products, gasoline, and liquor (which became a big source of revenue after Prohibition was repealed). Roosevelt was aware these were regressive but supported them out of necessity. And he distinguished between excise taxes on specific items, which were tolerable because they were narrowly focused, and broad consumption taxes, which he regarded as too sweeping and too great a burden on low-income Americans. (As governor of New York, he had supported a gasoline tax because its revenues were earmarked for road construction that benefited drivers paying the tax—a user fee.)

In the 1934 midterm elections, Democrats picked up enough seats to give them a three-to-one majority in the House and nearly that in the Senate, and Roosevelt felt emboldened to act. His principled view of taxation held that an individual's taxes should correspond to his or her "ability to pay," and he declared to Congress in June 1935, employing phrases that could easily have been used by Jefferson 130 years earlier, that "our revenue laws have operated in many ways to the advantage of the few, and they have done little to prevent the unjust concentration of wealth and economic power." He proposed what he called a "wealth tax," comprised of a stiff levy on corporations, a hike in the marginal income tax on affluent individuals, and a higher inheritance tax. The New Dealers in Congress responded enthusiastically, including most aspects of this program in the Revenue Act of 1935. The legislation was strongly opposed by Republicans and conservative Democrats; both groups viewed the new measures as particularly harsh on high-income individuals. Also known as the "Wealth Tax Act," it marked the beginning of a sustained clash between the administration and the business community over fiscal issues that would carry over into the war years. That year, Congress also passed what became the most enduring legacy of the New Deal—the Social Security Act.

In 1936, at Roosevelt's urging, Congress enacted a graduated tax on undistributed profits as well as a new surtax on corporate incomes as part of his assault on "unjust concentrations of wealth." Again, this was done over the objections of Republicans, conservative Democrats, and the business community. But the president's influence carried a great deal of weight and he had a large number of supporters in the Congress. The country appeared to agree, and in November, FDR won a resounding victory in his quest for a second term, carrying all but two states. Punctuating his victory, the Democrats added to their majorities in Congress.

The political euphoria was short-lived. In 1937 and 1938, the economy suffered a recession, dubbed the "Roosevelt Recession" by the president's critics. In 1938, a group of fervent New Deal champions, including Thomas Corcoran, Benjamin Cohen, and Leon Henderson, convinced FDR that the answer to the lingering recession was to embark on a new public-sector spending program, particularly for housing and highway projects. Congress went along with spending increases for these initiatives, recognizing that they would create jobs, but did not go forward with the president's requests to raise taxes to pay for them. Instead, an alliance of Republicans and conservative Democrats, mostly from the South and concerned about the weakening economy, eliminated the undistributed profits tax for small companies, reduced it for large companies, and made other probusiness adjustments. The president objected and refused to sign the bill, but he did not veto it because it contained a number of his spending initiatives. It became law without his signature in May 1938.

Due largely to the softening of the economy, a significant rise in joblessness, and the president's unsuccessful and widely criticized attempt to pack the Supreme Court, Republicans made substantial gains in the Senate and House in the 1938 midterm elections. In the primaries, Roosevelt attempted to engineer the defeat of a number of conservative Democrats he accused of undermining the New Deal. The strategy backfired and all were reelected. In 1939, a newly emboldened and enlarged group of Republicans joined conservative Democrats, including some the president had attempted to unseat, to eliminate the undistributed profits tax and give corporations greater flexibility to deduct capital losses. Recognizing that further tax increases on business and the wealthy were unlikely in this environment, and confronted with a sputtering economy, FDR embarked on a period of significant deficit spending aimed at reviving and then expanding growth.

A Looming War

On the eve of World War II, the political pendulum had swung away from Roosevelt. But events were occurring abroad that were to strengthen the president's hand. In 1933, Hitler had come to power in Germany. In 1936,

German troops reoccupied the Rhineland, which under the Treaty of Versailles that ended World War I was supposed to remain a demilitarized zone. In March 1938, Hitler forced his native Austria into a union with Germany known as the Anschluss, and in October he ordered his army to march into the German-speaking areas of Czechoslovakia known as the Sudetenland. On September 1, 1939, Hitler's troops invaded Poland; two days later, Britain and France declared war on Germany.

Soon after war broke out in Europe, Congress passed a series of measures, beginning in April 1940 with the National Defense Act, to increase the size of the army and the army air corps, to speed up ship construction, and to modernize aviation facilities in the Pacific and Alaska. Still, the country was officially neutral, and U.S. defense spending was but a fraction of the military budgets of Britain, Germany, Japan, and the Soviet Union.

In November, Congress amended the Neutrality Act of 1935, which prevented sales of munitions and other war equipment to belligerent nations. The change allowed warring countries to buy these items in the United States on a "cash and carry" basis. Their cash was accepted so long as they used their own ships to carry them. The primary aim was to help Britain, but to do so in a way that avoided drawing the United States into war simply because Americans held the debt of a belligerent (and thus had a financial stake in the nation's military success) or because a U.S. ship was sunk for running a blockade. America's factories now revved into action, producing enormous amounts of equipment and ammunition for the Allies. Combined with the stimulus from the 1939 tax cuts, these gave a boost to economic growth.

American military spending increased significantly after May 1940, when Germany launched its offensive on the Low Countries. In June, Congress passed three military spending bills that collectively raised defense appropriations by roughly $3 billion. In July, Roosevelt stepped up war preparations. To strengthen the army and navy, Congress budgeted $5 billion—double the 1939 amount—and authorized the Treasury to undertake additional borrowing. Soon after, FDR traded fifty American destroyers to Britain in exchange for bases in Bermuda and the Caribbean. He also pushed through appropriations to increase the size of the navy, rebase the Pacific fleet at Pearl Harbor, build additional combat aircraft, and enlarge the army through the draft. Even with these aggressive measures, defense spending accounted for just 17 percent of the budget in 1940—under 2 percent of GDP.

As preparedness accelerated, the administration sought new ways to increase revenues. The chief architect of the effort was Secretary of the Treasury Henry Morgenthau Jr. Like the president, Morgenthau was a believer in both balanced budgets and social equity. He had begun his career as an agricultural specialist and then became publisher of the *American Agriculturalist* magazine. Morgenthau owned a farm in Dutchess County, New York, and was active in state Democratic politics, developing a close friendship, beginning in 1913, with his neighbor and up-and-coming politician Franklin Roosevelt. When elected governor, Roosevelt appointed Morgenthau to chair the state's Agricultural Advisory Commission and subsequently named him state commissioner for conservation. He brought Morgenthau with him to Washington as chair of the Federal Farm Board and then appointed him undersecretary of the Treasury. In 1933, Morgenthau became secretary of the Treasury, a post he held for eleven years. Throughout his tenure, Morgenthau kept a detailed diary. While Roosevelt did not like to keep notes of his private meetings, and thus relatively few of his own records exist, Morgenthau's notes provide a rich, if occasionally self-serving, description of many of the most consequential financial policy discussions of the war.

In his January 1940 State of the Union address, Roosevelt reaffirmed his commitment to fiscal responsibility, even in the face of war, declaring his intention to seek additional funds for the military while also reducing non-security programs and cutting the budget deficit. Higher taxes would be necessary. "In the hope that we can continue in these days of increasing economic prosperity to reduce the deficit," he announced, "I am asking the Congress to levy sufficient additional taxes to meet the emergency spending." In his budget message the following day, FDR said he needed $460 million in additional taxes. Then, as the prospect of war loomed larger, he upped the figure to $1 billion. He also sought authority to raise the federal debt limit to permit increased borrowing.

The president's request quickly won support from congressional leaders. By June, the month Hitler's forces marched into Paris, Congress passed what came to be known as the First Revenue Act of 1940, which lowered personal tax exemptions, increased the surtax on the wealthy, raised corporate income taxes, imposed a 10 percent defense "super tax" on most existing taxes, and hiked a variety of excise taxes. To mollify taxpayers, some of the new levies were designated as "temporary" and slated to last for only five years. The act also authorized the Treasury to issue $4 billion in new bonds to finance the expanding defense buildup, despite vocal opposition from conservative Republicans, such as Representative Daniel Reed of New York, who criticized the additional borrowing as "an example of the deficit-financing, pump-priming scheme advocated by British economist John Maynard Keynes."

Morgenthau contended that the legislation did not do enough. He criticized Congress for a halfhearted effort, complaining that the bill was "little more than a gesture toward what was needed that year." What was really needed, in his view, was a new excess profits tax. The House Ways and Means Committee had considered including such a tax in the bill but concluded that devising a formula would be too controversial and that the process of reaching an agreement in committee would slow the progress of enacting other urgently needed revenue-raising measures.

Dissatisfied with Congress's unwillingness to impose stiffer taxes on businesses, FDR sent legislators a message calling for them to immediately take up the issue and enact a steep excess profits tax to "prevent defense profiteering and yield significant new revenue." Recalling the success of a similar tax during World War I, liberals in both the House and Senate strongly supported its revival. But conservative Democrats had major reservations. They did not consider it good policy or good politics to impose heavy burdens on corporations, especially in the defense industry. Senator Byron Patton "Pat" Harrison of Mississippi, the chairman of the Senate Finance Committee, coolly informed Morgenthau and Roosevelt that he preferred to avoid addressing the issue until after the November elections.

A stalwart of the 1930s Senate, Harrison had first been elected to the House in 1910, running as a Southern progressive, and was elected to the Senate in 1918 by defeating a critic of Woodrow Wilson. His political base was comprised of wealthy planters and merchants who opposed high taxes on business. Harrison had earned a reputation for moral rectitude during his contest with Alben Barkley for the post of majority leader. When the vote count appeared close, his advisers urged him to seek support from Mississippi's other senator, Theodore G. Bilbo, who had earned notoriety as a race-baiting demagogue. Harrison rejected the notion. "Tell the son of a bitch," he responded, "I wouldn't speak to him even if it meant the presidency of the United States." Harrison lost by one vote but reinforced his reputation as a tough and principled legislator.

Despite Harrison's power in the Senate, the president bucked his advice. Indeed, FDR saw the politics of the excess profits tax very differently.

For him, it was a way of inoculating the administration and the Democratic Party against the charge, leveled by populists in World War I, that they wanted to go to war for the benefit of big business and rich financiers. As historian John Morton Blum wrote, "Roosevelt was in a hurry to ban [war profits] so that Republicans could not call the Democratic Party a war party." This legislation, FDR informed Morgenthau, would be "the opening gun of the campaign."

The House Ways and Means Committee was also skeptical of the administration's revenue proposals. Its decidedly negative response was shaped largely by its legendary chairman, Robert Lee "Muley" Doughton, a longtime Democratic representative from North Carolina. Doughton, like Harrison, had first been elected to the House in 1910. He assumed the chairmanship of the committee in 1933 at the age of sixty-nine and had been a central figure in the passage of the Social Security Act and other New Deal tax legislation. But Doughton was foremost a Southerner. He had been born during the Civil War, and his father had served as a captain under Robert E. Lee and named his son after the general. He also was a staunch fiscal conservative who had earned his nickname "Muley" for "an image of a backwoods stubbornness that conveniently cloaked a shrewd ability to compromise without alienating either New Deal liberals or their conservative critics." Drawing on his "homespun philosophy," he often reminded colleagues that "the science of levying and collecting taxes is the science of getting the most feathers with the least squawking of the geese." He was one of a group of primarily Southern conservatives called "boll weevils," who generally supported the New Deal but opposed desegregation. (Doughton ultimately served as chairman of the Ways and Means Committee longer than any other man in history.)

The War Department played an active role in the debate over the bill. It urged Congress to go easy on corporations, especially military contractors, in order to induce them to invest more in defense-related production. Secretary of War Henry Stimson took the position that "if you are going to try to go to war or to prepare for war, in a capitalist country, you have got to let business make money out of the process or business won't work." That position also was consistent with the view that one of America's great strategic assets was its productive capacity. Taxes that damaged the defense industry—the "arsenal of democracy" on which the United States and its allies depended—would jeopardize the entire war effort.

With so many competing factions, progress on the bill was slow. The two main congressional committees could not reach agreement with the administration despite many conversations with Morgenthau and his colleagues in the Treasury. Then, "eager for action," and with Morgenthau on vacation, Roosevelt took an extraordinary step; he asked Harrison and Doughton to design an excess profits tax that would quickly pass Congress, taking the matter out of the hands of the Treasury. FDR explained to Undersecretary of the Treasury Dan Bell "that we must have an excess profits tax bill this season [and] that he did not want to be bothered with the details of the bill but would leave it entirely to the legislative branch." A significant reason for urgency was that Secretary Stimson and Secretary of the Navy Frank Knox—both of whom were prominent Republicans appointed to key positions to strengthen national unity—had told FDR that aspects of the existing legislation concerning amortization were holding up the signing of defense contracts. They, and Roosevelt, wanted a new bill that eliminated these impediments.

Given its mandate from the president, the Ways and Means Committee quickly reported out excess profits tax legislation. It was far less burdensome to business than its World War I predecessor, featuring amortization provisions that enabled many large businesses to avoid paying the entire tax and permitted defense industries to write off the cost of land, equipment, and buildings over five years. Morgenthau complained that it was "filled with loopholes permitting evasion, inadequate in raising revenue, harsh on small business." The Senate Finance Committee, in Morgenthau's view, responded no more constructively when it took up the legislation. It also enacted provisions that were far more favorable to the business community than he thought appropriate. The Treasury secretary criticized the committee for having "permitted almost a total escape from the excess profits tax for corporations with high earnings in recent years . . . and for corporations with huge capital structures."

Despite Morgenthau's displeasure, neither committee relented. On their recommendations, Congress passed a compromise bill in October that was very different from what the Treasury wanted. Excess profits were to be taxed on a graduated scale of 25 to 50 percent, but a company was permitted to choose whether its tax payment was based on its return on invested capital or on its average earnings during a base period (the years 1936 through 1939), whichever was more favorable. The legislation also permitted favorable amortization schedules for the construction of defense plants. Stimson and Knox welcomed it and their long-awaited contracts.

The bill pleased neither side completely. For many Republicans, it was too hard on business and too complicated. Senator Arthur Vandenberg, a prominent Republican from Michigan who would later play a key role in shaping foreign policy during the postwar period, quipped, "It would take a Philadelphia lawyer, a certified public accountant or an extraordinarily clever crystal gazer" to understand the bill. Congressman Allen T. Treadway, a Massachusetts Republican, criticized the legislation as a "monumental specimen of statutory incomprehensibility." Morgenthau characterized it as "a lousy bill" because it "sponsored the very kinds of discrimination that the President and the Treasury had for so many years opposed," and violated the basic tenets of the New Deal. Moreover, he believed profits would be high enough to induce sufficient new defense-related investment without incentives. Morgenthau urged Roosevelt to press congressional leaders for changes that imposed greater tax burdens on corporations and produced significantly more revenue. Interior Secretary Harold Ickes joined Morgenthau in criticizing the bill as a violation of New Deal principles.

The legislation posed a moral dilemma for FDR. He was passionately opposed to tax loopholes that gave special advantages to favored groups and permitted companies or individuals to avoid their fair share of taxation, but an election was on the horizon, defense requirements were mounting, and FDR recognized the need to provide incentives for U.S. industry to quickly gear up for military production. So he swallowed hard and signed the legislation. Morgenthau, who had become resigned to defeat, wrote in his diary that "in a campaign year," the president "had decided to accept an imperfect law that would encourage the defense program." The president also authorized the use of government loans for military plant construction, agreed to relax antitrust enforcement to permit greater collaboration within the defense industry, and permitted procurement to be done on a cost-plus basis that would virtually ensure profitability. Under normal conditions, all were measures a fervent New Dealer would have opposed as special advantages for business.

The Earliest Victory

In the 1940 elections, Roosevelt won an unprecedented third term, handily defeating Republican Wendell L. Willkie. The elections also produced enormous Democratic majorities in Congress—267 to 162 in the House

and 66 to 28 in the Senate. In January 1941, fresh from his electoral triumph, Roosevelt presented Congress with his budget request for 1942. It included nearly $11 billion in defense spending and total government expenditures of $17 billion. Later that month, he submitted legislation for what came to be known as the "Lend-Lease" program, authorizing the president to "sell, transfer title to, exchange, lease, lend, or otherwise dispose of " weapons, food, or equipment to any country "whose defense the President deems vital to the defense of the United States." As historian David Kennedy wrote in *Freedom from Fear,* "substituting military production and technology for [American] manpower" was the "essence of the 'arsenal of democracy' or short-of-war strategy during the period of neutrality." Transferring weapons might avert U.S. intervention, and if the nation did enter the war, the better equipped its allies were, the more fighting they could do—with American forces suffering fewer casualties. The proposal triggered a bitter congressional battle.

The Democrats' large majorities and Roosevelt's own decisive reelection did not prevent a group of isolationists opposed to American intervention from launching a vicious attack on Lend-Lease, charging that it inevitably would draw the nation into a conflict that should be left to the Europeans. Large numbers of Americans still ardently opposed intervention. FDR had to proceed carefully in his efforts to assist the nations fighting the Axis so that he would not be vulnerable to the charge that he was dragging the country into the conflict. Throughout 1940 and most of 1941, he engaged in a sustained effort to bring the public opinion around to support more direct assistance to Britain and its allies and to ensure that the United States was prepared for what he saw as an inevitable need to commit massive forces abroad.

He encountered vocal opposition in the Senate. Republicans Vandenberg and Robert Taft of Ohio teamed with Democrats Burton K. Wheeler of Montana and Bennett "Champ" Clark of Missouri to block the legislation. Wheeler went so far as to declare that "Lend Lease would be the military equivalent of the New Deal's agricultural program; it would plow under every third American boy." In time, as anti-Nazi feelings intensified, FDR rallied the majority of his fellow Democrats and a substantial number of internationalist Republicans to his side. The Lend-Lease bill was passed in March, by a two-to-one margin, opening the way for huge shipments to Britain and other nations. By year's end, $750 million in goods had been exported under this program. By the end of the war, nearly $50 billion had been sent to America's allies.

In May 1941, Morgenthau projected a budget deficit of $14 billion and announced the goal of covering two-thirds of the government's expenditures in the coming fiscal year with taxes and a third through borrowing. In June, as Germany began its invasion of Russia, the president threw his preparation plans into overdrive, announcing unprecedented military production objectives for the year: sixty thousand planes, forty-five thousand tanks, twenty thousand antiaircraft guns, and 18 million deadweight tons of merchant shipping, plus a large troop call-up. He also disclosed to Congress his plans to assist the Soviet Union.

In a speech explaining to Americans why he sought authorization to provide weapons for nations fighting the Axis powers, Roosevelt took the opportunity to warn the country about the threat the fascists posed to the country and of the necessity of preparing to meet that threat. "We must," he said, "prepare to make the sacrifices that the emergency . . . demands." He emphasized the need for "personal sacrifice," especially the "payment of more money in taxes," and indicated that in his forthcoming budget message he would recommend that "a greater portion of this great defense program be paid for from taxation than we are paying today. No person should try, or be allowed, to get rich out of this program; and the principle of tax payments in accordance with ability to pay should be consistently before our eyes to guide our legislation."

Shortly thereafter, Morgenthau sent Congress the details of the administration's revenue request, which included an increase in the personal and corporate income taxes and tightened loopholes in the excess profits tax. Congress began its deliberations in the late spring of 1941. By July, the Ways and Means Committee had passed legislation that would yield $13 billion in revenues, expected to cover 60 percent of the government's anticipated expenditures during the coming fiscal year. The committee's Republicans issued a minority report criticizing the bill, and took a potshot at the entire range of New Deal spending legislation. The Democratic "wastrels," it charged with considerable hyperbole, had "spent in eight years as much as the government had spent during its first 130 years." The full House was not moved. Amid intensifying concerns about adverse developments in Europe, it passed the committee bill, with minor changes, by a bipartisan vote of 369 to 40.

The Senate Finance Committee's version of the bill differed in several ways from that of the House. It lowered income tax exemptions and imposed new and higher taxes on estates. The bill also contained a revised excess profits tax, although one more modest than that proposed by the administration. A Treasury proposal for special taxes on nondefense items using materials needed for national defense was rejected by the committee.

In the midst of the committee's deliberations on the bill, in mid-June, Pat Harrison died. The chairmanship passed to Senator Walter George, a conservative Georgia Democrat who had grown up on a farm in Webster County and had served as an associate justice of that state's Supreme Court. Roosevelt had campaigned against George in the state's 1938 primary, calling him a "dyed in the wool conservative." George subsequently won the primary and the general election, but he bore a deep grudge. When someone later remarked that Roosevelt was his own worst enemy, George sarcastically responded, "Not as long as I am alive." Yet the accelerating threat of war overcame his resentments, and he worked hard to report out a revenue bill. The Senate passed the legislation, again by a bipartisan majority, 67 to 5.

In September, FDR ordered the U.S. Navy to "shoot on sight" German warships in waters "the protection of which is necessary for American defense." That month, the two chambers reconciled their bills and presented the Revenue Act of 1941 for the president's signature. It reduced the personal tax exemption from $2,000 to $1,500 for married couples and from $800 to $750 for individuals, increasing the tax rolls by 30 percent. It also raised the excess profits tax, although with corporate loopholes that the administration opposed, steepened the corporate tax rate, and made permanent a number of the taxes contained in the First Revenue Act of 1940. The 1941 act was intended to yield revenues at the level originally recommended by the Ways and Means Committee—$13 billion. It was the largest revenue bill in American history.

The New York Times proclaimed the act to be "by far the heaviest and most broadly based tax levy ever adopted by the country" and "the most important contribution to solving the paramount economic problem of rearmament: how to finance the tremendous government spending without plunging the country into a disastrous inflation." As effusive as the Times's language was, the act, as the country would shortly discover, was just the beginning.

America at War

The real explosion in appropriations and revenues took place after December 7, 1941. The following day, the United States declared war on Japan. On December 11, Germany declared war on the United States, hoping the move would solidify its alliance with Japan and lead the Japanese to attack the Soviet Union, relieving some pressure from Germany's eastern front. Japan refused, but the German action removed the last residue of American resistance to joining the European Allies against the Nazis. America fully mobilized for all-out war. Congress passed a series of measures that catapulted military spending from less than half the budget and nearly 6 percent of gross domestic product in 1941 to 90 percent of the budget and roughly 38 percent of GDP in 1944.

Following the attack on Pearl Harbor, Adolf Hitler belittled the United States' ability to respond to the Axis military challenge by calling it a "decayed nation," with "racial problems, and problems of social inequalities." "How," he asked rhetorically, "can one expect a state like that to hold together—a country where everything is built on the dollar?" Soon, he would see how well the United States did hold together, and how quickly and effectively it mobilized hundreds of billions of those dollars to produce a superiority of weapons that would ultimately defeat the Führer's once seemingly invincible Third Reich.

The attack on Pearl Harbor, and Germany's declaration of war, shifted American military production into high gear. In his January 1942 State of the Union message to Congress, Roosevelt declared, "It will not be sufficient for us [and our allies] to produce a slightly superior supply of munitions to that of Germany, Japan, and Italy. The superiority . . . must be overwhelming . . . a crushing superiority of equipment in any theater of the world war." American strategists, as David Kennedy described, recognized that large-scale military production was the "route that would claim the smallest toll of American lives" by ensuring that American troops had unquestioned superiority of weapons in the field and that the United States could provide its allies with the arms to do a large portion of the fighting.

The prospect of massive amounts of production and hiring to achieve this superiority swept away Roosevelt's concerns that higher taxes would weaken the economy. Once the government confronted the enormous revenue needs and spending requirements of active U.S. participation in the war, FDR insisted that Americans make far greater economic sacrifices. "War costs money," FDR stressed in his 1942 State of the Union address. "That means taxes and bonds and bonds and taxes. It means cutting luxuries and other non-essentials. In a word it means an 'all-out' war by individual effort and family effort in a united country. So far we have hardly even had to pay for it. We have devoted only 15 per cent of our national income to national defense." He predicted that the war soon would consume more than half of the nation's income. But Roosevelt's fiscal strategy was focused not only on raising money; it was part of a broader economic and political strategy of convincing Americans that the sacrifices they were making were equitably shared and, in particular, that neither wealthy Americans nor special interest groups were using loopholes to avoid paying their fair share at the expense of the average citizen.

In his budget message to Congress, FDR explained that with full and immediate mobilization under way, federal spending for the coming fiscal year would reach almost $59 billion, nearly double that of the previous year. The army, which numbered roughly 1.6 million at the beginning of December 1941, grew to 5.4 million by the end of 1942. Other services saw similar increases. The administration called for a tax increase that would produce an additional $7.6 billion in revenues (later raised to $8.7 billion). Another $2 billion was to be generated from extra Social Security payroll tax collections, which could be used for the war because payments into the system were greater than outlays at the time. Together, they would boost revenues to $19 billion, which still left $40 billion to be raised through borrowing.

The staggering increase in revenue requirements triggered a series of intense and often bitter political struggles in Washington. Not the least of these took place between congressional Democrats and the administration. Powerful members of the Congress, at the time firmly in Democratic hands, were deeply involved in the prolonged debates, with Chairmen Doughton and George playing central roles. There were constant tensions between them and the president, who, they felt, did not demonstrate sufficient respect for Congress's historically preeminent role in the area of tax policy.

At its core, the debate was between those who favored a tax system that drew a large portion of wartime revenues from a broad base and those who favored a highly progressive tax system that imposed a very large share of the tax burden on the wealthy. Advocates of the first approach supported a comprehensive national sales tax and a lower personal income tax exemption in order to draw a larger portion of additional revenues from wage earners, including those with modest incomes. Advocates of the second insisted on a sharply graduated tax schedule, consistent with New Deal principles. Roosevelt and Morgenthau stood in the latter camp; they favored a steep tax on the wealthy along with higher taxes on corporate profits and inheritances.

Morgenthau set three broad goals for financing the war. As he later wrote in his diary, one was "to persuade the balky Congress to raise taxes high enough to cover one half of the expenses." The second was to undertake a "tremendous program to defray the balance of expenses by borrowing." The third was to prevail in the "continual controversy with various federal agencies about the Treasury's effort to keep the purchase of bonds on voluntary basis." Throughout the war, Morgenthau urged Congress to levy higher taxes to soak up potential consumer spending, stressing that the taxes were needed to hold down inflation, although his faithful allegiance to New Deal principles made him reluctant to tax low-income workers.

The challenge Morgenthau faced in controlling inflation was different from the one confronted by McAdoo when the United States entered World War I. Then the economy was growing at a moderate pace due in part to large sales of supplies and equipment to the European belligerents. For many of those same reasons, the pickup in exports to Western Europe under "cash and carry" and Lend-Lease, as well as the 1939 tax cut, the U.S. economy achieved robust growth in 1940 and 1941. But the Great Depression had created massive job losses and a wave of factory closings, leaving the country with enormous excess productive capacity and millions of unemployed workers. So on the eve of World War II, nearly 15 percent of the labor force—about 8 million people—were jobless, less than the 30 percent peak at the height of the Depression, but still a very large number. The availability of unemployed or underemployed workers provided room for a significant increase in military recruitment and defense factory hiring early in the war without a commensurate increase in inflation. According to David Kennedy, "As much as 50 percent of capacity stood idle in manufacturing plants alone [and] all those dormant resources could be swiftly directed to martial purposes with minimal disruption to the fabric of peacetime life." In this sense, the Depression had "poised the economy for phenomenally rapid conversion to war production."

But Morganthau and his economic team were well aware that inflationary pressures would rise sharply when U.S. war production reached a fever pitch. The problem they would face was already being confronted by the British, so American officials studied the measures they were taking to address it. The most influential British voice urging tough action was that of the eminent economist John Maynard Keynes. In his seminal November 1939 article in *The Times* of London, "How to Pay for the War," Keynes cautioned British authorities, "The problem we face is that the aggregate of purchasing power is increasing faster than the available supply of goods. Increased defense spending is bringing about much fuller employment and with it rising income." He warned, "An excessive rise in prices will . . . spark off the vicious spiral of wage-price inflation, as well as being a cause of great social injustice." Keynes was skeptical of the benefits of rationing; he pointed out that although it halted price increases on some products, it channeled inflated spending into others. A better approach, he suggested, was to extend "taxation . . . to the working class, since 3/5ths of net expenditure on consumption is by those who earn less than £250 a year." He also proposed a highly progressive but paternalistic twist on taxing low-income workers: the entire share of their payments would be forced savings in the form of bond purchases, drying up their excess purchasing power but allowing them to eventually benefit when their bonds were redeemed after the war.

Roosevelt and Morgenthau were familiar with Keynes's work, but they did not accept the notion of forced savings. They initially were reluctant to embrace the concept that working-class citizens had to be taxed in order to check inflation.

Roosevelt and Morgenthau both favored a highly progressive tax system with a minimum burden on those with low incomes. The president noted that he had to accept high excise taxes earlier in his administration because the government needed the money; now the costs of the war necessitated keeping these taxes. However, as the tax historian Joseph Thorndike wrote, he believed that if "low and middle income Americans were necessarily saddled with regressive excise taxes, they had to be assured that those with more money would pay higher income and estate taxes." Roosevelt's sense of tax justice, according to Thorndike, was "intensely individualistic; he wanted each person to pay his or her 'fair share.'" To him, that meant the rich should shoulder most of the burden. But over time he came to accept Keynes's view that if inflation was to be contained, low-income workers had to pay more taxes.

Within a month after the attack on Pearl Harbor, Roosevelt and Morgenthau began forging their legislative strategy to generate $8.7 billion in taxes and the remainder in borrowing. On a gray and chilly morning in early March 1942, Morgenthau's limousine rolled up Pennsylvania Avenue from the Treasury to the Capitol building. There he would present the administration's plans for wartime financing. The Ways and Means Committee hearing room was packed. Morgenthau, underscoring the gravity of the situation, opened his remarks by outlining the immensity of the challenge. "The task before us," he said, "is to decide how this desperately serious war is to be financed and how its gigantic cost is to be distributed. . . . To defeat the strongest combination of enemies in our history, we shall have to spend on a scale for which there is no precedent."

The nation's wartime tax program, Morgethau emphasized, "should accomplish more than the raising of a huge amount of resources." It should also be "an instrument of victory." The task, in his view, was "to frame the new revenue act so wisely . . . that it will facilitate the maximum production of war materials, hasten the mobilization of our resources, strengthen the unity of our people for waging total war, and prepare us for the new economic and social problems that will face us when the war is won."

Echoing William McAdoo a quarter of a century earlier, Morgenthau warned that inflation must be restrained. The first task of revenue legislation, he underscored in his testimony, should be "to check inflation, for nothing in the economic field can interfere with the war effort so much as an uncontrolled rise in prices." That, in his view, would be "a source of social injustice." It would also "undercut morale . . . impede war production . . . and strike at random without consideration of equity or ability to bear the hardships which it imposes." Once inflation acquired momentum, it would be "extremely difficult to control and leave a heritage of post-war stresses and strains that will haunt us for decades." Thus, he argued, taxes should be used to "withdraw the greatest possible volume of purchasing power at this time, when many incomes are high and the quantity of goods for consumers is shrinking day by day because of the demands of our war effort."

But Morgenthau also made sure to reaffirm the administration's dedication to New Deal principles. He implored Congress to ensure that new taxes were "fair and non-discriminatory and imposed in accordance with ability to pay." In particular, he insisted that "taxes which cannot be adjusted to differences in income or family responsibilities, such as a general sales tax, should be avoided" and "undue profits should be recaptured when they occur." Consistent with these principles, Morgenthau supported hefty increases in the income tax for the most affluent Americans and recommended a hike in the corporate excess profits tax, with the maximum rate increasing from 60 to 75 percent, a "special surtax" of 31 percent on corporate profits in excess of $25,000, a significant increase in the estate tax, and higher excise taxes on luxuries such as distilled spirits, gasoline, cigarettes, soft drinks, candy, and gum. All told, $3 billion were to come from the higher personal income tax, the same amount from the increase in corporate taxes, and roughly half that from additional excise taxes. To eliminate "special privileges," Morgenthau recommended rescinding the tax exemption for interest on state and local bonds and the removal of depletion benefits for mines and oil wells. To reduce the impact of the higher taxes on those with modest incomes, he suggested deductions for medical expenses and tax credits for child care to help the many mothers working in war production factories. Responding to members who criticized the administration's tax request, he noted pointedly, "War is never cheap, but it is a million times cheaper to win than to lose."

The Sales Tax Fight

As Congress considered Morgenthau's proposals, the secretary had to fight a rearguard action against other members of FDR's administration. The opponents were led by the director of the Budget Bureau, Harold D. Smith, who favored broadening the tax base and proposed a high national sales tax and a lower personal exemption, both of which would hit the working class. His approach had strong support from the financial community, notably the influential Russell C. Leffingwell, who had been assistant secretary of the Treasury during World War I and had since become a partner at J. P. Morgan and Company. Leffingwell and Morgenthau engaged in an extensive wartime correspondence, featuring a debate on the merits of progressive taxation. Leffingwell strongly opposed imposition of a steep excess profits tax; instead he advocated a sales tax, arguing that this would enable the burden of wartime taxation to be "widely spread among all the people." He also supported an "income tax that taxed people to the very limit of their endurance" and hit all classes, not just the wealthy.

Boosters of the sales tax argued that it was needed not only to generate additional revenue but also to restrain inflation more aggressively. For most of them, it had one more important advantage: it was an alternative to higher taxes on corporations. They continued to argue that putting too great a tax burden on American business would jeopardize its ability to make essential investments in plants to produce military equipment and munitions during the war and would weaken the private sector's ability to generate new jobs once hostilities ended, raising the specter of a recession similar to the one of the early 1920s. The Treasury countered that the sales tax would violate New Deal principles of fairness to low-income Americans.

Today we tend to assume that high income and corporate taxes were inevitably destined to be the major source of World War II funding, but this was not obvious at the time. In the bureaucratic confrontations over fiscal policy early in the war, there were few predictable outcomes. A national sales tax was a real possibility and Roosevelt's ability to determine the course of fiscal legislation was anything but absolute. Morgenthau's was even less so.

Since the early 1930s, the idea of a national sales tax had enjoyed strong support among leading Republicans, but many Democrats also had advocated it. Among them was John Nance "Cactus Jack" Garner, who was to become FDR's first vice president and before that Speaker of the House. He had championed progressive causes in Congress during Mellon's tenure at the Treasury in the 1920s but had also voted in favor of a decidedly nonprogressive national sales tax in 1932 in order to reduce the post-Depression budget deficit. Garner and other fiscal conservatives had a strong aversion to big deficits; they believed that a national sales tax would generate a lot of revenue and that by supporting it they would demonstrate their commitment to fiscal responsibility.

When the United States entered the war, many in the business community—led by the U.S. Chamber of Commerce, which ran its own budget analysis and advertised that a sales tax would raise nearly $6 billion and stifle inflation—pressed the idea and found allies among Republicans and Democrats alike. Machiavellian legislative maneuvering followed. Congressional proponents tried to block key components of the administration's revenue-generating proposals from being included in the draft 1942 tax bill. Had they succeeded, they were prepared to argue that the revenue could be made up only by enacting a hefty sales tax.

Morgenthau advised Roosevelt to reject the sales tax proposal. "We feel strongly," he wrote FDR, "that it would be a mistake to yield to the clamor for a sales tax. . . . A sales tax would get no more money [than the Treasury's plan] but simply have shifted the source of revenues to lower income groups." Roosevelt agreed. The national sales tax, he asserted, was "a 'spare-the-rich' tax."

In an effort to derail the sales tax, Morgenthau suggested Congress enact a "spendings tax"—a graduated tax (in addition to the income tax) geared to the amount a family, or an individual, actually spent, minus stipulated allowances for necessities. Morgenthau and his staff were particularly enamored of an important feature of the tax: it could be made highly progressive.

They believed that conservatives would support it as well, seeing it as an alternative to a stiffer tax on corporations. But the plan was torpedoed in Congress, where members of the key committees "regarded [it] as too radical economically and too threatening to the influence they enjoyed as gatekeepers for complex exemptions and deductions to the income tax." Senator Joseph F. Guffey, a Democrat from Pennsylvania, gleefully asserted, "The plan is dead. . . . Not a man on the committee is for it." Although originally a supporter, FDR decided not to push the tax; he considered the proposal to be primarily a bargaining tool. Its quick demise led the *Washington Post* to refer to it as "Morgenthau's Morning Glory."

Mass Sacrifice

As war production gained momentum, Morgenthau became increasingly alarmed about the potential for price and wage increases to spin out of control. He wrote the president urging that the administration "not leave a stone unturned to keep the cost of living as nearly as possible at the present level." Picking up on Morgenthau's concerns, on April 27, 1942, the president sent a strong message to Congress warning of the urgent need to curb what he feared could soon become runaway inflation. He revived some of the tax measures that had been suggested earlier by the Treasury but subsequently rejected by Congress, plus a request for a big increase in the excess profits tax, a limit on individual incomes to no more than $25,000 after taxes, rationing, and credit limits. In a broadcast to the nation the following day, Roosevelt emphasized "the blunt fact . . . that every single person in the United States is going to be affected by this program."

Rationing was a key ingredient in the administration's attempts to hold down prices and help expand the notion of shared sacrifice: everyone received the same allotment of ration stamps regardless of income or position. Certain foods were rationed, especially as shortages of labor and transportation increased the cost and difficulty of moving fruits and vegetables to market, and the planting of Victory Gardens was encouraged. Price and wage controls further arrested increases in inflation.

The House Ways and Means Committee, including Doughton, many of his Democratic colleagues, and almost all the Republicans, was "antagonistic toward almost every Treasury proposal" put forward by Morgenthau in his March testimony. It rejected his ideas for closing tax loopholes, increasing the surtax, and boosting tax rates on estates and gifts. When the committee reported out its bill without these provisions, it was expected to yield just over $6 billion—well below the $8.7 billion that Morgenthau had requested. In his diary, the exasperated Morgenthau commented, "Those fellows just don't know there's a war on."

To secure higher revenues, Morgenthau appealed to the Senate Finance Committee. On September 3, he testified that the tax measures he had requested were essential "to draw into the treasury substantial additional funds out of the earnings and savings of the people [and] reduce consumer spending directly by withdrawing funds otherwise available for expenditure." At the same time, and as part of his ongoing effort to kill the general sales tax, he revealed that the administration could accept "a further lowering of the exemptions from the income tax applying to family income." Roosevelt originally opposed this move on grounds that it was regressive. In the end, however, it was less objectionable to him than the sales tax. Moreover, he had accepted a reduction in the exemption level in the Revenue Act of 1941 and it had not produced a major political backlash; to his surprise, even the *New York Times* had supported it. Morgenthau recognized that this would cause the tax to "reach into the lowest income groups above the level of bare subsistence income," but reasoned that it would be less regressive than the sales tax. To reinforce his credibility as a staunch advocate of tax fairness, even as he supported a lower exemption level, Morgenthau also called for "high penalty rates for luxury spending."

As the debate continued, the president attempted to put pressure on Congress by emphasizing the threat of inflation and the theme of shared sacrifice. In his fireside chat on September 7, he told the American people that "failure to solve [the inflation] problem here and now will make more difficult the winning of the war. If a vicious spiral of inflation ever gets under way, the whole economic system will stagger. Prices and wages will go up so rapidly that the entire production program will be endangered. The cost of war, paid by the taxpayer, will jump beyond all present calculations." He soberly informed Americans that they would need to make more economic sacrifices for the war effort. "Battles are not won by soldiers or sailors who think first of their own safety," the president said, "and wars are not won by people who are concerned primarily with their own comfort, their own convenience, and their own pocketbooks."

After eight months of infighting and heated debate, the Revenue Act of 1942 was passed. It was the defining fiscal legislation of the war. It lowered the personal exemption for individuals (from $750 to $500) and for married couples (from $1,500 to $1,200). As a consequence, the number of Americans paying the income tax rose from 13 million to 28 million. The normal tax rate was increased from 4 to 6 percent. To demonstrate their continued commitment to progressivity, congressional Democrats included a more sharply graduated surtax, which was paid primarily by the most affluent; the increase was from 6 to 13 percent for taxpayers in the lowest surcharge paying bracket and from 77 to 82 percent for those in the top bracket. The estate tax was hiked significantly; so was the top corporate rate, from 31 percent to 40 percent. The peak excess profits tax was set at 90 percent (with a postwar rebate of 10 percent). As during the Civil War, interest on home mortgages was made deductible, as were state and local tax payments.

The revenue bill also created an entirely new tax, the brainchild of Senator George—a 5 percent "Victory Tax" imposed on top of the normal tax rate. Assessed on all incomes above $624—making it highly regressive and therefore objectionable to the administration—it was to be repaid by a partial tax credit after the war and was tantamount to a forced loan to the government. Its aim was to produce an additional $3.6 billion in revenues before the refund and a net $2.5 billion after the refund. Thirteen million Americans paid the Victory Tax who would not otherwise have paid any income tax.

At a cabinet meeting held after the bill's passage, Roosevelt joked that the highly complicated legislation "might as well have been written in a foreign language." He was reported to have signed the three-hundred-plus-page bill immediately upon receiving it because, he was informed, "a one-day delay would cost $60 million in lost revenues."

The 1942 Revenue Act represented a compromise between those who supported a sharply graduated tax system and those who wanted a more broadly based system. By combining a number of progressive features with a number of regressive ones, the bill "represented agreement between Congress and Roosevelt on what became the core of a new tax regime."

The New Deal Revolt

The spirit of compromise was not to last long.

Republicans gained seats in the House in the 1942 midterm election. Before the election, Democrats held a 267 to 162 majority; they emerged with a majority of only 218 to 208, although they retained a better than 2 to 1 advantage in the Senate. Many of the new Republican House members had campaigned on an anti-Roosevelt, anti–New Deal platform and once in office took tough stands against FDR's policies. On occasion they teamed up with conservative Democrats, who also resisted a number of the president's more liberal measures, especially those adversely affecting business. And many members from both sides of the aisle resented FDR's attempts to steamroll Congress on tax legislation.

The first major clash occurred over the Current Tax Payment Act of 1943. Before the war, taxpayers were required to pay their entire liability for a given year in March of the following year. But by 1943, the number of taxpayers had grown dramatically, and many first-time and low-income taxpayers were struggling to put aside the money to meet their future lump-sum tax obligations. The delayed payment system also meant revenue collections lagged actual incomes by many months, so that the broad-based tax, which was meant to curb inflation, was not cutting household purchasing power quickly. More aggressive tactics were needed.

To speed up tax payments and to reduce evasion, the administration and leading Democratic members of the Congress decided to resurrect a technique successfully applied during the Civil War—collection at source. They sought legislation mandating that businesses withhold 1943 tax payments from workers' paychecks and promptly forward the money to the Treasury. However, taxpayers complained that it was unfair for the government to withhold their taxes in 1943 while also requiring them pay their lump-sum 1942 liability in that same year. As a transitional device, a number of members favored a plan to forgive taxpayers' 1942 liabilities. The idea had been floated by Beardsley Ruml, the chairman of the board of the New York Federal Reserve and treasurer of R. H. Macy, the New York–based department store.

Roosevelt strenuously objected. He argued that the wealthy, who owed the bulk of the taxes, would benefit disproportionately from the write-off. Moreover, because many families with moderate income did not have to pay taxes in 1942, they would not benefit at all. The 1942 legislation that lowered the exemption rate had its main impact in 1943. Roosevelt understood the political implications. "I cannot," he declared, "acquiesce in eliminating a whole year's tax burden on the upper income groups during a war period when I must call for an increase in taxes and savings from the mass of our people." Doughton called it an "outrage."

For several months, Roosevelt was at loggerheads with congressional advocates of the Ruml Plan, but in June 1943 a compromise was reached. Like much bitterly negotiated legislation, it pleased neither side: the final act failed to provide as much tax forgiveness as Ruml and his supporters wanted, but was still too generous for Roosevelt's taste. Rather than a full write-off of 1942 tax bills, it forgave 75 percent of a taxpayer's 1942 or 1943 liabilities, whichever was lower; one-half of an individual's unforgiven tax bill was to be paid in March 1944 and the other half a year later. Withholding from current paychecks for 1943 tax liabilities would begin on July 1, 1943. Roosevelt signed the legislation, believing it to be the best he could get. Lower-income Americans, though, gave him credit for holding out for an act that they considered to be fairer than the Ruml Plan. The new withholding provisions substantially improved the efficiency of the tax system, speeding up collection and significantly increasing compliance. The nation's tax infrastructure was finally ready for the challenges of war and enormous wartime budgets.

The Great Clash of 1943

Each time Roosevelt and the Congress succeeded in pushing the budget rock a bit higher up the mountain, the increasing demands of the growing conflict required them to push it still further. While federal spending had risen from $13 billion in 1941 to $78 billion in 1943, the government's revenues had increased from $7.6 billion to only $22 billion. The administration calculated that expenditures would reach roughly $100 billion in 1944, with anticipated revenue collection, even after increasing taxes and the number of people paying them, of only $38 billion. Morgenthau estimated that an additional $12 billion in revenues was needed.

Roosevelt understood that obtaining public support for higher taxes would require a renewed emphasis on equity. Americans were making major sacrifices: rationing was limiting personal purchases and wages were stiffly controlled. FDR wanted to assure the middle class that wealthy individuals and businesses were paying their fair share. "I cannot," he declared, "ask the Congress to impose the necessarily heavy financial burdens on lower and middle incomes unless the taxes on higher and very large incomes are made fully effective. At a time when wages and salaries are stabilized, the receipt of very large incomes from any source constitutes a gross inequity undermining national unity. Fairness requires the closing of loopholes and the removal of inequities which still exist in our tax laws."

In the spring of 1943, Congress deliberated on the president's request, but failed to act. The White House urgently considered ways to speed up the torpid pace on Capitol Hill. In May, FDR instructed Morgenthau, "What we want is to get on the basis where we are paying for one-third of the war through taxes." While that target was similar to the one set by McAdoo during World War I, Morgenthau had more ambitious revenue goals. "Mr. President," he responded, "you are wrong on that. We're on that basis. We are trying to get to a 50 per cent basis." The president responded positively, "You can shoot at 50 percent. . . . Get all you can. . . . If I don't get more revenue before the end of this calendar year, I am going to put the blame on Congress." Morgenthau asked for the full $12 billion in new revenues that he thought were required.

Congress, however, was not quite as ambitious as the president or his Treasury secretary. It continued to hold up the legislation. With the need for additional revenues becoming more urgent, Morgenthau, after consulting with the president, lowered his request to $10.5 billion, with the difference to be made up in civilian spending cuts. Most of the new money would come from an increase in the personal income tax rate and in the Social Security tax, along with higher estate, gift, corporate, and excise taxes. The administration also wanted to repeal the Victory Tax, which had added millions of low- and moderate-income Americans to the tax rolls.

Congress, in the words of one observer, fell on the proposal "like Caesar's assassins." House Ways and Means chairman "Muley" Doughton flatly opposed the request. "The taxpayer," he warned, "is up against about all he can take." Focusing on the negative impact these proposals would have on private enterprise, he added that "if you strangle business and profits with taxes, you don't get any more taxes." Senator George declared that Congress was not willing to support an increase above $6 billion.

As substantial as the president's request was, the chairman of the Federal Reserve's board of governors, Marriner Eccles, considered it insufficient. He and others in the financial community argued that it did not eliminate the "inflation gap," a term made popular by Keynes. The administration, they feared, was not taxing away enough spending power to curb consumption. Eccles suggested a tax package of nearly $14 billion, with $4 billion of that to be returned after the war. Doughton dismissed it as

"amazing, fantastic, and visionary. I don't like it at all," he exclaimed, "if possible it is worse than the Treasury proposal."

The Ways and Means Committee opposed any additional taxes on business, reflecting Doughton's frequently expressed desire to "keep our corporations in sound financial condition so that they will be able to convert to peacetime production and provide employment to men leaving the armed services after the war." Members criticized the higher income tax on the grounds that it would threaten the "liquidation of the middle class." The ranking Republican on the committee, Harold Knutson of Minnesota, charged that the Treasury's proposal would have "wiped out the middle class and jeopardized the solvency of all business." The committee also believed that the administration had overestimated the need for new taxes and that much new revenue was already in the pipeline as the result of past legislation. Rather than raise taxes further, several committee members urged the administration to control inflation not through higher taxes but through reducing nonmilitary spending, imposing tougher price and wage controls, and tightening rationing.

Morgenthau then attempted to work with the Senate Finance Committee to forge an alternative that was closer to the administration's proposals. The effort went nowhere. Committee leaders, including Chairman George, held views similar to those of their House counterparts and would not bend to pressures to impose higher taxes on corporations and wealthy individuals.

Reflecting these congressional sentiments, the Revenue Act of 1943, finally passed in February 1944, fell more than $8 billion short of the president's final request. It was expected to generate just over $2 billion in additional tax revenue, about half from increased excise taxes. It raised the excess profits tax to 95 percent, but also increased the exemption level, relieving many companies of the requirement to pay. The Victory Tax was cut to 3 percent, but the promise of a postwar tax credit was eliminated. Congress, dominated by Roosevelt's own party, had defied the president, in the midst of the largest war in American history.

A furious FDR vetoed the legislation. He justified his decision on two grounds. First, it demonstrated fiscal irresponsibility because the expected revenues were only about a fifth of what the country needed. Second, it contained too many benefits to special business interests. The bill, he protested, was "wholly ineffective" in generating needed revenues and "replete with provisions which . . . afford indefensible special privileges to favored groups," singling out the lumber, mining, natural gas pipeline, and airplane industries as unworthy beneficiaries of special treatment given their booming wartime profits. This legislation, FDR protested, was "not a tax bill but a tax relief bill providing relief not for the needy but for the greedy." Taking another jab at Congress, tinged with a measure of sarcasm, Roosevelt addressed the difficulty the average American would have in understanding the changes in the tax code: "The forms were too complex. . . . Taxpayers, now engaged in an effort to win the greatest war this Nation has ever faced, are not in a mood to study higher mathematics." The president was especially concerned that the bill would create a widespread perception of unfairness in financing the war. The tough and derisory tone of his veto message was meant to underscore to working-class Americans his personal commitment to fairness, but it backfired in the House and Senate.

In a quick response, nineteen of the twenty-five members of the House Ways and Means Committee signed a letter declaring the administration's $10.5 billion objective "oppressive to taxpayers and dangerous to the national economy," as well as a threat to business. The Democratic majority leader in the Senate, Alben Barkley, who had been among the president's closest allies on the New Deal and a frequent champion of FDR's initiatives in Congress, had met with FDR twice to urge him to sign the bill; he called the veto message "a calculated and deliberate assault upon the legislative integrity of every member of Congress." He convened a caucus of Senate Democrats, tearfully resigned as majority leader in protest, and left the meeting. He was unanimously reelected. Congress overrode the president's veto by enormous margins in both chambers—299 to 98 in the House and 72 to 14 in the Senate.

As these battles raged, Roosevelt was meeting regularly with his key military advisers to plan the Normandy landings. He had less time to devote to financial issues and turned most of them over to Morgenthau. Tempers cooled and later that year Congress enacted the Individual Income Tax Act of 1944. It repealed the Victory Tax but lowered the income tax cutoff to $500, so that most of those who had paid the Victory Tax would remain on the rolls. This change simplified the tax system while further broadening the tax base. It also established the concept of the "standard deduction," which was set at $500.

A Shared Tax

Despite the rancorous debates and recriminations between the president and Congress, as well as within the administration itself, the tax code was completely reinvented by the relentless and pressing necessities of war. The war in Europe ended on May 7, 1945, with the unconditional surrender of Germany. After the United States dropped atomic bombs on Hiroshima and Nagasaki, President Truman received word of Japan's surrender on August 14.

By this time, the vast majority of Americans had made a major financial contribution to the effort. The number of taxpayers had risen to a level that could not have been imagined prior to the war—from below 4 million in 1939 to over 42 million in 1945, a staggering 60 percent of the workforce. (During World War I, only 13 percent of the labor force paid taxes.) Changes in the tax code produced a dramatic increase in revenues, which rose from 6.8 percent of GDP just before the United States entered the war to 20 percent by the war's end. According to W. Elliot Brownlee, tax collections "leaped from $2.2 billion to $35.1 billion." But despite the addition of some 38 million people to the tax rolls, "the richest 1 percent of the population produced 32 percent of the revenue yield of the personal income tax."

Taxes totaled $176 billion over the war years, supplying funds for nearly 45 percent of federal spending—short of Morgenthau's goal of 50 percent, but far above the level reached during World War I. Robust tax revenues enabled the federal deficit—which had increased from $5 billion (just over 4 percent of GDP) in 1941 to over $54 billion (30 percent of GDP) in 1943—to decline even before the war's end. It fell to $48 billion (23 percent of GDP) in 1944.

Paying taxes was portrayed as a patriotic duty. Irving Berlin wrote a song entitled "I Paid My Income Tax Today." Walt Disney produced an animated cartoon entitled "The New Spirit," starring Donald Duck. It conveyed the message that it is "your privilege, not just your duty" to pay your taxes. It was all part of the buoying "spirit of sacrifice," as one historical study called it, that "leads to a higher [tax] rate at the end than at the beginning of major wars." This was certainly the case in World War II.

From 1940 through 1943, corporate taxes exceeded individual income taxes as a source of federal revenue. In 1943, personal income taxes amounted to just under 30 percent of revenues, while corporate taxes reached over 43 percent. The latter figure reflected the high corporate tax rate, the ease of collecting taxes from businesses, and the booming wartime production. Later in the war, as more Americans entered the workforce, individual income tax rates escalated, and Congress reduced the exemption level, the ratio flipped; personal income tax receipts surpassed corporate tax revenues. During the last year of the war, personal tax payments amounted to nearly $20 billion; that figure accounted for 40 percent of all tax revenues. Corporate taxes amounted to roughly $16 billion, 33 percent of total tax revenues.

The shift in the balance between the personal income tax and the corporate tax was made possible by a more benign attitude in Congress, and among many Americans, toward business profits than existed during World War I. The term "redistribution of wealth," the mantra of many tax-reform advocates during World War I, was barely used during World War II. There were several reasons. During World War I, many Southerners, led by Claude Kitchin, were deeply suspicious that Northern financial and business interests had engineered American intervention to serve themselves. Driven by this suspicion, they sought to impose severe tax burdens on them to offset profits made during the war. In contrast, while some isolationists harbored similar feelings prior to Pearl Harbor, after that there was no ambiguity as to why the United States was at war and no logic for holding businesses responsible for American intervention. In addition, as Brownlee pointed out, "Fear of a return of the depression made the middle-class public more tolerant than it had been during World War I towards taxation that was favorable to corporations. This leniency may have seemed naive to radical New Dealers, but it expressed a widely shared commitment to the pursuit of enlightened self interest." Far more so than in World War I, Brownlee said, "Americans concluded that their nation's security was at stake and that victory required both personal sacrifice through taxation and indulgence of the corporate profits that helped fuel the war machine." Moreover, "because of the popularity of the war effort . . . it was less necessary to leverage popular support . . . for the war by enacting a highly redistributive tax system."

The wartime tax regime adopted a number of techniques used in the past, including excise taxes that went back to the time of Hamilton; a graduated payments schedule and withholding that had their origins in the Civil War; and business taxes similar to, although more modest than, those applied during World War I. But World War II's enormous revenue requirements demanded much more. The most dramatic change was the large portion of the American people who were added to the tax rolls. Before 1940, the income tax was paid largely by the financially well off and

considered a "class tax"; by the end of World War II, it was paid also by tens
of millions of Americans of modest means and had become a mass tax. So
even as Roosevelt and Morgenthau spoke repeatedly of the importance of
progressive New Deal principles as guidelines for tax policy, during their
tenure in office, and with their acquiescence, a large number of low-wage
Americans became subject to the income tax. The war also witnessed an
abandonment of tariffs as a significant source of government funds; duty
collections amounted to less than 2 percent of federal revenues—one-
twentieth of the amount generated by the personal income tax.

The dramatic broadening of the tax base and the incorporation of
withholding in the tax system reflected a considerably different approach
to checking inflation from the one used during World War I. Then, the
progressive philosophy had led to stiff taxes on upper-income citizens, but
these were largely paid out of surplus funds, so taxes forced very few
households to cut back measurably on consumption. During World War II,
many millions of working-class Americans were forced to curtail consumption to pay taxes. Moreover, withholding meant that they never actually saw the tax money they paid; it went straight to the government.

Early on, staunch New Deal advocates had resisted high taxes on the
working class. Many were fond of quoting Keynes's earlier work about the
virtues of deficits for stimulating growth and hoped to use the argument to
avoid raising taxes on low-income workers. Keynes cautioned that by failing to raise taxes on workers, American leaders were putting the country at
risk of higher inflation. To one passionate New Dealer who seemed too relaxed about deficits and inflation, Keynes whispered over dinner: "Well, I
have to tell you that you are more Keynesian than I am." As the war progressed and inflation concerns mounted, most of Roosevelt's team recognized the need for higher taxes on the working class.

The philosophy of the New Deal, predicated in part on the desire to protect low-income workers, had to be compromised; Roosevelt and Morgenthau both recognized that this was the price they had to pay to tame inflation.

"Lend Us Your Dollars"

As with tax policy, Morgenthau looked to the experience of World War I—
both the successes and the failures—to develop his plan for war borrowing.
He knew that even if he reached his goal of meeting 50 percent of wartime

expenditures through tax revenues, he would have to find ways to borrow an unprecedented amount of money; by the end of the war, the figure would amount to over $200 billion. He also realized that the money would have to come almost exclusively from Americans since so many of the nation's traditional creditors abroad were also embroiled in the war and had been called on to lend to their governments.

Mindful of strong and continuing populist pressures, Roosevelt feared a negative reaction if working-class Americans, including millions of returning veterans, were seen to be paying high taxes after the war so that wealthy investors could clip bond coupons. During World War I, the government aggressively promoted the sale of small-denomination securities to low-income Americans but it began late and lost an opportunity to give them a financial role in supporting the war immediately after U.S. intervention, losing valuable time in tamping down inflation. So during World War II, the administration quickly launched initiatives to enable low-income workers to participate in bond issues, thereby drawing off large amounts of their purchasing power early in 1942.

The formula chosen was to offer two categories of war bonds. One was for individual investors—reminiscent of those offered by Jay Cooke during the Civil War and by McAdoo during World War I—called Series E Bonds, the fifth, and by far the largest in dollar terms, in a series of bonds tailored to lower- and middle-income families that had been rolled out beginning with Series A Bonds in 1935. Morgenthau had introduced these small-denomination securities, nicknamed "Baby Bonds," to provide American families with a vehicle for boosting their savings. In a statement that reflected his awareness of the old Jeffersonian concerns about the excessive power of those who hold government debt, and echoing Lincoln's declaration eight decades earlier that Americans "cannot be much oppressed by a debt which they owe to themselves," the Treasury secretary noted that "every man and woman who owned a Government Bond . . . would serve as a bulwark against constant threats to Uncle Sam's pocketbook from pressure blocs and special interest groups." In short, said Morgenthau, "we wanted the ownership of America to be in the hands of the American people."

The smallest denomination Series E bond was twenty-five dollars. But employing the savings certificate model of World War I, the administration launched a program to enable all Americans to buy ten-cent Defense Stamps at a post office; children could purchase them at school. The Defense Stamps were pasted in small booklets that, when filled, could be converted into small-denomination bonds. Series E Bonds were also offered on the Payroll Savings Plan, which permitted workers to make deductions from their paychecks on a regular basis to purchase bonds. These programs removed significant amounts of potential spending power from the economy, helping to contain inflation. Traditional Treasury Bonds were issued in larger denominations and tailored to wealthy investors and financial institutions.

Throughout the war, Morgenthau's approach to the sale of bonds, based on voluntary subscriptions, was opposed by a formidable array of adversaries, including Vice President Henry Wallace; Leon Henderson, the administrator of the Office of Price Administration; Harold D. Smith, the director of the Budget Bureau; Labor Secretary Frances Perkins; and Marriner Eccles of the Fed. James Byrnes, the head of the Office of Economic Stabilization, was especially vocal. He had given up a seat on the Supreme Court to contribute to the war effort, and he insisted that he would not take orders from Morgenthau. Byrnes had decided that Keynes's forced savings program would do a better job of fulfilling the mandate of his office—stabilizing prices—than voluntary savings, and he went so far as to give a radio interview urging a "large compulsory lending program" at the time the administration was actively promoting voluntary bond sales.

Roosevelt was repeatedly lobbied by these officials to reject Morgenthau's plan in favor of a "forced savings tax" similar to, but much larger than, the Victory Tax. Advocates contended that this approach would do a better job of restraining inflation. Because the money received by these workers would be promptly rebated after the war and then be spent quickly, they argued that it would stimulate postwar consumption and avoid a sharp economic downturn. But Roosevelt preferred to let workers choose, publicly endorsing Morgenthau's voluntary savings plan as a noncoercive way to accomplish the same objective. However, he also made it clear that his support would last only as long as voluntary bond purchases produced adequate sums of money.

Both Roosevelt and Morgenthau viewed voluntary bond drives as part of a bigger campaign that went beyond fighting inflation and collecting billions of dollars. Like McAdoo, they believed patriotic marketing campaigns would rally public support, "make the country war minded," and wipe out any remaining vestiges of isolationist resistance. Fred Smith, an advertising executive who assisted Morgenthau in organizing the sales campaign, summed it up: Morgenthau's "most important advertising decision [was] to use bonds to sell the war, rather than vice versa."

The president put enormous pressure on his Treasury secretary to increase bond sales. Morgenthau responded with a bold set of measures, launching massive drives every few months. He stressed the importance of such drives in giving Americans a significant role in the war effort. "There are millions of people," he noted, "who say, 'What can I do to help?' . . . Right now, other than going in the Army or Navy, or working in a munitions plant, there isn't anything to do. . . . Sixty percent of the reason I want to do this thing is . . . to give the people an opportunity to do something."

The First War Loan, marketed at the end of 1942 in what was called the Victory Loan Drive, raised nearly $13 billion, surpassing its goal of $9 billion. Morgenthau called it "the biggest amount of money ever raised by any government in such a short time." As the war effort intensified, he relentlessly launched new drives and Americans faithfully funded them. The Second War Loan, in April 1943, raised over $18 billion, $5 billion above its announced objective. The Third War Loan, in the fall of 1943, raised $19 billion; the Fourth War Loan, in the spring of 1944, raised $16.7 billion; and the Fifth War Loan, in the summer of 1944, raised $20.6 billion. All exceeded their announced targets by several billion dollars. Three subsequent drives produced resounding results as well.

Part of the drives' successes came from the sophistication of the government's sales pitch. The Treasury commissioned a massive advertising campaign stressing the importance of patriotic sacrifice. Illustrated with GIs in combat, the posters read: "He didn't count the cost . . . should you?" and "What did you do today for your country?" and "They give their lives; you lend your dollars." As in World War I, America's top entertainers weighed in, using radio to support the war effort. Singer Kate Smith—who popularized the song "God Bless America"—raised the then enormous sum of $40 million on a single CBS radio broadcast.

In addressing the American people, the president specifically linked the success of bond sales directly to the success of American troops: "Every dime and dollar not vitally needed for absolute necessities," he insisted, "should go into War Bonds and Stamps to add to the striking power of our armed forces." In a radio address to launch the Third War Loan, he told his fellow citizens, "Every dollar that you invest in the Third War Loan is your personal message of defiance to our common enemies." By 1945, over 85 million Americans had bought war bonds. Small investors accounted for roughly a quarter of the funds raised from bond sales. Although the war saw record levels of taxation, it also saw record levels of borrowing. The federal debt in the hands of the public (as opposed to government agencies, such as the Social Security Trust Fund) was $45 billion in 1940, which was 50 percent of GDP. It reached nearly $280 billion in 1946—a staggering 110 percent of GDP, compared to about 40 percent at the end of World War I and 50 percent at the end of the Civil War.

Throughout the war, the Federal Reserve's chief policy objective was to maintain low interest rates and thus hold down the cost of borrowing for the Treasury. To do so, it agreed to a process known as "pegging," placing an interest rate ceiling of ⅜ percent on short-term Treasury bills and 2½ percent on long-term Treasury bonds, with intermediate interest rates set for medium-term securities. It accomplished this by standing ready to buy Treasury securities in the market at prices that would sustain these low rates. This was important to the bond sales campaign because it eliminated market volatility and thus reassured Americans that the price of these securities would not drop as ever increasing amounts of bonds were issued. The Fed ended up holding 10 percent of the debt issued by the Treasury during the war. In contrast, during World War I the Fed did not buy Treasury bonds directly; instead, it maintained a low discount rate (the rate at which it lends short-term money to banks) that encouraged banks to buy bonds or to lend money to their customers at low rates so that their customers could purchase bonds.

The Federal Reserve's efforts to restrain interest rates on war bonds enabled the Treasury to hold down the cost of servicing the government's prodigious debt. At the war's end, the average interest rate on the debt was just under 2 percent, compared to over 4 percent after World War I. However, debt service amounted to 3.5 percent of GDP after World War II, compared to only 2 percent after World War I, with the difference reflecting the disparity in the scale and duration of the two wars.

When wage and price controls were ultimately removed after the war, pent-up consumer demand was let loose and businesses began to draw down savings and utilize postwar excess profits tax credits to convert factories to civilian production. A surge in inflation followed. Measured by wholesale prices, inflation remained at a relatively tame annual rate of 4 percent during the war, but jumped to 15 percent annually from mid-1945 through mid-1948. Though this "inflation tax" on bonds decreased their value to holders, it also helped reduce the Treasury's debt in real terms because the government serviced and repaid the bonds in inflated dollars.

★

In President Roosevelt's words, World War II required "the shifting of the major part of American industry from the products of peace to the weapons of war." As war expenditures mounted, the government's nondefense spending was reduced by an average of 11 percent annually. Early in the war, the Treasury recommended cutting $1 billion in budget line items that "compete with war production and add unnecessarily to the value of purchasing power in the hands of the people . . . especially the immediate reduction of expenditures on highway construction, rivers and harbors, non-defense vocational training and federal subsidies aimed at boosting the price of agricultural products." To emphasize his commitment to curtailing nonessential spending throughout the economy, FDR vetoed a large highway construction bill and a very generous agricultural bill. For its part, the Democratic Congress repealed authorizations for several of Roosevelt's pet New Deal initiatives: the Works Progress Administration (WPA), the National Youth Administration (NYA), the National Resources Planning Board (NRPB), and the Farm Security Administration (FSA). All told, nondefense spending was reduced from 7.2 percent of GDP in 1940 to 3.0 percent by 1945, including sharp budget cuts for surviving New Deal agencies.

Roosevelt accepted the need for sizable reductions in social programs, but he also insisted that there were limits to how much their budgets could be slashed. "We are," he asserted, "fast approaching the subsistence level of government—the minimum for sustaining orderly social and economic processes." This is no time "for any of us to stop thinking about . . . social and economic problems," he insisted. Instead, "we should bring more citizens under the coverage of old-age pensions and employment insurance. We should widen the opportunities for adequate medical care." Domestic prosperity and social progress, FDR emphasized, made the armed forces "conscious of their individual stakes in the preservation of democratic life in America." This would give them "the stamina and courage which come from unshakable faith in the manner of life which they are defending."

Throughout the war, Roosevelt attempted to focus public attention on the connection between advancing social justice at home and maintaining the morale of the armed forces abroad. The social roots of America's political and military strength have been themes of other presidencies as well. For Roosevelt—as for Lyndon Johnson two decades later—they came together not just in rhetoric but also in the budget. Roosevelt repeatedly admonished Congress that there were limits to his support for cuts in nonwar spending.

The titanic tax confrontations between Roosevelt and members of his own party in Congress had little effect on the war effort; what mattered was that the money the armed services needed and the defense industry required to run full bore was always there. And as bitter as Roosevelt felt toward Congress, and it toward him, there is no evidence that the president ever accused legislators of a lack of patriotism in denying his revenue requests. While there were sharp debates over how much money should be raised through taxation, and how the tax system should be structured, patriotism was not under debate. There is also little evidence that the morale of the troops suffered from the clashes at home over wartime finance.

For the most part, the tax debates during the war helped Roosevelt demonstrate to Americans—or at least a sufficient majority of them—that he was committed to ensuring that the war was financed equitably and that the massive sums of money the administration requested were in fact essential to defeat the mortal threat to the nation from the Axis Powers. Even as he asked millions of Americans to make great economic sacrifices—living under severe rationing and wage controls, shelling out a large portion of their wages to meet tax obligations, in many cases paying income taxes for the first time in their lives—he retained their support.

The public's acceptance of these tough measures resulted in part from the country's wartime economic boom and massive job creation. It was commonly accepted and quietly celebrated that the war had pulled the country out of the Great Depression. Indeed, World War II deficits were seen by many as the ultimate demonstration of the validity of Keynes's theory that deficits are a robust tool for lifting countries out of depressions or recessions. In 1939, there were nearly 10 million Americans without jobs; by 1944, there were fewer than 700,000. It was also easier for Americans to sacrifice during the war because the administration was successful in keeping inflation relatively low. Those who had suffered from the higher rates of inflation during World War I were quick to recognize the difference.

FDR brought to its pinnacle the Hamiltonian vision of a strong and assertive central government, utilizing to the fullest extent its borrowing and taxing power during wartime and binding Americans together in a commitment to the success of the war effort through massive bond sales. At the same time, the president confronted a challenge similar to the one Madison posed for Hamilton: he had to wrestle and ultimately make major accommodations with influential members of Congress who resisted his financial initiatives. In the end, FDR—the great wartime leader and New York patrician—was forced to accept the fact that legislators from small farm towns in North Carolina, Mississippi, and Georgia held the ultimate power to determine the way in which the war was funded and to deny him a portion of the revenues he sought.

But Roosevelt was a Jeffersonian in the way he viewed the tax system. The New Deal approach to taxation placed enormous emphasis on fairness to lower-income Americans and avoidance of loopholes that gave powerful business and financial interests what FDR considered unfair benefits. And while such objectives often were compromised, out of wartime necessity and political pragmatism, and taxation on business was less stringent than during World War I, Roosevelt held firm against measures, such as the national sales tax, the Ruml Plan, and breaks for special interests, that offended his core political principles and those of his main constituencies. This strong stance solidified his wartime leadership as well as his political base—the New Deal constituency.

Despite this intense political and philosophical wrangling, the government mobilized enormous sums of money for the war in a remarkably short period of time. As the American war-production engine turned out colossal amounts of ships, planes, ammunition, weaponry, and matériel, and Americans paid tens of billions of dollars in taxes and lent the government even more, the country unified around the common purpose of winning the war. McAdoo's observation that patriotism manifests itself in a willingness to make economic sacrifices during a war, and that such sacrifices contribute to the cohesiveness of society during wartime, was fully realized during World War II.

6

"A Prolonged and Complex Struggle"

THE THREAT OF AMERICAN BANKRUPTCY IN THE COLD WAR

COMMUNIST GUNS . . . HAVE BEEN AIMING AT AN ECONOMIC
TARGET NO LESS THAN A MILITARY TARGET.

—DWIGHT D. EISENHOWER

The Soviet Union had just tested an atomic bomb and instigated a coup in Czechoslovakia. Berlin was becoming a postwar hot spot. Yet in late 1949, under the chairmanship of George Mahon, a conservative Democrat from Texas, the House Appropriations Subcommittee on Defense cut the Pentagon's 1950 budget request. The Senate Appropriations Committee did the same. At the time the Soviet threat—played out in a series of provocations—was very much on the minds of members of Congress. But these legislators nonetheless voted against a large increase in America's defense spending because they, like many officials in Washington, including President Truman, believed that Soviet strategy was not to engage in an all-out war but to bankrupt the United States.

Many members of Congress feared that if the country were to engage in a massive military buildup in preparation for a major global war, it would mean large-scale borrowing, destabilizing inflation, and the accumulation of enormous amounts of new debt. That, in turn, would play into Moscow's hand by weakening America's long-term economic strength and sapping its will and capacity to defend its political and security interests. Congressman

Mahon cautioned, "Nothing would please our potential enemy better than to have us bankrupt our country and destroy our economy by maintaining over the years complete readiness." In its report to the full Senate, the Finance Committee declared, in a similar vein, "A nation which exhausts itself in enervation over preparation . . . may well fall prey to a cunning and patient enemy who fully realizes the debilitating influences of a war-geared economy over a long period of time."

The Cold War was dramatically different in its budgetary requirements from any previous war in American history. Prior to it, the United States did not have a tradition of maintaining a large peacetime military force. There had been distinct periods of mobilization and demobilization. War was declared, fought, and then ended. During earlier wars, troop levels and weapons procurement increased; large military spending bills were enacted along with legislation to increase taxes and borrowing. When a war was over, military spending and force levels dropped sharply, as did taxes and borrowing.

The Cold War changed that. A chronic war characterized by the mass mobilization of troops and extensive overseas deployment, it necessitated a large peacetime defense budget. In the two decades prior to World War II, military spending had averaged around 1 percent of GDP; during the Cold War, it averaged around 7.5 percent. With the world seemingly teetering between nuclear war and an uneasy peace, defense appropriations remained high. For the first several years of the Cold War, military spending was more than double nonmilitary domestic spending.

During the "shooting war" portions of the Cold War, the Pentagon's budget increased sharply, but the country also maintained high and sustained defense spending during the "nonshooting war" periods. Yet there were also presidential and legislative checks on excesses. Annual defense outlays rose or fell depending on the perception of the Soviet threat, the risks posed to the economy, and the attitudes of individual administrations and Congresses about the adequacy of military spending at the time.

In the early years of the Cold War, the country enjoyed a sustained period of fiscal stability. Although defense spending rose considerably during the Korean War, from just under 5.0 percent of GDP in 1949 to over 14 percent in 1953, and remained high thereafter, Presidents Harry S. Truman and Dwight D. Eisenhower insisted on budget discipline. To them, a strong economy and sound national finances were vital to the country's security. Both believed that allowing deficits to spin out of control, and inflation to spiral, would damage the productive sectors of the nation's economy as well as weaken the willingness of Americans, many of whom were prepared to revert to isolationism, to support sustained defense spending and a global security role for the country. They aimed to keep annual budgets in surplus, or at least in only modest deficit. The national debt dropped from roughly 110 percent of GDP at the end of World War II to just below 60 percent in 1960, when Eisenhower left office. It was a particularly impressive accomplishment given the costs of Cold War armaments.

Recovering from War

In his first State of the Union address, in January 1946, President Truman warned Americans that they could not withdraw from the world, as they had after World War I. He cautioned Congress, "We will not measure up to [our] responsibilities by the simple return to 'normalcy.'" Later that year, in Fulton, Missouri, in one of the historic addresses of the twentieth century, former British prime minister Winston Churchill alerted the West that the Soviet Union was erecting an "iron curtain" across Europe. At the time, many Americans, who had only recently seen the United States and Soviet Union as allies in defeating the Nazis, regarded the speech as alarmist, but soon the danger would become apparent. Threats to Greece and Turkey, a Communist coup in Czechoslovakia, challenges to Western interests elsewhere in Europe, the Berlin crisis, the discovery that the Russians had tested an atom bomb, and the Communist Revolution in China were profoundly unsettling to Americans who wanted to return to their prewar lives.

With the end of World War II in August 1945, government spending declined sharply. By January 1947, President Truman could report that federal outlays had fallen by roughly 40 percent over the past year and that the size of the civilian federal workforce had been halved. And despite resistance from the top leaders in the military, the size of the armed forces was cut dramatically. Public pressure in favor of rapid demobilization was widespread and intense, forcing substantial cuts.

In 1946, concerned about Soviet activities and growing instability abroad, the Pentagon decided to slow the rate of return of overseas troops. Servicemen and -women in such places as the Philippines, Germany, and Britain immediately protested, forcing the Defense Department to resume a fast rate of repatriation.

In the postwar period, domestic programs that had been starved of funds from 1940 through 1945 received increased appropriations. Although the philosophy of Keynesian fiscal management had not yet achieved wide acceptance in the United States as a peacetime technique for stimulating growth and employment, the general concept of utilizing deficit spending to stimulate a weak economy did find its way into one important piece of legislation. The Employment Act of 1946 required the government to pursue low rates of unemployment and to engage in deficit spending if necessary. President Truman, nonetheless, saw fiscal prudence as sound policy and was reluctant to follow that course.

In yet another "big wave" election of the twentieth century, the once-secure Democratic hegemony in Congress collapsed. Republicans won control of both the House and Senate in the 1946 midterms, the first time since the Great Depression they held majorities in both chambers. The party's platform had featured a commitment to cut government spending across the board, reduce taxes by 20 percent, raise tariffs, and decrease the nation's debt. It also called for reductions in military spending. During the campaign, leading Republicans had accused Truman of practicing "big government" and the party's tax study committee denounced the administration for its "reckless spending of the public's money."

In early 1947, the president asked the just-seated Congress to authorize spending of nearly $38 billion for 1948, with just over $11 billion for the military. The Joint Committee on the Legislative Budget recommended that the overall request be cut by $6 billion. That would have required significant cuts in appropriations for the army and the navy, as well as for overseas relief programs. This action prompted Secretary of War Robert Patterson to comment that enactment of such legislation would mean "that we will travel down the same old road, disarming while the other major powers remain armed." Through the leadership of Senator Arthur Vandenberg, who as an isolationist had caused so many headaches for Roosevelt and Morgenthau but now supported the country playing a robust international role, the Senate trimmed the cut to $4.5 billion. During subsequent negotiations, Vandenberg worked with other internationalists to improve the number still further. The final bill was aimed at producing revenues of $34.7 billion, only $3.3 billion less than the president's request.

By mid-1947, the army was down to less than 1 million compared to over 8 million in 1945, the navy to below 500,000 from over 3 million, and the marines to below 100,000 from nearly 500,000. Military spending fell from $50 billion in 1946 to just $11 billion in 1948. Cuts in defense spending, from 37.5 percent of GDP in 1945 to 5.5 percent in 1947, helped to produce a budget surplus of nearly 2 percent of GDP, despite a significant downturn in the economy that slashed revenues. In 1948, the country recorded an even greater surplus of over 4 percent of GDP—a figure not equaled since.

The Truman Doctrine

Because conservative Republicans were committed to reducing the size of the government after the war, they also opposed Truman's requests for foreign aid to enable poorer countries to counter Communist pressures. They aimed to cut funds for these programs even as they were chastising the president for not doing enough to thwart the Kremlin's global objectives. In the run-up to the 1946 elections, a GOP White Paper had criticized Truman for neglecting "the true aims and methods of the rulers of Soviet Russia," and failing "urgently to build strong American armed forces." Much of the spending these Republicans wanted to cut was aimed at achieving precisely the foreign policy objective their party advocated—resisting Communism.

At the time, however, the extent of the danger posed by the Soviet Union was not clear, and large numbers of Americans believed that the enormous sums that the United States had devoted to European reconstruction in 1945 and 1946 had been wasted. Republicans seized on this sentiment to argue that taxes should be reduced rather than squandered in overseas assistance programs. Internationalist Republican Henry Cabot Lodge of Massachusetts, who had resigned from the Senate in 1944 to serve in the army—the first senator to do so since the Civil War—likened the approach of his conservative colleagues to "a man wielding a meat ax in a dark room [who] might cut off his own head." Columnist Joseph Alsop stated, "The world is about to blow up in our faces, and the damn fools in the Congress behave as though there was nothing worse to worry about than their richer constituents' difficulty in paying their taxes." The unyielding insistence among conservative Republicans on tax cuts, regardless of their security implications, was to plague Presidents Truman and Eisenhower throughout the early years of the Cold War.

In 1947, Truman established the National Security Council (NSC) to better coordinate foreign and national security policy. Statutory members included the president, the vice president, the secretary of state, and the secretary of defense. The chairman of the Joint Chiefs of Staff was designated the principal military adviser. Others with key roles in foreign and military policy were often invited to sit in, and senior economic officials took part in meetings from time to time. In testifying before Congress on the NSC's role, James Forrestal, who became secretary of defense shortly after the council was established, noted, "Both world wars showed . . . that modern total warfare requires more than an army and a navy. It requires the use of agencies of Government other than the military departments. . . . Military strength today is not merely military power but it is economic and industrial strength. I might also say it's financial strength." The creation of the NSC reflected a recognition on the part of Truman and his advisers that marshalling domestic economic resources, especially the manufacturing and financial sectors, was essential to maintaining American military superiority and strategic power. An important portion of the NSC's original mandate was to coordinate with agencies responsible for mobilizing the country's industrial capabilities and manpower in the event of another war.

That year, Truman also sought congressional support for $400 million to assist Greece and Turkey, then under threat of Communist subversion, after Britain had proved unable to continue its financial support. Truman was advised that to obtain funds for these countries, he would have to persuade Congress and the public that it was part of a broader strategic initiative aimed at combating the worldwide forces of authoritarianism. Truman presented the initiative before a joint session of Congress on March 12, declaring, "It must be the policy of the United States to support free peoples who are resisting attempted subjugation by armed minorities or by outside pressures, [and] that our help should be primarily through economic and financial aid which is essential to economic stability and orderly political processes." He observed that "the seeds of totalitarian regimes are nurtured by misery and want. They spread and grow in the evil soil of poverty and strife. . . . The free peoples of the world look to us for support in maintaining their freedoms." This policy came to be known as the "Truman Doctrine."

At first, Truman's initiative and his request for funds met with a cool response. Many of his fellow Democrats in Congress felt vulnerable to the charge that they had spent too much money. And congressional Republicans characterized Truman's plan as "an assumption of Britain's empire."

Moreover, as Walter Isaacson and Evan Thomas wrote in their book *The Wise Men*, "to an ordinary Congressman, determined to cut budgets, spending billions and billions to rebuild a war-ravaged foreign continent was political madness. Most of their constituents had barely recovered from sacrificing their sons to save Europe; foreign aid was widely viewed as 'Operation Rat Hole.'"

Funding for the Truman Doctrine, and other programs to follow, would likely have failed to get through Congress had it not been for Vandenberg's dedication. He endorsed Truman's aid package and utilized his powerful position as chairman of the Senate Foreign Relations Committee to rally bipartisan support for it. In Congress, Vandenberg built what Isaacson and Thomas called an "internationalist consensus that future presidents would look back on with wistful longing." As Secretary of State Dean Acheson, one of a group dubbed the "wise men," succinctly put it, on the pressing foreign policy issues of the late 1940s, "advice and consent of the Senate" meant "consult with Vandenberg." With Vandenberg's backing, the bill authorizing aid for Greece and Turkey passed in April 1947 by margins of more than two to one in both chambers. Despite their desires to cut the budget, congressional Republicans had been persuaded by Vandenberg that they could not "appear soft on Communism."

The ambitious Marshall Plan for reconstruction of Europe initially faced considerable opposition, as well. Speaking at Harvard in June 1947, with Europe in the grip of a major economic crisis, Secretary of State George C. Marshall announced that it was the administration's aim to combat "hunger, poverty, desperation, and chaos" on that continent and encourage "agreement among the countries of Europe as to the requirements of the situation." What ultimately became one of the most consequential initiatives in American history immediately met vocal criticism. Detractors protested that the plan would require creating a new bureaucracy and thus enlarge the size of the government; in doing so, it would also thwart efforts to cut taxes and balance the budget. Adding to the ammunition of opponents was the problem of inflation. It had risen at a 15 percent annual rate after the war and was a national preoccupation. Opponents played to these concerns, arguing that by financing large exports of food, raw materials, and equipment, the Marshall Plan would push up already high prices for such items in the United States. Vandenberg warned the administration, "We're headed for the storm cellar on the Marshall Plan." Republican detractors labeled it a "bold Socialist blueprint."

Then, in February 1948, the Soviet Union sponsored a coup to over-throw the pro-Western government in Czechoslovakia. Truman saw this as his cue to go on the offensive and laid out in the starkest and most urgent tones the immediate need to fund the Marshall Plan. Addressing a joint session of Congress on March 17, the president denounced Moscow's "ruthless action" and described how "the Soviet Union and its agents have destroyed the independence and democratic character of a whole series of nations in Eastern and central Europe." He went on to warn of Moscow's "clear design" to dominate "the remaining free nations of Europe." With the Kremlin's actions becoming more ominous and Europe's circumstances becoming increasingly precarious, Congress acted. The European Recovery Act—the bill incorporating the funds and authorities required to implement the Marshall Plan—moved quickly, with the isolationists joining the internationalists in responding to the Communist threat. To keep maximum control over the $13 billion provided to fund the Marshall Plan, Congress agreed only to annual appropriations, rather than the four-year package the president had requested. Truman's 1949 Point Four initiative to provide economic assistance to help poorer nations resist Communist-provoked instability, although held up by Republican opposition in Congress for eighteen months, also ultimately received bipartisan support.

The Cost of Containment

In 1950, as the early skirmishes of the Cold War continued, a team of top State and Defense Department officials convened to prepare a report to the president and the National Security Council on the new strategic threat. The document they produced—known as National Security Council paper number 68 (NSC-68)—spelled out a bold strategy for "containment" of the Soviet Union. NSC-68 described the world as divided into free and totalitarian nations, with the United States as the principal power center in the free world and the bulwark of opposition to Soviet expansion. It predicted that in the event of war, the Soviet Union could capture much of Western Europe as well as the oil fields of the Middle East. Even more alarmingly, it warned that the Kremlin was capable of launching a nuclear attack on America. It reported that the United States was spending 6.5 percent of its GDP on defense, with other allies devoting 5 percent, while the Soviet Union was spending 14 percent.

NSC-68 urged "a substantial and rapid [military buildup] to support a firm policy intended to check and roll back the Kremlin's drive for world domination," which would require significantly strengthening the country's conventional and nuclear capabilities. The report emphasized that the United States "must have substantially increased air, ground, and sea strength, atomic capabilities, and air and civilian defenses, to deter war and to provide reasonable assurance, in the event of war, that it could survive the initial blow and go on to eventual attainment of its objectives."

The report did not attempt to estimate the precise cost of implementing the recommended strategy, but State Department representatives in the drafting group estimated that it would cost between $30 billion and $40 billion a year. These officials cited the economic stimulus provided by military spending during World War II and argued that additional defense outlays would give the economy a big boost. They inserted language into the report stating, "The American economy, when it operates at a level approaching full efficiency, can provide enormous resources for purposes other than civilian consumption while simultaneously providing a higher standard of living." Among the Keynesians whose work they drew upon was Leon Keyserling, who soon became chairman of Truman's Council of Economic Advisers. As described by John Lewis Gaddis in *Strategies of Containment*, Keyserling advanced the notion that "the nation could sustain more vigorous growth rates if the government would stimulate the economy and tolerate short-term budget deficits until tax revenues from increased economy activity begin to roll in." He argued that "if the government could expand the pie there would be less need to make tough choices about how to allocate the pieces," an idea that bears a close resemblance to that advanced by later supply-side economists in support of tax cuts, although the emphasis immediately after World War II was on spending increases.

Keyserling, according to Gaddis, had the president's domestic spending program in mind when he advanced his argument, but he endorsed the same conclusion for defense outlays, asserting that it was important to combat the widespread impression that "increased defense must mean equivalently lower living standards, higher taxes and a proliferation of controls."

The Pentagon had a very different view. Defense Secretary Louis A. Johnson had promised the president to rid his department of what he described as its "costly war-borne spending habits." Specifically, he had pledged to keep defense spending below $13 billion in 1950. Johnson was following Truman's lead; the president was concerned that increased defense spending would produce big deficits and harm the economy. He also believed that tight Pentagon spending would be politically helpful at a time when public opinion was strongly antideficit. Pentagon staff also recognized that there was a pervasive belief among senior congressmen—given voice by Representative George Mahon—that the Soviet Union hoped to force the United States to overspend on defense in order to undermine its economy.

Top military brass shared these concerns. General Omar Bradley, the chairman of the Joint Chiefs, told the Senate Appropriations Committee in early 1950 that the Pentagon recognized that "the eventual strength of the economy depends upon its industrial capacity," which could be undermined by big deficits. Accordingly, he went on, should he come to the committee asking for $30 billion or $40 billion, "maybe you should get a new Chairman." Reflecting such frugality, Johnson's representatives in the group came up with estimates roughly half those of the State Department.

The gap between the State and Defense Department cost projections was only one reason that a specific dollar cost estimate was not included in NSC-68. The report's authors also believed that attaching a price to this strategy would divert public attention from their primary objective—to make the nation's leaders aware of the consequences if they did not mount a resolute response to the increasingly dangerous Soviet threat.

When NSC-68 was presented to him in April 1950, Truman immediately asked for a thorough study of the costs of the individual programs proposed. In his 1949 inaugural address, he had promised to balance the budget, reduce the nation's debt, and, in what he called the Fair Deal, address pressing social issues such as health care, housing, and civil rights. To fulfill these objectives, Truman needed to restrain defense spending. Members of his administration—particularly key officials in the Bureau of the Budget—believed that the authors of NSC-68 had exaggerated the Soviet threat. At the time, the bureau was operating on the principle of "domestic objectives first," or what came to be known as the "remainder method," for determining the size of the defense budget. The bureau worked back from an assessment of "what the economy could stand in taxes," and subtracted from that "essential domestic expenditures and foreign aid." The Defense Department received the "remainder." In 1950, the "remainder" came to $13 billion.

During the early months of 1950, the political climate in the United

States had turned ugly in reaction to a string of bad news relating to the Cold War: a bitter debate raged over who had "lost" China and the country was exposed to revelations about prominent Soviet spies in the government. Taking advantage of all of this, and fanning the flames, was Senator Joseph McCarthy, a Wisconsin Republican who gained notoriety through his anti-Communist investigatory excesses and who repeatedly accused the administration of being "soft on communism." Major publications—including the widely read *Life* magazine—harped on the military imbalance between the Soviet Union and the United States: noting that 2 million Soviets were under arms compared to only six hundred thousand Americans.

Despite the dire warnings in NSC-68 and harsh criticism from the press and members of Congress, the administration still sought to hold military spending in check. Secretary Johnson pressed his subordinates to meet his $13 billion target for 1950, although the final figure was closer to $14 billion.

From Cold to Hot

On June 25, 1950, North Korea invaded South Korea. The terms of the debate changed dramatically. After World War II, the Korean Peninsula, which had been occupied by Japan since 1910, was divided along the thirty-eighth parallel under an agreement between the Soviet Union and the United States. Skirmishes between North Korean and South Korean troops had repeatedly taken place along the line. The June attack, supported by the Kremlin, forced South Korean forces into a full retreat. The North Korean army captured Seoul in just over a week. There were no American combat forces on the peninsula, but there were in Japan. Without asking Congress for a declaration of war, Truman dispatched them, followed by large numbers of troops from the United States, to South Korea to stem the invasion. American soldiers engaged in their first battle with North Korean forces on July 5. The United States also secured a UN resolution urging members to support South Korea, and significant numbers of British, Australian, and other national forces soon arrived.

Following the invasion, the administration was forced to reorder its priorities. Any illusions that the country could continue its policy of relying on a small peacetime military establishment were shattered. Truman soon accepted the recommendations contained in NSC-68 and sought sharply higher defense appropriations. When Chinese troops crossed the Yalu River into North Korea and entered the war in October 1950, official Washington felt an even greater sense of urgency. Many feared it might be the beginning of World War III. Defense appropriations shot up to almost $48 billion in 1951 and $60 billion in 1952.

In his first State of the Union message after the outbreak of hostilities, Truman spelled out the challenge: "The threat of world conquest by Soviet Russia endangers our liberty and endangers the kind of world in which the free spirit of man can survive." He stressed the need to make tough choices. "In the months ahead," he insisted, "the government must give priority to activities that are urgent—like military procurement and atomic energy and power development. It must practice rigid economy in its non-defense activities. Many of the things we would normally do must be curtailed or postponed." His message was hardly popular in a country just emerging from a period of austerity and sacrifice.

From an economic and financial perspective, the Korean conflict bore little resemblance to World War II. During World War II, military outlays at their peak reached over 37 percent of GDP, while their high-water mark during the Korean War was just below 15 percent. The number of Americans who served during the war was only a third the number who served during World War II, but the conflict was serious enough to require quick and substantial mobilization: in mid-1950, the army had a force strength of under 600,000, which rose to over 1.5 million by mid-1951; the navy went from 380,000 to 825,000, the marines from 74,000 to 231,000. The economy was also in better condition than before World War II. After experiencing a steep recession immediately after that war, the country had entered a period of modest growth. Unemployment was just over 5 percent in the year prior to the Korean War, far lower than just before World War II. Under these circumstances, officials concluded that engaging in large-scale deficit spending to finance the Korean War would have been inappropriate and harmful to the economy. And Truman was a fiscal conservative, who did not like deficits if they could be avoided.

Korea was also different from previous American conflicts because it was not an all-out war and had not been sanctioned by Congress. The president called it a "police action." For the military, the notion of fighting a limited war came as a surprise. Army historian Robert W. Coakley notes that "existing mobilization plans at the beginning of the Korean War . . . were all framed in terms of an all-out war. The Department of Defense had no plans for limited war. Thus the entire mobilization process was one of improvisation."

Though many American officials privately harbored concerns that the conflict might trigger a series of military engagements with the Soviet Union or its allies in other parts of the world, the administration was careful not to portray the North Korean or Chinese attacks as harbingers of World War III. Truman tried to balance his awareness that the war would cost a lot of money with a desire to resist the pressures for a massive military buildup.

Acheson insisted that the administration "must ask for money and if it is a question of asking for too little or too much . . . [we] should ask for too much." Truman readily accepted this advice, recognizing the need to make a strong statement in his first budget request after the conflict had begun, demonstrating that he was prepared to mobilize whatever resources were needed to prevail. A more tentative approach, he believed, would leave him vulnerable at home to the charge that he was underfunding the military. It would also convey a signal of weakness to Moscow, thus inviting a test of America's resolve elsewhere. A few days later, the president requested a $10.5 billion "emergency supplemental" appropriation—a request made outside the normal budgeting process and not contained in the administration's original proposed budget—for additional munitions and supplies and to meet the enormous costs of troop deployment across the Pacific. This was followed in early August by two more supplemental requests totaling $5.6 billion. Appropriations for the military that year amounted to $48 billion, more than 350 percent above the prewar request of $13.5 billion. But Truman refused to support more Pentagon spending on grounds that it would produce huge budget deficits. As Keyserling sized up the numbers, the president's program fell "about halfway between 'business as usual' and a really large-scale dedication of our economic resources."

The outbreak of war triggered a significant surge in speculative buying as businesses and individuals feared a return to wartime shortages. Wholesale prices rose by 16 percent from June 1950 through February 1951. The administration responded by imposing wage and price controls, but did not implement a new regime of rationing. At the outset, the Federal Reserve agreed to maintain its policy of stabilizing interest rates by pegging long-term Treasury securities, which it had continued after World War II. But as the Korean War progressed and the economy became overheated, senior Fed officials became concerned that continuing to peg would produce too great an increase in the money supply, which would accelerate inflationary pressures. They pressed the administration to be relieved of their commitment.

Truman resisted. He wanted the Fed to continue to stabilize interest rates on Treasury securities and thus the value of those securities. He feared, but did not say so publicly, that the country might become involved in a wider war against Communist powers, making massive additional financing necessary. And like Secretary McAdoo thirty years earlier, he worried that deterioration in the bond market could undermine the confidence of Americans and their allies. To underscore his determination that the Fed continue its practice of pegging, Truman took the unprecedented step of summoning the Federal Reserve's Open Market Committee to the White House on January 31, 1951. The Fed had been established as an independent body removed from the pressures and demands of the political system. No president had ever taken such an action. In the meeting, as reported by Allan H. Meltzer in *The History of the Federal Reserve*, Truman "recalled his experience in the 1920s when the value of government bonds fell to 80 before rising to a premium." But, according to Meltzer, neither the Fed chairman, Thomas Mc-Cabe, the former chairman of the Scott Paper Company and later the official in charge of disposing of excess war materials, nor the president touched directly on the dispute with the Treasury over pegging. Truman simply insisted, "We must combat Communist influence on many fronts. . . . If the people lose confidence in government securities, all we hope to gain from our military mobilization . . . might be jeopardized."

Following the meeting, the White House press office announced that the Fed's board of governors had agreed to continue pegging for "as long as the emergency lasts." In a sharp rebuke to the administration, the fiercely independent-minded Marriner Eccles, who had been Fed chairman under Roosevelt (he had not been reappointed to the job by Truman but remained on the Fed board), informed reporters from the *New York Times* and the *Washington Post* that he and his colleagues on the Open Market Committee had made no such commitment. In the weeks that followed, Fed officials and members of the executive branch engaged in an acrimonious and politically unsettling public debate. The White House and Treasury insisted on the need for the Fed to continue to stabilize the price of government bonds, while the Fed insisted that it needed to assert its independence in order to curb inflation. Senator Joseph O'Mahoney, a Democrat from Wyoming, appealed to McCabe's patriotism, writing to him to resolve the impasse since "the Soviet dictators are convinced that the capitalistic world will wreck itself by economic collapse arising from the inability or unwillingness of different segments of the population to unite upon economic policy."

In March 1951, an accord was reached between the Federal Reserve and the Treasury. The Fed would continue to maintain its current discount rate for the remainder of the year and temporarily support the price of five-year government notes; the Treasury would use the cushion of time to exchange marketable bonds for nonmarketable ones. After that, the Fed would shift its policy focus from artificially stabilizing interest rates to fighting inflation. Interest rates on government securities rose just after the accord was implemented, but efforts to hold down government deficits and the market's comfort with the long-standing 2.5 percent interest rate on long-term Treasury securities enabled bond yields to remain remarkably steady. A combination of government controls, budgetary restraint, and moderately tighter monetary conditions caused a drop in inflationary pressures from mid-1951 through 1952.

To Tax or Not to Tax

After World War II, a bipartisan consensus had quickly emerged that the government no longer needed the high level of revenues it had required to sustain the war effort. As after World War I, Congress repealed the excess profits tax as well as a number of excise taxes and lowered the levy on personal income.

Republicans, who had won control of Congress in 1946 on a platform promising tax cuts, proceeded with fervor to deliver on their promises, in part to stimulate the economy, in part to reward their wealthy supporters, and in part to deprive Truman of the funds to carry out his ambitious Fair Deal social reforms. Robert Lee Doughton's Republican successor as chairman of the Ways and Means Committee, Harold Knutson of Minnesota, explained their perspective: "For years we Republicans have been warning that short-haired women and long-haired men of alien minds in the administrative branch of government were trying to wreck the American way of life and install a hybrid oligarchy at Washington through confiscatory taxation." Now, Knutson believed, it was the Republicans' chance to end the "oligarchy" and proposed legislation to do so.

However, the Republican bill ran into stiff resistance from the White

House. Truman vetoed it on grounds that the tax cuts would increase the deficit, add to inflationary pressures, and provide disproportionate benefits to the wealthy. "The time for tax reduction," the president asserted, "will come when inflationary pressures have ceased." The motion to override narrowly failed in the House.

New tax legislation, drafted in early 1948, found broader support, including among Democrats. It provided greater benefits to lower-income Americans than did Knutson's 1947 proposal, reducing individual taxes, increasing the personal exemption from $500 to $600, permitting married couples to split their income for tax purposes, and providing benefits for individuals over sixty-five years of age. Truman vetoed that bill, too, but was overridden—the second time in U.S. history this had occurred on a revenue bill

Truman's surprise victory over New York's governor, Thomas Dewey, in the 1948 election was accompanied by a return of Democratic majorities to the House and Senate. Yet this did not guarantee smooth sailing for the president with Capitol Hill on tax issues. No major tax legislation was passed in 1949, and in 1950 the president was concerned about insufficient revenues. In his January 1950 State of the Union address, he asked for higher taxes, reporting that "more than 70 percent of the government's expenditures are required to meet the costs of past wars and to work for peace." At the same time, he noted, the government had to "make substantial expenditures which are necessary to the growth and expansion of the domestic economy." He lamented that "largely because of the ill-considered tax reduction of the 80th Congress [the Republican Congress that had overridden his veto] the Government is not receiving enough revenue to meet its necessary expenditures." To address the shortfall, he announced that the administration intended to hold down spending and submit legislation that would "yield a moderate amount of additional revenue." During the summer of 1950, Truman pressed Congress to raise the income tax, but it was an election year and there was little support. On the contrary, leading legislators were hoping to lower excise taxes and enlarge tax breaks to enhance their chances of victory.

Congress was in the midst of considering tax legislation when the Korean War broke out. The House had just passed legislation reducing a wide range of excise taxes; to make up the lost revenues, it increased other taxes, particularly the levy on corporate profits, and closed some loopholes. It had sent these measures to the Senate; the Finance Committee was debating them when North Korean troops poured into the South. Shortly afterward, Truman sent a letter to Chairman George asking him to revise the bill. He suggested that the "revenue-raising provisions of the pending bill be retained and supplemented by increases in the corporate and individual income tax rates." He further requested that the committee "eliminate the excise tax reductions made by the House but retain the loophole-closing, dividend-withholding" provisions. He further encouraged the chairman to "make every effort to finance the greatest possible amount of needed expenditures by taxation . . . and design taxation methods which prevent profiteering and distribute the tax burden fairly among the different groups of our people."

The Finance Committee and then the full Senate promptly increased the personal and corporate income tax as requested and the House concurred. The Revenue Act of 1950, signed in October, contained these changes, but Congress deferred Truman's request for a restoration of the excess profits tax until after the midterm elections. In those elections, the Democrats held on to both chambers. They enjoyed a thirty-five-seat majority in the House, but scrounged out a majority of only one seat in the Senate. Upon their return to Washington, with only a minor objection from the Republicans, Congress passed the Excess Profits Tax Act and the president signed it into law in January 1951. Intent on maintaining a balanced budget even if military costs doubled, Truman also pushed Congress for deep spending cuts in nonessential civilian programs. In 1950, civilian spending was nearly 9 percent of GDP; by 1952, Truman's last full year in office, it had been cut to 5 percent.

Despite the rapid run-up in military appropriations and troop mobilization, both lagged behind the public mood. In August 1950, a Gallup poll found that a resounding 70 percent of respondents would endorse even higher taxes to fund an even larger increase in the military: "Rarely has the Institute in its fifteen years of measuring public opinion found such heavy majorities to pay more taxes for any public purpose."

The following January, the president addressed the double challenge of restraining inflation and paying for the military buildup. Mobilization was proceeding rapidly. Immediately before the war, modest numbers of Americans were under arms; with the outbreak of the Korean War and Communist challenges elsewhere in the world, force strength shot up. To support these increases, the president asked Congress for an additional $10 billion in taxes—$4 billion from higher income taxes, $3 billion from additional corporate taxes, and the remaining $3 billion from new excise taxes. The debate that followed mirrored the one that had taken place early in World War II; labor groups lobbied for higher taxes on corporations, and business interests wanted a sales tax as an alternative to the corporate tax. Doughton, back in the chairmanship of the Ways and Means Committee since 1949, sarcastically commented that while all representatives of key interest groups said that "those they represented or spoke for wanted to do their full part in producing the revenue necessary to finance emergency expenditures, they usually . . . claimed that any additional revenue should come from some other source."

In a message to Congress on February 2, 1951, Truman applied more pressure, stating, "During World War II, taxes were not high enough, and the Government was forced to borrow too much. As the result, when controls were taken off after the war, prices skyrocketed . . . we must not let that happen again." In an effort to avoid greater borrowing and higher inflation, he recommended adopting a pay-as-we-go program reminiscent of the position taken by progressives during World War I.

The House Ways and Means Committee resisted. It cut the administration's requested tax increase to $7.2 billion. According to Doughton, this was "as large an amount as can be safely collected from the economy under present conditions." House Minority Leader Joseph Martin of Massachusetts quipped that the argument that a tax increase would curb inflation was "economic voodoo talk" (a phrase George H. W. Bush would later apply to then governor Ronald Reagan's support for big tax cuts in the 1980 presidential campaign). Other Republicans railed that the funds would only go to support the "socialist planners within the Truman Administration." The Revenue Act of 1951 pushed the top income tax rate up to 91 percent and the top corporate tax rate to an all-time high of 70 percent. Revenues escalated from just over 14 percent of GDP in 1950 to 19 percent in 1952.

Resistance to increased taxes and to significantly higher defense spending came primarily from the isolationist, conservative wing of the Republican Party. Its leaders argued, in Jeffersonian terms, that those measures would excessively augment the role of the government. The administration's emphasis on the "limited nature" of the conflict, and the absence of a formal congressional declaration of war or presidential statement that the country faced an urgent threat—so familiar to Americans during World War II—were seized on by fiscal conservatives as a reason to provide the administration with only limited financial support.

From the opposite side came criticism that the administration was providing too little funding for the armed forces. Moderate Democrats, as well as internationalist Republicans, including prominent House members Richard M. Nixon of California and Gerald R. Ford of Michigan, insisted on a more resolute war effort, backed by considerably greater funding. Together with thirteen like-minded colleagues, they wrote a public letter declaring that the situation in Korea "has exposed the fact that a tragic diplomatic and military inadequacy exists," and called for "complete mobilization." Their frustration with what they regarded as a lack of adequate military preparedness was echoed by General Omar Bradley, who lamented that although there were sufficient funds to fight in Korea, the military was not prepared to address the broader challenge from the Soviet Union. "It is a bruising and shocking fact," Bradley wrote later, "that when we Americans were committed in Korea we were left without an adequate margin of military strength with which to face an enemy at any other specific point. Certainly we were left without the strength to meet a general attack . . . except for the atomic bomb."

Despite significant increases in taxes and defense appropriations, a public opinion survey early in the war indicated that 83 percent of Americans polled favored continuing the high levels of spending on rearmament and 52 percent favored continued economic assistance to allies. One of the major charges by internationalist critics of the administration was not that its spending on the war was excessive, but that the money and the war effort in general were failing to produce satisfactory results. Sizable numbers of Americans were critical of Truman's unwillingness to make an all-out effort to retake the entire Korean Peninsula. Powerful voices in both parties—including future presidents Johnson, Nixon, and Ford—called for the commitment of a greater number of troops to bring the fighting to a quick and decisive end.

Truman had originally supported a strategy of driving all the way to the Yalu River to completely defeat the North Korean forces, but after China's intervention he settled on pushing Communist troops out of South Korea. For more hawkish Americans, this was far too modest an objective; they championed forcing a total surrender, and some saw the war as an opportunity to take on China and the Soviet Union, believing it was better to act against them decisively in 1951 than wait until they were stronger. This attitude, historian Walter Russell Mead noted, was in the Jacksonian tradition, which holds that "either the stakes are important enough to fight for, in which case you should fight with everything you have, or they aren't important enough to fight for, in which case you should mind your own business and stay home."

American and allied forces under the command of General Matthew Ridgway halted the Chinese advance and recaptured Seoul in March 1951. In the summer, after North Korean and Chinese troops were driven north of the thirty-eighth parallel, the war appeared to reach a stalemate. Large numbers of Americans became frustrated with the lack of progress. George Marshall, now secretary of defense after leaving the State Department in 1949, commented that early in the war there was "a general feeling of the majority of people with whom we came into contact, publicly and on the Hill, that we were not seeing the problem in its enormity and danger, and therefore not asking for enough." But after the Chinese advance was rebuffed, public opinion turned and congressional support for appropriations and the war dropped substantially. Early in 1951, reflecting on the reversal, Marshall said he had thought "there'd be a change in public opinion and we'd have a hard time with appropriations though possibly we might even get it in September, but I never dreamed that we'd get it in February." Fortunately for the war effort, the main appropriations requested for the Defense Department had already been passed and many of the arms and supplies required could be supplied from World War II surplus still stored in the Pacific Islands.

During 1952, the war had turned into an expensive and bloody standoff. Two-thirds of the American people disapproved of the administration's policies and so did most of the Congress. Peace talks had been under way since July 1951 but had achieved little. Even supporters of the war were frustrated at the extensive loss of life and a strategy that would not produce a clear victory or, at a minimum, a dignified exit strategy. In the early months of the year, Lyndon B. Johnson, a first-term Democratic senator and former House member from Texas who chaired the Senate Defense Preparedness Subcommittee, charged that the military did not have adequate weaponry and the administration was not sufficiently hardnosed in the face of the Soviet threat. He and his committee colleagues pressed the White House and others in Congress to allocate vastly greater sums to the military in anticipation of a global confrontation with the Soviet Union. In his book *Master of the Senate*, Robert Caro described the subcommittee's work as "a demand for greatly expanded mobilization, a placing of the nation on an all-out war footing almost as if it were engaged in a global conflict."

In May 1952, the widely respected *Washington Post* reporter Alfred "Al" Friendly investigated Johnson's charges that the administration was spending too little on the military. He concluded, "The Truman Administration had decided against full immediate mobilization . . . not because of any lack of toughness or of concern about the Russian threat but partly because such a mobilization cannot be maintained over a long period in the absence of war itself." Citing Friendly's report, a *Post* editorial concluded that the amount of resources being devoted to the military was correct "if rearmament is directed at the long pull." The point was similar to that made by Mahon and the Senate Finance Committee: overreacting to the Soviet threat with excessive military spending and borrowing would lead to high inflation and big deficits, damage the economy, and, in time, undermine the nation's ability to resist the spread of Soviet influence.

An Economic Target

The election of 1952 swept Dwight D. Eisenhower into office and produced Republican majorities—albeit very narrow ones—in both the House and Senate for only the second time since 1933. Fresh off their victory, congressional Republicans pressed the new president to cut taxes as soon as possible. But before he took office, Eisenhower, meeting with his top officials on the cruiser *Helena* off of Wake Island, was given the bad news by his budget director–designate Joseph Dodge that Truman's proposed 1954 budget of about $80 billion could not be cut significantly without jeopardizing national security. Moreover, Dodge reported, numerous, long-term commitments made by the Truman administration would require military spending to remain at high levels in future years. "We all expected that the budget we inherited for fiscal year 1954 would once again be out of balance," Eisenhower later wrote. "What we did not previously know was that our predecessors had piled on top of this mountainous debt additional C.O.D. purchases—largely in defense contracts." That, he noted, limited his administration's ability to reduce taxes without causing the federal government "to mire itself deeper in debt."

As irked as Eisenhower was at the Truman administration, he was equally irritated that "we had Republican promises to contend with—the promises of some lawmakers to balance the budget immediately and cut taxes, no matter what the result." Early in his administration, Eisenhower cautioned Congress that tax reductions would have to wait; they would be "justified only as we show we can succeed in bringing the budget under control. . . . Unless we can determine the extent to which expenditures can be reduced, it would not be wise to reduce our revenues."

In April 1953, three months after his inauguration, Eisenhower and his Treasury secretary, George M. Humphrey, met with the congressional leadership of the Republican Party in the White House. It turned out, in the president's words, to be "one of the worst days . . . [he had] experienced" since taking office. The president had known in advance that this would not be a pleasant meeting because he and Humphrey planned to inform the group that, contrary to their wishes and to Republican campaign promises, there would be no balanced budget and no tax cut in the coming fiscal year because of the continuing costs of fighting in Korea and other significant defense requirements.

Eisenhower wrote in his diary on the following day that upon receiving the bad news, Senate Majority Leader Robert Taft of Ohio, a staunch fiscal conservative who had contested Eisenhower for the Republican nomination and had been a bitter critic of Truman's deficits, "broke out in violent objection." He used, according to Eisenhower, "adjectives . . . that were anything but complimentary" and accused the administration of "merely adopting a Truman strategy . . . [and] said he would have to go on record as fighting and opposing it." Eisenhower, who admitted that his "temper was getting a little out of hand at the demagogic proceeding," expressed astonishment that in Taft's "tirade . . . not once did he mention the security of the United States."

The exchange was a foretaste of the highly emotional budget confrontations Eisenhower was to face over the next eight years. Ultraconservative Republicans, including Taft, relentlessly insisted on slashing taxes and spending, which would have meant big cuts in the defense budget. On the other end of the spectrum, a group of internationalist Democrats, led by Lyndon Johnson, alternately supported the president in his efforts to override the archisolationists in his party and badgered him for not putting more money into the military. Then there were the officials in the Pentagon and their allies in the business community, who sought government funding for their favorite defense programs, often by going around the executive branch directly to Congress.

Eisenhower had to walk a fine line between holding firm in his insistence that Congress appropriate sums sufficient to meet the nation's security needs and resisting unwarranted increases that would widen the budget deficit and undermine the economy, weakening the country's long-term defense. He warned those who advocated what he considered wasteful spending, "There is no defense for any country that busts its own economy" and that the country could be bankrupted by excessive military spending. In an address to the nation on the nature of the Soviet threat, he observed that the Kremlin's leaders "have plainly said that free people cannot preserve their way of life and at the same time provide enormous military establishments. Communist guns, in this sense, have been aiming at an economic target no less than a military target." Invoking one of the frequently repeated themes of his presidency, he warned Congress that "to amass military power without regard to our economic capacity would be to defend ourselves against one kind of disaster by inviting another." His secretary of state, John Foster Dulles, was more blunt: "If economic stability goes down the drain, everything goes down the drain."

While a Jeffersonian in his concerns that excessively close ties between business and government would harm the average citizen, Eisenhower was a Hamiltonian in his insistence that strong finances and a robust economy were vital to the nation's security. In a conversation with advisers early in his administration, he stressed, "The relationship between military and economic strength is intimate and indivisible," reminding them that the country could "spend itself into bankruptcy." Eisenhower's premise was that the maintenance of sound government's finances was basic to a sound economy, which in turn was vital to national security. He insisted that members of his national security and economic teams work together to "plan not for some short-run crisis period, when Soviet power might exceed that of the United States in some categories, but rather for the 'long haul,' balancing essential military power with a healthy economy." This balance came to be known as the "Great Equation."

In May 1953, the administration sent a budget to Congress that aimed to reduce the $10 billion deficit in Truman's 1954 budget request by roughly $4 billion, but kept defense spending at about 13 percent of GDP. Republican conservatives wanted stiffer spending cuts, including reductions in the defense budget; their objective was to eliminate government borrowing entirely. Eisenhower objected. In his opinion, the defense budget had to remain large, despite the big deficit. "Regardless of the consequences," the president said, "the nation's military security will take first priority in my calculations." He emphasized that he "could never approve a plan to slash defense spending just to contrast Republican economy with Democratic fiscal irresponsibility."

The Partisan Threat

In the early 1950s, Senator Johnson convinced a number of his colleagues to support Eisenhower's defense requests. He pointed out that the main threat to the country did not come from within the White House but from the "Conservative Clique" in Congress that sought to block foreign assistance and sharply reduce America's military presence in Western Europe. In February 1953, shortly after LBJ was elected Senate minority leader, he warmly applauded Eisenhower's call in his first State of the Union address for a "spirit of true bipartisanship" and urged the Democratic caucus to heed it. Johnson went on to insist that "the issues of war and peace are far too serious to be settled in the arena of narrow, partisan politics." The House minority leader and former Speaker Sam Rayburn, at the time the most powerful Democrat in Washington and an admirer of Eisenhower, informed his party colleagues that he did not see their role as opposing simply for the sake of opposing. "Any old jackass can kick a barn down," he quipped, "but it takes a good carpenter to build one." This implicit pact drawn between a coalition of Democratic internationalists and moderate Republicans in Congress and the White House resulted in the passage of substantial defense budgets and foreign assistance programs during the first few years of the Eisenhower administration.

Early in 1953, Dan Reed, the chairman of the House Ways and Means Committee, proposed eliminating several of the tax increases enacted by the Democratic Congress in 1951. He also wanted to allow the Korean War excess profits tax to expire in mid-1953. Reed, a feisty Republican from upstate New York who had once been a football coach at Cornell University, had entered the House during World War I, alongside Claude Kitchin. He liked to boast that he had "voted against more New Deal measures than any other member of Congress." In pressing to rescind the 1951 Democratic tax hikes, Reed argued, as Mellon had in the 1920s, that large tax reductions would stimulate business activity, which, in turn, would produce higher revenues sufficient to make up for those lost from the lower tax rates. His frequent nostalgic reminiscences about the policies of Andrew Mellon earned him the nickname "Neanderthal Man." Eisenhower was, as he later wrote, "emphatic in my opposition" to Reed's legislation. He insisted that the six-month extension of the excess profits tax and the corporate income tax be maintained to pay for the Korean War.

A rancorous struggle ensued. Reed was fixated on stifling Eisenhower's wishes. Following Kitchin's example, he used the power of his chairmanship to persuade the committee to draft legislation blocking the extension and asserted that he would get his bill passed "no matter what Eisenhower or Humphrey, or anyone else had to say about it." But the now incensed Eisenhower and Speaker Joe Martin pushed back. Over Reed's vehement objection, Congress extended the two taxes and incorporated the administration's other revenue proposals. Eisenhower signed the legislation into law in July. He later wrote that he "could not agree that the country should have, or wanted, a tax cut ahead of a balanced budget or a balanced budget ahead of national security."

Permanent Insecurity

Because the Cold War military challenge differed dramatically from the kinds of acute, short-term wars Americans had recently experienced, Eisenhower believed that he and other leaders had the responsibility to explain the changed nature of defense requirements now facing the country. "Unhappily," Eisenhower warned, "the danger [the Cold War] poses promises to be of infinite duration." To confront this danger successfully, he observed, "There is called for, not so much the emotional and transitory sacrifices of crises, but rather those which enable us to carry forward steadily, surely, and without complaint the burdens of a prolonged and complex struggle—with liberty the stake." The Cold War threatened to last for generations, to linger as a multidecade state of insecurity. Eisenhower believed that one of his tasks was to prepare Americans to sustain these burdens.

The enormous expense of the Cold War and the resources it drained from the economy prompted Eisenhower to reflect that "the current problem in defense spending is to figure how far you should go without destroying from within what you are trying to defend from without." In confronting the complexity of the Cold War's fiscal challenge, he had to determine the correct balance between spending enough to meet America's essential security requirements and resisting excesses that could undermine the long-term strength of the nation's economy, its political and social cohesion, and, ultimately, its ability to pay for a strong military during a protracted period.

Before World War II, American military doctrine held that the United States did not need a large peacetime army. It had been widely assumed that if a war were to break out in another part of the world, the United States would have time to prepare, since America's allies in the region would be able to hold the line and engage the enemy until the United States mobilized its forces. That scenario had played out in World Wars I and II. But the Soviet threat and the Korean War made that notion obsolete. The United States was now the preeminent ally and could no longer assume it had time to mobilize if another major war broke out; it had to be in a continued state of preparedness. If NSC-68's doctrine of containment was to be credible, the country would need to sustain a large, powerful, and permanent force at home and abroad—one that could defend Western Europe, Japan, and other allies and quickly project American power anywhere in the world.

Recognition of this new challenge led Eisenhower to formulate the New Look doctrine, which was designed to produce a ready defense capability at a reasonable cost. The doctrine assumed that the United States was going to face a multidecade confrontation with the Soviet Union and its ideological adherents; accordingly, U.S. military spending should be geared to the long haul rather than fluctuate according to the perceived threat at the moment. Eisenhower urged administration officials to avoid exaggerating the near-term threat, since sharp increases in military spending would produce unnecessarily big deficits. Using the same reasoning, excessive domestic spending also had to be avoided. Thus, Eisenhower sought annual budgets that were in or close to balance and defense spending at a level that could be sustained "for a long and indefinite period."

Eisenhower was especially concerned about the effect of big deficits on public confidence and morale. "Unbalanced budgets and increasing costs have a reciprocal effect," he wrote. "As deficits deepen, prices tend to rise. . . . Such price increases, spiraling indefinitely upward . . . can eventually wreck the nation's security. At home, they promote discontent among our people. Overseas they can lead to a decline of the dollar . . . which vitiates our friends' confidence in us and tempts our enemies to see us as weaker than we are." In a letter to a friend, Eisenhower warned that inflation was a serious enemy to democracy. "With this thief and robber stalking across the country we can only have an apparent prosperity for a time, but not for long. Inflation must be avoided, and that means that the Federal government must not only live within its means but must, in time of prosperity, begin reducing the nation's debt." In his view, a weak American economy could cause the Kremlin to feel more confident that it could break the resolve of the American people to sustain the costs of the Cold War. If that happened, Soviet leaders might then take the opportunity to step up their military presence around the globe, expecting little or no challenge from the United States.

The key elements of the New Look were contained in National Security Council document 162/2, which the president approved in October 1953. It stated that the country required "a strong military posture, with emphasis on the capability of inflicting massive retaliatory damage by offensive striking power" and that the United States "will consider nuclear weapons as available for use as other munitions." This massive retaliation doctrine aimed to deter the Soviets and provide for a sustainable capability to strike back if the United States were ever attacked. To make NSC-162/2 a reality, defense budgets had to be shifted from conventional forces toward nuclear weapons. The air force's Strategic Air Command had to be enhanced and the army's and navy's tactical nuclear arsenals increased.

Because Eisenhower felt the Kremlin posed both an economic and a military threat, he insisted that the Pentagon pay for high-priority weapons and programs by cutting low-priority systems and ensuring rigorous economies in procurement. He understood that the military had to be well funded but was adamant about rooting out unnecessary spending, especially for programs or weapons systems initiated to satisfy powerful business interests or political constituencies rather than for hard-nosed security requirements. He believed they added to the deficit but not to the country's military strength. He was particularly critical of "members of Congress who so fearfully cater to the demand of selfish [military contractor] lobbies."

To ensure spending discipline at the Pentagon, Eisenhower instructed the National Security Council to estimate the cost of the defense programs it proposed rather than simply suggest new initiatives without considering their impact on the budget. A financial annex outlining the fiscal implications of various plans under deliberation had to be attached to NSC papers. He directed Treasury Secretary Humphrey to attend NSC meetings so security planners would "recognize the relationship between military and economic strength." "This country could choke itself to death piling up military expenditures," he warned, "just as surely as it can defeat itself by not spending enough for protection."

Eisenhower's budgetary restraint was all the more remarkable because he could have obtained legislation for much higher defense spending than his administration requested. As Sam Rayburn said, "He should know more about what it took to defend this country than practically anyone and . . . if he would send up a budget for the amount he thought was necessary to put the country in a position to defend ourselves against attack, I would promise to deliver 95 percent of the Democratic votes in the House."

Truces

Throughout the early months of his presidency, Eisenhower sought to negotiate an end to the war. "People grow weary of war," he said, "particularly when they see no decisive and victorious end to it." To the president, the cost of achieving a victorious end in Korea was excessively high, not only in economic terms but also in its impact on American society. "Victory," he asserted, "would require such an expansion of the present conflict as to demand practically a general mobilization. This would mean regimentation [the kind of economic controls and sacrifices experienced in World War II]—and the question arises as to the length of time we could endure regimentation without losing part of our free system."

America's active military engagement in the Korean War ended with a truce in July 1953. Now, in Eisenhower's assessment, the danger of inflation would give way to the danger of recession. With the high appropriations for the war no longer necessary, the president set about the task of reducing taxes.

Later that year, Humphrey crafted legislation to implement such reductions. Like many Republicans of his generation, he greatly admired Andrew Mellon, whose picture he displayed prominently in his office, and the tax cuts he suggested were modeled after those the Republicans had enacted in the 1920s. By this time, the president and Dan Reed had put their earlier differences behind them. The White House worked with Reed, other antitax Republicans, and a number of conservative Democrats to cut excise taxes on transportation and luxury items, such as jewelry and perfume; exempt a portion of dividend income from taxation; and improve depreciation allowances for business. The administration also secured legislation to liberalize deductions for dependents and medical expenses. By bipartisan consent, wartime increases in the income tax and excess profits tax were allowed to expire in January 1954.

The 1955 defense request, the first that fully reflected the priorities of Eisenhower's New Look, reduced the force size and budgets of the army and navy. The air force would receive modest budgetary increases and more personnel because of its enhanced role. The policies met with enormous resistance. Army Chief of Staff Matthew B. Ridgway resigned. Eisenhower had bluntly called Ridgway's views "parochial" because he refused to accept the administration's "new strategy of using the threat of atomic bombs delivered by airplanes as the nation's chief line of defense and deemphasizing the role of the foot soldier." Ridgeway later recalled, "I felt I was being called upon to tear down, rather than build up . . . a properly proportionate fighting force." Democrats seized on the frugal defense budget to complain that Eisenhower was creating a "bomber gap"; later they proclaimed he had allowed a "missile gap" to develop as well.

Leading Republicans sought to use the postwar budget surplus to enact another tax cut—a twenty-dollar deduction for each dependent. Eisenhower opposed the legislation, charging that it would be an electoral giveaway, "a private political relief bill for the Congressmen and Senators who attached their names to it." He lectured Congress, "We could not ignore . . . the obligation we had to future Americans to reduce the deficit whenever we could appropriately do so." Eisenhower triumphed, and the measure was defeated. In his 1956 State of the Union address, he cautioned Congress that "under conditions of high peacetime prosperity, such as now exist, we can never justify going further into debt to give ourselves a tax cut at the expense of our children." His warning would go unheeded during the next phases of the Cold War—and for much of the next fifty years.

Early in 1956, in a potential reprise of the confrontation between Truman and the Fed, the Federal Reserve chairman, William McChesney Martin Jr., the former president of the New York Stock Exchange who had been appointed by Truman in 1951, informed Treasury Secretary Humphrey that the prospect of increased inflation led him to conclude that an interest rate increase was needed. In an election year, Eisenhower feared that such a move could cause the economy to weaken and endanger his prospects at the polls. Martin nonetheless held firm, and the Fed increased rates in April. Humphrey pressed Eisenhower to publicly condemn the increase. Martin, however, explained to the president that inflation needed to be curbed or it would get out of hand; besides, he added, the Fed could always lower rates if the economy slowed. After weighing the arguments, Eisenhower made a remarkable statement that gave the Fed's independence an enormous boost. In a press conference, he responded to a question as to whether he believed the Fed should be accountable to the administration: "It is not under the authority of the President, and I really personally believe it would be a mistake to make it definitely and directly responsible to the political head of state." Despite the administration's concerns about the rate hike, the economy continued to grow, which helped Eisenhower win a landslide victory in 1956.

Another factor contributing to Eisenhower's electoral triumph was the country's budget surplus that year. In his campaign, Eisenhower proudly pointed to it as an important accomplishment. Once elected, he moved to use the surplus to implement what he called "modern Republicanism," which featured school construction grants, the national highway system (which had been launched in 1954 but remained underfunded), the development of water resources, and the expansion of federal welfare programs. Much of the incremental spending in his budget was for these items; defense and foreign assistance received only moderate increases. The White House requested higher appropriations for Eisenhower's initiatives, fully expecting that Congress would cut them back. It also was given economic forecasts that anticipated continued strong growth, which would generate revenue increases above those anticipated in the government's budget projections. The administration believed that these two factors combined would produce a balanced budget, but things did not turn out as planned. Democrats still held slim majorities in both chambers; they cut domestic spending as anticipated but also slashed defense spending far more than the president deemed prudent. And instead of growing rapidly, the economy slumped into recession. The resulting revenue losses exceeded the spending reductions instituted by Congress, throwing the budget into deficit.

Then the Soviet Union launched the world's first artificial satellite, Sputnik, on October 4, 1957, focusing new attention on the defense budget and the alleged missile gap. Sputnik demonstrated not only that the Soviets were ahead in the space race but that their missiles could reach the United States, creating a heightened sense of vulnerability among Americans. Congressional sentiment now turned sharply. Legislators appropriated more for defense in 1958 than the president had requested. By mid-January 1958, Congress, "which had exhibited such economy-mindedness in the previous year, had not only restored all the money it had cut from the Pentagon's . . . budget but had given the President substantial additional spending authority for military purposes." Sputnik "had served to unravel—not just loosen—Congressional purse strings, at least as far as the Democratic majority was concerned."

In presenting his budget for 1959, Eisenhower cautioned against getting carried away with military spending in the wake of the Sputnik shock. His budget request called for moderate increases in defense spending, but also cut back a number of the domestic programs that had been key features of modern Republicanism, which, as described by historian Charles Alexander, "had been a casualty of the missile and space age."

Despite the president's warnings, Congress appropriated more for defense and domestic programs than he had requested. In conjunction with the adverse revenue effects of the recession, the deficit hit $12 billion—2.6 percent of GDP—the largest of the Eisenhower presidency. The most important feature of modern Republicanism that survived was the national highway construction plan, which Eisenhower justified substantially on national security grounds, though it also enjoyed support throughout the country because it gave a big boost to jobs, commerce, and the domestic economy.

Eisenhower's farewell address is often cited for its warning about the "military-industrial complex," but it also resonated with another warning. The outgoing president counseled Americans "to avoid the impulse to live only for today, plundering for our own ease and convenience the precious resources of tomorrow." In a tone that harked back to the Founding Fathers' recognition of their obligation to "posterity," he warned, "We cannot mortgage the material assets of our grandchildren without asking the loss also of their political and spiritual heritage. We want democracy to survive for all generations, not become the insolvent phantom of tomorrow."

★

The early Cold War years posed complicated financial challenges for the Truman and Eisenhower administrations.

Truman's first challenge lay in asking a country that expected to return to some measure of "normalcy" after World War II to pay higher taxes to support assistance programs for Europe to contain Communist encroachment and Moscow's attempts to subvert friendly governments. His second challenge was to determine how to raise significant sums for a war that had caught the nation by surprise in mid-1950. He was remarkably successful in both—securing large appropriations with bipartisan support. His third challenge was to prevent too dramatic an expansion of the military, to avoid incurring big deficits and signaling to the Soviet Union or the American people that the country was preparing for an all-out war. Truman successfully did so by tamping down the public's and Congress's expectation of a quick and decisive victory in Korea—especially resisting pressures to assert America's nuclear superiority or take the war directly to China or the Soviet Union.

Finally, when the war reached an impasse and public sentiment had soured, the challenge shifted to sustaining support for the appropriations necessary to continue fighting. Truman's approach, as Secretary Marshall put it, was to prosecute the war with "determination but also with patience and calm deliberation," but that did not produce the clear-cut military results for which the public clamored. Congressional and public support ebbed significantly. Truman bequeathed to Eisenhower a limited war, a military stalemate, and stalled negotiations—plus a lot of military IOUs that the new president did not anticipate—but also a legacy of toughness in resisting the Soviets, fiscal rectitude, and organizational coherence in the form of the National Security Council system.

For an individual with little formal economic or financial training, Eisenhower demonstrated a remarkable grasp of the fiscal risks of the Cold War. He constantly had to contend with powerful factions in the Republican Party that demanded big cuts in taxes and spending, even if that meant significant reductions in the resources available for national defense. There were also times when the president faced intense pressures to raise Pentagon spending beyond levels he believed to be necessary for the nation's security. In the later years of his administration, he was subject to Democratic criticism that his efforts to maintain a lean defense budget produced a missile gap and other vulnerabilities. In the final analysis, Eisenhower successfully balanced the need for strong defense against the need for a responsible fiscal policy remarkably well.

Had another president with less credibility on defense been in office at the time, military spending and fiscal policy in general would likely have taken a very different course. For example, if Robert Taft had won the nomination in 1952 and gone on to win the presidency, he might well have slashed military spending and eliminated virtually all foreign assistance in the early 1950s to produce a balanced budget. That would have been interpreted in Moscow as a signal that the United States was unwilling to devote sufficient resources to protect its interests and those of other democracies—and the Cold War containment policy would have collapsed. Later in the decade, as Cold War concerns intensified, it is likely that a president with less experience as a military leader would have succumbed to pressures for considerably greater defense spending, thereby producing more sizable budget deficits, especially after the launch of Sputnik. Because of Eisenhower's fiscal conservatism and his willingness to oppose those who advocated considerably greater defense spending after the Korean War, defense budgets during the remainder of the 1950s were generally kept in check. The president harbored many of the reservations that Thomas Jefferson had expressed about large budgets, especially caused by self-serving economic ties between military contractors and the government.

Eisenhower learned from the experience of the Korean War. He saw how the country turned away from supporting high military budgets when the conflict stalled. He recognized the risk that a similar turn in support could occur later in the Cold War if there appeared to be a stalemate and the costs were deemed too high. With this lesson in mind, he attempted to educate Americans that they had to be prepared for sustained defense spending for many years. A key aspect of this education was to explain how the Cold War would differ from the two world wars that Americans had recently experienced. He recognized that the Cold War would require contained sacrifices rather than acute ones of the kind Americans had been asked to make during those wars. He lectured his administration colleagues and members of Congress that defense budgets had to be structured for a decades-long war, not a relatively quick conflict. In these circumstances, excessive defense spending in the short term would produce big deficits or require higher taxes or both and raise the risk that the public would weary and turn against the defense effort. Also, the inflation and deficits resulting from excessive spending financed by heavy borrowing would weaken and destabilize the economy.

Critics argued that Eisenhower did not ask for enough money for the military. In the 1960 presidential campaign, the Democratic Party's platform charged that "over the last 7 1/2 years, our military power has steadily declined relative to that of the Russians and the Chinese and their satellites . . . and that our military position today is measured in gaps—missile gap, space gap, limited-war gap." Many in the military shared the Democrats' concerns. During the early months of John F. Kennedy's administration, access to intelligence from U-2 spy planes convinced the president and his advisers that there never had been a missile gap. By the end of 1961, satellite intelligence showed that the United States was well ahead of the Soviets in operational intercontinental ballistic missiles, and, in December, President Kennedy pointedly stated, "In terms of total military strength, the U.S. would not trade places with any nation on earth." Another issue during the campaign centered on exaggerated projections, based on extrapolations of 1950 growth rates, that the Soviet economy would overtake the U.S. economy by the 1980s. That, of course, turned out not to be the case.

7

"Hard and Inescapable Facts"

THE GREAT SOCIETY VERSUS THE VIETNAM WAR

THE PRESIDENT SIMPLY DID NOT WANT TO RISK A CONGRES-
SIONAL TEST OF HIS VIETNAM POLICY IN THE FORM OF A TAX
POLICY TO PAY FOR IT.

—PAUL A. VOLCKER

In the late summer of 1967, Lyndon Johnson was a frustrated man. The war in Vietnam was going badly, necessitating a dramatic increase in troop levels, and the nation's budget deficit was growing rapidly, driven by the rising costs of the war and the president's Great Society social agenda. Johnson, however, had held off asking Congress to increase taxes, fearing a confrontation with legislators over the war and his domestic agenda.

The president did not want to abandon his social program in order to secure the tax increases he needed to cover the Pentagon's soaring budget. He knew that previous twentieth-century presidents—Woodrow Wilson, Franklin Roosevelt, Harry Truman, and Dwight Eisenhower—were unable to prevent defense spending from undercutting their domestic programs. Yet, as the federal deficit grew, Congress became increasingly divided and unhappy. Conservatives, such as Arkansas Democrat Wilbur Mills, the chairman of the House Ways and Means Committee, were willing to spend more for the war and increase taxes to do it, but they were unwilling to pay more for the president's ambitious social agenda. Liberals supported John-son's social agenda but objected to tax increases to finance the increasingly unpopular war. The simmering tensions had boiled over earlier in the year, when LBJ sought legislation to impose a 6 percent tax surcharge. As the president had anticipated, congressional leaders, especially Mills, insisted that he agree to large domestic spending cuts in return for the committee's critically needed support for the tax increase.

In August, the president laid out, in stark terms, what he called the "hard and inescapable facts." The impasse over taxes and spending had led to a deficit that, in his view, constituted a "clear and present danger to America's security and economic health" by threatening to cause "ruinous inflation," "brutally higher interest rates," and many other ills. Although he indicated a willingness to accept modest reductions in domestic spending, Congress still refused to act. Mills, in particular, would not budge. In March 1968, Johnson bluntly criticized Congress for its failure to address the deficit, which, he charged, had led to "the sharpest financial threat in the postwar era."

Johnson faced a dilemma. He hoped to finance escalating military costs without calling on the American people to pay higher taxes and now, with the need for more revenue, his social agenda was in peril. As deficits grew, congressional leaders—on a bipartisan basis—exercised their power over appropriations and revenues to force the matter. The defining battle was between a White House that did not want to cut social programs to free up resources for a costly war and a Congress whose leaders wanted to curb the growth in the deficit primarily by cutting domestic spending. As a result of the prolonged impasse between the two branches, both the deficit and inflation spun out of control.

Amnesia and Ambivalence

Virtually all the lessons previously and painfully learned about how to pay for a war were tossed aside, at least for a time, during the Vietnam conflict. Where past wartime administrations had looked to the successes and the mistakes of their predecessors, the Johnson administration chose to ignore past experience for several years and imagined that Vietnam was an entirely different sort of war, in an entirely different circumstance, in which old lessons did not apply.

The John F. Kennedy and then Johnson administrations took a different approach to military matters than had Eisenhower. As John Lewis

Gaddis wrote, "Eisenhower, they believed, had relied too heavily on the threatened use of nuclear weapons.... His attachment to solvency as an interest co-equal with security not only reflected outdated economics, it also ran needless risks by leaving the nation with too few options for action below the nuclear level." Kennedy wanted to have a broader range of options, a wider choice than humiliation or all-out nuclear war. He also took a different approach to paying for this broader range. Whereas "Eisenhower's assumption had been that because means were inelastic, interests had to compete with one another: resources allocated to defense could only come at the expense of other priorities whose neglect might defeat the purposes of defense in the first place. But in the 'new economics' of the Kennedy administration, domestic and foreign interests were assumed to be complementary: the economy could withstand, even benefit from, increases in spending for *both* national defense and domestic reform." This was a plausible economic argument when the economy was underperforming, but, taken to its extreme, it led to overheating and inflation.

Kennedy, and then Johnson, turned away from Eisenhower's New Look, focusing the military more heavily on the army. From 1961 through 1964, the army's size was increased from about 850,000 to nearly 1 million. Only 23,000 troops were stationed in Vietnam at the end of that period, but that soon changed, and the U.S. military presence there leapt to 184,000 by the end of 1965, and to 536,000 by the end of 1968. Defense spending increased by nearly 50 percent. All told, nearly 9 million Americans served during the war, roughly 4.3 million in the army, 1.8 million in the navy, 1.7 million in the air force, and 800,000 in the marines.

Far from asking the nation to sacrifice during the early stages of escalation, Johnson reassured Americans that no major tax or spending changes were necessary, calmly asserting that the conflict in Vietnam would not divert resources from Medicare, Medicaid, Head Start, and other domestic programs. Johnson frequently remarked to his assistant Joseph Califano that the massive financial demands of World War II had killed the New Deal and the increase in funding for the Korean War had killed Truman's Fair Deal, and he was concerned a similar fate would befall the Great Society. To avoid having to make trade-offs between the two, he eagerly embraced the Keynsian philosophy that Keyserling had advanced in the 1940s and 1950s and that became a hallmark of the Kennedy administration's economic approach: if growth were strong, the economy could absorb rising defense costs as well as those of more activist social policies without requiring tough prioritization. As the military buildup accelerated, LBJ proclaimed, "We can continue the Great Society while we fight in Vietnam." As late as January 1967, he professed confidence that the country was on "a sensible course of fiscal and budgetary policy that we believe will keep our economy going without new inflationary spirals; that will finance responsibly the needs of our men in Vietnam and the progress of our people at home."

But the realities of the budget told a different tale, undermining the credibility of LBJ's words. Government spending continued to climb: military outlays accelerated from 8.5 percent of GDP in 1964 to 9.4 percent in 1968, while nonmilitary spending also increased, from 8.7 percent of GDP in 1964 to 9.8 percent in 1968. As Arthur Okun, a member of the president's Council of Economic Advisers (CEA), observed, "The economists in the administration watched with pain and frustration as fiscal policy veered off course."

Johnson thought that the strong economic growth the nation was experiencing in the mid-1960s would prevent him from having to choose between the war and the Great Society. A highly stimulative tax cut passed in 1964 gave the economy a big boost, but by December 1965, the chairman of the CEA, Gardner Ackley, advised the president that he could not rely on growth alone to avoid making tough budgetary choices. "Unless expenditures could be contained," he told Johnson, "a significant tax increase would be necessary to prevent an intolerable degree of inflationary pressure." However, as Johnson biographer Doris Kearns Goodwin explained, LBJ was in "no mood to listen to such warnings at the moment when the American people were enjoying all the favorable consequences of the boom. . . . He flatly refused to consider a tax increase, sticking to his initial position that the American nation could afford guns and butter alike."

No Internal Coordination

Johnson's "cardinal rule in his conduct of the war," Goodwin observed, "was to keep it as painless and concealed as possible." Deliberately avoiding new taxes, he drew upon existing revenues and borrowing to finance his bombs and his troops. But the rising costs of the war and his social programs, combined with robust consumer demand, were conspiring to create what economists dubbed the "Great Inflation"—a surge in prices that would help to doom the president's Vietnam policy and much of his Great Society as well.

In the spring of 1966, LBJ and his defense secretary, Robert S. McNamara, knew that military spending would be much higher than the $10 billion previously allocated. Yet "they refused to admit how much defense spending would rise, limiting their public statements to vague pronouncements." In contrast to the approach taken by Wilson, Roosevelt, and Truman, Johnson's finely honed political instincts failed him, and he did not call upon Americans to make sacrifices for the war. When he could no longer ignore the financial hazards and had to ask for tax increases, his stubborn refusal to prepare Americans for hardship left him vulnerable to public and congressional criticism and unable to muster sufficient support to sustain his programs. "When inflation set in," Goodwin noted, "in the absence of a wartime mood of sacrifice, the centers of power in Congress responded with a conventional call to cut the budget."

But it was not only the public and Congress that were kept in the dark. Within the administration, historian Jeffrey Helsing observed in his book *Johnson's War/Johnson's Great Society,* "there was a complete lack of overall economic coordination." Defeating the purpose of Truman's National Security Council and ignoring the benefits that Eisenhower had recognized when he directed Treasury Secretary George Humphrey to attend its meetings, Johnson maintained a decision-making structure in which "domestic and military policies were simply kept apart. No one was responsible for looking at the big picture. The president never asked his economic advisers for specific analysis of the military escalation." Most of the planning for the war took place not in the National Security Council but in LBJ's Tuesday lunch group, which included the secretaries of state and defense, the special assistant for national security affairs, the director of the CIA, and the chairman of the Joint Chiefs of Staff. LBJ preferred this handpicked group because, in his words, "the National Security Council meetings were like sieves. I couldn't control them." Notably absent was Treasury Secretary Henry "Joe" Fowler. Fowler, a New Deal veteran, had overseen production during both World War II and the Korean War and had served as the undersecretary of the Treasury during the Kennedy administration. Although he helped steer the president's policies through Congress, where he enjoyed excellent relations, neither he nor anyone else on the president's economic team were privy to information on the anticipated size or costs of Vietnam. The awkward isolation of Johnson's Treasury Department was underscored when William McChesney Martin, the chairman of the Federal Reserve board, learned of the prospect of much higher defense costs not from the

White House but from the chairman of the Senate Appropriations Committee, Richard Russell. A surprised Martin noted, "I had more information than the Treasury had."

Within the Tuesday lunch group, the man who knew most about economics and finance was Defense Secretary Robert S. McNamara. McNamara had earned a reputation as a corporate whiz, returning to his business school alma mater, Harvard, to become its highest-paid assistant professor at the time. After applying modern business efficiency principles to World War II bombing campaigns, he was hired by the Ford Motor Company, and served briefly as its first president from outside the Ford family before joining the Kennedy administration at the Defense Department. In 1965, recognizing that the cost of the war was escalating, McNamara sent LBJ a private memo recommending a tax increase to avert a rise in inflation and the deficit. The "president flatly refused my advice," he recalled. Johnson and McNamara chose not to circulate the memo to Fowler and the rest of the administration's economic advisers. "I submitted my spending estimate and proposed tax increase in a highly classified draft memorandum," said McNamara, adding that "not even the Treasury Secretary or the chairman of the Council of Economic Advisers knew about it." Fowler, out of the loop, "firmly stated throughout most of calendar year 1966 . . . that the budgetary deficit for 1967 will not exceed $1.8 billion." The actual figure was nearly triple that.

In addition to rejecting McNamara's recommendation, Johnson scolded him. "Obviously you don't know anything about politics," he lectured his defense secretary. "I'll tell you what's going to happen. . . . In the course of the debate they'll say, 'You see, we've been telling you so. You can't have guns and butter, and we're going to have guns.'" Later, LBJ predicted that, once the issue was raised, "all those conservatives in the Congress would use it as a weapon against the Great Society. . . . Oh, they'd use it to say they were against my programs, not because they were against the poor . . . but because the war had to come first." That is just what happened two years later.

Troubles with the Congress

A particular source of contention between the White House and Congress was the administration's repeated use of "emergency" supplemental appropriation requests for military spending. In August 1965, the administration submitted the first such request, an appeal for $1.7 billion in additional funds for the war. McNamara was called up to Capitol Hill by the Senate Appropriations Committee to defend the figure. In the course of an acrimonious hearing, he was pressed for future cost estimates and replied that the Defense Department could not provide them. Senator John Stennis, a senior Democrat from Mississippi on the committee who was known by the nickname "Mr. Integrity" and had been the first in his party to criticize Joseph McCarthy for his red-scare tactics, shot back, "It would make more sense to finance the war through congressionally authorized appropriations up front rather than emergency supplemental appropriations requests along the way." An exasperated Stennis bluntly stated his annoyance that Congress had been given so little information about the administration's calculations of future costs for the war in Vietnam. "We are entitled to know more than we now do about it," he insisted. Then, underscoring the discomfort that he felt in trying to defend the president's policy in the Senate, Stennis added, "I do not want to tell the Senators on the floor that you had no idea."

McNamara cited two major reasons for submitting the supplemental request. First, predicting the cost of the Vietnam War with precision was difficult. This doubtless was true, as it is in most wars, but there is considerable evidence that senior administration officials recognized well in advance that the conflict would cost more—much more—than the figures they supplied to Congress. Members of Congress suspected that McNamara, who was famous for his number crunching, probably knew a lot more than he was telling them. McNamara's posture also stemmed from his not wanting "to give the military a blank check," believing that in order for the civilian leadership at the Defense Department "to keep control over the costs and the programs, the best course was to authorize money with little lead time." Accordingly, he sought to maintain a tight rein "to avoid the unnecessary production and stockpiling of military equipment that was the experience at the conclusion of the Korean War."

This approach soon lost credibility with Congress and the American people. As the troop level reached 365,000 in 1966—double that of 1965—the war's costs were soaring and public discontent was rising. With this escalation under way, Helsing wrote, the assumption embedded in the administration's budget request "that the war would wind down or end after June, 1967" was met with incredulity. To most members of Congress, that "did not reflect either military or economic reality" and was seen as just another example of the administration "downplaying the extent of the costs of the war and the significance of the commitment that would require American sacrifices." Most observers expected the cost would be twice the administration's request, and that expectation was borne out when it asked for a $12 billion supplemental appropriation to obtain the extra money.

In July 1967, the Congressional Joint Economic Committee issued a report that took the administration to task for hiding information from Congress. "The lack of accurate expenditure data during calendar 1966," it stated, "handicapped the Congress seriously in reaching appropriate tax, spending and other economic policy decisions." The pressure tactic worked. In its 1968 budget request, the administration asked for $20 billion, followed by just one supplemental of $3.8 billion. In the following year, it asked for one supplemental of merely $1.3 billion. The rest of the war was paid for with no supplemental requests.

But much of the damage had already been done. Because the Defense Department had underestimated expenditures in 1965 and 1966, no effort was undertaken within the administration to set spending priorities and reduce other programs to pay for the war. By keeping Congress, which was in Democratic hands, uninformed, senators and representatives were forced to constantly react to the administration's surprises rather than work with Johnson to find the most politically acceptable way to raise the money needed.

By pretending that the war would be relatively inexpensive, Johnson also failed to prepare Americans for the additional tax burdens that eventually would come and heightened their distrust of the administration. This approach ran counter to FDR's constant warnings that sacrifice was necessary for victory during World War II and Truman's insistence that the Korean War be paid for with higher taxes. Instead of using the war to explain the need for additional funds—and sell it to the American people—Johnson shied away from any budget talk. Thus, as appropriation requests for the war rose, so did the number of people who concluded that the financial commitment was too costly.

But there was another, less cynical, reason for the administration to downplay the budgetary cost of the war, at least in 1965 and 1966. Prior to the Korean War, American leaders believed that the country needed only a modest-sized army on the assumption that if and when the country needed to mobilize a larger force, it would have time to do so. However, as Helsing wrote, "ever since the Korean War, the U.S. military had maintained a peace-time deployment, and a level of readiness and equipment on hand that had never been achieved prior to any other military conflict in American history." As a result, on the eve of the Vietnam escalation in the mid-1960s, a large number of Americans were already in the armed forces and big military stockpiles were in place. Thus, Johnson's war planners concluded that a "huge [new] military buildup was . . . unnecessary, unlike with Korea or the two world wars. It was assumed that the United States could quickly respond to any contingency and deploy forces whenever and wherever necessary—with little need for major buildup and additional financial sacrifice." Reflecting this point of view, Arthur Okun noted, "the Vietnam conflict found us well prepared and required a relatively small buildup in total military procurement."

The conventional wisdom in the administration was that, unlike past wars, mobilization for Vietnam would not create inflationary pressures. Defense and economic planners, including Okun, believed that the country's "strong defensive posture during peacetime would limit the disruption to the civilian economy if war came."

In fact, there was little economic disruption from 1960 through 1965; military spending increased by only a modest 11 percent, from $45 billion to $50 billion. But as the war intensified, expenditures jumped by more than 50 percent, to $78 billion in 1968. Because the economy was already growing at a rapid rate and approaching full capacity, the surge in military purchases triggered inflationary pressures. The consumer price index soared from 1.9 percent in 1965 to nearly 5 percent in 1968 and to 6 percent in 1969. Borrowing costs rose sharply. Especially painful to many Americans was the spike in the mortgage interest rate to nearly 7 percent—a figure that had not been seen since World War II.

The Fed and LBJ—David Confronts Goliath

While the administration's relations with Congress were strained, they were downright acrimonious with the Federal Reserve. LBJ repeatedly pressed Chairman Martin to keep interest rates down so that the economy would continue to grow at a rapid rate and generate sufficient tax revenues to pay the mounting costs of his domestic and military programs. And because inflation pushed taxpayers into higher brackets, Johnson did not mind a bit of that as well.

In mid-1965, the consumer price index was rising at an annualized rate of 2.6 percent, more than double the rate in the previous twelve months. Martin became alarmed.

In early October, Martin tried to convince Johnson that an increase in interest rates would "sustain and stretch out the expansion" by containing inflationary pressures. Johnson attempted to delay the Fed's action, telling Martin, "I'm scheduled to go into the hospital for a gall bladder operation. You wouldn't raise the discount rate while I'm in the hospital, would you?" Martin assured him, "We'll wait until you get out." A month later, having postponed action, Martin concluded that inflation posed too great a risk to delay further. He told his colleagues that "if the system waits until mid-January," as Fowler and Ackley advocated, "and if the budget turns out as I think it will, it will be too late for monetary policy to have any effect." A key ally of Martin's on the Federal Reserve board was retiring in January, and the chairman feared that the replacement might not be as sympathetic to a rate increase.

Even more of a concern to Martin was the impression that the Fed was knuckling under to pressure from the White House. When the president summoned Martin down to his ranch for a meeting in early December, Martin worried that his independence would be completely compromised. It was, Martin said, "a question whether the Federal Reserve is to be run by the administration in office." He decided to take preemptive action. On December 3, 1965, at the urging of the chairman, the Fed, by a 4–3 vote, upped the discount rate (the rate charged to banks for short-term loans). Joe Califano described Johnson as "burning up the wires to Washington, asking one member of Congress after another, 'How can I run the country and the government if I have to read on a news-service ticker that Bill Martin is going to run his own economy?'"

When Martin arrived at the ranch, there were fireworks. According to his account, Johnson "was very disagreeable," accusing him of "harming his presidency." LBJ railed, "You've got me in a position where you can run a rapier into me and you've done it." Martin calmly responded, "We were not precipitous about this. I warned you about it. We discussed this and you asked me to give you another chance. I did, and we couldn't wait any longer." Martin also reminded the president that the Federal Reserve Act vested him with a responsibility for the economy separate from the president's authority. In the end, Johnson did not resort to his long-practiced tactic of rallying powerful allies in Congress against his adversaries. Martin had enemies in Senator Russell Long of Louisiana, the chairman of the

Finance Committee, and Congressman Wright Patman of Texas, the chairman of the House Banking Committee; the president could have tried to persuade them to challenge the Fed's independence. He refrained from doing so. Still, the effects of Martin's bruising battle with Johnson lingered. Offsetting his rebukes from Johnson was consolation from a former president: from his retirement farm in Gettysburg, Dwight Eisenhower wrote of "the intense pride I have in seeing you stand 4-square for what you know to be right" and predicted that "history will evaluate your career in the Federal Reserve Board something like it does for John Marshall on the Supreme Court."

As heroic as Martin's stand was, the Fed's move was too little too late, and inflation surged in 1966, even as the Fed continued to tighten credit. Higher inflation and a growing deficit weakened confidence in the nation's financial markets and in the dollar and encouraged Congress to put more pressure on the administration to take bold action. In the fight against inflation, counseled Martin, "Monetary policy has done about all that it properly can." It was time for tougher fiscal policy. The looming showdown in the "guns and butter" debate had arrived.

LBJ's Tax Surcharge

As Martin had his "go-rounds with Johnson," the president was weighing the possibility of requesting a tax increase. But in January 1966, Chairman Wilbur Mills flatly told him that it was "out of the question." Mills, a staunch fiscal conservative, wanted domestic spending cuts, not tax increases, to close the budget gap. Later that year, Bill Martin pressed Johnson to address the tax issue. "You should," urged Martin, "go forward with the tax increase on the assumption that expenditures in Vietnam are going to rise." LBJ resisted. Given Mills's ultimatum, he was sure that asking for a tax increase would be an invitation to conservatives to cut appropriations for the Great Society.

As spending on the war mounted, the deficit swelled at an alarming rate. In 1967, the cost of the war leaped from an original forecast of just under $6 billion to $13 billion, and the budget deficit was projected to widen from $4.5 billion to nearly $12 billion, hitting $19 billion in 1968, an astronomical amount at the time. Martin tried the president again, suggesting he go to the American people and make the case for a wartime tax increase. A "candid presentation of the facts, giving full weight to the costs of our efforts in Vietnam . . . would ensure prompt enactment," he advised Johnson. "I am far more concerned about the effects at home and abroad of a failure to propose an increase in taxes than I am about the effects of proposing one."

LBJ held the line against tax increases as long as he could. As Paul Volcker, at the time a senior official in the Treasury, noted, Johnson was keenly aware that by allowing a debate on the financing of the war, he would be opening a larger debate on the war itself and on his entire program. Heightened concerns about widening budget deficits and rising inflation, along with enormous political pressures from members of his own party in Congress, ultimately produced a change of heart. In his 1967 State of the Union address, Johnson recommended a 6 percent surcharge on individual and corporate income taxes to "last for two years or for so long as the unusual expenditures associated with our efforts in Vietnam continue." Single taxpayers with incomes below $1,900 were to be exempt, as were married couples with two children earning below $5,000.

Johnson reminded Americans that even with this tax increase, they would face a lower tax burden than before he took office: "If Americans today still paid the income and excise taxes in effect when I came into the Presidency, in the year 1964, their annual taxes would have been over $20 billion higher than at present tax rates, so this proposal is that . . . your government asks for slightly more than one-fourth of that tax cut each year in order to hold our budget deficit for fiscal 1968 within prudent limits and to give . . . our fighting men the help they need in their hour of trial."

The surcharge proposal found few friends in Congress. Democrats had lost forty-seven seats in the House in the 1966 midterm elections, and the survivors were largely unsympathetic to pleas from the White House. Wilbur Mills joined with the House minority leader, Gerald R. Ford, a moderate Michigan Republican, and Chairman Long to resist Johnson's initiative. If LBJ thought the Democratic Congress would simply register its criticisms before standing behind their president, he was disappointed. Mills refused to set aside his qualms. He was skeptical that the president's proposals were sufficient to close the deficit. The administration had argued that the economy would recover in the second half of 1967, and so the tax increases could be easily accommodated. Mills refused to hold hearings on the proposal, telling Ackley, "You can't legislate on the basis of economic forecasts; you have to legislate on the basis of reality."

In addition, Mills insisted that for any tax increase to pass the House it must be accompanied by significant spending cuts. Inflation was sapping the country's economic strength and Mills believed that it was largely due to rising costs, or "cost-push inflation." In Mills's view, sharply reduced government spending, which the president resisted, was the key tool for alleviating inflationary pressure, not tax increases, which, he had concluded, would be wholly ineffective. Mills lectured administration officials that tax increases were a tool for curbing "demand-pull inflation," from which, he asserted, the country did not suffer. It was a battle both of economic analysis and, perhaps more to the point, of two powerful Washington egos. Mills refused to budge from his position; so did the president.

Mills also took advantage of the tax debate to openly scold Johnson on the administration's general lack of budget discipline, noting that "the fact of the matter is that the budget has not set tough priorities. The United States is simultaneously battling Communist aggression in Vietnam and trying to give help not only to the poverty stricken but to many other groups as well." Mills said this inability to choose between spending for the military or for a range of domestic programs, or even to set clear priorities among such programs, was the reason the United States was running a growing budget deficit—a deficit that in 1968 would reach 3 percent of GDP, higher than at any time since World War II. Further evidence of LBJ's failure to prioritize was the upsurge in the federal government's share of GDP. Having skyrocketed to nearly 45 percent at the end of World War II, it had dropped to just 16 percent five years later; now it stood at 20 percent, a distressing figure to fiscal conservatives.

Mills dominated tax policy in Congress during the 1960s in much the same way as Claude Kitchin had in the Wilson era and Robert Doughton had during the 1930s and 1940s. In a 1987 interview in which he reflected back on his dispute with LBJ, Mills emphasized that he "was never opposed" to the surcharge itself. "What I wanted to do was to see if we couldn't balance the budget. . . . I wanted [the president] to withhold money." Specifically, he wanted Johnson to withhold $6 billion from previously appropriated funds and cut $14 billion from the next fiscal year's budget. He told the president that without these reductions, he just could not muster sufficient votes in the House for the income tax surcharge. At this point, congressional action came to a halt. As Arthur Okun lamented, "The nation had an excellent chance to get on a path of non-inflationary prosperity. That chance depended on prompt congressional enactment of the tax increase, and the entire strategy failed when legislative action did not take place."

Not known for being subtle when he wanted something, LBJ pushed hard for his tax proposal. "I know it doesn't add to your polls and your popularity to say we have to have additional taxes to fight this war abroad and fight the problems of our cities at home," he chided, but "we can do it with the gross national product we have."

As the financial situation deteriorated and inflation threatened, new voices arose within the administration in favor of a larger tax increase. Treasury Secretary Fowler had been lukewarm about a tax hike. Now he advised Johnson, "The overwhelming preponderance of economic opinion is that there is no longer any real danger that the imposition of this temporary increase will cause an economic downturn." LBJ agreed to go back to Congress to request a 10 percent surcharge, a level recommended by Martin. Still, Mills remained fixed on spending cuts, which he insisted must accompany any tax increase. "I am distancing myself from the legislation until the president delivers spending cuts," he told Califano.

Now Johnson's rhetoric took on a more urgent tone. In early August 1967, he sent a somber "state of the budget and the economy" message to Congress, entitled "The Hard and Inescapable Facts." In it, he predicted that without a "tax increase and tight expenditure control," the deficit would exceed $28 billion, posing a "clear and present danger" to the United States. "If left uncorrected," he warned, it could cause "a spiral of ruinous inflation," lead to "brutally higher interest rates," and produce "an unequal and unjust distribution of the cost of supporting our men in Vietnam." Invoking a "call to the sense of obligation felt by all Americans," LBJ asked for a "temporary surcharge of 10%" on individual and corporate taxes, which "would expire on June 30, 1969, or continue for so long as the unusual expenditures associated with our efforts in Vietnam require higher revenues." He raised the surcharge request from his original 6 percent because deficit projections had gone up. Appealing to patriotic sentiment, LBJ asserted that "the inconveniences this demand imposes are small when measured against the contribution of a Marine on patrol in a sweltering jungle, or an airman flying through perilous skies." Yet he also stuck to his position that the Great Society should not be shortchanged, stating that "the Nation's unfinished agenda here at home must be pursued as well."

Johnson then took his message directly to the American people via the media. He called a press conference to describe the budget trade-offs that had been available to him. He had, he said, rejected two options for addressing the gaping $28 billion deficit: to "borrow it all" or to "tax it all." Instead, he explained, he had decided to "borrow a part of it, tax a part of it and save a part of it." He aimed to raise $7.4 billion through the surcharge. Roughly the same amount was to be saved by curbing the growth of domestic programs. The remaining funds were to be borrowed. Because the new surcharge would not apply to families with incomes below $10,000, the 16 million Americans in the lowest tax brackets would be spared.

Until this point, Johnson had resisted significant domestic spending cuts, proclaiming, "We cannot permit the defense of freedom abroad to sidetrack the struggle for individual growth and dignity at home." He frequently called on Americans to demonstrate the "staying power" that was needed to defeat Communism overseas while supporting his domestic policy agenda. According to a Harris poll, 48 percent of Americans in early 1968 agreed that the country could do both; 39 percent did not. Those polled gave priority to financing the war over domestic programs.

During much of the war, many Americans were upset that the United States was not using more of its military power to achieve a decisive victory, a sentiment similar to the one expressed by critics during the Korean War. And, as was the case during that earlier conflict, while it appeared that victory in Vietnam was within reach, public support remained strong and ample financial resources were available to the president. As Walter Russell Mead observed, "American public opinion was generally more exercised over Washington's failure to apply all available force to Vietnam than it was over the necessity for the war altogether." As late as the middle of 1968, when the American force level rose to over five hundred thousand, support for appropriations ran high. However, when a victory in Vietnam seemed elusive, Americans began to see it as a quagmire and grew frustrated that more power was not being deployed to bring the conflict to a quick and decisive end. Support dropped. Among those expressing frustration was the governor of California, Ronald Reagan. In mid-August 1967, Reagan argued that the United States should pull out of Vietnam not because he opposed the war, but because he thought that the country could not win because "too many qualified targets had been put off limits to bombing."

Johnson was furious when Mills suspended hearings on tax legislation—which were scheduled to begin in mid-August—and Ford halted any further movement on the matter by the House. "Mr. Ford and Mr. Mills have taken the position that they cannot have any tax bill now," Johnson said. "They will live to rue the day when they made that decision because it is a dangerous decision." Mills's office curtly replied, "The president will rue the day he made that statement."

Early in 1968, the Ways and Means Committee reported out a bill that contained no surcharge at all. Mills felt that Johnson's proposed spending cuts were halfhearted and that for any tax increase to be successful, it needed to be coupled with expenditure control in "spirit and deed." As the debate raged, the deficit grew and inflationary forces mounted, convincing many investors to sell dollars to buy gold. There was a sharp fall in the value of the currency.

Johnson also was discovering that support for the war was collapsing. It turned sharply negative during the Tet Offensive, the series of attacks by the North Vietnamese army and the Viet Cong Communist guerrillas in the South in hundreds of cities and towns that began on the Vietnamese lunar new year, January 30, 1968. The American public became increasingly sensitive to the high rate of casualties and the rising number of draftees. Moreover, a growing unease emerged that the United States no longer had a clear path to victory. It did not help that the substantial economic cost of the war translated into a big increase in the budget deficit, which, in turn, was associated in the public mind with higher inflation and rising borrowing costs. Soon, more than half of all Americans believed the country was spending too much on the war.

In a national television address on March 31, Johnson increased the pressure on Congress. "Failure to act—and to act promptly and decisively—would raise very strong doubts throughout the world about America's willingness to keep its financial house in order," he warned legislators. He pulled no punches, declaring that because "Congress has not acted . . . tonight we face the sharpest financial threat in the post-war era—a threat to the dollar's role as the keystone of international trade and finance in the world." In a slight sweetener to the budget hawks, he added, "[As] part of fiscal restraint that includes a surcharge, I shall approve appropriations reductions in the January budget when and if Congress so decides that should be done." At the conclusion of his address, the president, having only narrowly defeated his antiwar challenger, Senator Eugene McCarthy, in the New Hampshire primary, and facing probable defeat in Wisconsin, pulled out of the presidential race, announcing, "I shall not seek, and I will not accept, the nomination of my party for another term."

The country was dumbstruck by the announcement. Shock waves reverberated throughout Congress. In the frenetic aftermath, two senators took the initiative. Republican John Williams and Democrat George Smathers saw an opportunity to wrest the tax and appropriations issues from Mills and his colleagues in the House. Without Mills's prior knowledge, they attached an amendment to a completely unrelated piece of legislation—an automobile and telephone excise tax bill—to impose the 10 percent tax surcharge that LBJ had requested the previous August and cut spending by $6 billion. That led to an agreement among the leaders of the tax and appropriations committees of the House and Senate on a package that embodied these measures. Most of the spending cuts were to come out of Great Society social programs. Experts estimated that the package would reduce the deficit by $20 billion for 1969.

Johnson, who had earlier expected Mills to ultimately accept just $4 billion in domestic spending cuts, initially argued that the $6 billion reduction was too large. When liberal Democrats attempted to restore some of these funds in the House, Mills blocked their efforts. Several of Johnson's advisers recommended a veto, but Fowler pointed out that it would be irresponsible to allow a difference of $2 billion in spending to derail a reduction in the deficit of $20 billion. After a contentious debate, Johnson decided not to back congressional liberals in their campaign to defeat Mills. He concluded that "any further confrontation would risk serious economic problems." In his mind, the country's economic crisis would worsen significantly in that circumstance. "This is a question of survival," LBJ insisted. "It is not public relations; it is a matter of survival for this country."

The Revenue and Expenditure Control Act of June 1968 gave the president his tax surcharge and produced a $6 billion cut in current-year spending, with more than double that scheduled for the following fiscal year. Notably, while domestic spending was slashed, military appropriations were protected by conservative legislators and continued to rise. Mills insisted that though he favored spending cuts, "I am certainly not talking about [Vietnam-related] expenditures. We simply have to do what is necessary there, whatever the cost as far as spending is concerned." Following that legislation, domestic outlays declined and revenues surged. The country even enjoyed a slight budget surplus in 1969—the last it would see for three decades. But inflation, which had gained momentum in 1967 and 1968, continued to climb.

Pulling Out

With reports on Vietnam casualties and the economy delivering a drumbeat of bad news through 1968, the Republicans won the White House and gained a few seats in Congress in the November elections. After he took office in 1969, President Richard M. Nixon presided over a gradual deescalation in Vietnam, removing 25,000 troops by the middle of 1969, another 90,000 later that year, and 150,000 in the spring of 1970. As the result of the Paris Peace accords, all American troops were withdrawn by the end of March 1973. Nixon's Vietnam policy sought, in the words of Henry Kissinger, his national security adviser, to disengage the United States in a way that did not "doom the millions who had relied" on American military support over the previous decade or lead to the impression of an "abject failure" that would "vindicate neo-isolationist trends at home."And Nixon "realized that for economic reasons the war was simply costing too much, and for the sake of domestic tranquility, he had to cut back on the American commitment to Vietnam."

The budget surplus in 1969, his first year in office, handed Nixon an opportunity to reduce taxes. The Tax Reform Act of 1969 extended Johnson's surcharge—at a rate of 5 percent—through June 1970, after which it was allowed to expire, but it also reduced the tax burden on low-income citizens, raised the personal exemption level, and increased the minimum standard deduction, thereby dropping large numbers of Americans from the tax rolls. The president then reduced military spending as a portion of GDP, from 8.7 percent in 1969 to 5.9 percent in 1973.

The economic damage, however, was already done. In 1970, inflation climbed to 5.5 percent, a legacy of delayed tax increases and spending cuts along with tardy tightening by the Fed. To stabilize the economy, Nixon imposed controls on prices and wages in 1971. But the measures were applied unevenly and caused major imbalances in the goods and commodities markets. Higher oil prices stemming from an Arab embargo and subsequent price hikes during and after the Arab-Israeli Yom Kippur War in 1973 accelerated the rise in inflation, which plagued the economy for the remainder of the decade.

In order to further limit U.S. activities in Vietnam, in 1974 Congress imposed legislative ceilings on the number of American personnel authorized to be in the country and cut off all military funding to the government of South Vietnam. Together, these actions contributed to the collapse of the

Saigon government and the fall of the capital to Communist forces on May 30, 1975.

Following the war, military spending dropped to 5.5 percent of GDP in the mid-1970s, but nonmilitary spending accelerated. A deficit spending mind-set had settled over the country in the 1960s and 1970s, and neither party appeared willing to reverse the trend. As Mills later put it, the "idea has developed over the years that everybody, whether he can afford it or not, is entitled to this and that, and if he can't afford it the government has to make it available." From 1975 through 1979, annual budget deficits exceeded $50 billion, considerably higher than during any of the Vietnam War years.

Congress was unwilling to raise taxes to keep pace with increasing domestic spending. Notably, during most of the 1950s, military outlays were double domestic civilian outlays, while during the Vietnam War, they were about even. During the Nixon administration, civilian spending was roughly double military spending and would remain so through much of the rest of the century.

★

Johnson was fixated on history. He dwelled on the fact that the financial demands of World War II had killed Roosevelt's New Deal and those of the Korean War had killed Truman's Fair Deal. But in the final analysis, LBJ could not protect his social programs either. When American troops are deployed on the battlefield, Americans tend to want to ensure that the military is well funded before supporting generous domestic programs. By tightly protecting domestic expenditures and refusing to make substantial spending cuts, Johnson allowed the budget deficit to get out of hand—and provoked a fight with Congress that essentially guaranteed that his dream for the Great Society would unravel. Johnson's stubborn stance against tax increases in 1965 and 1966, his refusal to level with the American people about the cost of maintaining both the Vietnam conflict and the Great Society, and years of confusing budget numbers and cost underestimates destroyed congressional and public trust in the president and his fiscal policies.

The lack of coordination within his administration deprived the president's economic advisers of the ability to give him timely advice to avoid the financial crisis that emerged, although given LBJ's reluctance to accept counsel he did not wish to hear, it is questionable whether he would have changed course any sooner. As it turned out, the economic official with the most information and the most courage—Fed chairman Martin—had little success in persuading LBJ to tackle the budget and inflation.

As during World War II, Congress played a decisive role in shaping the nation's fiscal policy. In the spirit of James Madison, it fulfilled its constitutional responsibility to exercise oversight and used its taxation and appropriation powers to force Johnson to change his economic and foreign policy. Of course, the Democratic Congress handled Nixon even more bluntly, cutting funding for the Vietnamese government altogether.

Johnson's dilemma was not unique during the Cold War. Two decades later, President Ronald Reagan faced a similar problem. In 1982, Congress balked at continuing to make available the additional sums of money he sought for his large military buildup. And it refused to further reduce social spending in order to free up additional funds for the military, forcing the president to accept higher taxes to narrow the yawning budget deficit.

8

Bankrupting Communism

THE REAGAN REARMAMENT AND DEFICIT FINANCE

> THE SOVIETS ENGAGED IN AN UNRELENTING BUILDUP OF THEIR
> MILITARY FORCES. THE PROTECTION OF OUR NATIONAL SECU-
> RITY HAS REQUIRED THAT WE UNDERTAKE A SUBSTANTIAL PRO-
> GRAM TO ENHANCE OUR MILITARY FORCES.
>
> —RONALD REAGAN

The Reagan years saw the greatest peacetime military buildup in American history, but Ronald Reagan did not see it as a time of peace. He fully considered the Cold War to be the strategic equivalent of the two world wars fought earlier in the century. After entering office, the president moved swiftly to express his long-held contempt for the Soviet Union. In his first press conference, on January 29, 1981, he stated that "during the course of the Cold War, [the Soviets] have openly and publicly declared that the only morality they recognize is what will further their cause, meaning that they reserve the right to commit any crime, to lie, to cheat." Confronted with what he considered to be a severe Soviet threat, Reagan concluded that a stronger American military was essential and, consequently, so was a great deal more defense spending.

At that time, most Americans shared his view. During the height of the Vietnam War, 52 percent of the U.S. public believed the country was spending too much on defense; similar figures were recorded in polls throughout the immediate post–Vietnam War period. But as the 1970s came to an end, the mood changed. Concerns about the Communist threat mounted after the Soviet Union invaded Afghanistan in December 1979 to preserve the pro-Soviet government that had been established by a coup the year before. Coupled with a perceived impotence in the Iran hostage crisis, during which Iranian student radicals held sixty-six U.S. diplomats and embassy staff hostage for over fourteen months, Americans were convinced that the country needed to project a tougher image to the world. A large majority felt the military had received insufficient resources during President Jimmy Carter's administration. Lou Cannon wrote in his biography *President Reagan: The Role of a Lifetime* that in 1981 "a consensus rare in American peacetime history favored . . . huge increases in military spending."

Reagan captured and articulated the new public sentiment in his first State of the Union address: "In the last decade, while we sought the moderation of Soviet power through a process of restraint and accommodation, the Soviets engaged in an unrelenting buildup of their military forces. The protection of our national security has required that we undertake a substantial program to enhance our military forces." Where the main thrust of American Cold War strategic doctrine since the 1950s had been containment, Reagan set out not simply to hold the line, but to roll back the Soviet Union's global influence and capabilities. In May 1982, the National Security Council decided on a strategy—laid out in National Security decision document 32—"to contain, and reverse the expansion of Soviet control and military presence throughout the world, and to increase the costs of Soviet support and use of proxy, terrorist and subversive forces." The NSC document asserted that the 1980s were likely to see "the greatest challenge to our survival and well-being since World War II." Reagan was fully prepared to mobilize whatever resources were necessary to meet this challenge and make this strategy succeed.

But obtaining funds for the military on a sustained basis proved to be a significant challenge in the latter part of the Cold War—and one very different from that of past twentieth-century wars. In previous conflicts, news from the front lines and the need to support troops in the field significantly affected the atmosphere in which major decisions on financing were made in the executive branch and in Congress and gave a sense of immediacy to the process. "Shooting wars" focused the attention of policymakers in ways that the less visible challenges of the late Cold War did not.

Building Up the Deficit

Military spending had begun to rise in the last two years of the Carter administration. In 1980 it rose by 20 percent, to nearly 5 percent of GDP, in response to the Soviet invasion of Afghanistan. Under Reagan, it climbed further, to a peak of 6.2 percent of GDP in 1986. Although nowhere near the high point of the Vietnam War, when military spending reached over 9 percent of GDP, the circumstances were now profoundly different. Vietnam had required the mass mobilization and dispatch, halfway around the world, of more than half a million troops for a prolonged conflict.

The fact that there was no compelling "hot war" to justify the boost in military spending when Reagan took office did not deter him from arguing for a bigger defense budget. He saw it as necessary for conducting a war of economic attrition that would, over time, diminish the Soviet Union's capacity to sustain a large and strategically potent military capability and to challenge America's global influence. During the 1980 campaign, he told the *Washington Post* that a military buildup would be "of great benefit to the United States" because "the Soviets were too weak economically to compete in an expanded arms race and would come to the bargaining table instead." He also believed there were compelling strategic reasons for such a buildup. James R. Schlesinger, who had served as secretary of defense under Richard Nixon and Gerald Ford, and Carter's director of Central Intelligence, Admiral Stansfield Turner, had informed him that the Soviets were spending more on their military than the United States. Turner reported that "all of the best studies have shown that the balance of strategic nuclear capabilities has been tipping in favor of the Soviet Union."

Reagan campaigned for the presidency on a platform that featured a strong commitment to substantially increase America's military strength. Proclaiming the need for a bold rearmament plan and equally bold tax cuts, he won a landslide victory and Republicans picked up a large number of seats in Congress. In 1980, they had been in a 58 to 41 minority (with one independent) in the Senate; the elections gave them control of the Senate for the first time in twenty-six years, by a 53 to 46 majority, and they picked up thirty-four seats in the House, although the Democrats retained the majority.

Upon assuming office, Reagan gave David Stockman, the director of the Office of Management and Budget (OMB), and Defense Secretary Caspar

Weinberger the primary roles in recommending how much Pentagon spending should grow. "A man of restless intellect and swiftly changing visions," Stockman had a "knack for putting deft and insightful budgetary analysis into political context." He had impressed Reagan when he served as a surrogate for John Anderson and then Jimmy Carter during preparations for the 1980 presidential debates. Weinberger had managed California's budget when Reagan was governor and had earned the nickname "Cap the Knife" for his zeal in cutting spending as OMB director in the Nixon administration.

In his biography *President Reagan: The Triumph of Imagination*, Richard Reeves recounted that Stockman and Weinberger initially agreed to a 7 percent increase in defense spending over Carter's budget. But Stockman had used Carter's 1980 budget figure as his baseline, while Weinberger had used Carter's proposed 1981 budget, which included a congressionally mandated 9 percent increase imposed after a failed effort to rescue the American hostages in Iran. In the event, Reagan pushed even further than Weinberger. In what he termed a "get well" package, he ordered a 12 percent increase in the 1981 budget and a 15 percent increase the following year.

Former president Richard Nixon urged Reagan to free up at least a portion of budgetary funds for his new military programs by reducing fraud and waste in the Defense Department. During his eight years as vice president, Nixon had doubtless heard Eisenhower insist on the need to impose spending discipline on the military, and he had worked toward the same goal during his own administration. Though Reagan sought to curb such practices in other departments, he ignored Nixon's advice. According to Cannon, he chose instead to keep "military spending in a separate mental compartment tucked safely away from his bedrock belief that government was inevitably inefficient." The president "exempted the Pentagon from the strictures on excessive spending imposed on other departments." That was something his Cold War predecessors Eisenhower and Truman never did.

Most Americans initially agreed with Reagan's emphasis on building a more robust military, even if it meant more spending. So did most members of Congress; the Senate approved the main features of the president's budget proposals along with substantial increases in military spending and cuts in domestic social programs by an 80 to 15 majority. The House upheld it 232 to 192. This major legislative victory for the president highlighted the bipartisan support his proposals initially enjoyed.

Taking the Supply Side

Americans were especially willing to support the president's bold rearmament plan because they were not asked to endure higher taxes to pay for it. On the contrary, they were treated to a significant tax cut, in the form of the Economic Recovery Act of 1981. The legislation was inspired by a 1977 bill sponsored by two leading Republican tax cut advocates: Congressman Jack Kemp, an early champion of supply-side economics who was also well known for his first career as a quarterback for the Buffalo Bills, and the chairman of the Senate Finance Committee, William "Bill" Roth of Delaware, a fiscal conservative who endeared himself to his constituents by appearing at his stump speeches accompanied by his mascot, a huge Saint Bernard dog. Kemp and Roth proposed an across-the-board 30 percent tax cut, phased in over three years; it called for lowering the top tax rate from 70 to 50 percent and the bottom rate from 14 to 10 percent. They argued that their initiative would provide a potent tonic for a country mired in "stagflation"—high inflation and sluggish growth. Kemp and Roth blamed stagflation on "tax bracket creep"; since wage increases awarded to compensate workers for higher prices pushed them into higher tax brackets, the government took more of their money even though their real (inflation-adjusted) wages remained at basically the same level. Allowing workers to keep a larger portion of their earnings, they contended, would enable them to hold on to more of the rewards from their efforts, and that, in turn, would boost productivity and growth.

Reagan modeled his dramatic first-year fiscal initiative on the Kemp-Roth plan. His initial proposal was to cut taxes by 30 percent over three years; it also called for establishing a cost recovery program for businesses designed to stimulate investment. The legislation that ultimately emerged from Congress lowered marginal tax rates for most Americans by an average of 25 percent over three years (5 percent in the first year and 10 percent in each of the next two). It also cut corporate taxes, provided incentives for increased savings, indexed individual income tax rates to prevent bracket creep, and improved depreciation rates for business. The legislation enjoyed bipartisan support; Republicans and moderate-to-conservative Democrats—including the group of Southerners known as "boll weevils," whose predecessors were part of the old Roosevelt New Deal coalition—came together to pass the bill by majorities of 89 to 11 in the Senate and 238 to 195 in the House. Administration officials

predicted that by stimulating job creation and investment, the tax cuts would generate enough additional revenue to compensate for the significant losses initially caused by the reduction in taxes. Reagan promised Americans that in future years the budget deficit would decline significantly even as tax rates were lowered and military spending escalated rapidly.

The Reagan tax cuts marked the culmination of growing public discontent with big government and the poor performance of the economy in the 1970s. They represented a new twist on the populist pressures for tax reform of the early years of the twentieth century. At that time, large numbers of Americans rebelled against the excessive concentration of wealth in the hands of a relatively few businessmen and financiers and the regressive taxes paid by the average citizen in the form of tariffs and excise taxes. This time, advocates of reform rebelled against what many Americans considered a bloated Washington bureaucracy as well as the high—some argued confiscatory and unjust—income taxes required to pay for it. The so-called welfare state had grown at a rapid pace since the 1960s, and the sprawling government bureaucracy it had created was expensive and inefficient. Perhaps more significantly, the public increasingly doubted the government's ability to remedy the nation's social problems and improve welfare by spending large sums of money. Shrinking the size, role, and cost of government—and especially reducing the onerous tax burden required to foot the bill—was a popular cause. For many Americans, cutting their taxes was a matter of simple justice.

Reagan understood this sentiment and felt it to his core. He was very much a Jeffersonian in his disdain for big government. It was anathema to him. In his first inaugural address, he bluntly stated that "government is not the solution to our problem; government is the problem." So, too, he believed, were the taxes needed to pay for it. He frequently commented on how, while making movies during World War II, he had paid out 91 percent of his salary to the government in taxes. On this issue, he was passionate. "It is a myth that our graduated tax system has any resemblance to proportionate taxation," he said. "The entire structure was created by Karl Marx. It is simply a penalty on the individual who can improve his own lot; it takes his earnings from him and redistributes them to people who are incapable of earning as much as he can."

The strongest advocates of tax cuts were members of a new cadre of supply-side economists and journalists who differed sharply from the pre-

vailing economic wisdom of the time, Keynesianism. Keynesians saw tax cuts as a device to stimulate growth in a weak economy, whereas supply-siders believed that tax cuts were desirable in virtually any circumstance—whether the nation was in a recession or not—to enhance the overall strength and productivity of the economy. Robert Bartley, who ran the editorial page of the *Wall Street Journal*, was a formidable proponent of that philosophy, arguing, as Andrew Mellon had in the 1920s, that large tax cuts would generate an economic boom that in turn would provide healthy increases in revenue flows. The supply-side doctrine was attractive to Reagan, who saw it as a way to dismiss the criticism that his tax cuts would lead to a dangerous increase in the budget deficit.

Not all Republicans, even within the administration, bought into supply-side thinking. Paul Volcker, then chairman of the board of governors of the Federal Reserve, described the administration's economic team as "an odd mixture of hard-boiled monetarists, 'supply-siders,' . . . and a few pragmatists." More traditional fiscal conservatives, who were barely visible in the White House yet constituted the majority of Republicans in the House and Senate, were enthusiastically supportive of tax cuts, but were at least as focused on slashing the growth in federal spending and reducing the deficit.

Reagan sought to pull his administration team and Republican congressional factions together in support of one policy. According to the *New York Times*, he "declared new guidelines for public policy that stress stimulating not demand [as Keynes preached] but production and supply, mainly by lowering business taxes, while relying on other measures—budget cuts and tight money—to rein in inflation." To cut domestic spending and the deficit, Reagan advocated "tighter eligibility rules and reduced spending on food stamps, student loans, aid to the arts, humanities, sciences, public service jobs." "The Reagan economic program, like the Reagan constituency and economic team," wrote William Niskanen, a member of the president's Council of Economic Advisers, "reflected a range of views on economic policies."

The controversy surrounding the president's motives in proposing aggressive tax cuts became a major source of political friction between Reagan and his critics. The 1981 act led to accusations from liberal Democrats that he was set on fulfilling the conservative goal of "starving the beast," cutting taxes to the point that the deficit would dry up funds for social spending. Opponents called it the "planned deficit" theory,

though Cannon, who then covered Reagan for the *Washington Post*, considered that a "wild assertion which does not withstand an examination of economic and political evidence." Planned or not, the deficits were enormous.

The Reagan tax cuts ultimately boosted growth and job creation and increased the portion of income taxes paid by the wealthy, as the president and supply-side advocates predicted, but they also produced shockingly large deficits, which they had not. Originally, the administration believed that, in the words of budget director David Stockman, "you could have a big tax cut and a big defense buildup, and still have a balanced budget by 1984," which Reagan promised would be followed by a big surplus. But it all depended on what the Reagan team playfully termed "Rosy Scenario." Reagan's economists, along with many in the private sector, had projected robust growth for 1982. Instead, the economy and revenues slumped. Throughout that year, the country was mired in a persistent recession—a term Reagan, who preferred euphemisms, never used, instead calling it a "soggy economy." Stockman privately projected that by 1984, "the tax cut and the defense buildup would create the greatest budget deficit in history, growing to $130 billion in that year alone." But as biographer Richard Reeves observed, Reagan was still projecting a "breezy optimism," stating publicly that the budget could be balanced by 1983, or at least by 1984.

As the deficit outlook deteriorated, so did the administration's fiscal credibility. In one short year, Reagan's public approval rating fell by 20 percent, and with it support for his military buildup. By 1982, 41 percent of Americans thought the United States was spending too much on the military; just 18 percent said it was spending too little. In this environment, a number of prominent Democrats and Republicans refused further support for Reagan's military-spending initiatives.

Alarmed at the rapidly climbing deficit, Stockman suggested that the administration reduce defense spending. Weinberger strenuously objected. So, too, did Reagan, who declared, in language Eisenhower might have used in the 1950s, that "if it comes down to balancing the budget or defense, the balanced budget will have to give way." Of course, Eisenhower would have also required tougher standards for making military spending decisions and objected to budget-busting tax cuts. Reagan did neither, and dismissed the suggestion that a portion of his recently passed tax cuts should be delayed.

One reason for Reagan's tenacity in pressing for high levels of defense

spending was his understanding that the Soviet Union was facing serious economic difficulties. On March 26, 1981, he wrote in his diary, "They are in very bad shape . . . and if we can cut off their credit they'll have to yell 'uncle' or starve." It was a fresh and correct assessment. Earlier in the Cold War, U.S. military and congressional leaders had expressed concern that the Soviets were attempting to bankrupt America by forcing the United States to spend so much on defense in the short term that its economy would be weakened and the public's will to devote large sums to the military in the long term would be broken. Later, Democrats suggested that under the Eisenhower administration the differential between Soviet and U.S. growth was so great that, if sustained, the Soviet Union's economy would surpass that of the United States in the 1980s. But new numbers supplied to Reagan by the CIA showed a "50 percent decline in the growth rate of the Soviet economy over the past thirty years."

Early on, Reagan had cast aside concerns—of the type Eisenhower had so often expressed—that massive defense spending would lead to large budget deficits and render the United States more vulnerable economically. If large U.S. military spending forced comparable outlays by Moscow, he believed, that was money well spent, as it would enfeeble the Soviet Union's economy to the point that the USSR would cease challenging American power or, better yet, collapse. He also believed that the same ends could be achieved by confronting the Soviets in the client states to which they were providing economic and political support, thus raising the cost of their actions.

Signed on May 20, 1982, NSC decision directive 32 described the administration's strategy of weakening the Soviet economy by "forcing the USSR to bear the brunt of its economic shortcomings." To this end, it called for an effort to "increase the cost of Soviet support and use of proxy, terrorist, and subversive forces," and thereby impose heavy new financial burdens on an already teetering Soviet economy. That strategy was also financially attractive because the costs were asymmetrical in America's favor; the Kremlin would have to spend far more money to prop up its client governments than the United States would to undermine them. A further step in weakening the Soviet economy was taken in March 1983, when the president announced that he was directing "a comprehensive and intensive effort to define a long-term research and development program to achieve our ultimate goal of eliminating the threat posed by strategic nuclear missiles," which came to be known as the "Strategic Defense Initiative" (SDI), or, as its detractors often referred to it, "Star Wars." SDI would be costly for the

United States, but Reagan concluded that it would also force the Soviets to ramp up their military spending significantly.

The economic attrition strategy was pursued further by the Director of Central Intelligence, William "Bill" Casey. Casey had rescued Reagan's presidential campaign from insolvency and, as a reward, the shrewd and tough-minded loyalist was put in charge of "cleaning up the CIA." He was a strong advocate of bolstering the human resources of the intelligence community and proposed stepping up covert American support for resistance movements against the Soviets in places such as Afghanistan, Angola, and Nicaragua. "We need to be backing these movements with money and muscle," Casey insisted. "If we can get the Soviets to expend enough resources, it will cause fissures in the system. We need half a dozen Afghanistans." The effort to weaken the Soviet economy was one of the defining features of the conduct of the Cold War under Reagan—and fraught with irony considering that four decades earlier many American officials believed that the Soviets were pursuing a similar approach to diminish the global role of the United States.

Casey's tactics were validated by the Soviet Union's difficulties in consolidating its hold on Afghanistan. As George Crile noted in his book *Charlie Wilson's War*, in April 1986 "the United States was escalating. . . . It was no longer clear that the Soviets could pay the price of this war." More broadly, he observed, "the Soviet economy was on the verge of collapse; it couldn't afford the expense of keeping up with Reagan's menacing nuclear and conventional arms race." General Valentine Varennikov, commander of the Red Army in Afghanistan, "was convinced that his own colleagues on the General staff . . . had virtually bankrupted the country. As he saw it, they had fallen into a U.S. trap of building totally unnecessary weapons systems that the country couldn't afford just because the United States was building them." That was precisely as the president and Casey had hoped.

The Congressional Challenge

Financial pressures were mounting in the United States as well. Republicans and Democrats began to balk at Reagan's budget numbers and his wildly optimistic deficit projections. In 1980, the deficit had been 2.7 percent of GDP; by 1982, it was 4 percent—and rising. Many thought the culprit was

increased defense spending. Although most Americans supported a larger Pentagon budget, doubts were being cast as to whether the administration's appropriations requests had been well thought out and whether they were supported by a compelling strategic rationale.

A significant source of trouble was the administration's inability to explain satisfactorily the relationship between its appropriations requests and its strategic objectives. Because this was not a shooting war, it was harder to sell a big run-up in military spending in the terms that had been employed during the two world wars or even Korea; the case had to be made by identifying the direct linkage between the Pentagon budget and specific strategic objectives, which often proved difficult to do. In the fall of 1982, the administration encountered difficulty in convincing the Republican-controlled Senate to appropriate funds to deploy an intercontinental ballistic missile known as the MX, or Peacekeeper. Senator Bill Cohen, a Maine Republican—flanked by Sam Nunn, a conservative Democrat from Georgia, and John Tower, an even more conservative Republican from Texas—explained to Reagan's national security adviser Robert "Bud" McFarlane, a veteran of the Marine Corps who previously had served as a deputy to Henry Kissinger, that "your problem is your witness." Defense Secretary Weinberger was not able to persuade the Senate Armed Services Committee to support the administration's request. Cohen said, "The secretary could never make a coherent case for how the appropriation request for specific systems and hardware correlates to your military strategy." The lack of clarity in the administration's reasoning behind its budget numbers was becoming apparent even to its congressional allies.

Republicans and Democrats alike also realized that the administration's deficit projections were way off the mark. As Reeves noted, many members of Congress concluded that "the president's numbers just had not added up." In 1982, the Congressional Budget Office (CBO) forecast $650 billion in deficits over the next three years. Fiscal conservatives, including the president's close friend Senator Paul Laxalt of Nevada, urged him to act promptly to narrow the gap. The Republican chairman of the Senate Finance Committee, Robert Dole of Kansas, announced his plan to introduce a bill to hike taxes. *Time* magazine's Lawrence Malkin reported that the chairman of the Senate Budget Committee, Pete Domenici of New Mexico, "warned the President that he had to raise taxes.... Domenici stated that 'you're just going to have to have some more revenue to pay for all those things that we want or don't have a prayer of getting rid of.' Reagan responded that he refused to accept 'the same kind of talk we've heard for forty years.' "

Unable to convince Republicans in Congress to accept his proposed budget for 1983, Reagan was forced to consider the economic trade-offs. In a July 1982 briefing paper prepared by the White House staff and marked "Extremely Confidential," he was informed that deficits were growing to dangerous levels: "The administration's fiscal program is in danger of pulling apart at the seams." It pointed out that the president's "national security buildup programmed for 1981 through 1985 now nearly doubles the Vietnam buildup" and that "our current long-term fiscal policy does not generate the tax resources to finance it even under ideal economic performance."

Tighter Monetary Policy

Public discontent over sky-high interest rates added to the pressures. The real interest rate on a corporate bond in 1982 was roughly 10 percent, compared with 4 percent at the height of the Vietnam War. The 4 percent figure (which had appeared disturbingly high to Americans at the time) had helped force President Johnson's hand on taxes and spending. Double-digit interest rates in the early 1980s, however, were hardly Reagan's fault. They resulted from the tough-minded efforts of the Fed chairman, Paul Volcker, to tame the inflation that had plagued the economy since the 1960s. Volcker, who had been appointed by Carter in 1979, significantly restrained growth in the money supply, causing U.S. interest rates to rise to levels unseen in the twentieth century. With the pain of high interest rates widely felt, he was roundly criticized for his assertive measures. Criticism came from the public, Congress, and within the administration—but not from Reagan. There were no theatrics or confrontations between the president and the chairman of the kind that had exploded between LBJ and William McChesney Martin Jr. in the 1960s.

The president was under pressure from the supply-siders to ditch Volcker. But Reagan understood the importance of the chairman's tough stance. As Peggy Noonan, special assistant to the president who was widely credited with a deep understanding of his views, observed, he "believed inflation was 'a thief in the night' and stopping it was a high priority." He judged Volcker's policy squeeze to be the best chance of achieving that objective. In addition, Reagan and his key advisers, James Baker and Richard Darman, were politically shrewd. Noonan noted that in refusing to join the criticism of Volcker, Reagan "showed his independence from the wilder eyed supply-siders . . . which was, among other things, reassuring to the economic establishment. And establishments matter." Reagan's willingness to go along with Volcker's policies produced enormous benefits; the rate of inflation fell from nearly 10 percent in 1981 to roughly 3 percent in 1988.

Despite being a deficit hawk, Volcker avoided a direct assault on Reagan's fiscal policies. In testimony before the House Committee on Banking, Finance, and Urban Affairs in the summer of 1982, he stated, "I certainly want to see some more action to reduce the deficits in coming years." But he did not take the bait of Democrats on the committee, who tried to persuade him to endorse their proposal for deferment of the last year of the 1981 income tax cut. Instead, Volcker suggested that Congress "reduce expenditures . . . or look to other forms of revenue raising."

The chairman's position was consistent with Reagan's. In repeated messages to Congress, the president urged tighter restraints on nonmilitary spending, taking on a Democratic Party heavily beholden to constituencies that demanded the creation and expansion of social programs. He was, to a certain degree, successful: nondefense outlays fell from 15 percent to 12.5 percent of GDP during his terms in office. Reagan also recognized that compromises had to be made on the revenue side to rein in the budget deficit, and he was willing to do his part—so long as that did not involve raising the income tax rate. He successfully thwarted Democratic efforts on that front, but went along with eliminating or reducing tax deductions, exemptions, and credits. This pragmatic approach was incorporated first in the Tax Equity and Fiscal Responsibility Act of 1982 (TEFRA) and then in the Deficit Reduction Act of 1984; they increased taxes, but did so in a way that was less visible to the average American than a boost in the marginal income tax rate.

Reagan justified the change in direction, or at least his support for congressionally initiated change, by referring to the increases as "tax reforms" or "revenue enhancers." They were sold as legislative refinements designed to increase equity and reduce corporate loopholes. The public largely accepted them; most Americans recognized that the deficit had to be reduced. In going along, Reagan tacitly acknowledged that his expanded military programs had to be paid for with increased taxes because he could not get support for significantly greater nondefense spending cuts.

Signed into law in September 1982, TEFRA was based on principles outlined by Senator Dole, a traditional fiscal conservative who was profoundly skeptical of supply-side economics and was a strong advocate of balanced budgets. It aimed to increase revenues by $99 billion over three years, and included higher levies on cigarettes, telephone calls (readopting the tax first applied during the Spanish-American War), travel, investment income, and certain business activities. Reagan was obliged to campaign actively for the legislation among Republicans because the Democratic Speaker of the House, Thomas "Tip" O'Neill, had laid down an ultimatum: the administration had to deliver a hundred votes in the House or the Democrats would not muster sufficient votes from their own members to pass it. As part of the brokered agreement, Democrats accepted a reduction in appropriation levels for a number of their pet domestic programs and Republicans pared back some of the president's defense spending initiatives. Reagan also supported other revenue-boosting initiatives. In November, he asked Congress to add five cents a gallon to the federal gas tax, a user fee to finance the government's bridge and highway repair program. This more than doubled the existing four-cent levy. The legislation was passed and signed the following March.

Having already accepted the need for tax increases, Reagan could have justified higher taxes to the American people by describing the costs of strengthening the military, rallying them to the need for sacrifices to pay the bill, as Wilson had done during World War I and Roosevelt during World War II. Instead, he turned to euphemisms, losing an opportunity to sell a tax increase in patriotic terms and to persuade Americans to buy into the notion that additional military spending was needed. Doing so might have headed off some of the later congressional cuts in defense spending.

At the same time, Congress and the administration set to work to restore solvency and public confidence in one of the most popular surviving programs of the New Deal: Social Security. The National Commission on Social Security Reform, headed by the former chairman of President Gerald R. Ford's Council of Economic Advisers (CEA), Alan Greenspan, recommended increasing the payroll tax and the retirement age as well as delaying the scheduled cost of living allowances for retirees. With substantial bipartisan agreement, Congress adopted Greenspan's proposals. The plan boosted revenue inflows and slowed the growth of payments to retirees, placing the system on a firmer footing.

The improvement in the Social Security system not only restored its solvency for several decades but, in the process, provided the government with a large pool of funds, in the form of an expanded Social Security surplus, that it could draw on to cover increases in the regular operating deficit. And American leaders did not hesitate to raid those funds on a regular basis, relieving the pressures on the president and Congress to slash the deficit.

By this time, even prominent figures within the White House accepted the need for further tax increases and spending cuts to reverse the dangerous budgetary trend. Voicing what was obvious to most, Martin Feldstein, a highly respected Harvard economist who was chairman of Reagan's CEA, told a group of reporters in February 1984, "We can't grow ourselves out of these deficits. . . . We're going to have to have the additional tax revenue, we're going to have to trim back on the size of defense authorizations, and we're going to have to have domestic spending cuts." Feldstein was quickly reprimanded by White House Chief of Staff James Baker, who insisted that administration officials religiously toe the administration line. But it would not be long before even the president had to admit the need for bolder action.

Within a few weeks, under pressure from congressional leaders, Reagan consented to another three-year deficit reduction package—the Deficit Reduction Act of 1984—aimed at increasing tax revenues by more than $50 billion and cutting spending by $11 billion, including a reduction in the Pentagon budget. Moderates in the Republican Party, led by Senate Majority Leader Howard Baker of Tennessee, had become increasingly distressed at the rising deficits and were instrumental in pushing through the legislation. They also resisted further deep reductions in social programs, sensing that the majority of Americans would not support them. Reagan accepted the need for the taxes but wanted bigger spending cuts.

Throughout the debate, Reagan was battling Tip O'Neill. Reagan had a close personal relationship with O'Neill, but they had entirely different political and spending philosophies. O'Neill warned, "We are not going to let [the Republicans] tear asunder programs we've built over the years," and groups such as the Congressional Black Caucus and organized labor prepared for combat. Yet Reagan knew when to compromise. The president was an old admirer of Roosevelt and, as a boy in Dixon, Illinois, had helped his father, who had been able to get a job during the Depression because of the New Deal, distribute leaflets supporting FDR. He was also a pragmatist who recognized the strong public support New Deal programs enjoyed and wanted to avoid a head-to-head confrontation with Congress on these issues. Against this backdrop, Reagan focused primarily on cutting "discretionary" spending programs that were left over from Johnson's Great Society. As he wrote in his diary, "The press is trying to paint me as trying to undo the New Deal. I'm trying to undo the Great Society." But he also ended up protecting some of LBJ's programs. He "ruled out cuts in two Social Security programs and any substantial reduction in five others: Medicare, veterans' benefits, school lunches, Head Start and summer youth jobs."

With so many programs protected and revenues as a portion of GDP running well below their levels of the early 1980s, the deficit remained disturbingly large through 1984 and 1985, troubling antideficit Republicans. The largest budget line was the Department of Defense. The call to reduce military spending further came from conservatives, liberals, and moderates alike. Congressman Dick Cheney, a Wyoming conservative, cautioned that if the president "doesn't cut defense spending he will become the No. 1 special pleader in town." He encouraged Reagan to "reach out and take a whack at everything to be credible." Unless he was willing to reduce Social Security or raise taxes, said Cheney, he had "to hit defense."

In 1985, the deficit hung stubbornly above 5 percent of GDP and more than 15 percent of the budget was devoted to paying interest on the federal debt, much of which had been accumulated during the Reagan administration. In April, the president addressed the nation, describing the progress he had made in shifting resources from domestic spending to defense. He insisted that the main reason for the accumulation of huge deficits was the cost of domestic programs.

That assertion did not square with the numbers. Nonmilitary spending fell from 15 percent of GDP in 1980 to roughly 13 percent during the mid-1980s, while the deficit rose from 2.7 percent to 5 percent of GDP. So domestic spending could hardly have been the main reason for the enormous fiscal imbalance. Of the several causes of the large deficits, the revenue shortfall due to the 1981 tax cut was the greatest.

Budget Reform

Having raised taxes twice, there was little congressional or executive branch appetite for another increase. The focus turned to broader fiscal reform. In the forefront of the process were Republican senators William Philip "Phil"

Gramm of Texas and Warren Rudman of New Hampshire and Democratic senator Ernest "Fritz" Hollings of South Carolina. Gramm, a former economics professor, had supported Reagan's tax cuts in 1981, when he was a Democratic member of the House. He then switched to the Republican Party and was elected to the Senate in 1984. Rudman and Hollings, army veterans of Korea and World War II, respectively, were passionate advocates of budget reform. The focus of these three senators was not directly on tax increases or spending cuts, but on creating an "automatic" formula to eliminate deficits over time.

The product of their work was the Balanced Budget and Emergency Deficit Control Act of 1985 (better known as the Gramm-Rudman-Hollings Act), which aimed to balance the budget in six years by establishing annually declining deficit targets. If the deficit exceeded the target in a given year, automatic spending cuts, called "sequesters," would kick in. This meant that unless the president and Congress could agree on legislation that would produce a deficit below the target level, an across-the-board percentage cut in all discretionary programs would be automatically imposed to meet the required target. Defense and nondefense programs were to be cut by roughly the same percentage.

It was a rare example of bipartisan legislation, worked out between a Democratic House and a Republican Senate, that satisfied both sides, though for very different reasons. Because roughly half of the automatic sequesters would be in the defense budget, the Democrats believed they would "force the president to choose between punishing cuts in the Pentagon budget or a long-resisted boost in tax revenues" and that he would choose the latter. The Republicans, on the other hand, were convinced that the sequesters would give the "president the leverage to crunch . . . domestic programs down to the size he always intended." The *Baltimore Sun* despaired: "What's especially striking is that these views pass each other in the dark, with no one knowing which . . . will prevail."

That year, another event took place that would have an even greater impact on the future American budget than the Gramm-Rudman-Hollings Act. In March 1985, the Soviet president, Konstantin Chernenko, died and was replaced by Mikhail Gorbachev—who promptly began a policy of *glasnost* (opening) and *perestroika* (restructuring). He was to be Reagan's main interlocutor in the waning days of the Cold War. He recognized, as he later explained, that "in the eyes of the people, especially the educated . . . the totalitarian system had run its course morally and politically. People were waiting for reform" and that the Soviet system and its ability to compete with the United States in the arms race were unsustainable.

The Gramm-Rudman-Hollings Act became the high-water mark of fiscal cooperation between Congress and the administration during the period. However, its enforcement mechanism was found to be unconstitutional and it had to be redrafted. A new version, engineered in 1987 by the now fully Democratic Congress, extended the deadline for eliminating the deficit to 1993. It also exempted a larger number of domestic programs, which meant a greater portion of any sequesters would come from defense. The legislation also modified the formula to regulate how cuts could be made within individual departments.

A reluctant Reagan signed the bill, largely because it included an increase in the national debt ceiling that was required to keep the government open for business. But he blasted Congress for attempting to set a "trap" by "telling me that we must pay for its uncontrolled domestic spending by endangering our national security or by raising your taxes, or both." He vowed that he would "not allow the American people to be blackmailed into higher taxes." He declared, "To those who say we must weaken America's defense: They're nuts. To those who say we must raise the tax burden on the American people: They're nuts." (He was alluding to a message sent by American commander General Anthony McAuliffe when he was asked to surrender to the Germans during the Battle of the Bulge and defiantly responded, "Nuts.") Reagan then insisted that the right response was "to cut the excesses from the domestic budget, to impose on the domestic budget, once and for all, a sense of responsibility." The president never had to make tough choices because deficits during the latter years of his administration did not exceed the target levels at which the automatic sequesters would kick in.

As disinclined as Reagan was to slice defense spending further, he ultimately succumbed to necessity. In 1987, the country saw its first $1 trillion budget and total debt rose to over $2 trillion. In the fall, Frank Carlucci replaced Weinberger as defense secretary and, to the irritation of the military commanders, set about chopping more money from the Pentagon's budget. Carlucci recognized that under the tenure of "Cap the Knife," the knife had not been very sharp nor had it been wielded very much, so that a lot of uneconomic and unnecessary spending had taken place. He focused primarily on reducing personnel levels and cutting what he considered to be unnecessary weapons and ships, although he provided a healthy sum for the president's Strategic Defense Initiative. But Democratic majorities in Congress wanted even further reductions. They passed a bill that denied Reagan a substantial portion of the SDI budget and placed restrictions on funding for space-based interceptors, a key component in the program. The president vetoed the bill. Ultimately, Congress and the White House reached a compromise that dropped the restrictions on the interceptor but retained the cuts on SDI. With deficits remaining high, the president was forced to swallow this bitter pill. From 1987 onward, military spending declined as a portion of GDP. It was difficult for the administration to sustain high levels of Pentagon spending in the presence of budgetary problems and the absence of the kind of patriotic support for military appropriations that would normally be evident during a hot war. Yet the results of earlier U.S. military spending were now becoming clear; in December 1987, Reagan and Gorbachev signed the Intermediate Range Nuclear Forces (INF) treaty, which eliminated these nuclear missiles.

The 1980s marked the first time in American history that the ratio of debt to GDP had increased in peacetime—or, depending on one's perspective, in a period without a "hot war." The ratio grew from 26 percent in 1980 to 42 percent in 1989, compared to a peak of 34 percent at the height of troop deployment during the Vietnam War. Though taxes were raised substantially in 1982 and 1984 and the revenues they produced, coupled with economic growth, helped to reduce budget imbalances in the latter years of the administration, they remained at a still-high 3 percent of GDP in 1988. The significant spending cuts the president constantly requested did not take place on the scale that he and conservative Republicans in Congress had hoped for. The best he could achieve was a reduction in nonmilitary spending of 2.5 percent of GDP. Truman had engineered a reduction of 4 percent during the early 1950s, but then the country had been fighting a hot war and the public was willing to make sacrifices; support for social spending had also grown markedly since that time. More aggressive domestic spending cuts were blocked primarily by Speaker O'Neill and other liberal Democrats, but also by moderate Republicans. But Reagan never lost sight of his objective: in 1987, he vetoed a transportation bill because it contained 152 earmarked projects inserted by members of Congress for their local constituencies.

Debtor to the World

Since World War I, the United States had been the world's largest creditor nation. Under the weight of the Reagan administration's budget deficits, it became the world's largest borrower and debtor, a decisive shift in the country's external balances. A rise in the dollar's exchange rate, caused in part by high interest rates, reinforced this shift by reducing the international competitiveness of American goods. The foreign money came largely from Western Europe. The turning point was not missed by the ninety-year-old former Conservative prime minister of Great Britain, Harold Macmillan. During his lifetime, his country had been a major lender to, and then a major borrower from, the United States. Commenting in the House of Lords on the Reagan deficits, Macmillan noted that the president had "broken all the rules" by cutting taxes while increasing defense spending. "They have had the sense," he observed admiringly, "to make somebody else pay for it. In a word, Reagan has called in resources from the old world to finance the expansion of the new."

Early in the administration, the net international investment position of the United States was a positive $360 billion; in 1988, it was a negative $198 billion. The consequences of heavy dependence on foreign capital became clear on October 19, 1987, known as "Black Monday," when the Dow Jones Industrial Average dropped 508 points. A number of factors caused the market to tumble, including the announcement of a large trade deficit, the suggestion by Treasury Secretary James Baker—who had moved from the White House to that job in 1985—that the dollar would have to fall further to correct it, and Baker's criticism of Germany for not doing enough to reduce its trade surplus. These events persuaded some investors that the recently cobbled arrangements among the major industrialized nations to stabilize the currency markets would unravel, which would cause the dollar to plummet, foreigners to withhold or withdraw investments in U.S. securities, and American bond prices to drop sharply. Such apprehensions badly rattled investor confidence.

America's heavy dependence on external capital in the late 1980s would have been familiar to Hamilton, who emphasized the special effort necessary to maintain the confidence of foreign creditors; he would have been disappointed to see that Reagan administration officials seemed little concerned about the budget deficits.

★

President Carter spent $160 billion on defense in his last full year in office. In his last year, Reagan had doubled that. All told, Reagan's defense budgets came to over $1.5 trillion. A strong case can be made that military spending and the tough negotiating approach of the Reagan administration shortened the duration of the Cold War. Reagan saw, more clearly than most, the deep economic and political flaws in Soviet Communism and the importance of a resolute U.S. approach to Moscow's repressive policies and its abuses of human liberties. But a crucial financial question is whether the end of the Cold War could have been achieved without the massive budget deficits and a tripling of the publicly held national debt—from $711 billion to $2.1 trillion—during the Reagan administration. If one accepts Gorbachev's explanation, internal factors were primarily responsible for his desire to develop a new relationship with the West. But, at the same time, the Red Army's top general in Afghanistan said that the Soviet Union's attempts to match the American military buildup had a decisive impact on its economic strength; consequently, the Kremlin's inability to sustain the arms race must have also played a key role. But even if the high costs of SDI and other components of Reagan's weapons program were necessary to end the Cold War, deficits could have been better controlled through a less aggressive initial tax cut, greater reductions in entrenched social programs by Congress, and more rigorous privatization and discipline in defense budgeting.

Initially, Reagan's fiscal policies commanded widespread support and helped to boost growth and job creation. Yet they also produced major imbalances. The frequent shifts in the administration's tax policy reflected contradictions in economic philosophy within the White House and among Republicans in Congress. Looking back over the 1980s, Paul Volcker observed that "the more starry-eyed Reaganauts argued that reducing taxes would provide a kind of magic elixir for the economy that would make the deficits go away or at least not matter." The "elixir" did not work. From 1983 through 1989, annual deficits exceeded $150 billion. The highest, in 1983, amounted to 6 percent of GDP. Even in 1984, when the country recorded an impressive 7.6 percent growth rate, the deficit was nearly 5 percent of GDP, well above the peak recorded during the Vietnam War, when Johnson was harshly criticized for fiscal irresponsibility. As a percentage of GDP, deficits were higher than any seen since World War II. In addition, the supply-side tax cuts disappointed on other grounds. As *BusinessWeek* columnist Michael Mandel later wrote, "Rather than increasing savings, as the supply-side advocates had hoped, the national savings rate had dropped. And business spending on equipment hardly rose, despite a strong recovery."

When Reagan was obliged to acquiesce to tax increases, he failed to argue that they were a patriotic sacrifice. It is far from clear whether the president's failure to address the revenue problem more forthrightly was due to a lack of political courage or a false hope that growth would ultimately solve the problem. He certainly had the political courage to go along with Volcker's highly controversial approach to curtailing inflation. Yet he never confronted the American people with the equally stark need for increased taxes to pay for military spending and to reduce the budget deficit when it became clear that cuts in civilian spending would not do it alone. It is plausible that he recognized that without the compelling pressures of a shooting war, making the case for tax increases would have been a lot more difficult than it was for Roosevelt or Truman. In the final analysis, key presidential advisers believe that Reagan had such a visceral distaste for taxes that he simply could not bring himself to make the case for any increase, of any kind, on any grounds. He profoundly believed that Americans had been overtaxed for decades.

By redefining populism, Reagan also changed the way the administration approached the financing of his defense buildup. At the outset of World War I and World War II, national leaders believed that a substantial portion of military costs had to be paid for by higher taxes, mostly on businesses and wealthy individuals. Because Reagan cut taxes for both of these groups and was unable to reduce domestic programs enough to fill the gap, most of the additional military spending had to be covered with borrowed money. Moreover, by promoting a supply-side approach to fiscal policy at the outset of the administration, Reagan's officials did not feel they had to make the kind of hard choices that Lyndon Johnson confronted in 1967 and 1968. Their assumption that the tax cut would essentially pay for itself and shortly produce surpluses enabled them to duck the responsibility for setting fiscal priorities. When reality struck, they found this hard to do.

During the more tranquil periods of Cold War, the country lacked a broad and sustained consensus on the degree and severity of the Soviet threat. World War II had produced a heightened spirit of national unity in support of large military budgets, big tax increases, and sharp domestic spending cuts. In contrast, public opinion on military spending and how to obtain funds to support it was sharply divided during much of the Cold War; that was true during the latter years of the Reagan administration when U.S.-Soviet tensions flared up only occasionally. Americans often were split over

the proper size of the Pentagon's budget and how to pay for it. During the 1980s, these issues were thrashed out in a highly disorderly and often highly partisan way. But, in the end, Reagan achieved most of his grand designs. In addition to undermining the Soviet Union's ability to continue the Cold War, he made it far more difficult for subsequent Congresses or presidents to raise taxes, as his vice president, George H. W. Bush, would soon discover.

Within a year of Reagan's departure from the White House, the Berlin Wall had fallen; within four years, the Soviet Union was officially dissolved. A meaningful portion of the credit for that collapse and for ending the Cold War on terms favorable to the United States appropriately belongs to Reagan, but a significant portion must be more broadly shared. Former president Gerald Ford, who as a Republican leader in Congress early in the Cold War supported the internationalist defense and foreign assistance policies of several administrations, put the U.S. success in historical perspective. "I feel very strongly," he observed, "that our country's policies, starting with Harry Truman and those who followed him—Democratic and Republican presidents and Democratic and Republican Congresses—brought about the collapse of the Soviet Union."

Notwithstanding periods of obvious excess, U.S. fiscal policy following World War II generated the resources and contributed to the underlying growth and stability in the American economy that enabled the country to prevail in the Cold War. The United States mobilized enormous sums that enabled the Pentagon to contain Soviet expansionism for over forty years. But America's success was due not only to its military strength. Following World War II, America also financed the colossal costs of reconstruction in Europe and the Pacific, enabling former enemies to prosper, join the democratic, free-market world, and become U.S. allies. The economies and societies of many nations vulnerable to Communist-sponsored insurrections received large amounts of U.S. aid. The North Atlantic Treaty Organization (NATO) bolstered American and allied security. The World Bank, the International Monetary Fund, and the General Agreement on Tariffs and Trade promoted U.S. and global prosperity. In time, these efforts permitted America to spread the costs and responsibilities for containing the Soviet Union among other countries.

Throughout the Cold War, the United States enjoyed robust domestic economic growth, job creation, and expansion of economic opportunity. It avoided the trap that its early Cold War leaders feared: economic decline triggered by unsustainable defense spending. However, these very fears served a purpose; they had created a cautious approach to defense spending under Truman and Eisenhower. After that, the checks and balances that are so central to the American political system, forces that since the time of Jefferson and Madison have curbed military spending in the absence of a compelling threat, reasserted themselves periodically, reining in excesses. The Soviets had no checks, balances, or restraints. In the end, the USSR undermined its already struggling economy by trying to match American arms spending. Reagan read the situation in the Soviet Union correctly and understood that in the 1980s the Communist system was becoming dysfunctional because of its inherent economic and political flaws. These, he correctly anticipated, would force the Soviet Union to end its participation in the arms race and its support for regimes that sought to undermine U.S. interests.

However, Reagan's fiscal legacy is mixed. His string of deficits and debt accumulation left the country more vulnerable financially. Had the 9/11 attacks taken place a decade earlier, around the time of the truck bombing of the World Trade Center in 1993, the country would have had far less room in the budget to stimulate the economy, finance reconstruction, fight a war in Afghanistan, and pay for the war on terrorism at home. On the other hand, the collapse of the Soviet Union allowed a steep reduction in American military spending, from 6 percent of GDP in the mid-1980s to 3 percent a decade later. That enormous peace dividend contributed significantly to the budget surpluses the country enjoyed at the end of the 1990s, and these surpluses would in turn give President George W. Bush great financial latitude to respond to Al Qaeda's attacks in 2001.

9

New Enemies

ASYMMETRICAL THREATS AND THE LONG WAR ON TERRORISM

AMERICANS SHOULD NOT EXPECT ONE BATTLE, BUT A LENGTHY
CAMPAIGN, UNLIKE ANY WE HAVE EVER SEEN.

—GEORGE W. BUSH

In August 1990, an unusual meeting took place at the White House. President George H. W. Bush called together his National Security Council to consider how to finance America's coming effort to liberate the oil-rich country of Kuwait, which had just been invaded by Iraq. The meeting was strikingly different from White House gatherings held during previous wars. In the conflicts of the nineteenth and twentieth centuries, the Treasury had to raise virtually all of the necessary funds from American sources. During the two world wars, it even had to finance a considerable amount of the military needs of America's allies.

Now, the United States was planning to ask its coalition allies—Kuwait itself, its wealthy neighbors, and the major industrialized nations that were heavily dependent on Middle East oil—to assume a large share of the Gulf War's costs. The NSC decided that Secretary of State James Baker and Treasury Secretary Nicholas Brady should visit Europe, the Middle East, and Asia to persuade "our allies and friends [to] help defray our defense costs." Bush called it the "tin cup" mission.

At the time, America's intervention was highly controversial, with several influential members of Congress opposed to committing U.S. forces in what was seen as another region's territorial dispute. Further, following the Soviet Union's collapse, many Americans believed that the United States would not need to get involved in another major war anytime soon. Strong voices also argued that, with a large budget deficit, the country could not afford the multibillion-dollar cost of the exercise.

The Cold War as it evolved during the Reagan era presented one face of post–World War II conflict, one that directly affected American strategic interests, but with no direct military engagement. The Gulf War, during the administration of President George H. W. Bush, presented another, one with a clearly defined battlefield but a less direct threat to U.S. strategic interests. The international military coalition forged by President Bush, a UN vote that endorsed his actions, and substantial foreign financial contributions played key roles in creating and sustaining support for carrying out the president's promise to evict Iraqi forces from Kuwait. The conflict demonstrated the financial value to the United States of building strong coalitions and obtaining international legitimacy for its military actions, both of which encouraged other nations to pay a large portion of the costs.

When the United States was preparing to go to war with Iraq again, in early 2003, President George W. Bush assembled a coalition that, except for a handful of countries, did not play a major military role, and there was no affirming UN vote. The war was seen as largely a unilateral American effort supported by a few allies, and no Islamic nations were directly involved. Nor was there a real prospect that coalition members would contribute to the Pentagon's expenses. And there was yet another difference. While President George H. W. Bush had contained civilian spending during the Gulf War and raised taxes to relieve building fiscal pressures, George W. Bush pressed for a large multiyear tax cut and Congress voted for significant nonsecurity spending increases during the Iraq War.

At the outset of most major U.S. military engagements in the twentieth century (with the obvious exception of the Vietnam War), Congress and the White House engaged in a reassessment of American fiscal policy to help muster the resources needed to meet additional wartime expenditures. Although massive borrowing was required, efforts were made to limit that through spending and tax adjustments. In the early stages of the Iraq War, however, the American people were assured that the cost would be low, and no reassessment or resource reallocation took place. The administration also cast aside worries about the potential bill for postwar reconstruction, promising that Iraqi oil revenues would defray much of the expense. Accordingly, both the Bush administration and its allies in Congress downplayed the budgetary implications of going to war or securing the country against terrorists.

Initially, American officials found it relatively easy to sidestep questions about tax increases and nondefense spending cuts. While military appropriations in 2003, in inflation-adjusted terms, were roughly the same as during the high defense spending years of the Korean and Vietnam Wars, the exponential growth of the U.S. economy over the previous half century meant the figure amounted to a far smaller portion of the nation's GDP than in the 1950s or 1960s. Military outlays were roughly 15 percent of GDP during the peak of the Korean War and 10 percent during the most intense years of the Vietnam War, but only 4 percent at the outset of the Iraq War.

As it was fighting in Iraq, the United States was also engaged in a broader war, which the Pentagon refers to as the "Long War" on terrorism. It bears certain financial similarities to the Cold War in that it requires a long-term commitment of resources. But the competition for those resources will be much more intense than during the Cold War. Agencies charged with protecting America's security against terrorists seeking nuclear, chemical, or biological weapons will have to compete for budgetary resources with entitlement programs that will cost trillions of dollars over the coming decades. While military outlays were the major driver of government spending early in the Cold War, the Pentagon's portion of the budget has steadily receded. The driving force has become Social Security, Medicaid, and Medicare—and their costs will mushroom as the 79 million post–World War II baby boomers retire and draw benefits. Unchecked, these programs will crowd out discretionary spending, of which the largest portion is for the military, and will limit the government's flexibility to reallocate resources to meet urgent security threats.

This fiscal reality—so different from the challenges of the previous century—has yet to intrude on national life. It appears to have played only a limited role in the way President George W. Bush and Congress have structured taxes and spending policy during the Iraq War and positioned the country to meet the financial challenges of the war on terrorism.

Mobilizing Foreign Money

On August 2, 1990, Iraqi president Saddam Hussein's troops invaded Kuwait. Five days later, President George H. W. Bush launched Operation Desert Shield, a deployment of U.S. naval and air forces to deter a subsequent invasion of Saudi Arabia and began preparations to liberate Kuwait. In late August, the National Security Council decided on its plan to obtain foreign funding to pay for American military costs and to aid countries such as Egypt, Jordan, and Turkey, whose trade was adversely affected by the economic sanctions imposed on Iraq by the United Nations.

Estimates of the costs of the coming war came to tens of billions of dollars. As Bush later wrote, "Congress demanded to know who else was going to put up money for Gulf defense efforts and how much." Legislators pressed the administration to obtain guarantees of substantial contributions from other nations. The president later noted that their insistence "reflected a widespread domestic feeling that we were doing the lion's share of work in responding to Saddam and were acting on behalf of the world's interests, not just our own." He agreed that this was "not an unreasonable position" given concerns in the United States about the size of the budget deficit, which was running at close to 4 percent of GDP. Political capital at home was to be gained by securing financial capital abroad.

For five months, the administration and Congress grappled with the question of whether to launch an effort to push Iraqi forces out of Kuwait. A heated public debate took place as well. Many Americans opposed military intervention, fearing large numbers of casualties from chemical weapons attacks. Saddam was known to have used poison gas on separatist Kurds in the north of Iraq and on Iranian troops. Opponents of going to war advocated reliance on UN sanctions to force Iraq to leave Kuwait, but Bush had no faith in the effectiveness of sanctions, pointing out that there was little evidence that they had any impact.

With no sign that Saddam would retreat, the president launched Operation Desert Storm on January 16, 1991, to preserve the principle, as he put it, that "no nation will be permitted to brutally assault its neighbor." After a massive air campaign, the United States and its allies launched an all-out ground assault. More than 540,000 American troops were deployed to the Persian Gulf region to serve alongside 270,000 coalition troops—the largest collective deployment of land troops and air power since World War II. They confronted roughly 550,000 Iraqi soldiers in and around Kuwait. The coalition made quick work of the Iraqis; a mere one hundred hours after the land war commenced, resistance collapsed and Kuwait was liberated. On February 27, Bush called a cease-fire and a halt to American advances.

The war was brilliantly executed and brilliantly financed. In the end, most of the bill for the incremental cost of America's participation was paid by coalition partners: of the $61 billion spent by the United States, more than $48 billion was repaid—in cash—by foreign governments, notably Kuwait, Saudi Arabia, Japan, Germany, and South Korea. These nations also made "in-kind" contributions of equipment, fuel, and other supplies amounting to nearly $6 billion and provided assistance to poorer countries of the region whose economies had been hurt by lost trade and the cutoff of Iraqi oil due to the sanctions against Saddam's regime. As Bush later observed of the economic assistance, "It was not initially planned that way, but it worked out that way because of the nature of the coalition."

Twenty-five nations participated in the Gulf War coalition, including a number in the Arab world. Iraq had attacked a neighboring state, and oil-producing nations in the area had strong reasons to support, both militarily and financially, American efforts to prevent Iraqi forces from moving south into Saudi Arabia, to force Saddam's troops out of Kuwait, and to protect the neighborhood from future Iraqi incursions. America's non–Middle East allies had a similar interest in a U.S. military success and provided considerable amounts of funding. The war proved to be an object lesson that effective coalition building was good fiscal policy as well as good security policy. And UN backing for the war created legitimacy in the minds of many nations, which encouraged their contributions of troops and funds.

The Budget Confrontation

As the war was unfolding, George Bush was also grappling with a large budget deficit. At his initiative, Congress and the administration launched a renewed attack on it in 1990, and that would turn out to have an important impact on fiscal policy during and after the war.

Bush had come into office in January 1989 with a commitment to fiscal responsibility. Richard Darman, who had been assistant to the president and deputy secretary of the Treasury under Reagan and was highly regarded for his financial and budget expertise, spearheaded the effort as Bush's budget director. In a widely publicized speech at the National Press

Club, he condemned what he termed "now-now-ism," including the failure
to invest adequately for the future, the failure to restrain the predictable
growth of entitlements, and the failure to limit the use of long-term debt to
finance consumption. Bush and Darman agreed that large deficits undermined domestic and foreign confidence in America's fiscal governance.

In his budget message to Congress less than a week after his inauguration, Bush called for the formation of a "special leadership group" aimed at
reducing the 1990 deficit by 40 percent and meeting the targets in the
Gramm-Rudman-Hollings Act. He also extended an olive branch to the
Democrats. Their support was essential to any solution, since they held a 55
to 45 majority in the Senate and a 260 to 175 majority in the House. In
keeping with his campaign promises, the president vowed not to raise
taxes. However, at the urging of Democrats he agreed to freeze the defense
budget for one year and to increase spending for some social programs.

But the discord that had surrounded budget issues during the latter part
of the Reagan administration carried over into the Bush presidency. Although the bipartisan leadership group agreed in principle on a series of
measures to cut nearly $30 billion in spending, the Democratic Congress
failed to enact many of the reductions that its leaders had promised. Early
projections for 1991 were alarming; the Congressional Budget Office anticipated a deficit of $130 billion, more than double the Gramm-Rudman-
Hollings target of $64 billion. Later, it projected a deficit of more than $230
billion.

Allowing the sequesters to kick in would have devastated the budgets
of most agencies. Yet if Congress could not agree on other ways to produce
substantial deficit cuts or on an alternative to the Gramm-Rudman-Hollings
legislation, the sequester provisions would automatically take effect, depriving most government departments of large sums of money and forcing
them to shut down many functions. The president, as Darman later recounted, "did not believe that the political system would allow such a dire
outcome to occur, in what amounted to a 'game of chicken.'"

Bush originally hoped that the threat of massive government disruption would force Congress to agree to a comprehensive deficit reduction
plan. When Congress balked, he called for talks with its leaders in an attempt to find a responsible alternative to the sequesters. The Democrats
agreed to go along, but insisted on a precondition—that the president accept a tax increase as one component of a final package.

Congress felt it had the White House over a barrel. Both sides recognized that to avoid a sequester and achieve meaningful deficit restraint, entitlement spending had to be controlled. But Democrats would not agree to that unless the president accepted a tax increase, and most Republicans dared not take the political risk of cutting entitlements without the cover of Democratic support. Bush had to make some accommodation with the Democrats, who drove a tough bargain, challenging the Republicans to first produce a program that could avoid a sequester without raising taxes or cutting entitlements. If the Republicans supported either of these measures, the Democrats would exact a high political price; if they did not, Republicans would have to bear the costs—substantive and political—of appearing to cause the sequesters to kick in. The debate between the White House and Congress in 1990 was almost a mirror image of that between Lyndon Johnson and Wilbur Mills in the mid-1960s. Then, Mills insisted on spending cuts and Johnson wanted tax increases; this time, Bush wanted spending cuts and Congress insisted on tax increases.

For several weeks, negotiations proceeded at a torpid pace. Pressure for a budget deal intensified when Federal Reserve board chairman Alan Greenspan told the administration that he "would pursue tight monetary policies until a meaningful deficit reduction package was enacted." To break the impasse, the president met with bipartisan leaders of Congress in June to give a push to the stalled negotiations. That group released a general statement that put everything on the table for further negotiation, noting that "both the size of the deficit problem and the need for a package that can be enacted require all of the following: entitlement and mandatory program reform, tax revenue increases, orderly reductions in defense expenditures, and budget process reforms." Two of these four elements were of great importance to the Republicans and had not previously been agreed to by the Democrats—mandatory program reform and budget process reform. But a group of anti-tax Republicans saw the reference to "tax revenue increases" as a betrayal of the president's pledge of "no new taxes" and reacted with bitter attacks.

Negotiations were still under way in August when Saddam's army invaded Kuwait and American forces were deployed to the region. At this point, members of the Bush national security team became extremely concerned about the possible use of the defense sequester, and their concerns leaked. That weakened the administration's hand in the game of chicken it was playing with Congress. It was clear to legislators that the administration had to make a deal. President Bush saw it the same way. "When push came to shove and our troops were moving overseas," he recalled, "we needed a fully functioning government. I simply had to hammer out a compromise to keep the government open, but I paid a terrible price."

In late September, the president and Democratic congressional leaders reached an agreement on comprehensive deficit reduction. They floated a new legislative proposal, aimed at slashing the deficit by $500 billion over a five-year period, that included modest tax increases (although not on individual incomes), substantial reductions in entitlements, and a cut in defense spending. On October 5, the resolution containing the bipartisan agreement was voted down in the House by an alliance of conservative Republicans, who resented the tax increases, and liberal Democrats, who complained that a number of the taxes, particularly one on energy, and the cuts in social spending hit low-income Americans too hard. Leading the charge for the conservative Republicans was House Whip Newt Gingrich, who had been part of the negotiating group but who then disagreed with the outcome. As the president later wrote, "I was very disappointed that one of our top leaders in Congress . . . very influential with the Republican right, at the last minute backed away from a compromise he had all but agreed to."

Congress soon passed a "continuing resolution" to keep the government open and suspend the Gramm-Rudman-Hollings sequester for another week. Upping the ante, Bush vetoed it, saying that Congress should devote its energy to passing an acceptable budget compromise. The House failed to override by six votes, and the government was forced to shut down over the Columbus Day weekend. A few days later, Congress passed a new budget resolution that called for less of a reduction in entitlements and greater tax increases, and thus was able to attract more Democratic support. With a compromise in sight, Congress passed and the president signed a series of continuing resolutions to keep the government running.

The outcome of this convoluted and painful process was the Omnibus Budget Reconciliation Act of 1990, finally passed at the end of October. It contained modest restraints on entitlements, but far less than the ill-fated September compromise. Much to the anger of conservative Republicans, it also contained tax increases, including a small hike in marginal rates on high-income taxpayers. As Darman later wrote, the tax increases only amounted to one-fifth of the package and "were less than half the size of the tax increases signed by President Reagan in 1982." Though the legislation was expected to reduce the deficit by roughly $480 billion over the following five years, a weak economy caused the deficit to widen rather than narrow, reaching 4.7 percent of GDP in 1992.

Darman observed that although the administration "had very much wished that we could use the across-the-board sequester as a means to force a satisfactory resolution of the budget debate, as events developed, in the context of Gulf War preparations . . . attempting to use sequester would simply result in calling our own bluff." In this respect Bush, like earlier presidents, found himself in a position in which the government's need for wartime funds forced him to make compromises with Congress that he otherwise might have avoided.

The fate of the proposed gas tax was a particularly disappointing footnote to the story. The short-lived September consensus included an immediate five-cent-per-gallon increase in the federal gas tax, with further hikes to be phased in over several years. It also included a new tax on heating oil. A federal gasoline tax was among the taxes that had passed White House muster during the Reagan years, and Greenspan had endorsed a new energy tax to raise revenues and decrease the deficit. A gas tax increase found influential supporters in the House, notably the Democratic chairman of the Ways and Means Committee, Dan Rostenkowski of Illinois. Rostenkowski had proposed an even more aggressive fifteen-cent-per-gallon increase. In defending the gas and heating oil taxes, Bush noted that they "had the virtue not only of contributing to deficit reduction, but also, over time, of decreasing America's dependence on foreign oil, an objective whose importance was made increasingly evident . . . in the face of the Iraqi invasion of Kuwait."

In asking for this sacrifice in the interest of national security, Bush invoked the tradition of earlier wartime presidents. However, narrower politics prevailed. The energy taxes were attacked by conservative Republicans and liberal Democrats; the former objected to any tax increase, the latter to their regressivity. The final act did not contain the levy on heating oil and cut the gas tax increase in half.

The Omnibus Act was bolder on long-term fiscal reforms. Title XIII, known as the Budget Enforcement Act, contained three process restraints designed to serve as successors to the Gramm-Rudman-Hollings Act. For the first time, it required that the budget take into account the true costs of federal credit and debt-subsidy programs. These had been proliferating since they were not subject to Gramm-Rudman-Hollings, and their growth was producing a large amount of hidden liabilities in the budget. The act also placed enforceable caps on future spending on defense, international affairs, and domestic discretionary programs. Congress could appropriate

funds up to the set limit for each category but could not underfund one category and shift the remaining funds to another. There were self-executing
limits on the ability to exceed the caps and stiff penalties for doing so.

Further, the act established the mechanism of pay-as-you-go budgeting (PAYGO), requiring that new entitlement benefits and new tax cuts
be offset by higher taxes or entitlement reductions elsewhere in the budget.
For example, if Congress were to pass legislation cutting the income tax by
an amount estimated to lose $10 billion in revenue, it would have to in-
crease another tax, say the inheritance tax, or cut entitlement spending, by
an amount sufficient to produce an additional $10 billion. During the
1990s, these rules proved highly effective and, according to the Congressional Budget Office, accounted for much of the deficit control.

The September 12 World

A decade after the liberation of Kuwait, America was again involved in a
war with Iraq, but this one was embedded in the context of a much broader
conflict—the war on terrorism. The United States was plunged full force
into this war, much as it had been into World War II, by attacks that caught
the country by surprise. The war on terrorism, the war in Afghanistan to
root out Al Qaeda and its protector, the fundamentalist Taliban, and the
Iraq War must be considered together, not only because President Bush
and his supporters closely linked them but also because they must be paid
for at the same time.

The war on terrorism was thrust into the American political dialogue
within hours of Al Qaeda's attacks on New York and Washington on September 11, 2001. Nine days later, George W. Bush told a joint session of
Congress that, in this war, "Americans should not expect one battle, but a
lengthy campaign, unlike any we have ever seen." Secretary of Defense Donald Rumsfeld, underscoring the point in a *New York Times* op-ed piece,
wrote, "This will be a war like none other our nation has faced. . . . Our opponent is a global network of terrorist organizations and their state spon-
sors. . . . Even the vocabulary of this war will be different." He might well
have added, "so must be the way we finance it."

The most contentious budget issue in Washington in the weeks before
the 9/11 attacks had been whether the government would dip into the "Social Security lockbox," that is, draw money from the Social Security surplus

to cover deficits in the regular budget. Much of the projected $3.1 trillion ten-year regular budget surplus had already been eaten up by the June 2001 tax cut, lower revenues, higher government benefit payments resulting from the weak economy, and an earlier budget resolution that had mandated large amounts of additional spending for farm subsidies and Medicare prescription drug benefits. Responding to the attacks, Congress immediately passed a $40 billion emergency national security, humanitarian aid, and reconstruction package. It also appropriated $15.6 billion for airline relief and additional funds later for the campaign against Al Qaeda and the Taliban in Afghanistan. The Federal Reserve, which had been lowering interest rates since early in the year to combat an ongoing recession, quickly lowered them again.

Then, on October 4, the chairmen and ranking members of the House and Senate Budget Committees produced a bipartisan document containing principles for the new stimulus measures that they believed would be required to boost growth after 9/11. They stated that the "terrorist attacks have created a national emergency, instigated a war on terrorism, and exacerbated a slowdown in the economy." They went on to declare that "the Congress and the President clearly will provide the resources necessary to respond to these events," but they also emphasized the need "to ensure that those resources [did not] . . . erode fiscal discipline in the future." They laid down a compelling principle to guide post-9/11 fiscal policy: "Long-term fiscal discipline is essential to sustained economic growth" and "measures to stimulate the economy should be limited in time." They explicitly noted that the Social Security surplus should not be raided to offset deficits in the normal operating budget and that "all economic stimulus proposals should sunset within one year, to the extent practicable." In addition, they asserted, "To uphold the policy of repaying the greatest amount of national debt feasible," spending cuts and revenue increases should be planned for the subsequent ten years to "make up for the cost of near term economic stimulus." It was to be an admonition soon forgotten.

Lowball Estimates

Before 9/11, the government had recorded four years of surplus, in 1998, 1999, 2000, and 2001, with the latter two being the largest as a portion of GDP since 1951. These surpluses—which had emerged during the high-growth years of President Bill Clinton's administration and owed a lot to the post–Cold War peace dividend, fiscal discipline, and spending caps—had enabled the Treasury to pay down a portion of the federal debt. They also provided room in the budget for George W. Bush and Congress to meet the financial requirements of responding to the terrorist attacks.

After 9/11, the federal government devoted billions of dollars to assist the victims and restore economic growth. Beyond that, however, the administration and most members of Congress suggested no substantial alteration of fiscal policy. Although U.S. leaders had solemnly declared a war on terrorism, Congress and the president continued to pursue fiscal policies established in the pre-9/11 peace, even as the need for additional resources for recovery, homeland security, and the military became apparent. Unlike in past wars, there were no bipartisan calls for patriotic sacrifice. Instead, Americans were encouraged to increase spending to boost the economy.

Mobilizing the financial resources to respond to the attacks, topple the Taliban, and round up or kill Al Qaeda forces did not require the enormous tax increases, domestic spending cuts, or patriotic bond drives seen during World Wars I and II, but the new security challenge should have triggered a reassessment and revision of the nation's fiscal priorities to determine what portion of the tax cuts and spending commitments that seemed affordable before 9/11 were no longer so. In addition, there was an opportunity to rally Americans to participate in the modern equivalent of the world war bond drives—a national drive to develop new sources of domestic energy, more extensively exploit old sources, and engage in comprehensive conservation efforts. Such measures would have reduced the country's oil dependence on the volatile Middle East, from which the terrorists and their financing came and which was increasingly vulnerable to disruption. To the contrary, in March 2002, only six months after the attacks, sixty-two senators rejected higher fuel efficiency standards, which would have reduced U.S. dependence on foreign oil. Although the United States faced a wholly new threat, its leaders seemed content with business as usual on the financial and energy fronts.

That fall, the United States and the United Kingdom began a lengthy diplomatic effort in the United Nations aimed at mobilizing support to confront what they considered to be a serious threat from allegedly hidden weapons of mass destruction in Iraq, one of the countries named earlier by the president as a member of the "axis of evil" that supported global terrorism and threatened the nation's security. American and British diplomats maintained that Iraq was in violation of UN Security Council resolution 1441, which required it to destroy all weapons of mass destruction. American officials insisted that because Saddam Hussein had not complied, the weapons must be captured or destroyed through military action. Unable to obtain a Security Council resolution to sanction the use of force—the French, Russians, and Chinese all threatened to veto one if it came to a vote—President Bush ordered an "attack of opportunity" without the support of the United Nations.

On March 20, 2003, Operation Iraqi Freedom commenced, with America leading a "coalition of the willing." It began with an intense bombing campaign, dubbed "shock and awe," to destroy the morale of the Iraqi military, and a nearly simultaneous ground assault. More than 100,000 American soldiers and marines, 26,000 British troops, and small numbers of Australian, South Korean, Italian, Polish, and other forces rolled over the outgunned and outmaneuvered Iraqi forces.

The following day, Bush informed Congress that he had acted because "further diplomatic and other peaceful means alone will neither adequately protect the national security of the United States against the continuing threat posed by Iraq, nor lead to enforcement of all relevant United Nations Security Council resolutions regarding Iraq." He had "reluctantly concluded . . . that only the use of armed forces will accomplish these objectives and restore international peace and security in the area." On April 9, Baghdad fell. Afterward, massive violence perpetrated by internal and foreign jihadis, militias engaged in internecine struggles, and escaped criminals mired the country in a prolonged state of insurrection and civil war.

As the United States prepared for the conflict, the question of cost was debated. Some in the administration were more candid—or accurate— than others. In September 2002, White House economic adviser Lawrence Lindsey publicly estimated that a war with Iraq would cost roughly $100 billion to $200 billion. Promptly, the director of the Office of Management and Budget, Mitch Daniels, shrugged off the estimate as "very, very high" and indicated that $50 billion to $60 billion was more likely. In January 2003, Secretary Rumsfeld, appearing on ABC's *This Week with George Stephanopoulos,* asserted that "the Office of Management and Budget estimated [the cost of the war] would be something under $50 billion." Stephanopoulos noted that "outside estimates say up to $300 billion," which Rumsfeld dismissed as "baloney."

In May 2003, Daniels asserted, "The United States is committed to helping Iraq recover from the conflict, but Iraq will not require sustained aid." Deputy Defense Secretary Paul Wolfowitz dismissed the comments of an anonymous administration official, quoted in the *Washington Post*, that the war and its aftermath would cost $95 billion. "I don't think he or she knows what he is talking about," Wolfowitz retorted. The head of the U.S. Agency for International Development insisted that the U.S. contribution to rebuilding Iraq would be just $1.7 billion. In fact, by the end of 2006, the Defense Department's budget totaled over $290 billion, and foreign aid combined with diplomatic operations totaled $28 billion. In early 2007, the administration estimated that another $270 billion would be required.

In addition to misjudgments about the strength, staying power, and determination of the insurgents, the administration based much of its analysis of Iraq's future resource requirements on inflated expectations and wishful thinking about that country's future oil revenues. High-level officials assured the American people that Iraqi oil would enable the United States to avoid a significant reconstruction bill. Testifying before the House Committee on Appropriations after the start of the war, Wolfowitz confidently claimed that Iraq's "oil revenues . . . could bring between $50 and $100 billion over the next two to three years. We're dealing with a country that can really finance its own reconstruction, and relatively soon." That April, Vice President Cheney predicted that Iraq's oil production would reach 3 million barrels per day at the end of 2003. As of the end of 2006, it was averaging around 2.3 million barrels.

These statements were made even though staff reports available to Wolfowitz and Cheney indicated that Iraq had a major oil problem. Before the war, a Pentagon task force warned that the decade-long UN embargo, which limited imports of drilling and exploration equipment, had damaged Iraq's oil industry and hobbled its production capacity. Other reports substantiated the Pentagon's assessment and stressed that enormous amounts of outside investment in the oil industry would be required to bring Iraqi production up to a level that would provide sufficient revenues for a major reconstruction effort. In September 2003, L. Paul "Jerry" Bremer, the head of the Coalition Provisional Authority charged with managing the U.S. occupation of Iraq, submitted a candid report alerting the White House that oil revenues would be insufficient to rebuild the country.

The Bush administration, of course, was not unique in underestimating war costs. History demonstrates the difficulty most administrations have had in determining the cost and duration of a war at its outset. In virtually every case, military spending has been far greater than originally anticipated. But the administration should have been aware of the oil problem and learned from the mistakes of its predecessors about the unpredictability of early wartime spending projections rather than dismissing those who offered higher cost estimates. Perhaps because of its optimistic forecasts, the administration did not feel compelled to limit either appropriations requests for other programs or the depth and duration of the tax cuts it had proposed just before the war. It made no effort to adjust spending so that more funds would be available if hostilities lasted longer than expected or if postwar occupation, peacekeeping, and reconstruction turned out to be more expensive. During the Johnson administration, the lack of such adjustments reflected an absence of coordination between the national security and economic officials; that was not the case in 2003. In his first National Security Presidential Directive (NSPD-1), Bush had made the secretary of the Treasury a formal member of the National Security Council. This permitted useful coordination in blocking terrorist funds, but seemed to make little difference in setting fiscal strategy.

The weakness of the coalition cobbled together for the war and its unwillingness to shoulder any of the U.S. financial burden also failed to induce a note of caution in the administration's budget outlook. On March 27, 2003, in a press conference with British prime minister Tony Blair at Camp David, President Bush boasted, "We've got a huge coalition. As a matter of fact, the coalition that we've assembled today is larger than the one assembled in 1991, in terms of the number of nations participating." Larger it may have been, but unlike the 1991 coalition, it provided little financial help to the United States, primarily because, as *Washington Post* reporter Thomas E. Ricks wrote in his book *Fiasco*, "It wasn't a solid alliance, based on common interests, as the father's had been, but rather a jerry-rigged series of deals that couldn't survive much pressure." The Bush administration considered a "tin cup" mission, but it did not pursue the idea because it expected a lackluster response. The best that could be managed was a donor conference in Madrid in October 2003, during which foreign governments pledged $13 billion in loans and grants for Iraqi reconstruction; as of the end of 2006, however, less than one-third had been disbursed. Ricks wrote that there were political and strategic costs in "being

backed by a phony coalition." There also was an economic cost—the absence of substantial foreign financial support for America's military operation or postwar assistance. The unwillingness of the French or German
governments to back the war effort was especially costly, as it eliminated
two potential sources of support during the considerably longer and far
more costly post-invasion phase of the conflict.

In September 2003, the administration asked Congress for an $87 bil-
lion emergency supplemental appropriation, the first of several such requests to pay for operations in Iraq and Afghanistan. It was submitted as
separate legislation even though a $400 billion defense bill was under con-
sideration at the time. In 2003, such a request was generally regarded as appropriate, since predicting the actual sums required for the war at the time
the original Defense Department budget was submitted would have been
virtually impossible. The supplemental requests that followed in 2004,
2005, and 2006, which contained most of the funding requests for Iraq,
were more controversial.

Supplemental appropriation requests were not a new phenomenon.
They had been used to finance the initial stages of most military operations
during the Korean War, Vietnam War, and the war in Bosnia. However, as
the Congressional Research Service noted, "past Administrations have requested . . . funding for ongoing military operations in regular appropriations bills as soon as even a limited and partial projection of costs could be
made." For example, the Johnson administration submitted a supplemental
request for 1965 and a budget amendment for 1966, but after that most of
the funding for the Vietnam War was through regular appropriations bills,
with only small, unforeseen amounts sought through supplementals.

The serial, routine use of supplemental appropriation requests to finance
the cost of the Iraq War was unprecedented, undermined budget planning,
and confused the process of congressional oversight. A look at the timing of
the supplemental requests suggests that they were delayed so that they would
not be considered during the general appropriations process. In February
2005, the president submitted his 2006 budget request, and only a week later
requested an $82 billion supplemental for Iraq and Afghanistan. Much the
same occurred in 2006. Bush administration officials defended their approach, using arguments that earlier had caused the Johnson administration
to lose its credibility. "The nature of the War on Terror continues to make it
difficult to predict with precision future funding needs," declared the Office
of Management and Budget's spokesman in September 2006. But the money

being requested was largely for Iraq and Afghanistan, not the broader war on terror, and by that time it was possible to apply some degree of forward planning to those conflicts that would have yielded reasonable cost estimates for use in annual appropriations requests.

The process became even more mired in confusion because spending that had little to do with urgent national security requirements was included in supplemental requests. A *Washington Post* editorial noted, "The Bush administration has chosen to fund operations in Iraq and Afghanistan, along with a grab bag of other programs, outside the normal appropriations process. To call this emergency spending is farcical. . . . There is no reason, especially as the war continued, not to budget for most, if not all, of it in the ordinary course of business." Even congressional Republicans became annoyed at the practice. An exasperated Republican member of the House Appropriations Committee, David Hobson of Ohio, told a *Los Angeles Times* reporter, we need to be "really straightforward about what we're funding and where it's coming from." Retired Lieutenant General John M. Riggs, an expert in army modernization, commented, "We're fighting a war on supplementals and it's a hell of a way to do business. The basic budget of the U.S. Army needs to be adjusted to fight the war on terror, and I have no idea where the money is going to come from." The Iraq Study Group, chaired by James Baker and Lee H. Hamilton, complained that "because most of the costs of the war showed up not in the normal budget but in requests for emergency supplemental appropriations, [they] are not offset by budgetary reductions elsewhere [and erode] budget discipline and accountability." In early 2007, the president indicated that requests for new funds for Iraq in 2008 and 2009 would be made through the normal budget process.

Lower Taxes, More Money?

In June 2001, George W. Bush had secured passage of a comprehensive package of tax reductions, the Economic Growth and Tax Relief Reconciliation Act (EGTRRA). It reduced taxes on incomes and capital gains, expanded the child tax credit, increased subsidies for education and retirement savings, lowered the levy on estates and gifts, and repealed certain limitations for itemized deductions. Several provisions were scheduled to "sunset," that is, revert to the status quo ante, in ten years unless subsequent legislation made them permanent. The measures did not give the expected boost to the stalled economy, however, and consumer confidence, retail sales, and industrial production were still in decline when the terrorists struck on 9/11. In 2002, Congress enacted a smaller tax cut in the Job Creation and Worker Assistance Act, but the economy remained sluggish.

While the administration was preparing for war with Iraq, Congress and the White House considered another round of tax reductions. On January 7, 2003, the president proposed legislation to increase "the pace of the recovery and job creation" by speeding up implementation of the 2001 tax cuts, ending double taxation of dividends, extending unemployment benefits, and creating new "re-employment accounts to help displaced workers to get back on the job." The congressional Joint Committee on Taxation estimated that the proposal would cost as much as $726 billion between 2003 and 2013. In addition, it anticipated that if the tax cuts passed in 2001 were made permanent, rather than lapsing as called for in the legislation, the cost in lost revenues would amount to nearly $625 billion by 2013.

Congress was in the midst of considering the tax bill as the administration was making its case for war against Iraq. Senator John McCain, a decorated war hero who had studied military history at the Naval Academy and knew of the numerous examples of war costs being underestimated, indicated that he was open to the idea of a new tax cut, but would not support it "until Congress and the Administration have a better understanding of the costs of war and peace." On the other hand, Republican House majority leader Tom DeLay, known as "the Hammer" for his forceful approach to party discipline and political retribution, declared, "Nothing is more important in the face of war than cutting taxes." The president insisted that a large tax cut was needed to revive the still weak economy. "I heard somebody say, 'Well, what we need is a tax increase to pay for this.' That is an absurd notion. . . . Lower taxes will help enhance economic recovery."

Notwithstanding presidential pressure and support among Republican congressional leaders, Senators Olympia Snowe of Maine and George Voinovich of Ohio insisted on a tax reduction no greater than $350 billion over ten years. One week before the war began, they joined Democrats Max Baucus of Montana and John Breaux of Louisiana in a letter to both parties' Senate leaders opposing any tax cut beyond $350 billion because of "international uncertainties and debt and deficit projections." A few days after the attack on Iraq was launched, Voinovich was even more explicit: "I happen to believe that we'll have troops [in Iraq] for one year or two years. You're going to at least probably have to spend $2 billion a month next year . . . just to provide security there." Breaux declared Bush's tax proposals bad public policy: "When you have a $300 billion deficit and . . . we're at war and we don't know how much it's going to cost." The chairman of the Senate Budget Committee, Republican Don Nickles of Oklahoma, countered that the large tax cut was needed because "we need to be growing our economy." Democrats advanced a more modest package of cuts that would have benefited primarily low- and middle-income families.

Given the narrow GOP majority at the time, this small coalition of moderate Republicans and Democrats forced the administration to scale back. After three months of bargaining capped by a final day of "unusually tense negotiation and a series of stormy meetings" brokered by Vice President Cheney, a deal was worked out that met its demands but also enabled the president to claim a victory for having accelerated earlier income tax reductions and cut the tax on stock dividends. The legislation, the Jobs Growth Tax Relief Reconciliation Act (JGTRRA), passed on May 23, 2003, two months after the war in Iraq began. In contrast to the sense of bipartisanship on fiscal policy that had been exhibited in the early stages of most American wars and despite the agreement among the moderate Democratic and Republican senators, the final vote was largely along partisan lines; all but one Republican in the House and three in the Senate (McCain, Snowe, and Lincoln Chaffee of Rhode Island) voted in favor, while all but seven Democrats in the House and two in the Senate voted against. Congress had become more polarized since 2001, when eleven Democrats in the Senate and twenty-eight in the House voted for JGTRRA. (McCain and Chaffee had voted against that, too.) The act's tax reductions amounted to $318 billion over ten years, but that figure assumed that its cuts for married couples, benefits for families with children, elimination of the inheritance tax, and lower taxes on dividends and capital gains would be allowed to expire as scheduled. Bush and most of the Republicans in Congress, however, pursued the cuts with the explicit intention of seeking another round of legislation to make them permanent, which would double the act's cost. Advocates of the tax cut pointed to reductions in the rates on capital gains and dividends as ways to increase investment and thus productivity, and rejected the argument that the uncertainties of war spending argued for a more cautious approach. But the additional spending measures passed during this period could not be justified on similar grounds. Despite the administration's claim that it was committed to fiscal discipline, it made no effort to secure congressional agreement to curb spending. Neither party would push for major spending cuts to offset the loss in tax revenues, whether short or long term, or to cover the added cost of the war.

By this time, the October 2001 memorandum written by top members of the House and Senate budget committees apparently had been forgotten. The great majority of the supporters of the 2003 legislation made little distinction between cuts needed to stimulate growth immediately and those that would produce deficits in future years, long after the economy had recovered and required no fiscal stimulus, at which time the loss of revenues would impose a constraint on the government's ability to pay for other national priorities, including the war in Iraq and the war on terrorism. Supporters of the legislation maintained that tax cuts would produce so much growth that revenue increases would sharply diminish the deficit. In looking back on these tax cuts in 2006, Bush observed, "Some in Washington say we had to choose between cutting taxes and cutting the deficit. . . . That was a false choice. The economic growth fueled by tax relief helped send our tax revenues soaring." Republican Senate majority leader Bill Frist of Tennessee went even further, proclaiming, "When done right, [tax cuts] actually result in more money for the government." This philosophy, it seemed, relieved legislators and the president from having to make hard choices about either spending or taxes; if one is willing to assume that growth will eliminate a large deficit, politicians can conveniently avoid cutting popular programs or raising taxes.

The 2003 legislation helped to revive the economy, boosting investment and employment in 2004, 2005, and 2006, which in turn increased revenues in these years. But, because it was not accompanied by spending restraints, it also increased the deficit at a time when the country was engaged in fighting costly wars in Iraq and Afghanistan as well as the larger war on terrorism. If the war on terrorism was considered the nation's highest priority, it was not reflected in U.S. fiscal policy, which was not altered to free up resources to pay for it. There was no attempt to make nonsecurity spending adjustments or impose tighter sunset provisions to ensure long-term fiscal discipline as taxes were cut to respond to short-term stimulus requirements. Even when events made it clear that the Iraq War would last a lot longer and be a lot more expensive than originally assumed, no adjustment in fiscal policy took place.

Earmarked for Insecurity

The 9/11 attacks on the World Trade Center and the Pentagon required heightened spending for national security and economic recovery. Along with the subsequent wars in Afghanistan and Iraq, they led to significant increases in the Pentagon's outlays, from just under $300 billion in 2001 (roughly 3 percent of GDP) to nearly $500 billion in 2005 and $522 billion in 2006 (more than 4 percent of GDP). Homeland security spending also rose dramatically—especially after the bipartisan creation of the Department of Homeland Security in 2002—albeit from a low base. Together, military and homeland security spending accounted for nearly 5 percent of GDP by 2006.

At the outset of most other wars, Congress and the administration reevaluated existing budgetary strategies and priorities. Presidents Roosevelt, Eisenhower, and Truman explicitly called for cuts in nonmilitary spending to make money available for war. And during the War of 1812, the Civil War, World Wars I and II, and the Korean War, the Treasury secretary decided on and informed Congress of the portions of wartime spending he proposed to cover by borrowing and taxation.

In sharp contrast, when it came to the Iraq War and the war on terrorism, the administration was silent on a fiscal strategy. There was no evident financing plan. Spending for discretionary programs unrelated to security increased by nearly 5 percent in the first three years after 9/11—a rate of increase even higher than that under Lyndon Johnson, who was spending generously on the Great Society during the Vietnam War. The additional money went to farm subsidies, education, and transportation, as well as for a cornucopia of earmarked projects—also known as "pork"—for the benefit of influential political constituencies.

The number of earmarked projects grew significantly after 2001. Rather than seeing the war on terrorism or Iraq as reasons to forgo such spending, legislators engaged in more of it. During the three years after the beginning of the Iraq War in 2003, the cost of these programs rose by 29 percent. Using 2001 as a base, the growth in earmarks was similarly steep, costing taxpayers $18.5 billion in 2001 and $29 billion in 2006—a 55 percent run-up. Even in the midst of war, the Defense Department budget was not immune. The Congressional Research Service identified nearly 2,900 such projects costing $9.4 billion in the 2006 defense budget, compared to roughly 1,400 projects costing $7.2 billion in the year before 9/11. Although these pork projects are hardly the cause of recent budget deficits and constitute a relatively small portion of overall government spending (for instance, earmarks comprise just over 2 percent of the defense budget), they create an impression that legislation is rigged toward special interests and that Congress is unwilling to practice the types of fiscal prudence and sacrifice that came into play during prior conflicts. As Roosevelt recognized, it is unrealistic to ask Americans to sacrifice for the common good if they believe their money is being used for the benefit of special interests.

Congress continued to appropriate large sums for nondefense purposes based on budget resolutions enacted before the 9/11 attacks, and to channel funds into earmarked projects even though a number of important facets of homeland security were inadequately funded. Stephen Flynn, an authority on antiterrorism, pointed out that due to lack of adequate security, "The transportation, energy, information, financial, chemical, food, and logistical networks that underpin U.S. economic power and the American way of life offer the United States' enemies a rich menu of irresistible targets. And most of these remain virtually unprotected." A task force of the Council on Foreign Relations reported in the summer of 2003 that "overall expenditures must be as much as tripled to prepare emergency responders across the country." It estimated that an additional $37 billion would be required to strengthen preparations to respond successfully to a hazardous materials attack; an additional $15 billion to prepare fire departments and EMS workers for rescue operations and to enhance the Federal Emergency Management Agency's national search and rescue teams; an additional $10 billion to enhance 911 systems; and an additional $30 billion to improve hospital preparedness. Although some of these initiatives are functions of state and local governments, much of the funding can come only from the federal government. Relying so greatly on local governments to provide the funding to protect U.S. facilities against terrorist attacks is reminiscent of Madison's reliance on state militias to protect the country during the War of 1812; that turned out to be an enormous mistake, as the country learned when much of Washington was put to the British torch.

Five years after 9/11, money for homeland security continued to be distributed with a pre-9/11 mind-set, based on political influence rather than on risk assessment. To cite one example, in early 2005, the inspector general of the Department of Homeland Security reported that the department had allotted hundreds of millions of dollars to protect ports of low priority, without sufficient focus on those that were the most vulnerable, and the money "had not yet achieved its intended results in the form of actual improvement of port security." Later that year, the 9/11 Commission noted that Congress had made "minimal progress" in dealing out homeland security funds based on risk and vulnerability and lamented that they "continue to be distributed without regard to risk, vulnerability, or the consequences of an attack."

A Debt for Future Generations

After 2001, the budget deficit climbed. In 2000, the United States recorded a surplus of 2.4 percent of GDP; in 2004, it had a deficit of 3.6 percent of GDP, a deterioration of 6 percent of GDP over four years and the largest such drop in the past fifty years. Only four other times in American history has a weakening of this magnitude occurred—during the Civil War, World War I, the Great Depression, and World War II.

However, this time, the United States could not point to a depression or massive wartime spending as the source of its fiscal reversal. A weak economy and high military spending were, to be sure, contributing factors, but the country certainly was not in a depression and defense spending increased only modestly by historical wartime standards, from under 3 percent of GDP in 2001 to roughly 4 percent in 2004. The bright side of this picture was that the budget deficit remained low as a portion of GDP compared to earlier wars, and the fiscal situation improved considerably after 2004. Federal revenues rose from 16 percent of GDP in 2004 to 18.4 percent of GDP in 2006 as the economy recovered. And pressures for more stringent fiscal policy caused a deceleration in the growth in appropriations for nondefense discretionary spending. As a result, the deficit declined to $248 billion, or less than 2 percent of GDP, in 2006. But earlier tax cuts and spending excesses still weighed on revenues. The Center on Budget and Policy Priorities calculated that "even with the spending for the wars in Iraq and Afghanistan and the response to Hurricane Katrina, the federal budget would essentially be in balance if the tax cuts had not been enacted or if they had been offset by either increases in other taxes or cuts in [other] programs."

But even as some economists celebrated the lower deficit, others pointed to the likelihood of future increases. In 2006, the Congressional Budget Office (CBO) estimated that based on current legislation—which included the sunsets of recent tax reductions—the cumulative deficit between 2007 and 2016 would amount to $1.76 trillion. If the recent tax cuts were to be made permanent, as Republican leaders urged, relief from the Alternative Minimum Tax was extended, and spending continued to rise in tandem with overall growth, the CBO forecast that the cumulative ten-year deficit would total nearly $3.5 trillion, even if the U.S. military presence in Afghanistan and Iraq were phased down. The bipartisan Concord Coalition was even more pessimistic, predicting a $5.16 trillion cumulative federal deficit over the next ten years. In coming to this figure, it projected that all expiring tax cuts would be made permanent, relief from the Alternative Minimum Tax would be extended, appropriations would rise at the same rate as economic growth, and Congress would continue to prevent scheduled cuts in Medicare spending for doctors.

Faith in the ability of tax cuts to drive the economy and dramatically reduce or eliminate deficits, which heavily influenced the thinking on fiscal policy at the turn of the twenty-first century, caused many officials to take a relatively relaxed view of these problems. Significant reductions of the deficit in 2005 and 2006 have been cited as validating the fiscal benefits of the 2001 and 2003 tax cuts. That success reinforced the prevailing view in Washington that no hard budgetary choices are needed, no reconsideration of wartime tax or spending policy. Yet even administration economists recognized that tax cuts do not pay for themselves. The 2003 *Economic Report of the President* noted, "Although the economy grows in response to tax reductions, it is unlikely to grow so much that lost revenue is completely recovered by the higher rate of economic activity." A report prepared by Jane Gravelle for the Congressional Research Service made the point even more explicitly, concluding that the "supply side effect [from the tax cuts] arising from increased work and savings are unlikely to have [revenue] feedbacks of over 10%." Basing future budgetary projections on overly optimistic assumptions reduces Congress's willingness to take tough corrective measures. Once such benign assumptions are made, the need to set priorities on taxes and spending can be sidestepped—at least for a time.

If the projections of the Concord Coalition prove correct and the country accumulates deficits exceeding $5 trillion through 2015, the publicly held debt will build from below 40 percent of GDP in 2006 to 43 percent in 2010 to 53 percent in 2015. During the early 1950s, the federal debt stood above 50 percent of GDP, but that was a legacy of the massive borrowing to pay for World War II. And, just as important, it was also on its way down due to the sound fiscal policies of the Truman and Eisenhower administrations. In 2006, debt was on its way up and appeared likely to stay on that course without fundamental policy changes. If Congress were to make recent tax cuts permanent, and failed to enact significant entitlement reform, the country would face a very steep rise in the debt burden in the next decade.

During his first term, President Bush also made an attempt to reform Social Security with a plan that featured personal savings accounts. As frequently occurs in such debates, the subject was instantly polarized, with each side attempting to attribute malevolent intentions to the other. With no meaningful reform in the works, the prospect of a dramatic deterioration in the nation's finances in the next decade became all the more real. The Social Security trustees have projected that the system's costs will grow from 4.3 percent of GDP in 2005 to over 6 percent in 2030; Medicare trustees predict that over the same period hospital insurance and supplementary medical insurance will grow from 2.7 percent of GDP to 6.5 percent. These increases alone will be greater than the portion of GDP accounted for by all national security spending today.

Low interest rates held down the cost of servicing the federal debt in 2004 and 2005, but with rates rising in 2006, that relief ended. In 2006, debt service amounted to a relatively low 1.5 percent of GDP. The CBO estimated that it will edge up to 1.6 percent of GDP in 2016 under its optimistic "baseline scenario," but the Concord Coalition's scenario puts the figure at 2.5 percent by 2016, more than half the portion of GDP expected to be spent on the military. A number of this magnitude could cut into defense and other programs.

Recent deficits have not set off alarm bells in Congress or the financial markets of the kind heard during the Korean War, the Vietnam War, and the Reagan rearmament. In part, this was because they remained only a modest portion of GDP in historic terms; in part, because inflation and interest rates were at or near post–World War II lows. Moreover, deficit spending in 2003 and 2004 proved a useful technique for stimulating growth. And, more recently, deficits have shrunk.

These felicitous circumstances have allowed the Bush administration to avoid the kinds of clashes over fiscal policy experienced during previous wars. In the 1950s, Korean War spending was linked to high inflation, providing fodder for critics of the Truman administration. The Vietnam War contributed to big budget deficits and was associated in the public mind with high interest rates and inflation, adding to the political pressures on the Johnson administration to change course. Critics pointed to Reagan's deficits in the 1980s as a reason to curb his defense buildup. The defense costs and budget deficits of the Iraq War are not associated in the public mind with rising interest rates or increased inflation, and without a complaining public, there is little incentive for Congress to put a check on the administration or itself.

★

While the Gulf War will not go down in history as a major military encounter, it nonetheless provided valuable lessons regarding the financial importance of strong alliances and international legitimacy. Despite the initial political opposition to the United States' involvement, George H. W. Bush was able to bolster domestic support and alleviate the budgetary impact by forging an international coalition to wage the war and provide financing for it. Bush and Baker rallied more than two dozen nations to the coalition, each with a stake in America's military success. This well-crafted military and financial alliance with other wealthy countries that benefited from American military protection lowered the cost of the war to U.S. taxpayers. Turning to external sources for wartime funds contrasted sharply with the experience of previous wars in the twentieth century, in which the United States was called upon to support its allies both militarily and financially. And it stands in sharp contrast to the Iraq War, in which the United States assumed the lion's share of military and reconstruction costs. The example of George H. W. Bush's administration offered a template for the future conduct of war in a world in which the United States is the sole power capable of large-scale military action, though it occurred in the context of a special set of circumstances.

The budgetary confrontations during the Gulf War also produced innovative measures designed to instill fiscal discipline in Washington. PAYGO and spending caps forced Congress and the administration to set clear priorities and to make fiscal trade-offs when enacting tax cuts and entitlement increases. As with Roosevelt, Eisenhower, and Johnson, George H. W. Bush received some of the harshest criticism on fiscal matters from members of his own party, but in the final analysis, moderate members of Congress, on both sides of the aisle, were able to work with the White House to craft solutions to curb a spiraling deficit. They left the country with procedure that produced greater fiscal discipline than it had seen since the 1950s. But PAYGO—forged in a desperate attempt to curb a widening deficit in 1990—was allowed to expire in 2002. During the George W. Bush administration, the White House and the Republican leadership in Congress strongly opposed efforts to reinstate PAYGO in its original version that applied to both spending and taxes, insisting that it only restrict spending.

The Iraq War was managed very differently from the Gulf War. The absence of a robust coalition virtually eliminated the prospect of substantial foreign funding. Without a demonstrable willingness in Washington to take the views of other nations into account before final decisions were made, there was no agreement on a broad-based military response and no commitment among U.S. allies to contribute large sums of money for the war and reconstruction.

From a fiscal perspective, the Iraq War and the broader war on terrorism departed from the pattern of U.S. wars of the twentieth century. Following 9/11, American authorities failed to follow the path set by their World War I, World War II, and Korean War predecessors of reassessing and reordering the nation's fiscal policy. Restraint in nonsecurity spending would have been appropriate to redirect funds to protect the nation's security and prosecute the war in Afghanistan. Instead, many legislators saw in 9/11 what their predecessors in the 1950s had seen in the launch of Sputnik: an opportunity to increase spending. There was a key difference, however. After Sputnik, the new money went largely for security, whereas after 2001, a large portion went for purposes that had little or nothing to do with national security.

At the beginning of the Iraq War, Congress and the White House had another chance to adjust taxes and spending in light of wartime requirements. They missed that as well. A few members argued that because of the expected financial requirements of the war, Congress should take a more modest approach to tax cuts than the administration favored, and by a narrow vote margin they prevailed. But there was no overarching process for forging a long-haul strategy that encompassed taxes, discretionary spending, and entitlement reform to free up funds for the military, intelligence, homeland security, and nonmilitary international programs to prosecute the war on terrorism.

Testifying about the Iraq War before the House Ways and Means Committee in March 2003, Treasury Secretary John Snow did not suggest any alteration in the president's January tax cut proposal, then being considered in Congress, or in government spending. Instead he asserted, "The cost of the war will be small. We can afford the war, and we'll put it behind us." His prediction followed the tradition of many of his predecessors, who had also grossly underestimated the costs of war.

Pressures to withdraw troops intensified in 2006, primarily because to mounting casualties and a growing frustration that enormous mistakes had been made and victory was becoming highly improbable. Arguments that war-related spending was diverting budgetary resources from more popular or more essential programs were a secondary reason cited by those who favored prompt disengagement. Americans have consistently demonstrated a willingness to support the appropriation of sufficient sums to keep the nation's troops well supplied and armed when they are engaged in combat, but when the public becomes convinced that victory is not possible, the cost factor constitutes an additional argument against sustaining the military effort and in favor of bringing troops home, as demonstrated in the 1950s and 1960s.

During the Iraq War, the administration took the view that the best defense was a good offense. It justified pursuit of the war on grounds that it would help prevent a terrorist attack in the United States; consequently, as the war consumed $8 billion a month, programs to strengthen homeland defense and the nation's antiterrorist military and intelligence capabilities in other parts of the world went underfunded.

In the long war on terrorism, extended periods without an attack might mislead the public into thinking that high levels of security preparedness can be realized at lower levels of security spending. This could lead to cuts in homeland defense and international security programs from an already low base. That sentiment could grow as these expenses compete, under chronic deficit conditions, with domestic constituency-driven spending as well as with the coming flood of entitlement payments to the baby boomers. As a result, future presidents and Congresses may find themselves without the resources, the military capacity, the intelligence capabilities, the foreign assistance programs, or the homeland security apparatus required to thwart or cope with dangerous new security threats.

The *New York Times*'s veteran reporter R. W. "Johnny" Apple Jr. highlighted this concern a month after the 9/11 attacks. "The danger, over the long term," he noted, "is loss of interest. With much of the war to be conducted out of plain sight by commandos, diplomats and intelligence agents, will a nation that has become used to easy self-indulgence stay focused?"

Conclusion

THE PRICE OF A LONG WAR

Henry Kissinger has written that "America's journey through international politics has been a triumph of faith over experience." For much of the nation's history, however, U.S. fiscal policy has been the reverse—the triumph of experience over faith. Time and again, policymakers have demonstrated that they have learned from the successes and failures of their predecessors.

When terrorists attacked New York and Washington in 2001, the American people found themselves once again at war—not a conventional war but a unique conflict in which the enemy is neither a government nor even a single entity. Its methods are different from those of others the United States has confronted; it aims to inflict massive death and destruction on the American homeland and on countries friendly to the United States, and its fighters, often motivated by religious fanaticism, are willing to engage in suicidal acts to accomplish their objectives.

Yet the war on terrorism does not pose a unique fiscal challenge. In one fundamental way it is similar to the Cold War: it is likely to last for decades and, consequently, will require a long-term financial strategy. To manage the Cold War's financial challenge, early Cold War presidents Truman and Eisenhower reached deep into America's history, following George Washington's imperative that policy should serve the needs not only of the current generation but also of future generations and Alexander Hamilton's principle that sound national finances are a prerequisite for sustaining the country's military strength and security, and thereby reducing its vulnerability to its enemies. In keeping with these tenets, both presidents attempted to strike a balance: provide the military with large sums to meet the Soviet challenge but avoid fiscal excesses that would saddle the country with enormous debt, which would undermine its long-term stability and its capacity to mobilize sufficient resources to resist, contain, and reverse the spread of Soviet influence and troop presence over a sustained period.

The war on terrorism calls for a similar long-term approach, but the specific budgetary issues are very different. In the 1950s, defense spending dominated the budget. Today, Social Security, Medicare, and Medicaid dwarf defense spending and all other parts of the budget, and their costs are accelerating rapidly; they pose a budgetary risk similar to that some feared from expanding military spending five decades earlier. During the middle of the twentieth century, the country had a savings surplus; in the early twenty-first century, it relies heavily on foreign capital to fund annual budget deficits and make up for its chronic shortage of domestic savings. In the 1950s, the United States did not suffer from severe energy dependence; in the early twenty-first century, it imports 60 percent of its oil requirements, much of it from potentially vulnerable suppliers, and, by contributing to high world oil prices, bolsters the resourses of countries and groups hostile to the United States.

American officials face a complex fiscal challenge: to successfully prosecute the global war on terrorism while also meeting the growing costs of retirement and health-care benefits. At the same time, they must ensure that the nation's finances become a source of strength in the war on terrorism and retain the critically important confidence of domestic and foreign investors.

Five years after the 9/11 terrorist attacks, neither the president nor Congress had come to grips with this challenge, let alone faced up to the dangers inherent in maintaining a fiscal policy that in the next decade will result in massive deficits, declining budget flexibility, and further dependence on foreign capital. It is often said that 9/11 "changed everything." In the area of fiscal policy, however, it changed nothing. The country is pursuing a pre-9/11 fiscal policy in the post-9/11 world.

The Fiscal Challenge

Over the next several decades, the country will face the threat of catastrophic attacks from enemies seeking to obtain and deploy increasingly lethal weapons. Shortsighted fiscal policy will financially constrain the government's ability to avert and respond to these threats. Large multi-year tax cuts, a proclivity for domestic spending for parochial purposes, and lack of a national consensus on whether and how to reform balloon-ing mandatory retirement and health benefits will leave coming genera-tions with massive debt and hundreds of billions of dollars in obligations. Without significant changes, future leaders will find it difficult to obtain sufficient resources for national security, the country will be rendered increasingly vulnerable to economic disruption in the event of another terrorist attack, and the government will face a reduced financial capac-ity to cope with other extraordinary events, such as a major new military deployment, a calamitous hurricane, or a flu pandemic.

After 9/11, as the costs of the government's response mounted, the long-term terrorist threat became clear, and projections for future annual deficits grew, political leaders did not review or revise earlier tax legislation and spending commitments in light of the dramatically altered fiscal land-scape. Neither the president nor Congress stopped to consider whether commitments that seemed affordable in a time of peace and budget sur-pluses were still affordable in a time of war and projected large budget deficits. Indeed, they pushed through multiyear tax cuts in 2002 and 2003, and Congress appropriated large amounts of additional money for nonse-curity purposes, even as the added expenses of the war on terrorism, homeland security, and the conflicts in Afghanistan and Iraq were impos-ing new demands on the budget—and were projected to do so for years to come. There was no attempt to offset the impact of additional security spending by sharply cutting other programs or imposing tight "sunset" provisions on the tax cuts, as the bipartisan, bicameral budget committee leaders had suggested in October 2001.

This unwillingness to reset budget priorities stands in marked contrast to the past. During most of America's wars, parochial desires—such as tax breaks for favored groups or generous spending for influential constituencies—have been sacrificed to the greater good. The president and both parties in Congress have come together—albeit occasionally after con-tentious confrontations—to cut nonessential spending and increase taxes. Because levels of defense spending and annual deficits early in the twenty-first century were low by historical standards, it was easy to sidestep such matters after 9/11 and even at the beginning of the Iraq War. But this attitude reflected a fiscal myopia, because while short-term budget issues were manageable, the country faces a serious long-term problem. Much higher deficits are expected in the next decade and beyond due to the anticipated explosion in mandatory spending—for example, Social Security is projected to experience an annual shortfall of over $250 billion by 2030 versus a surplus of $70 billion in 2005. Financial prudence argues that the country enter the coming decade with budget surpluses and a lower national debt rather than with chronic deficits and a rising debt.

A multiyear fiscal strategy is needed to protect the country against the threat from global terrorism and to provide retirement support and health benefits to a rapidly aging and often needy portion of the population. The current course risks conflict—or, at a minimum, considerable friction—between these two objectives. Avoiding a clash requires a reprioritization of budget policy, including cuts in nonessential spending in all budget categories, reforms in entitlement programs to ensure their financial sustainability, sufficient tax revenues to cover anticipated expenses, and room in the budget to meet emergencies.

The war on terrorism requires a great deal of spending by the defense department, but it also necessitates significant outlays for intelligence, diplomatic initiatives, efforts to interdict terrorist financing, foreign assistance, first responders, police departments, homeland protection authorities, and efforts to gain support in the Islamic world. If the United States remains on its current course, it will be painting itself into a financial corner: officials charged with ensuring U.S. security and conducting these programs will find it increasingly difficult to obtain funds. Social Security, Medicare, and Medicaid—mandatory programs with outlays determined by prior legislation—and interest payments on the government's rising debt will constrain the government's budget flexibility to meet these needs.

In August 2006, the Congressional Budget Office (CBO) alerted Americans to this emerging problem. The deficits of the coming years, it noted, will "occur not because the government is trying to pull the economy out of a recession, fight a war, or allocate resources to investment, but because it is spending more and more on programs for the elderly and on interest payments on accumulated debt." No matter how optimistic one is that domestic discretionary spending will continue to decelerate and that tax cuts will substantially boost revenues, the long-term trajectory for the nation's deficit and debt is sharply upward. That jeopardizes its security and its ability to meet other essential needs. Two hundred years ago, Hamilton recognized the connection between sound long-term finances and national security, but today it appears to have been forgotten.

The Long War and the Cold War

In preparing for the financial challenges of the war on terrorism, the Cold War offers an instructive lesson: threats—and perceptions of threats—will ebb and flow. As they do, public support for the funding of key security programs is likely to ebb and flow as well.

During the Cold War, periods of relative tranquility produced public pressures to reduce military spending. Sometimes cuts were appropriate, since more than a few military programs were overfunded and some were simply included in the budget because they were initiated or sustained by what President Eisenhower called the "military industrial complex." But there also were times when demands for cuts intensified as the result of congressional or public frustration with the size of military spending, the lack of progress of a war, or general dissatisfaction with the policies of the administration in office. Often these cuts were made without a strategic assessment of their impact on national security.

During the Cold War, when public support declined, budget cuts generally took place from a high base. But that is not the situation for many homeland security programs today. Many areas of homeland defense have not received sufficient funding from the start. As noted by the 9/11 Commission, in several areas, including infrastructure protection, spending is frustratingly inadequate. Any cuts are likely to come from a low base, adding to the nation's vulnerability.

Future leaders could confront problems like those faced by President Truman early in the Cold War, when members of Congress, intent on reducing the budget deficit, attempted to thwart his requests for funds to assist nations threatened by the Soviet Union. If the United States suffers from bloated deficits, future presidents will be hamstrung in funding vital initiatives to help other countries build participatory political institutions, strengthen internal security capabilities, address basic human needs, establish free market institutions, improve secular education, and mount antiterrorist security campaigns. All are essential components of the war on terrorism.

Yet although there are numerous similarities between the financial challenges of the Cold War and those of the war on terrorism, there also are significant differences. The Cold War involved massive military spending on both sides; the war we face today is financially asymmetrical. Terrorist acts generally cost the perpetrators only a few hundred thousand dollars but cost the victim country much more. In a highly publicized videotape released in October 2004, Osama Bin Laden underscored this point by referring to the estimate of a British diplomat that Al Qaeda "spent $500,000 on the event [9/11]" while the United States "lost . . . more than $500 billion." Describing his efforts to oust the Soviet army from Afghanistan, Bin Laden boasted that "the Mujahadeen bled Russia for ten years until it went bankrupt and was forced to withdraw in defeat. . . . So we are continuing this policy of bleeding America to the point of bankruptcy."

The United States will have to spend hundreds of billions of dollars on intelligence, weapons, technology, and homeland protection to prevent subsequent attacks. Many billions more will be needed for recovery should an attack occur. The notion of bankrupting enemies into collapse or submission, an important part of America's eventual Cold War strategy, will not be available in the global fight against terrorism.

And there is yet another difference. What came to be known as the "balance of terror" in the Cold War deterred each side from directly attacking the other. As we have so painfully observed, there is no such constraint in the war on terrorism. Indeed, one of the terrorists' main goals is to attack the United States, perhaps with chemical, biological, or nuclear weapons capable of killing enormous numbers of people and seriously disrupting the American economy. As devastating as the 9/11 attacks were, they did not impact critical transportation or communications infrastructure. Exploding a "dirty" nuclear bomb in a major port or transportation center, in addition to inflicting large numbers of casualties, would be far more harmful to the economy than the 9/11 attacks because it could shut down the supply chain for vital energy, food, manufacturing components, and other items for a prolonged period and throw hundreds of thousands of people out of work. Such infrastructure is likely to be a choice target in the future. Magnus Ranstorp, the director of the Center for the Study of Terrorism and Political Violence at St. Andrews University in Scotland, has pointed out that Al Qaeda has "an acute awareness of where to hit, where it hurts the most. . . . There's an awareness of the benefits of targeting critical infrastructure."

2001 VS. 2006

A substantial budget surplus in 2001 gave the United States government considerable flexibility to mobilize large sums of money for relief, reconstruction, and economic stimulus after the 9/11 attacks as well as for the war in Afghanistan and enhanced homeland defense. In addition, there were minimal adverse effects on the stock and bond markets. After a few days of financial jitters, foreign investor confidence and the dollar firmed up and capital flows into the United States resumed. A Congressional Research Service (CRS) report noted, "Panic selling of dollar assets did not occur as some had feared. In many respects currency and financial markets remained steadier than many had expected and regained their pre-attack levels within weeks." In part, this stability resulted from fast action by the Federal Reserve Bank of New York, which injected tens of billions of dollars into the banking system overnight, as well as from close coordination by American financial officials with their counterparts in Europe, Japan, and other major countries to support the dollar. But the sound state of America's domestic finances was an essential factor.

The next time could be very different. Years of large fiscal deficits afford less room in the budget to respond to another attack. In that event, spending for reconstruction and relief measures would increase sharply, while revenues would plunge due to a pronounced economic downturn, causing the deficit to mushroom. New borrowing could quickly add up to hundreds of billions of dollars, placing enormous stress on a budget already in deficit and what would likely be a shaken financial market. Moreover, even substantial increases in liquidity by the Fed to boost demand would be of little benefit if the ability of the economy to meet such demand were disrupted by the prolonged incapacitation of large swaths of the transportation network or significant portions of the nation's manufacturing sector.

The financial dangers would be all the greater because the United States has become more heavily dependent on foreign capital. In 2001, foreign capital inflows totaled $780 billion; by 2005 (the last full year for which statistics are available as this book goes to press), that figure had doubled to nearly $1.5 trillion. In 2005, foreign investors purchased more than half of the Treasury securities issued (over 55 percent versus 46 percent in 2001), meaning that foreigners financed over half of the government's deficit. At the end of that year, foreigners held $2 trillion in American securities. Dollar assets accounted for 70 percent of foreign central bank reserves. In 2006, the U.S. economy and government were more dependent on foreign capital than at any time since that of Hamilton—who recognized the financial risks of such dependence.

Former Federal Reserve board chairman Alan Greenspan warned that at some point "international investors will adjust their accumulation of dollar assets or, alternatively, seek higher dollar returns to offset concentration risk"—that is, they will reduce purchases of dollar assets or demand a higher interest rate to continue to invest in them. By increasing the budget deficit and producing severe economic dislocations, a major terrorist attack would elevate foreigners' fears about concentration risk. Billions of dollars of capital inflows could dry up, and money now invested in the United States could flow elsewhere, causing American interest rates to soar and the dollar to plummet. Because the United States has become far more dependent on foreign capital than it was in 2001, the financial impact of such actions will be significantly greater.

As the Founding Fathers recognized more than two hundred years ago, in the economic as well as the military realm weakness invites aggression. For them, a sound economy and sound finances were as much a part of the nation's defense as a strong military. That remains true today. Chronic deficits, rising debt, and significant dependence on foreign capital make the United States vulnerable and offer an added enticement to terrorists who think they can severely disrupt the U.S. economy.

Financial Competition on the Home Front

During the 2004 presidential campaign, Democratic candidate Senator John Kerry argued that the Iraq War diverted funds from urgent needs at home. That argument appealed to some Americans, though many others understood that there was not necessarily a one-for-one trade-off. However, if the defense budget continues to grow for the indefinite future, the question of resource diversion will become more prominent and divisive, as it was during the Vietnam War.

Senator George V. Voinovich of Ohio, who was instrumental in scaling down the proposed 2003 tax cut, also had reservations about the president's request that year for an $87 billion supplemental appropriation for Iraq and Afghanistan. Voinovich noted, "It's hard to say to everybody, 'Well, we don't have money for sewers or water, but we're going to put all that money over there.' What everyone's looking for is a sense of equity and fairness." In making this argument, he was in good company. President Eisenhower made a similar point five decades earlier: "Every gun that is made, every warship . . . every rocket fired signifies . . . a theft from those who hunger and are not fed, those who are cold and are not clothed."

The fiscal challenge to the defense budget posed by these trade-offs cannot be brushed aside. For 2007, Pentagon spending adjusted for inflation is projected to be equivalent to the peak annual levels of the Korean War and the Vietnam War. But, because of the enormous growth in the U.S. economy over recent decades, defense spending as a percentage of GDP is less than one-third the peak of the Korean War and less than half that of the Vietnam War. As a portion of the overall federal budget, it has declined from 70 percent at the height of the Korean War, to below 50 percent at the height of the Vietnam War, to less than 20 percent in 2007. But as a portion of *discretionary* spending, the drop is much less: from nearly 75 percent during the Korean War to roughly 50 percent in 2007. So although military appropriations account for a relatively small portion of current GDP and of the overall budget, they consume a very large share of discretionary spending. And that is where budget cutters will look first for reductions, because obtaining legislative coalitions and public support to slow the growth of mandatory payments is considerably more difficult, and these will remain on automatic pilot if no action is taken to alter their sharply upward trajectories.

Unless mandatory payments are reined in or inflows are significantly increased, discretionary appropriations, including America's defense and homeland security expenses, will be squeezed. In 2006, spending on Social Security, Medicare, Medicaid, and interest on the federal debt amounted to just under 60 percent of government revenues; if they continue on their current path, they will account for two-thirds in 2015. The CBO's "baseline projections" indicate that Social Security spending alone will grow from $550 billion in 2006 to $960 billion in 2016; steeper increases will occur in Medicare, which is expected to balloon during this period from $372 billion to over $900 billion, and Medicaid, which is projected to more than double, from $181 billion to over $390 billion. And these increases are only the beginning; the numbers will soar further in the next several decades. The nonpartisan Concord Coalition warns that "unless Congress is willing to raise taxes considerably, future taxpayers will have to accept much lower spending for other public purposes—including homeland defense and national security—or they will face larger and larger deficits and the resulting negative consequences for the economy and future standards of living."

The CBO projected that even if revenues remain at their thirty-year average of 18.3 percent of GDP and spending grows on an intermediate path, the federal debt will rise from 40 percent of GDP to 100 percent of GDP over the next twenty-five years. This would be close to the level reached at the end of World War II. Interest payments would reach 4.6 percent of GDP at that time, well above World War II levels. The CBO also projected that if half of the predicted deficit in twenty-five years were to be eliminated by cutting discretionary spending—including defense—it would have to be cut by nearly 80 percent from its baseline level. A Government Accountability Office (GAO) report cautioned, "Continuing on this unsustainable path will gradually erode, if not suddenly damage, our economy, our standard of living, and ultimately our national security."

Franklin Roosevelt recognized that even under the intense pressures of World War II, military requirements had to be met without abandoning core programs that promoted social justice. Likewise, in the current environment it is unlikely that the public and Congress will support large cuts in Social Security and Medicare to boost security spending. But meeting national security and entitlement needs requires prioritizing resource allocation within each area and paring back outlays in other programs, as was done during the Roosevelt, Truman, Reagan, and George H. W. Bush administrations.

In curbing explosive Social Security and Medicare growth, America's leaders should apply the very simple yet politically essential principle that has governed the country's fiscal policy during other challenging periods: equity. Those who can pay more for, or whose financial circumstances enable them to rely less on, these programs should be called upon to do so. America's leaders must begin a candid national dialogue on these issues, laying out the costs of mandatory programs over the next several decades alongside those of defense, debt service, and other needs, and examine how these figures stack up against the revenues that will be available.

Who Should Pay for the War on Terrorism?

History holds important lessons about how to approach the financial challenges facing the country as it confronts the war on terrorism. The underlying issues are age-old questions: who should pay and how should they pay.

Finding the answers never has been easy, but the nation's leaders have always found it necessary to seek them.

For much of America's history, the White House and Congress have recognized the inevitability of massive borrowing when the nation's security has been threatened, and for the most part they have tried to structure that borrowing to strengthen national unity. Hamilton called a well-funded debt a "national blessing" because it gave Americans who held federal securities an interest in supporting the fledgling post-Revolutionary government. Lincoln saw bond sales as a way to more closely tie greater numbers of Northerners to the Union's cause. William McAdoo and Henry Morgenthau initiated patriotic bond drives to enable Americans not directly engaged in the world wars to make a contribution; bonds were issued in low denominations to enable middle-class families to buy them as easily as the rich.

But U.S. policymakers also have attempted to restrain debt accumulation by following, when possible, the "pay-as-we-go" principle to avoid transferring excessive burdens on future generations or heightening tensions between investors who owned bonds and the broader population of taxpayers whose money went to service them. Through taxes, Wilson met a third of the incremental costs of World War I, Roosevelt paid for nearly half of World War II, and Truman covered virtually all of the costs of the Korean War. During the world wars, income and business taxes fell primarily on the wealthy, to demonstrate the government's commitment to equity.

When American troops have fought on the battlefield, U.S. leaders have generally sacrificed low-priority spending and special-interest tax benefits, accepting the principle that Americans who were not fighting abroad should be asked to make sacrifices at home. For the most part, the American people have supported such changes. And, until recent decades, after a war the nation's leaders have attached enormous importance to paying down debt as quickly as possible. A century and a half after Washington urged Americans not to "ungenerously" transfer war debt to the next generation, Eisenhower warned against doing the same thing.

Of late, the precedents and experiences of past generations have been cast aside. The 9/11 attacks were seen by many legislators as a license to spend more money on nonsecurity programs, and Americans have not been called to make sacrifices. Tax cuts and spending increases on politically popular but security-irrelevant domestic programs have been enacted as if there were no expensive defense programs to be funded. Hard choices were not necessary, most thinking went, because the cost of the war as a portion of the nation's GDP was modest in historic terms and, in any case, growth would shrink the deficit. Using rosy assumptions, advocates of the 2001 and 2003 tax cuts wanted to make them permanent while at the same time arguing that the war on terrorism would last for decades—with little acknowledgment that the costs of prosecuting it would last for decades, as well.

When it comes to fiscal matters, the country now appears to be relying on faith over experience, hoping that sustained growth will erase deficits and that the ballooning costs of Social Security, Medicare, and Medicaid will be manageable in the coming decades without difficult reforms. Failing to reform these programs will cause acute fiscal problems down the road, but the current generation of politicians devotes little attention to the matter; few appear willing to pay the political price of supporting controversial alterations. But if such corrections are not made now, America's leaders will find it more difficult to pay the bills for the nation's defense. Unbridled mandatory spending and a growing budget deficit pose a threat to national security in the twenty-first century, much as Eisenhower feared unbridled defense spending and a growing budget deficit would in the mid-twentieth century.

The current situation calls for a reassessment of short- and long-term budgetary priorities and a government and public review of how taxation, borrowing, and spending should be managed over coming decades. As George H. W. Bush suggested in 1990 when he brokered the budget reforms of that year, all items should be on the table. The test should not be which among a multiplicity of competing interest groups, economic ideologies, or political constituencies can win the battle of the moment for a favored tax cut or spending program. It should be whether the allocation of the nation's budgetary resources coincides with its highest security and social priorities, whether enough revenues will be available to meet those priorities over coming decades, and whether the current generation is assuming a sufficient share of the responsibility or, instead, is transferring an inordinate burden to future generations.

Paying Future Debts

The first prerequisite for an honest and effective dialogue is recognition that the country will not be able to grow out of its deficits. The CBO has warned that "tough choices will be required . . . traditional incremental approaches to budgets will need to give way to more forceful and periodic reexaminations—ultimately covering discretionary and mandatory programs as well as on the revenue side of the budget." It also has warned that "substantial reductions in the projected growth of spending or a sizable increase in taxes as a share of the economy—or both—will probably be necessary to provide a significant likelihood of fiscal stability in coming decades." As Fed chairman Ben Bernanke pointed out, "Crucially, whatever size of government is chosen, tax rates must ultimately be set at a level sufficient to achieve an appropriate balance of spending and revenues in the long run."

Such an exercise is essential to avoiding the transfer of heavy burdens to future generations. President George W. Bush stated that he "came to this office to confront problems directly and forcefully, not to pass them to future presidents or future generations." If every decision in Washington were guided by this principle, policymakers would leave the country in sound economic shape, with greater resource flexibility to protect the nation's security. But, of late, few if any decisions have followed this principle.

Several steps can be taken to put the country's finances on a firmer long-term footing. Few measures would be more effective than restoring the pay-as-you-go (PAYGO) provisions contained in the 1990 Budget Act, along with tight definitions of what constitutes emergency spending (a provision used to evade PAYGO limits). In January 2007, the newly seated Democratic-controlled House passed legislation to restore the PAYGO process in a step to implement budget reform. Greater use of the presidential veto—one of the most powerful tools in producing legislative restraint—should be employed regardless of the party in control. A good template would be Roosevelt's veto of the 1943 tax act, which was riddled with benefits for special interests; FDR called it a "tax cut for the greedy, not for the needy." Legislators must also reassert their strong oversight role vis-à-vis the executive and use it to force greater spending discipline, as during the Vietnam War and the Reagan rearmament. Congressional oversight often has been a powerful tool for ensuring more rigorous fiscal standards. A return of checks and balances between the branches is essential to sustaining sound national finances.

Specific areas of the budget should be attacked at once. The Democratic-led House has taken a measure to increase transparency in the earmarking process by requiring that each proposal show the names of the legislators who introduced it. In his 2007 State of the Union address, President Bush proposed cutting the number and cost of earmarks at least in half; accomplishing this goal would help to restore fiscal responsibility. Another advance would be to require that every earmark proposal be accompanied by a five- to ten-year CBO cost estimate. An end to runaway earmarking would reduce waste and demonstrate a commitment to fiscal evenhandedness. Asking some Americans to give up favored programs or tax benefits to pay for the war on terrorism or balance the budget is much harder if those who are well connected continue to receive funds for pet projects. As the Concord Coalition argued:

> No economic group except for the very needy should be exempt from contributing to eliminating the federal budget deficit. Those who can more readily shoulder the burden should be asked to do so. Narrowly targeted tax breaks or spending provisions for business or individuals do not belong in a deficit reduction plan. Even if fully offset, such political "pork" diverts resources from more pressing national needs and increases public cynicism about the fairness of the federal budget process.

Earmarks in the defense budget should not be immune to scrutiny. Indeed, they should be subjected to especially close oversight to ensure that resources are focused on the Pentagon's most vital priorities. Each proposal should receive an evaluation of its military benefits by an objective, outside consultant and the Defense Department, along with a requirement that all earmarked contracts be subject to competitive bidding.

A Realistic and Accountable Pentagon

Given the pressures from other parts of the budget, the Pentagon bears a heavy responsibility to show that it is using its funds with maximum efficiency and effectiveness. The 2006 Quadrennial Defense Review (QDR), the third conducted by the U.S. Department of Defense since Congress mandated the process, and the first one prepared while the country was at war, sought to realign resources, training, equipment, and troop allocations to the changing security threat. In the wake of the 9/11 attacks and the Iraq War, the QDR recommended that the military devote greater effort to battling terrorists and insurgents and less to preparing for conventional military challenges.

Along with the Defense Department's five-year budget projections, the

QDR made the case for substantially greater military outlays in the coming years. The CBO also projected that core defense spending will increase significantly and identified several of what the Pentagon refers to as "cost risk" probabilities, new and unexpected requirements that could push the figures higher. The GAO has cautioned that defense spending will be "running head-on into the nation's unsustainable fiscal path."

In anticipation of that headlong clash—and to avoid a slump in support similar to that experienced late in the Vietnam War and during the Reagan rearmament—the Pentagon should subject its budget to tough internal tests so that the amounts requested are clearly linked to priority security needs. (Although its budget is much smaller, the Department of Homeland Security should do the same.) In late 2005, the White House began to apply pressure "to rein in rapidly rising [Pentagon] spending" due to its "growing awareness that the nation cannot afford to pay for new weapons systems costing hundreds of millions of dollars, fight wars in Iraq and Afghanistan and cover major domestic demands." Scrutiny of Pentagon spending will only get tougher.

To ensure that defense budgets are credible, the Pentagon will have to constantly reallocate resources to meet fundamental priorities and jettison less vital systems and programs. Cold War programs designed for a different era will need to be dropped in favor of systems to fight contemporary wars. The GAO observed that the Pentagon's "requirements process generates more demand for new programs than fiscal resources can support" and warned that if these practices continue "draconian, budget driven decisions will have to be made later." Echoing Eisenhower's insistence on spending discipline, it called for "constraining individual program requirements by working within available resources [and] establishing clear business cases for each individual investment." If mandatory social programs are to be brought under greater fiscal discipline, Defense Department spending must be subject to a similar effort. As Eisenhower recognized, cutting waste and inefficiency out of the Pentagon's budget is neither unpatriotic nor harmful to American security. To the contrary, undisciplined military spending weakens the nation's security by wasting money that could go to higher security priorities and by undermining the public's support.

The government must also renew its commitment to heeding Eisenhower's warnings regarding the military-industrial complex. The allocation of funds to contractors during the Iraq War has led to charges of waste and favoritism, and the public and Congress need to be reassured that taxpayer money is being used to maximum efficiency. While American servicemen and -women are sacrificing their lives, the thought that companies are making untoward profits due to the mismanagement of contracting and procurement damages Pentagon credibility. All contracts should be subject to competitive bidding and scrutinized closely. Further, the Pentagon's resource requests for Iraq will need to be judged against the needs of other national security objectives. In 2005, a CRS report stated, "If [overall] deficits remain stubbornly difficult to control, as they have proven to be in the past, then it may be optimistic to expect defense budgets to grow at even the moderate pace the Administration is now projecting." If that is the case, trade-offs will have to be made to most effectively utilize the limited resources available for national security. In this respect government authorities will need to guard against the tendency for any one war, such as that in Iraq, to be considered such a high priority that they turn a blind eye to assessing the efficiency of the funds devoted to it and thereby divert resources from other priorities in the war on terrorism. Putting resources into one area out of inertia and then insisting that it is a strategic decision undermines credibility and starves other major national security programs.

Tough questions will need to be asked and publicly debated: Which national security programs are vital? Are some vital programs being underfunded while less important ones are provided disproportionately large amounts? Is homeland security money being allocated based on risk assessments or on political influence? Are important measures to improve security at home and abroad being sacrificed because so much money is going to the Iraq War? Are other agencies' national security programs suffering shortfalls because such large sums go to the Pentagon? What process is in place to ensure that funding for the war on terrorism is comprehensively addressing infrastructure, diplomacy, intelligence, and other needs?

Because of the overarching nature of homeland security, funds are provided through a variety of military services and government agencies. Fiscal planning and resource prioritization has not been carried out effectively. The first step toward an improvement should be to reorganize the fragmented congressional oversight. Congress's slowness in consolidating and coordinating the various aspects of homeland security has led to fiscal waste, spending duplication, large gaps, and failure to identify the entire range and urgency of risks facing the country. The 9/11 Commission emphasized that funding for homeland security should not simply be a revenue-sharing program but instead should be budgeted based on risk and vulnerability assessments. Early in the Cold War, Truman established the National Security Council to ensure coordination among the various security agencies, which had, in the past, only come together in response to a shooting war. He realized that a new apparatus was necessary to meet a new threat. A similar vision should guide the Congress in reorganizing for the war on terrorism.

Energy Patriotism

Among America's greatest vulnerabilities is its enormous dependence on foreign oil. Supply interruptions have the potential to severely disrupt the U.S. economy. The high world oil prices that result in part from America's massive oil imports strengthen the hand of countries hostile to the United States and discourage its allies from standing up to oil-producing nations. Because of their energy wealth, Iran and Venezuela are in a stronger position to challenge the United States and support insurgencies elsewhere. Moreover, the billions of dollars spent for imported oil unwittingly provide funds to groups that support terrorism or seek to undermine the stability of the United States and other nations. Cutting U.S. oil dependence and helping other nations, including China and India, to do the same will curb world oil prices and help constrain the flow of oil revenues to countries and organizations antagonistic to American interests. In the major wars of the twentieth century, Americans repeatedly have demonstrated a remarkable willingness to make patriotic sacrifices, but they have not been called on to do so in the current war. During World War II, Treasury Secretary Morgenthau saw patriotic bond drives as a response to the question, "What can I do to help?" Today the answer lies not in buying more bonds but in buying less gasoline.

The United States responded well to the oil crises of 1973–74 and those that followed during the 1980s. Since 1975, oil consumption as a percentage of GDP has been cut in half. But progress has slowed considerably since the mid-1990s. To restore the momentum, a concerted and urgent national effort is required to substantially increase the efficiency of oil use in all forms of transportation.

Further, 40 percent of the enormous growth in the U.S. trade deficit between 2001 and 2006 resulted from an increase in the country's already outsized oil bill. Large volumes of imported oil are also closely intertwined with the country's increased buildup of foreign debt. A high oil-import bill means a big outflow of funds; the resulting increase in the nation's trade and current account deficits requires larger amounts of foreign borrowing.

Oil independence is not a near-term likelihood, but major steps can be taken to reduce the country's oil vulnerability by expanding potential supplies of a wide range of domestic energy sources and reducing oil use. Close arrangements with neighboring countries possessing substantial oil resources, such as Canada and Mexico, are vital to tapping secure sources of energy.

With energy as with overall fiscal policy, the country is operating with a pre-9/11 mind-set. The Energy Policy Act of 2005 provided loan guarantees, tax credits, and funding for new technologies and nonconventional energy initiatives, but these were not commensurate with the urgency of the country's energy challenge. There appears to be too little understanding of the national security dangers of high oil dependence and too little willingness to reconcile long-standing political, philosophical, ideological, and economic differences between those who focus on boosting supplies of conventional energy and those who focus on the need for conservation.

The next threat to American security could well be global warming, and the United States must incorporate that prospect into its energy policy. The summary of the British government's seven-hundred-page report on global warming, the Stern report, begins with this ominous sentence: "The scientific evidence is now overwhelming: climate change presents very serious risks, and it demands an urgent global response." This should be a powerful guide to future American energy policy. For the decade ahead, a well-funded effort is needed to develop alternative transportation fuels, such as biomass, and hybrid automobile technologies as well as to fully utilize nuclear, wind, and solar power in order to help reduce the country's emissions.

In 1977, with the nation importing about 40 percent of its oil needs, President Jimmy Carter called an effort to reduce energy dependence "the moral equivalent of war." It is even more so now, with America importing 60 percent of its oil and fighting the war on terrorism. As Senator Joseph Biden, the chairman of the Senate Foreign Relations Committee, noted, "Our oil dependence fuels the fundamentalism we're fighting. . . . It limits our options and our influence around the world, because oil-rich countries pursuing policies we oppose can stand up to us, while oil-dependent allies may be afraid to stand with us." The committee's ranking Republican, Richard Lugar, wrote, "The global trend of foreign governments asserting greater control over oil and gas reserves allows unfriendly regimes to use their oil and gas exports as leverage against the United States."

As during the two world wars, Americans must drastically alter their saving and spending habits. A combination of market and government incentives and a massive public relations effort using the media, schools, and the clergy—as were utilized to sell bonds and encourage tax payments during past wars—can accelerate the reduction in American oil use by producing substantial changes in day-to-day energy consumption, encouraging the purchase of more efficient cars, and promoting the modification of driving practices. An all-out effort to cut foreign oil dependence and exert downward pressures on world oil prices would reduce energy constraints on American foreign policy, weaken the flow of funds to American adversaries, and curb the massive outflow of petrodollars. A national effort to enlist large numbers of Americans behind such measures, for patriotic and economic reasons, should be a top national security priority. For more than two hundred years the government has mobilized massive amounts of capital for national security; during the new war on terrorism, it must mobilize a massive public effort to reduce oil use and dependence.

The Price of Liberty Today

The 9/11 Commission warned that Al Qaeda "could . . . scheme to wield weapons of unprecedented destructive power in the largest cities of the United States." Future attacks could impose enormous costs on the entire economy. Having used up the surplus that the country enjoyed as part of the Cold War peace dividend, the U.S. government is in a weakened financial position to respond to another major terrorist attack, and its position will be damaged further by the large budget gaps and growing dependence on foreign capital projected for the future. As the historian Paul Kennedy wrote in his book *The Rise and Fall of the Great Powers*, too many decisions made in Washington today "bring merely short-term advantage but long-term disadvantage." The absence of a sound, long-term financial strategy could bring about a deterioration that, in his words, "leads to the downward spiral of slower growth, heavier taxes, deepening domestic splits over spending priorities and a weakening capacity to bear the burdens of defense."

Decades of success in mobilizing enormous sums of money to fight large wars and meet other government needs have led Americans to believe

that ample funds will be readily available in the event of a future war, terrorist attack, or other emergency. But that can no longer be assumed. Budget constraints could limit the availability or raise the cost of resources to
deal with new emergencies. If government debt continues to pile up,
deficits rise to stratospheric levels, and heavy dependence on foreign capital grows, borrowing the money needed will be very costly. Hamilton understood the risks of such a precarious situation. After suffering through
financial shortages, lack of adequate food and weapons, desertions, and
collapsing morale during the Revolution, he considered the risk that the
government would have difficulty in assembling funds to defend itself all
too real. If America remains on its dangerous financial course, Hamilton's
gift to the nation—the blessing of sound finances—will be squandered.

The U.S. government has no higher obligation than to protect the security of its citizens. Doing so becomes increasingly difficult if its finances are
unsound. While the nature of this new brand of warfare, the war on terrorism, remains uncharted, there is much to be gained if our leaders look to the
experiences of the past for guidance in responding to the challenges of the
future. The willingness of the American people and their leaders to ensure
that the nation's finances remain sound in the face of these new challenges—
sacrificing parochial interests for the common good—is the price we must
pay to preserve the nation's security and thus the liberties that Hamilton
and his generation bequeathed us.

Notes

INTRODUCTION

xiv "price of liberty": Alexander Hamilton, U.S. Department of the Treasury, *First Report on Public Credit*, January 9, 1790.

xvi "vigorous exertion in time of peace": George Washington, Farewell Address, *Independent Chronicle* (Boston), September 26, 1796.

xix "in the heart": Osama Bin Laden, Videotape, Al Jazeera TV, October 29, 2004.

1. HAMILTON'S VISION

2 "operate injuriously": Alexander Hamilton, U.S. Department of the Treasury, *First Report on Public Credit*, January 9, 1790.

3 "a monopoly that will take place": Henry Lee to James Madison, April 3, 1790, in James Madison, *Papers,* ed. Robert Rutland et al., vol. 13 (Charlottesville: University of Virginia Press, 1963), p. 136.

3 "our credit": Thomas Jefferson to James Madison, June 20, 1790, in *The Papers of Thomas Jefferson,* ed. Julian P. Boyd et al., vol. 18 (Princeton, N.J.: Princeton University Press, 1950), pp. 536–37.

3 "The possession of a good credit": Thomas Jefferson to James Madison, 1788, in *The Writings of Thomas Jefferson*, ed. Andrew Lipscomb and Albert Bergh, vol. 6 (Washington, D.C.: The Thomas Jefferson Memorial Association, 1904), p. 455.

4 "compromise which was to save the union": Thomas Jefferson, *Account of the Bargain,* http://www.gwu.edu/~ffcp/exhibit/p14/p14_3.html.

4 "While Madison and Jefferson": Joseph Ellis, *Founding Brothers: The Revolutionary Generation* (New York: Alfred A. Knopf, 2000).

4 "As Washington's aide-de-camp": Ibid, p. 199.

5 "presidents in wartime remained objects": Arthur Schlesinger Jr., *War and the American Presidency* (New York: W. W. Norton, 2004), p. 80.

6 "Loans in times of public danger": Hamilton, *First Report on Public Credit.*

7 "borrow, at pleasure": *The Works of Alexander Hamilton*, ed. Henry Cabot Lodge, vol. 3 (New York: G. P. Putnam's Sons, 1904), pp. 295–96, in Robert J. Shapiro, *Coin of the Liberal*

Realm: The Political Character of the American Monetary System (PhD diss., Harvard University, 1980), p. 80.

9 "Do you think, gentlemen": Albert S. Bolles, *The Financial History of the United States: 1774–1789* (New York: D. Appleton, 1884), p. 38, in Paul Studenski and Herman Edward Kroos, *The Financial History of the United States* (Washington, D.C.: Beard Books, 2003), p. 27.

9 "There is at present no absolute necessity": Bolles, *Financial History*, p. 201, quoting the *Pennsylvania Packet*, January 20, 1780.

10 "There is scarcely anything that can wound": [Alexander Hamilton], "The Federalist No. 15," *Independent Journal*, December 1, 1787, http://www.constitution.org/fed/federa15.htm.

10 "lay and collect Taxes": U.S. Constitution, art. 1, sec. 8, cl. 1.

10 "No money shall be drawn": U.S. Constitution, art. 1, sec. 9, cl. 7.

12 "the oppression arising from [federal] taxation": Patrick Henry, quoted in Tax History Museum, "1777–1815: The Revolutionary War to the War of 1812," http://www.tax.org/Museum/default.htm.

12 "assumption of this power of laying direct taxes": Ibid.

13 "it is evident": Alexander Hamilton quoted in Tax History Museum, "1777–1815."

13 "direct taxes are not necessary": James Madison, "Speech on Ratification of the Federal Constitution," June 6, 1788, http://www.constitution.org/rc/rat_va_05.txt.

13 "direct taxes shall be apportioned": U.S. Constitution, art. 1, sec. 2, cl. 3.

13 latest census: U.S. Constitution, art. 1, sec. 9, cl. 4.

14 "A public debt supported by public resources": Udo Hielscher, *Financing the American Revolution* (New York: Museum of American Financial History, 2003), p. 43.

15 "tax on importation . . . falls exclusively": Thomas Jefferson to Samuel DuPont De Nemours, 1811, in Lipscomb *Writings of Thomas Jefferson*, vol. 13, p. 391.

15 "necessary for the support": *The Impost Act of 1789* ("Duties on Merchandise imported into the United States"), *United States Statutes at Large*, vol. 1 (1845).

17 "would be ruinous to the public credit": Hamilton, *First Report on Public Credit*.

17 "a breach in the public faith": *Papers of Alexander Hamilton*, ed. Harold C. Syrett et al., vol. 6 (New York: Columbia University Press, 1969–1987), p. 33, in Ron Chernow, *Alexander Hamilton* (New York: Penguin Press, 2004), p. 296.

17 "discrimination between the different classes": Hamilton, *First Report on Public Credit*.

17 "distinction" between the "transferee" and the "original proprietor": Ibid.

17 "no time, no state of things": Lodge, *Works of Alexander Hamilton*, vol. 3, p. 295, in Shapiro, *Coin of the Liberal Realm*, p. 79.

18 "to be provided for according to the precise terms": Ibid.

18 "one of the great determining factors": Walter Russell Mead, *Special Providence: American Foreign Policy and How It Changed the World* (New York: Alfred A. Knopf, 2001), p. 67.

19 "in an Agricultural Country like this": Beverley Randolph to George Washington, January 4, 1791, in *The Papers of George Washington: Revolutionary War Series*, ed. Abbott and Dorothy Twohig, vol. 7 (Charlottesville: University of Virginia Press, 1985), p. 178, in Ellis, *Founding Brothers*, p. 205.

20 "national blessing": Hamilton, *First Report on Public Credit*.

20 nation's gross national product (GNP): It is worth noting that at the time neither the concept nor the term "GNP" existed. It entered into common use during WWI and was replaced after WWII by the term GDP. Retroactively, we use the term to measure the size of the economy, but contemporaries did not have such figures available

and therefore they could not have been a guide to either policy or to market opinion.

20 "the most bitter and angry contest": Alan Greenspan, "U.S. Treasury Securities: Lessons from Alexander Hamilton," The Annual Public Securities Awards Dinner of the Public Securities Association, New York, N.Y., October 7, 1996.

21 "still more generally obnoxious": Chernow, *Alexander Hamilton,* p. 342

21 "we are already obliged": George Washington to Alexander Hamilton, July 29, 1792, in *Papers of Alexander Hamilton,* vol. 12, p. 131.

22 "Whenever the government appears in arms": *Papers of Alexander Hamilton,* vol. 26, pp. 552–53.

22 "to see it incorporated as a fundamental maxim": Hamilton, *First Report on Public Credit.*

22 "as the vicissitudes of nations beget": Alexander Hamilton, U.S. Department of the Treasury, *Report on Manufactures,* December 5, 1791.

23 "extinguish" the federal debt: Alexander Hamilton, U.S. Department of the Treasury, *Report on a Plan for the Further Support of Public Credit,* January 16, 1795.

23 "purchased, redeemed or paid": Ibid.

24 Government debt rose: Studenski and Kroos, *Financial History,* p. 55.

24 debt declined as a portion of GNP: James Macdonald, *A Free Nation Deep in Debt: The Financial Roots of Democracy* (New York: Farrar, Straus, and Giroux, 2003), p. 306

25 the Committee on Ways and Means: Studenski and Kroos, *Financial History,* p. 49.

26 "Anger at these and similar measures": Mead, *Special Providence,* p. 242.

26 "discharge the debts which unavoidable wars may have occasioned": George Washington, "Farewell Address," *Independent Chronicle,* September 26, 1796.

27 "In those simpler times": Greenspan, "U.S. Treasury Securities."

2. THE FIRST GREAT TEST

28 Randolph . . . assaulted: John Randolph, *Annals of Congress,* 12th Cong., 1st sess., 1811–12, pp. 1390–81, in Richard Buel Jr., *America on the Brink: How the Political Struggle over the War of 1812 Almost Destroyed the Young Republic* (New York: Palgrave Macmillan, 2005), p. 152. The *Annals of Congress* covers the 1st Congress in 1798 through the 1st session of the 18th Congress in 1824; they were followed by the *Register of Debates* (1824 through 1837) and the *Congressional Globe* (1833 through 1873). Each played the role that the *Congressional Record* plays today.

29 "meant to abandon creditors": *Annals of Congress,* 13th Cong., 1st and 2nd sess., 1813–14, p. 461, in Buel, *America on the Brink,* p. 182.

29 "almost destroyed the young Republic": Buel, *America on the Brink,* p. 182.

30 "add a single amendment": Thomas Jefferson to John Taylor, November 26, 1798 in *Writings of Thomas Jefferson,* vol. 10, p. 24.

30 "public curse": James Madison to Henry Lee, April 13, 1790, in James Madison, *Papers of James Madison,* vol. 13 (Chicago: University of Chicago Press, 1977), p. 147.

30 " 'danger to democracy' ": Mead, *Special Providence,* p. 187.

30 "the creditor class": Ibid., p. 188.

30 "Wars cost money": Ibid.

31 In the early 1800s, nearly a third: Caroline Webber and Aaron Wildavasy, *A History of Taxation and Expenditure in the Western World* (New York: Simon and Schuster, 1966), p. 378.

31 "Though I am an enemy of the system of borrowing": To the Commissioner of the Treasury, 1788, in *Writings of Thomas Jefferson,* vol. 6, p. 378.

32 Negotiation between Hamilton and Bayard: Sean Wilentz, *The Rise of American Democracy: Jefferson to Lincoln* (New York: W. W. Norton, 2005), p. 94.

32 "the most perfect system": James Hamilton, *Reminiscences of James A. Hamilton* (New York: Charles Scribner, 1869), p. 23, in Chernow, *Alexander Hamilton*, p. 647.

34 "Mr. Randolph goes to the House": William Plumer, *William Plumer Papers, 1778–1854*, ed. Frank C. Mevers et al. (Sanford, N.C.: Microfilming Corp. of America, 1982), p. 61.

34 "to strike at the root of the evil": Albert Gallatin to President Jefferson, November 1802, in *Writings of Albert Gallatin* (Philadelphia: J. B. Lippincott, 1879), p. 71.

35 "We are able": Thomas Jefferson, Second Annual Message to the Congress, December 15, 1802, in *A Compilation of the Messages and Papers of the Presidents, 1789–1897*, ed. James D. Richardson, vol. 2 (Washington, D.C.: U.S. Government Printing Office, 1907), p. 489.

35 "the return to peace": Albert Gallatin, *American State Papers*, vol. 3, *Finances* 6:248.

37 "believed that eliminating the public debt": Buel, *America on the Brink*, p. 99.

37 "The Genevan Secretary": C. C. Stagg, *Mr. Madison's War* (Princeton, N.J.: Princeton University Press, 1983), p. 54, in Wilentz, *Rise of American Democracy*, pp. 143–44.

37 "If we go to war now": Thomas Jefferson, "Last Trail for Peace," letter to James Monroe, in *Jefferson: Writings*, ed. Merrill D. Peterson (New York: Library of America, 1994), pp. 1199–20, in Mead, *Special Providence*, p. 187.

38 "the evils inseparable from it": Albert Gallatin to Thomas Jefferson, March 10, 1812, in *The Life of Albert Gallatin*, ed. Henry Adams (New York: J. B. Lippincott, 1879), pp. 455–56.

38 "chill the war spirit": Donald R. Hickey, "The War of 1812," in *The American Congress: The Building of Democracy*, ed. Julian E. Zelizer (New York: Houghton Mifflin, 2004), p. 1988.

39 "Go to war without money": John Randolph, *Annals of Congress*, 12th Cong., 1st sess., pp. 1380–81, in Buel, *America on the Brink*, p. 152.

40 "People will pay the proposed taxes": The New Federalists, *The American Almanac*, in Anton Chaitkin, "Henry Clay's War Hawks Win a Victory over British Terrorism," *Executive Intelligence Review*, February 28, 1986, p. 4.

40 The internal taxes that Gallatin: Buel, *America on the Brink*, p. 101.

41 masterful document: Alexander Hamilton to James Duane, September 3, 1780, in *Papers of Alexander Hamilton*, vol. 2, p. 414.

41 "necessary and proper": Alexander Hamilton, "Opinion on the Constitutionality of an Act to Establish a National Bank," February 23, 1791, in *Papers of Alexander Hamilton*, vol. 8, p. 97.

42 "the first and fatal blow": Henry Adams, *History of the United States During the Administrations of James Madison* (New York: Library of America, 1986), p. 886, in Garry Wills, *Henry Adams and the Making of America* (New York: Houghton Mifflin, 2005), p. 293.

42 "fully adequate to the support": Gallatin, *Finances* 6:497.

43 "sap the foundations of": Report of the House Ways and Means Committee, *Annals of Congress*, 13th Cong., 1st sess, p. 1375.

43 "the government was broke": Gordon, *An Empire of Wealth*, p. 119.

43 "were still unwilling": Hickey, "War of 1812," p. 1988.

43 "we have hardly enough money": Wilson, *Stephen Girard*, p. 266, in Gordon, *An Empire of Wealth*, p. 119.

44 "more stable": George W. Campbell, *American State Papers*, vol. 3, *Finances* 6:624.

44 "approached the subject with fear": Hickey, "The War of 1812," p. 103.

45 "the sum to be borrowed": *The Debates and Proceedings of the Congress of the United States,* 13th Cong., 1st and 2nd sess., 1813–14, pp. 1271 and 1404, in Buel, *America on the Brink,* p. 197.

45 "the best moment to arrest" the war: Daniel Sheffey, November 18, 1814, in Buel, *America on the Brink,* p. 197.

45 "freed from having to sustain": Buel, *America on the Brink,* pp. 208–9.

45 "pleaded for unity": Diary of William Bentley, vol. 4, p. 280, in Buel, *America on the Brink,* p. 210.

46 "inadequacy of the existing provisions": James Madison, State of the Union, September 20, 1814, The American Presidency Project, http://www.presidency.ucsb.edu/ws/index.php?pid=29456.

46 "offensive war": *Niles' Weekly Register* 1, p. 232, in Buel, *America on the Brink,* p. 134.

46 "Will Federalists lend": Benson J. Lossing, *Lossing's Field Book of the War of 1812* (1869), ch. 42, n. 2, http://freepages.history.rootsweb.com/~wcarr1/Lossing2/Contents.html.

47 "warned potential investors": *New England Palladium* (Boston), March 16, 19, 23, 26, 30, and April 6, 1813, in Buel, *America on the Brink,* p. 182.

47 "Napoleon Bonaparte himself ": Wilentz, *Rise of American Democracy,* p. 155.

48 "most Federalists in Congress": Buel, *America on the Brink,* p. 220.

48 "pains . . . taken to excite every suspicion": *Independent Chronicle,* November 24, 1814, in Buel, *America on the Brink,* p. 210.

49 "embarrassment arising": James Madison, State of the Union, December 5, 1815, The American Presidency Project, http://www.presidency.ucsb.edu/ws/index.php?pid=29457.

50 "In their own mind": Wilentz, *Rise of American Democracy,* p. 165.

51 Madison proposed higher tariffs: Webber and Wildavasy, *History of Taxation,* p. 84.

51 "early extinguishment of the public debt": James Madison, State of the Union, December 3, 1816, The American Presidency Project, http://www.presidency.ucsb.edu/ws/index.php?pid=29458.

51 five years following the war: James Monroe, State of the Union, November 14, 1820, The American Presidency Project, available at http://www.presidency.ucsb.edu/ws/index.php?pid=29462.

51 "an immense tax": Buel, *America on the Brink,* p. 220.

52 "We cultivate": John C. Calhoun, December 19, 1828, "Excerpts from the South Carolina Exposition and Protest," http://social.chass.ncsu.edu/middleton/hi251/CourseMaterial/SCExpositionProtest.pdf.

55 "improved conditions of the public revenue": Madison, State of the Union, December 5, 1815.

55 "even within a short period": Madison, State of the Union, December 3, 1816.

55 "well-founded hope": James Monroe, State of the Union, December 7, 1824, The American Presidency Project, http://www.presidency.ucsb.edu/ws/index.php?pid=29466.

3. THE FIERY TRIAL

56 "the fiery trial": Abraham Lincoln, Annual Message to Congress, December 1, 1862, The American Presidency Project, http://www.presidency.ucsb.edu/ws/index.php?pid=29503.

56 "manifest equity": Salmon P. Chase, U.S. Department of the Treasury, *Report of the Secretary of the Treasury on Finances,* 37th Cong., 1st sess., 1861, Senate Executive Document 2 (Washington, D.C., 1861), p. 1112, in Joseph J. Thorndike, "An Army of Officials: The Civil War Bureau of Internal Revenue," Tax History Museum, December 21, 2001, p. 7, http://www.tax.org/Museum/default.htm.

57 "wealthy capitalists": Owen Lovejoy, *Congressional Globe*, 37th Cong., 1st sess., 1861, p. 248.

57 "I cannot go home": *Congressional Globe*, 37th Cong., 1st sess., 1861, p. 306, in Thorndike, "An Army of Officials," p. 8.

57 "that we have laid taxes": Ibid., pp. 247, 250, in Thorndike, "An Army of Officials," p. 9.

57 "internal duties or direct taxation": Edwin R. A. Seligman, *The Income Tax: A Study of the History, Theory and Practice of Income Taxation at Home and Abroad*, 3rd edition (New York: Augustus M. Kelly, 1970), p. 431, in Weisman, *Great Tax Wars*, p. 32.

60 "We demand": *New York Tribune*, in George W. Van Vleck, *The Panic of 1857: An Analytical Study* (New York: Columbia University Press, 1943), p. 104, and *Tribune Almanac 1859*, pp. 52–53, in James M. McPherson, *Battle Cry of Freedom: The Civil War Era* (New York: Ballantine Books, 1988), p. 189.

60 "the problem was not whether": John Sherman, *Recollections of Forty Years in the House, Senate, and Cabinet: An Autobiography*, vol. 1 (Chicago: Werner Co., 1895), p. 259, in Jane Flaherty, "The Perceived Power: Government and Taxation during the American Civil War," doctoral thesis, Texas A&M University, December 2005, p. 83.

61 "lowest for necessities": Weisman, *Great Tax Wars*, p. 33.

61 "his ability, firmness, and purity": Abraham Lincoln to Lyman Trumbull, January 7, 1861, in *Collected Writings*, vol. 4, p. 171, in Doris Kearns Goodwin, *Team of Rivals: The Political Genius of Abraham Lincoln* (New York: Simon and Schuster, 2005), p. 292.

61 a salve for the merchant class in New York: Goodwin, *Team of Rivals*, p. 292.

62 Chase's consuming ambition: Ibid., p. 293.

62 "to take charge of the finances": Sidney Ratner, *American Taxation: Its History as a Social Force in Democracy* (New York: W. W. Norton, 1942), p. 62.

62 "heedless of the abyss": Salmon P. Chase, *The Salmon P. Chase Papers*, ed. John Niven, vol. 1 (Kent, Ohio: Kent State University Press, 1997), p. 381, in Flaherty, "The Perceived Power," p. 228.

62 Chase family experience after War of 1812: Goodwin, *Team of Rivals*, pp. 35–36.

62 "danger that the protectionists": Abraham Lincoln to Lyman Trumbull, January 7, 1861, in *Collected Works of Abraham Lincoln*, ed. Roy P. Basler and Christian O. Basler, vol. 4 (New Brunswick, N.J.: Rutgers University Press, 1990), p. 171, in Goodwin, *Team of Rivals*, p. 292.

62 "Go to Secretary Chase": Donald R. Kennon and Rebecca M. Rogers, *The Committee on Ways and Means: A Bicentennial History, 1789–1989* (Washington, D.C.: U.S. Government Printing Office, 1989), p. 148.

63 "finance . . . war costs": William G. Sumner, *A History of American Currency* (New York: Henry Holt and Company, 1876), p. 197, in Johnson, *History of the American People*, p. 197.

63 "Public credit can only be supported by public faith": Chase, *Report of the Secretary of the Treasury*, p. 112, in Thorndike, "An Army of Officials," p. 7.

63 "despotic ruler of the House": Alphonse B. Miller, *Thaddeus Stevens* (New York: Harper and Row, 1939), pp. 133–34, in Kennon and Rogers, *Committee on Ways and Means*, p. 145.

63 "The capitalists must be assured": *Congressional Globe*, 37th Cong., 1st sess., 1861, p. 282, in Thorndike, "An Army of Officials," p. 7.

63 fairer to the average American: Chase, *Report of the Secretary of the Treasury*, p. 112, in Thorndike, "An Army of Officials," p. 7.

64 "The subjects of every state": Adam Smith, *An Inquiry into the Nature and Causes of The Wealth of Nations* (New York: Putnam, 2003), p. 1043.

64 "unwilling [to] increase": Ibid., pp. 1070–71.

65 The idea of a federal: *Congressional Globe*, 37th Cong., 2nd sess., 1861–62, p. 1196, in Thorndike, "An Army of Officials," p. 15.

65 "stocks, bonds, mortgages, money": Weisman, *Great Tax Wars*, p. 32.

66 "I am inclined very much to favor": *Congressional Globe*, 37th Cong., 2nd sess., 1861–62, p. 255, in Thorndike, "An Army of Officials," p. 12.

66 "millionaires like Mr. W. B. Astor": Ratner, *American Taxation*, p. 67.

66 "one of the most": Ibid., p. 68.

66 "seized every excuse": Ibid.

67 "Chase has no money": Donald, *Lincoln*, p. 330, in Weisman, *Great Tax Wars*, p. 36.

67 Rather than $318 million: Studenski and Kroos, *Financial History*, p. 142.

67 "just in its principle": Salmon P. Chase, *Report of the Secretary of the Treasury*, Washington, D.C., December 9, 1861, in Thorndike, "An Army of Officials," p. 14.

67 an innovative recommendation: Studenski and Kross, *Financial History*, p. 142.

67 "generation must be annually taxed": *Congressional Globe*, 37th Cong., 2nd sess., 1861–62, pp. 1040, 1194–97, in Ratner, *American Taxation*, p. 70.

68 "the modest tax": Thorndike, "An Army of Officials," p. 15.

68 "to find our way in the comparative dark": Francis Fessenden, *The Life and Public Service of William Pitt Fessenden* (Boston: Houghton Mifflin, 1907), p. 191, in Weisman, *Great Tax Wars*, p. 41.

69 "no burdens on those": *Congressional Globe*, 37th Cong., 2nd sess., 1861–62, pp. 1576–77, in Ratner, *American Taxation*, p. 71.

69 "one of the most obnoxious": *Congressional Globe*, 37th Cong., 1st sess., 1861, p. 247, in Thorndike, "An Army of Officials," p. 9.

70 "I know that the army of collectors": *Congressional Globe*, 37th Cong., 1st sess., 1861, p. 206, in Thorndike, "An Army of Officials," p. 11.

70 "Congress should not shrink": *Congressional Globe*, 37th Cong., 2nd sess., 1861–62, p. 1224, in Thorndike, "An Army of Officials," p. 19.

70 "In this emergency": Ibid., p. 255, in Thorndike, "An Army of Officials," p. 18.

71 "If we bleed": *Congressional Globe*, 37th Cong., 1st sess., 1861, p. 1196, in Ratner, *American Taxation*, p. 78.

72 "this inequality": Ibid., p. 1876, in Thorndike, "An Army of Officials," p. 21.

72 "The very best men in New York": Robert Stanley, *Dimensions in Law in the Service of Order: Origins of the Federal Income Tax, 1861–1913* (New York: Oxford University Press, 1993), p. 29, in Weisman, *Great Tax Wars*, p. 41.

72 "It is just, right and proper": *Congressional Globe*, 37th Cong., 1st sess., 1861, p. 1196, in Ratner, *American Taxation*, p. 83.

73 "an exclusive burden on industry": Ibid.

73 "at the same time [that] we": *Congressional Globe*, 37th Cong., 2nd sess., 1861–62, pp. 694–97, in Ratner, *American Taxation*, p. 97.

73 "in the dim future": Ibid., p. 837, in Ratner, *American Taxation*, p. 98.

74 to raise $400 million: Abraham Lincoln, "To the Senate and the House of Representatives," February 5, 1865, *Collected Works of Abraham Lincoln*, vol. 7, pp. 260–61, in Goodwin, *Team of Rivals*, p. 695.

75 "the stamping of paper": Alexander Hamilton, U.S. Department of the Treasury, *Report on the Bank*, December 13, 1790, in Chernow, *Alexander Hamilton*, p. 348.

75 "needed to establish a currency": Shapiro, *Coin of the Liberal Realm*, p. 174.

76 "legal money": Kennon and Rogers, *Committee on Ways and Means*, pp. 155–56.

76 "the wit of man": George Pendleton, *Congressional Globe*, 37th Cong., 2nd sess., 1861–62, p. 551, in McPherson, *Battle Cry of Freedom*, p. 446.

76 "I learn": Richard Nelson Current, *Old Thad Stevens: A Story of Ambition* (Westport, Conn.: Greenwood Press, 1980), p. 155, in Kennon and Rogers, *Committee on Ways and Means*, p. 157.

76 "be of greater advantage to the enemy": Miller, *Thaddeus Stevens*, p. 160.

76 "The Treasury is nearly empty": *Congressional Globe*, 37th Cong., 2nd sess., 1861–62, p. 618, in McPherson, *Battle Cry of Freedom*, p. 446.

77 "If nothing could be done": Miller, *Thaddeus Stevens*, p. 164.

77 "of doubtful constitutionality": Bray Hammond, *Sovereignty on an Empty Purse: Banks and Politics in the Civil War* (Princeton, N.J.: Princeton University Press, 1970), pp. 213–14, in McPherson, *Battle Cry of Freedom*, p. 445.

79 Southerners increasingly hoarded: Johnson, *History of the American People*, p. 463.

81 "What our Revolutionary Fathers": Macdonald, *A Free Nation Deep in Debt*, p. 397.

81 "The Working Men's Savings Bank": Ibid.

81 "to prevent a monied aristocracy": Robert V. Remini, *Andrew Jackson and the Course of American Freedom, 1822–1832*, vol. 2 (New York: Harper and Row, 1981), p. 34, in Gordon, *An Empire of Wealth*, p. 125.

82 "every person of small means": Abraham Lincoln, State of the Union, December 31, 1864.

82 "The great advantage of citizens being creditors": Ibid.

82 "these gentlemen from New York": John Wesley Hill, *Lincoln, Man of God* (New York: G. P. Putnam's Sons, 1920), p. 270.

82 "out of the three million subscribers": Macdonald, *A Free Nation Deep in Debt*, p. 398.

82 "Only a few years earlier": Ibid., p. 399.

83 Before the war: U.S. Senate, *History of the Committee on Finance*, 97th Cong., 1st sess., 1981, Senate doc. 97–5, p. 35, http://www.senate.finance.gov/history.pdf.

84 "Ought not men": Ratner, *American Taxation*, p. 70, in Weisman, *Great Tax Wars*, p. 39.

84 "filling all the customs house positions": Goodwin, *Team of Rivals*, p. 631.

85 "you and I have reached": Abraham Lincoln to Salmon P. Chase, June 30, 1864, in *Collected Works of Abraham Lincoln*, vol. 7, p. 419, in Goodwin, *Team of Rivals*, p. 633.

85 "Chase has two bad habits": Lucius Chittenden, *Recollections of President Lincoln* (New York: Harper and Bros., 1901), pp. 378–79, in Goodwin, *Team of Rivals*, p. 635.

85 "worse than another Bull Run": Ibid., p. 378–79.

85 "the great magician": *Chicago Tribune*, July 3, 1864, in Goodwin, *Team of Rivals*, p. 635.

85 "man of undoubted financial ability": *Chicago Tribune*, July 2, 1864, in Goodwin, *Team of Rivals*, p. 636.

85 warmly welcomed: Goodwin, *Team of Rivals*, p. 637.

86 "to clean up the corruption": Charles A. Jellison, *Fessenden of Maine, Civil War Senator* (Syracuse, N.Y.: Syracuse University Press, 1862), pp. 190–91.

86 "the validity of the public debt": U.S. Constitution, amend. 14, sec. 4.

86 "All debts contracted": U.S. Constitution, art. 6.

87 "Neither the United States": U.S. Constitution, amend. 14, sec. 4.

87 "the rapid reduction of taxation": *Congressional Globe*, 39th Cong., 1st sess., January 14, 1864, p. 216, in Flaherty, "The Perceived Power," p. 255.

87 "detrimental to the country": "Revenue System of the United States," House Ex. Doc. 34, 39th Cong., 1st sess., January 29, 1864, pp. 36–37, in Flaherty, "The Perceived Power," p. 255.

88 "was only considered and passed": *Congressional Globe*, 41st Cong., 2nd sess., 1870, p. 3993, in Thorndike, "An Army of Officials," p. 33.

88 "If you want to make this tax so odious": Ibid., p. 4717, in Thorndike, "An Army of Officials," p. 33.

88 "guarantee to bondholders": *Congressional Globe*, 41st Cong., 2nd sess., 1870, p. 4714, in Thorndike, "An Army of Officials," p. 33.

88 "In a republican form of government": *Congressional Globe*, 39th Cong., 1st sess., 1865, p. 2437, in Thorndike, "An Army of Officials," p. 34.

90 "to protect the national honor": Ulysses S. Grant, Inaugural Address, March 4, 1873, *Messages and Papers of the Presidents*, p. 396, in Macdonald, *A Free Nation Deep in Debt*, p. 395.

93 "the burden of taxes": Ratner, *American Taxation*, p. 139.

93 "The debt had been": Ibid., pp. 140–41.

93 "increased their margin of profits": Ibid., p. 139.

4. Capitalizing Patriotism

95 "excess profits tax": Weisman, *Great Tax Wars*, p. 326.

95 "the poor people throughout the country": Arthur S. Link, *Woodrow Wilson and the Progressive Era* (Norwalk, Conn.: Easton Press, 1982), p. 94, in Weisman, *Great Tax Wars*, p. 304.

96 "use America's . . . influence": 1896 Republican Party Platform, The American Presidency Project, http://www.presidency.ucsb.edu/showplatforms.php?platindex=R1896.

97 "piling up the public debt": Ibid.

97 "we are brethren": *Congressional Record*, 55th Cong., 2nd sess., 1898, vol. 31, p. 4356, in Ratner, *American Taxation*, p. 231.

97 "You count upon the heat of battle": Ibid., p. 4376, in Ratner, *American Taxation*, p. 231.

97 "the rich would receive the great benefits": Ratner, *American Taxation*, pp. 231–32.

98 "took from the rich only": Thomas G. Shearman, "The Owners of the United States," *Forum* (November 1889), pp. 262–73, in Ratner, *American Taxation*, pp. 219–20.

98 The Grangers, the Knights of Labor: Sheldon D. Pollock, *The Politics of Taxation: Who Pays What, When, How* (unpublished monograph, November 1998), p. 5.

98 sixty-eight bills: Ratner, *American Taxation*, p. 232.

99 "eschewed the easy": Benjamin M. Friedman, *The Moral Consequences of Economic Growth* (New York: Alfred A. Knopf, 2005), p. 133.

99 "The two competing": W. Elliot Brownlee, *Federal Taxation on America: A Short History* (Cambridge: Cambridge University Press, 1996), p. 35.

99 "open the door": Ratner, *American Taxation*, p. 232.

100 "beginning at nothing": Andrew Carnegie, "The Gospel of Wealth," *North American Review* 389 (June 1889), pp. 653–64.

100 "unpleasant but necessary": Randolph E. Paul, *Taxation in the United States* (Boston: Little, Brown, 1954), pp. 65–67, in Kennon and Rogers, *Committee on Ways and Means*, p. 244.

101 "intellectually keen, physically impressive": Ratner, *American Taxation*, p. 280.

102 "Nothing had ever injured the prestige of the Supreme Court": Archibald Butt, *Taft and Roosevelt*, vol. 1 (Garden City, N.J.: Doubleday, 1930), p. 134, in Ratner, *American Taxation*, p. 292.

103 In 1894, the richest 2 percent: Willford Isbell King, *The Wealth and Income of the People of the United States* (New York: The Macmillan Company, 1915), pp. 230–35, in Ratner, *American Taxation*, pp. 307–8.

103 "lay and collect taxes": U.S. Constitution, amend. 16.

103 "advance economic justice": Brownlee, *Federal Taxation*, p. 55.

103 "The country would be helpless": Cordell Hull, *The Memoirs of Cordell Hull* (New York: The Macmillan Company, 1948), p. 76, in Weisman, *Great Tax Wars*, p. 305.

104 Because average annual personal income was just over $600: Webber and Wildavasy, *History of Taxation and Expenditure in the Western World*, p. 421.

105 "The income tax law had been enacted in the nick of time": Hull, *Memoirs*, p. 76, in Weisman, *Great Tax Wars*, p. 305.

105 "America's Army for Empire": Graham A. Cosmas, *An Army for Empire: The U.S. Army in the Spanish American War* (College Station: Texas A&M University Press, 1971).

105 "were frequently called upon": Richard W. Stewart, ed., *American Military History, Volume I: The United States Army and the Forging of a Nation, 1775–1917* (Washington, D.C.: Dept. of the Army, 2005), p. 365.

107 "I did not get much in the way of inspiration": William G. McAdoo, *Crowded Years: The Reminiscences of William G. McAdoo* (Boston: Houghton Mifflin/Riverside Press, 1931), p. 373.

107 "did as well as anyone could have": Ibid., p. 374.
America's direct involvement: Studenski and Kroos, *Financial History of the United States*, p. 280.

107 "not believe that the people of this country": Woodrow Wilson, State of the Union, December 7, 1915, The American Presidency Project, www.presidency.ucsb.edu/ws/print.php?pid=29556.

108 "Every reform we have won": Ray Stannard Baker, *Woodrow Wilson: Life and Letters*, vol. 6 (Garden City, N.Y.: Doubleday, 1929–39), p. 506, n. 2.

109 "break the hold of corporate privilege": Hull, *Memoirs*, p. 61.

109 "A nation cannot go constantly into debt": U.S. Department of the Treasury, *Annual Report*, 1915, pp. 51–52, in Charles Gilbert, *American Financing* (Westport, Conn.: Greenwood Press, 1970), p. 77.

111 "clear triumph for the progressive and agrarian": Weisman, *Great Tax Wars*, p. 307.

111 "bring home to the minds of . . . voters": Ratner, *American Taxation*, p. 365, in Weisman, *Great Tax Wars*, p. 316.

112 "large, kind and affable man": Kennon and Rogers, *Committee on Ways and Means*, p. 253.

112 "sudden, rapid and stupendous": Elizabeth Saunders, "Economic Regulation in the Progressive Era," in Zelizer, *American Congress*, p. 340.

112 "belligerency would benefit": Joseph A. McCartin, "The First World War," in Zelizer, *American Congress*, p. 432.

112 "We are going to pile up debt": George W. Norris, "Speech Against Declaration of War," in Richard Hofstadter and Beatrice K. Hofstadter, *Great Issues in American History: From Reconstruction to the Present Day* (New York: Vintage Books, 1982), p. 214, in Mead, *Special Providence*, p. 187.

112 pay-as-we-go principle: Kennon and Rogers, *Committee on Ways and Means*, p. 253.

112 "graduated taxes upon income, inheritances": Ibid.

113 "You can tell your people": Roy G. and Gladys C. Blakey, *The Federal Income Tax* (New York: Longmans, Green, 1940), p. 123, in Weisman, *Great Tax Wars*, p. 318.

113 "involve the granting of adequate credits to the government": Woodrow Wilson, Address to Joint Session of Congress, "War with Germany," 65th Cong., 1st sess., April 2, 1917.

113 Troop level statistics: "Stewart, *American Military History*, p. 358.

113 Selective Service Act: Ibid., p. 367.

114 "I want the man who comes home": McCartin, "The First World War," in Zelizer, *American Congress*, p. 435.

115 "by a scale of taxation": McAdoo, *Crowded Years*, p. 383.

115 "perhaps be destructive": Ibid., p. 384.

115 "realized that a policy": Ibid., p. 374.

115 "place the United States on a wartime basis": Gilbert, *American Financing*, p. 83.

116 committee hearings: Ibid., p. 87.

116 "your children and mine": Alex Mathews Arnett, *Claude Kitchin and the Wilson War Policies* (Boston: Little, Brown, 1937), pp. 242–53, in Kennon and Rogers, *Committee on Ways and Means*, p. 255.

116 "the skin-deep dollar patriotism": Weisman, *Great Tax Wars*, p. 321.

116 "the current generation": *Congressional Record*, 65th Cong., 1st sess., August 16, 1917, pp. 662–63, in Gilbert, *American Financing*, p. 93.

116 "The concept of taxing": Weisman, *Great Tax Wars*, p. 326.

117 "manifestly equitable": Footnote in letter from Joseph Patrick Tumulty to Woodrow Wilson, August 2, 1918, in *Wilson Papers*, vol. 49, pp. 163–64; also Woodrow Wilson to Claude Kitchin, August, 2, 1918, in *Wilson Papers*.

117 "that distinguished stubborn": Diary of Josephus Daniels, August 14, 1918, *Wilson Papers*, vol. 49, p. 258, in Kennon and Rogers, *Committee on Ways and Means*, p. 257.

117 "government by the chairmen": Woodrow Wilson, *Congressional Government: A Study in American Politics* (Baltimore: Johns Hopkins University Press, 1956), pp. 82–83.

117 Joseph W. Fordney: Kennon and Rogers, *Committee on Ways and Means*, p. 255.

117 "seriously affect the cotton milling industry": *Congressional Record*, 65th Cong., 1st sess., August 16, 1917, p. 6067.

117 Underwood . . . fought against a war profits tax: Gilbert, *American Financing*, p. 93.

117 McAdoo raised his estimate: Ibid., p. 91.

118 "without a doubt": Ibid., p. 99.

118 "democratic principles": Ratner, *American Taxation*, p. 382.

118 "did not advise further tax increases": McAdoo, *Crowded Years*, p. 296.

119 "Congress is anxious": Gilbert, *American Financing*, p. 256.

119 "bear any burden and undergo any sacrifice": Wilson, Address to Joint Session of Congress, "War Finance Message," 65th Cong., 2nd sess., May 27, 1918, in Weisman, *Great Tax Wars*, p. 332.

119 "practically the whole of the burden": *Literary Digest* 38 (September 14, 1918), pp. 14–15, in Ratner, *American Taxation*, p. 390.

120 "piece of bungling absurdity": Gilbert, *American Financing*, p. 108.

120 "the greatest measure of taxation": "Washington Notes," *Journal of Political Economy* 27 (March 1919), p. 214, in Ratner, *American Taxation*, p. 391.

121 about 15 percent of American households: Brownlee, *Federal Taxation*, p. 63.

121 In 1920, the lowest: Gilbert, *American Financing*, p. 114.

121 "These burdens would": *New York Times*, August 1917, in Weisman, *Great Tax Wars*, p. 326.

121 "to make the larger public": Weisman, *Great Tax Wars*, p. 345.

121 While taxes did not produce: Ibid., p. 227; see also Seligman, *Income Tax*, in Studenski and Kroos, *Financial History*, p. 298.

122 "Chase was evidently afraid": McAdoo, *Crowded Years*, p. 374.

122 "on a commercial basis:" Ibid., pp. 117–19, 380–81.

122 ARE YOU 100% AMERICAN?: Macdonald, *A Free Nation Deep in Debt*, p. 403.

122 "The great financial operations": U.S. Department of the Treasury, *Annual Report*, 1917, p. 3, in Gilbert, *American Financing*, p. 118.

122 "largest authorization of bond issues": McAdoo, *Crowded Years*, p. 375.

122 "We knew that it was not going to be a cheap war": Ibid.

123 "man who could not serve": Ibid., p. 378.

123 "Member banks made loans to their customers": Milton Friedman and Anna Jacobsen

Schwartz, *A Monetary History of the United States, 1867–1960* (Princeton, N.J.: Princeton University Press, 1963), p. 220.

124 "to all intents and purposes": Ibid., pp. 216, 546.

124 "drafted into a role": Janeway, *Economics of Crisis*, p. 147.

124 "We cannot sell bonds": Gilbert, *American Financing*, pp. 126, 128.

124 "drew a smaller portion": Weisman, *Great Tax Wars*, p. 128.

124 "bonds could be sold": Ibid.

124 The fourth issue: Gilbert, *American Financing*, p. 135.

125 "Suppose hundreds of millions": McAdoo, *Crowded Years*, p. 380.

125 "every man, woman and child": U.S. Department of the Treasury, *Annual Report*, p. 19, in Gilbert, *American Financing*, p. 164.

125 "the humblest person in the land": William G. McAdoo, U.S. Department of the Treasury, "The Second Liberty Loan and the Causes of Our War with Germany," 65th Congress, 1st sess., Senate doc. 112 (Washington, D.C.: U.S. Government Printing Office, 1917), p. 14, in Gilbert, *American Financing*, p. 164.

125 Roughly half of all American families: Weisman, *Great Tax Wars*, p. 324.

126 "We went direct": McAdoo, *Crowded Years*, p. 378.

126 "Banks held for their own accounts": Janeway, *Economics of Crisis*, p. 154.

127 The annual rate of wholesale price inflation: Friedman and Schwartz, *Monetary History*, p. 546.

127 "the purchasing power of the public": Janeway, *Economics of Crisis*, p. 153.

127 "War-taxes should cease": *Literary Digest* 60 (February 22, 1919), p. 14, in Ratner, *American Taxation*, p. 300.

127 "No other single issue": Brownlee, *Federal Taxation*, p. 60.

128 "He fell as truly": Kennon and Rogers, *Committee on Ways and Means*, p. 250.

128 "encourages wasteful expenditures": U.S. Department of the Treasury, *Annual Report*, 1919, pp. 23–24, in Ratner, *American Taxation*, p. 403.

128 "strike down the vicious principle": *Congressional Record*, 67th Cong., 1st sess., 1921, p. 61, in Ratner, *American Taxation*, p. 410.

129 "The principle of income tax": Hull, *Memoirs*, p. 81.

129 "the Government . . . will receive more revenue": Andrew Mellon, *Taxation: The People's Business* (New York: Macmillan, 1929), p. 17.

129 "ability to pay": Ibid., pp. 56–57, in Brownlee, *Federal Taxation*, p. 76.

129 "the fairness of taxing more lightly": Ibid., in Brownlee, *Federal Taxation*, p. 77.

130 "catapulted the nation": Janeway, *Economics of Crisis*, p. 148.

5. A RIGHTEOUS MIGHT

134 "in their righteous might": Franklin D. Roosevelt, Address to Joint Session of Congress, "War with Japan" ("Day of Infamy"), 77th Cong., 1st sess., December 8, 1941.

136 "bold, persistent experimentation": Franklin D. Roosevelt, Commencement Address, Oglethorpe University, Atlanta, Georgia, May 23, 1932.

136 "would be inviting revolution": Robert A. Walker, *Rainey of Illinois: A Political Biography, 1903–1934* (Urbana: University of Illinois Press, 1977), p. 182, in Harold C. Relyea, "Speakers, Presidents and National Emergencies," House doc. 108–204, the Cannon Centenary Conference (Washington, D.C.: U.S. Government Printing Office, 2003), p. 207, http://www.gpoaccess.gov/serialset/cdocuments/hd108-204/browse.html.

137 "our revenue laws have operated": Franklin D. Roosevelt, Message to the Congress, June 1935, in Studenski and Kroos, *Financial History*, p. 444, in Ratner, *American Taxation*, p. 420.

137 Social Security Act: Kennon and Rogers, *Committee on Ways and Means*, p. 282.

140 "In the hope": Franklin D. Roosevelt, State of the Union, January 3, 1940, The American Presidency Project, http://www.presidency.ucsb.edu/ws/index.php?pid=15856.

140 First Revenue Act of 1940: Kennon and Rogers, *Committee on Ways and Means*, p. 297.

140 "temporary" taxes: Ratner, *American Taxation*, p. 494.

141 "an example of the deficit-financing": Kennon and Rogers, *Committee on Ways and Means*, p. 296, n. 39.

141 "little more than a gesture": John Morton Blum, *Roosevelt and Morgenthau: A Revision and Condensation from the Morgenthau Diaries* (Boston: Houghton Mifflin Company, 1970), p. 377.

141 "prevent defense profiteering": Ibid., p. 378.

141 Byron Patton "Pat" Harrison: Wikipedia.org/wiki/Pat Harrison.

142 "Roosevelt was in a hurry": Blum, *Roosevelt and Morgenthau*, p. 377.

142 Robert Lee "Muley" Doughton: Kennon and Rogers, *Committee on Ways and Means*, p. 276.

142 "if you are going to try to go to war": Diary of Henry L. Stimson, August 26, 1940, in Robert Higgs, "World War II and the Military Industrial Complex," The Future of Freedom Foundation, May 1995, http://www.fff.org/freedom/0595d.asp.

143 "eager for action": Blum, *Roosevelt and Morgenthau*, p. 378.

143 "that we must have": Ibid., p. 138.

143 It was far less burdensome: Kennon and Rogers, *Committee on Ways and Means*, p. 297.

143 "filled with loopholes": Blum, *Roosevelt and Morgenthau*, p. 379.

143 "permitted almost a total": Ibid., p. 377.

144 "It would take a Philadelphia lawyer": Kennon and Rogers, *Committee on Ways and Means*, p. 299.

144 "monumental specimen": Ibid., p. 298, n. 41.

144 "sponsored the very kinds": Blum, *Roosevelt and Morgenthau*, p. 379.

144 "in a campaign year": Ibid., p. 380.

145 "sell, transfer title to": Lend-Lease Act, *United States Statutes at Large*, 77th Cong., 1st sess., vol. 55, 1941–1942 (Washington: U.S. Government Printing Office, 1942), pp. 31–33.

145 "substituting military production and technology for [American] manpower": David M. Kennedy, *Freedom from Fear: The American People in Depression and War, 1929–1945* (New York: Oxford University Press, 2005), p. 619.

145 "Lend Lease would be": Patrick Maney, "The Forgotten New Deal Congress," in Zelizer, *American Congress*, p. 468.

146 In June, as Germany began its invasion: Studenski and Kroos, *Financial History*, p. 438.

146 "We must prepare to make the sacrifices": Franklin D. Roosevelt, State of the Union, January 6, 1941, The American Presidency Project, http://www.presidency.ucsb.edu/ws/index.php?pid=16092.

146 The Democratic "wastrels": Kennon and Rogers, *Committee on Ways and Means*, pp. 299–300.

147 "dyed in the wool conservative": Maney, "The Forgotten New Deal Congress," in Zelizer, *American Congress*, p. 464.

147 "Not as long as I am alive": Ibid., p. 486.

147 "shoot on sight": Franklin D. Roosevelt, Radio Address ("Fireside Chat"), September 11, 1941, The American Presidency Project, http://www.presidency.ucsb.edu/ws/?pid=16012.

147 Details of the Revenue Act of 1941: Kennon and Rogers, *Committee on Ways and Means*, p. 300.

147 "by far the heaviest": *New York Times*, September 18, 1941, in Ratner, *American Taxation*, p. 500.

148 "decayed nation": William L. Shirer, *The Rise and the Fall of the Third Reich* (New York: Simon and Schuster, 1960), p. 995, cited in Kennedy, *Freedom from Fear*, p. 615.

148 "It will not be sufficient": Franklin D. Roosevelt, State of the Union, January 6, 1942, The American Presidency Project, http://www.presidency.ucsb.edu/ws/index.php?pid=16253.

148 "route that would claim the smallest toll": Kennedy, *Freedom from Fear*, p. 619.

148 "War costs money": Roosevelt, State of the Union, January 6, 1942.

150 "to persuade the balky Congress": Blum, *Roosevelt and Morgenthau*, p. 426.

150 "As much as 50 percent of capacity": Kennedy, *Freedom from Fear*, p. 617.

151 "The problem we face": Robert Skidelsky, *John Maynard Keynes: Fighting for Freedom, 1937–1946* (New York: Penguin Books, 2000), pp. 54–55.

151 "low and middle income Americans": Joseph J. Thorndike, "The Price of Civilization: Taxation in Depression and War, 1933–1945," Tax History Museum, February 23, 2003, p. 4, http://www.tax.org/Museum/default.htm.

152 "The task before us": Henry Morgenthau Jr., U.S. Department of the Treasury, *Testimony of Secretary Morgenthau before the House Ways and Means Committee*, 77th Cong., 2nd sess., March 3, 1942.

152 "should accomplish more than": Ibid.

152 "to check inflation": Ibid.

152 "fair and non-discriminatory": Morgenthau, *Testimony before the Ways and Means Committee*.

152 Morgenthau's tax proposals: Kennon and Rogers, *Committee on Ways and Means*, p. 301.

153 "widely spread among all the people": Russell C. Leffingwell to Henry Morgenthau Jr., October 2, 1941, and June 11, 1942, in Russell C. Leffingwell Papers, Yale University.

154 sales tax would raise nearly $6 billion: Kennon and Rogers, *Committee on Ways and Means*, p. 301.

154 a hefty sales tax: Blum, *Roosevelt and Morgenthau*, p. 435.

154 "We feel strongly": Ibid., p. 452.

154 "a 'spare-the-rich' tax": U.S. Department of the Treasury, "Evils of the Sales Tax," Briefing Paper for the President by Treasury Division of Tax Research, doc. 96–6650, April 14, 1942, in Joseph J. Thornton, "The Tax That Wasn't: Mid-Century Proposals for a National Sales Tax," Tax History Museum, March 19, 1996, p. 3, http://www.taxhistory.org/thp/readings.nsf/cf7c9c870b600b9585256df80075b9dd/b2f82f1c5b44fdf285256e430078dbfd?OpenDocument.

155 "regarded [it] as too radical": Brownlee, *Federal Taxation*, p. 111.

155 "The plan is dead": Blum, *Roosevelt and Morgenthau*, p. 438.

155 "not leave a stone unturned": Ibid., p. 432.

155 "the blunt fact . . . that every single person": Franklin D. Roosevelt, Message to Congress, April 27, 1942.

155 "antagonistic toward almost every": Blum, *Roosevelt and Morgenthau*, p. 434.

156 "Those fellows just don't know": Ibid., p. 435.

156 "to draw into the treasury": Henry Morgenthau Jr., U.S. Department of the Treasury, *Testimony of Secretary Morgenthau before the Senate Finance Committee*, September 3, 1942.

156 "Battles are not won": Franklin D. Roosevelt, Radio Address ("Labor Day Fireside Chat"), September 7, 1942, The American Presidency Project, http://www.presidency.ucsb.edu/ws/index.php?pid=16303.

157 the Victory Tax: Blum, *Roosevelt and Morgenthau*, p. 439.

157 "might as well have been written in a foreign language": Ibid., pp. 302–3.

157 "represented agreement between Congress and Roosevelt": Brownlee, *Federal Taxation*, p. 112.

158 "I cannot acquiesce in eliminating": Dennis J. Ventrey Jr. and Joseph J. Thorndike, "The Plan that Slogans Built: The Revenue Act of 1943," Tax History Museum, September 1, 1997, p. 4, http://www.taxhistory.org/thp/readings.nsf/cf7c9c870b600b9585256df80075b9dd/671f701c110a19d985256e430079173d?OpenDocument.

159 "I cannot ask the Congress": Franklin D. Roosevelt, Budget Message, January 6, 1943, The American Presidency Project, www.presidency.ucsb.edu/ws/index.php?pid=16375.

160 "What we want is to get": Blum, *Roosevelt and Morgenthau*, p. 441.

160 "like Caesar's assassins": Joseph J. Thorndike, "Wartime Tax Legislation and the Politics of Policymaking," Tax History Museum, October 25, 2001, available at http://www.taxhistory.org/thp/readings.nsf/cf7c9c870b600b9585256df80075b9dd/f9cb12c7ca3ccf9185256e22007840e7?OpenDocument.

160 "The taxpayer is up against": Ralph Grizzle's Online Portfolio, undated, http://www.ralphgrizzle.com/.

161 "amazing, fantastic, and visionary": Thorndike, "Wartime Tax Legislation," p. 4.

161 "keep our corporations in sound financial condition": Ibid., p. 3.

161 "wiped out the middle class": Kennon and Rogers, *Committee on Ways and Means*, p. 305, n. 56.

161 It was expected to generate just over $2 billion: Thorndike, "Wartime Tax Legislation," p. 4.

162 "wholly ineffective" and "replete with provisions": Franklin D. Roosevelt, Tax Bill Veto Message, February 22, 1944, The American Presidency Project, www.presidency.ucsb.edu/ws/index.php?pid=16490.

162 "oppressive to taxpayers": Blum, *Roosevelt and Morgenthau*, p. 450.

162 "a calculated and deliberate": U.S. Senate History, http://www.senate.gov/artandhistory/history/common/generic/Senate_Historical_Office.htm.

163 "leaped from $2.2 billion": Brownlee, *Federal Taxation*, p. 115.

163 "your privilege, not just your duty": Ibid., pp. 118–19.

163 "spirit of sacrifice": A. T. Peacock and J. Wiseman, *The Growth of Public Expenditure in the United Kingdom* (Princeton, N.J.: Princeton University Press, 1961), p. 428, in Webber and Wildavasy, *History of Taxation and Expenditure*, p. 530.

164 "Fear of a return of the depression": Brownlee, *Federal Taxation*, pp. 116–17.

165 "Well, I have to tell you": Skidelsky, *John Maynard Keynes*, p. 121.

166 "every man and woman who owned a Government Bond": Henry Morgenthau Jr., *War Financing Policies: Excerpts from Three Addresses by Morgenthau* (Washington, D.C.: U.S. Government Printing Office, 1944), in Peter Tufano and David Schneider, "Reinvesting Savings Bonds," *Tax Notes*, March 3, 2005, p. 12, http://www.people.hbs.edu/ptufano/taxnotes.PDF.

167 "large compulsory lending program": Blum, *Roosevelt and Morgenthau*, p. 448.

167 "make the country war minded": Ibid., p. 427.

168 "There are millions of people": John Morton Blum, *From the Morgenthau Diaries: The Years of War* (Boston: Houghton Mifflin, 1967), pp. 19–20, in Macdonald, *Free Nation Deep in Debt*, p. 440.

168 "the biggest amount of money": Blum, *Roosevelt and Morgenthau*, p. 429.

168 "He didn't count the cost": Government posters available on the Internet.

168 "Every dime and dollar": Roosevelt, Message to the Congress, April 27, 1942.

168 "Every dollar that you invest": Franklin D. Roosevelt, Radio Address ("Fireside Chat"), September 8, 1943, in Macdonald, *A Free Nation Deep in Debt*, p. 442, http://www.presidency.ucsb.edu/ws/index.php?pid=16312.

170 "the shifting of the major part of American industry": Roosevelt, Message to the Congress, April 27, 1941.

170 "compete with war production": Morgenthau, *Testimony of Morgenthau before the Ways and Means Committee.*

170 "We are fast approaching": Ibid.

170 "for any of us to stop thinking": Franklin D. Roosevelt, State of the Union, "The Four Freedoms," January 6, 1941, The American Presidency Project, http://www.presidency.ucsb.edu/ws/index.php?pid=16092.

6. "A Prolonged and Complex Struggle"

174 "Nothing would please our potential enemy": *Congressional Record,* 81st Cong., 1st sess., vol. 95, 1949, pp. 4427–28, in Dennis S. Ippolito, "Federal Budget Policy and Defense Strategy," Strategic Studies Institute, U.S. Army War College, February 15, 1996, p. 7, http://permanent.access.gpo.gov/lps13638/lps13638/budget.pdf.

174 "A nation which exhausts itself ": *Congress and the Nation 1945–1964* (Washington, D.C.: Congressional Quarterly, 1965), p. 254, in Ippolito, "Federal Budget Policy," p. 7.

175 "We will not measure up": Harry S. Truman, State of the Union, January 21, 1946, The American Presidency Project, http://www.presidency.ucsb.edu/ws/index.php?pid=12467.

175 By January 1947: Harry S. Truman, State of the Union, January 6, 1947, The American Presidency Project, http://www.presidency.ucsb.edu/ws/index.php?pid=12762.

176 "reckless spending of the public's money": "Republican Party Tax Study Committee Report," *New York Times,* July 26, 1846, in Studenski and Kroos, *Financial History,* p. 476.

176 "that we will travel down the same old road": Robert Patterson to R. Nicholas Burns, February 11, 1947, in Robert Patterson Papers, box 18, Draper Manuscripts, Truman State University, Kirksville, Mo., in John Lewis Gaddis, *The Origins of the Cold War, 1941–1947* (New York: Columbia University Press, 1972), p. 345.

177 "the true aims and methods": "GOP Senators Statement Charging Foreign Policy Bungling in Europe, Asia," *New York Times,* August 14, 1950.

177 "a man wielding a meat ax": Joseph M. Jones, *The Fifteen Weeks* (New York: Harcourt, Brace, 1964), p. 91, in Gaddis, *Origins of the Cold War,* p. 345.

177 "The world is about to blow up": Joseph Alsop to Martin Sommers, February 25, 1947, MSS, box 1, in Gaddis, *Origins of the Cold War,* p. 345.

178 "Both world wars showed": Senate Armed Services Committee, *Testimony of Secretary of Defense James Forrestal,* March 18, 1947, in Janeway, *Economics of Crisis,* p. 215.

178 "It must be the policy of the United States": Harry S. Truman, Greek-Turkish Aid Policy, Address to Joint Session of Congress, 80th Cong., 1st sess., March 12, 1947.

179 "to an ordinary Congressman": Walter Isaacson and Evan Thomas, *The Wise Men: Six Friends and the World They Made—Acheson, Bohlen, Harriman, Kennan, Lovett, McCloy* (New York: Simon and Schuster, 1986), p. 406.

179 "internationalist consensus": Ibid., p. 399.

179 "advice and consent": Dean Acheson, *Present at the Creation: My Years at the State Department* (New York: W. W. Norton, 1969), pp. 223–24, in Isaacson and Thomas, *Wise Men,* p. 399.

179 "appear soft on Communism": Isaacson and Thomas, *Wise Men,* p. 401.

179 "hunger, poverty, desperation, and chaos": George C. Marshall, Commencement Address, "The Marshall Plan," Harvard University, Cambridge, Mass., June 5, 1947.

179 "We're headed for the storm cellar": Isaacson and Thomas, *Wise Men,* p. 428.

180 "the Soviet Union and its agents": Harry S. Truman, Address to Joint Session of

Congress, "National Security and Conditions in Europe," 80th Cong., 2nd sess., March 17, 1948.

181 "a substantial and rapid": "A Report to the National Security Council-NSC 68," April 12, 1950, President's Secretary's File, Truman Papers, http://www.trumanlibrary.org/whistlestop/study_collections/coldwar/documents/sectioned.php?documentid=10-1&pagenumber=1&groupid=1.

181 "The American economy": NSC-68, April 15, 1950, cited in John Lewis Gaddis, *Strategies of Containment: A Critical Appraisal of Postwar American National Security Policy* (New York: Oxford University Press, 1982), p. 93.

181 "the nation could sustain more vigorous growth": Gaddis, *Strategies of Containment,* p. 94.

181 "increased defense must mean equivalently lower living standards": Hamilton Q. Dearborn, Memorandum, approved by Leon Keyserling, May 1950, cited in Gaddis, *Strategies of Containment,* p. 94.

182 "the eventual strength of the economy": Senate Committee on Appropriations, *Statement of General Omar Bradley before the Committee on Appropriations,* 81st Cong., 2nd sess., March 15, 1950.

182 "domestic objectives first": Senate Committee on Appropriations, Supplemental Appropriations for 1951, *Hearings before the Committee on Appropriations,* 81st Cong., 2nd sess., 1951, p. 39, in Paul Y. Hammond, "NCS-68: A Prologue to Rearmament," in *Strategy, Politics, and Defense Budgets,* ed. Walter R. Schilling, Paul Y. Hammond, and Glen Snyder (New York: Columbia University Press, 1962), pp. 267–378.

183 policy of relying on a small: Herman S. Wolk, "The Blueprint for the Cold War," *Air Force Magazine Online* 83, no. 3 (March 2000), p. 9, http://www.afa.org/magazine/march2000/0300coldwar.asp.

184 "The threat of world conquest": Harry S. Truman, State of the Union, January 8, 1951, The American Presidency Project, http://www.presidency.ucsb.edu/ws/index.php?pid=14017.

184 "existing mobilization plans": Robert W. Coakley, "Highlights of Mobilization, Korean War," March 10, 1959, http://www.army.mil/cmh-pg/documents/Korea/kwmob.htm.

185 "must ask for money": Dean Acheson, Memorandum of Conversation, July 14, 1950, box 66, Dean G. Acheson Papers, Harry S. Truman Library and Museum, Independence, Mo.

185 vulnerable at home: George C. Marshall, Press Conference Minutes, March 27, 1951, box 206, folder 58, George C. Marshall Papers, George C. Marshall Foundation, Lexington, Va.

185 "about halfway between": Lester H. Brune, "Guns and Butter: The Pre-Korean War Dispute Over Budget Allocations," *American Journal of Economics and Sociology* 48, no. 3 (1989), p. 361.

185 Wholesale prices rose: Friedman, *Moral Consequences of Economic Growth,* p. 597.

186 "recalled his experience in the 1920s": Minutes of the Federal Reserve Open Market Committee, January 31, 1951, in Allan H. Meltzer, *The History of the Federal Reserve* (Chicago: University of Chicago Press, 2004), p. 25.

186 "We must combat": Board of Governors of the Federal Reserve System, minutes of the Federal Open Market Committee (FOMC), January 31, 1951, http://fraser.stlouisfed.org/docs/MeltzerPDFs/omc_013151b.pdf.

186 "the Soviet dictators": Joseph O'Mahoney to Thomas McCabe, February 13, 1951, minutes of the FOMC Executive Committee, February 14, 1951, p. 83.

187 "For years we Republicans": Kennon and Rogers, *Committee on Ways and Means,* p. 308.

188 "The time for tax reduction": Ibid., pp. 309–10.

188 "more than 70 percent": Harry S. Truman, State of the Union, January 4, 1950, The American Presidency Project, http://www.presidency.ucsb.edu/ws/index.php?pid=13567.

189 "revenue-raising provisions": Truman Presidential Museum and Library, July 25, 1950.

189 "Rarely has the Institute": Gallup, "Public Would Rather Risk War than Permit Red Expansion," *Washington Post*, August 4, 1950.

189 The following January: Kennon and Rogers, *Committee on Ways and Means*, p. 310.

190 "those they represented": Ibid., p. 311.

190 "During World War II": Harry S. Truman, Special Message to the Congress Recommending a "Pay as We Go" Tax Program, February 2, 1951, The American Presidency Project, www.presidency.ucsb.edu/ws/index.php?pid=12846.

190 "as large an amount as can be safely collected": Kennon and Rogers, *Committee on Ways and Means*, p. 311.

190 "economic voodoo talk": Ibid.

190 "socialist planners": Ibid.

190 The Revenue Act of 1951: Zelizer, *American Congress*, p. 87.

190 Revenues escalated: Iwan W. Morgan, *Deficit Government: Taxing and Spending in Modern America* (Chicago: National Book Network, 1995), p. 61, in Zelizer, *American Congress*, p. 87.

191 "has exposed the fact": "15 Republicans Urge Standby Control Setup," *Washington Post*, July 31, 1950.

191 "It is a bruising and shocking fact": Robert J. Donovan, *Tumultuous Years: The Presidency of Harry S. Truman, 1949–1953* (New York: W. W. Norton, 1982), p. 255, in Michael P. Riccards, *The Ferocious Engine of Democracy: A History of the American Presidency*, vol. 2 (Lanham, Md.: Madison Books, 1995), p. 227.

191 83 percent of Americans polled favored: Schwerin Research Corporation, "Domestic Public Opinion and the Achievement of National Objectives," June 5, 1952.

191 "either the stakes are important enough": Mead, *Special Providence*, p. 254.

192 "a general feeling": George C. Marshall, press conference minutes, Marshall Papers, box 206, folder 58, March 27, 1951.

192 "a demand for greatly expanded": Robert A. Caro, *Master of the Senate: The Years of Lyndon Johnson* (New York: Alfred A. Knopf, 2002), p. 347.

193 "The Truman Administration had decided": *Washington Post*, May 12–17, 1952, in Caro, *Master of the Senate*, p. 348.

193 "if rearmament is directed at the long pull": Caro, *Master of the Senate*, p. 347.

193 "We all expected that the budget we inherited": Dwight D. Eisenhower, *Mandate for a Change* (Garden City, N.Y.: Doubleday & Company, Inc., 1963), p. 128.

193 "we had Republican promises": Ibid., p. 130.

194 "justified only": Dwight D. Eisenhower, State of the Union, February 2, 1953, The American Presidency Project, http://www.presidency.ucsb.edu/ws/index.php?pid=9829.

194 "one of the worst days": Dwight D. Eisenhower diary, May 1, 1953, "The Presidency: The Middle Way," vol. 14, pt. 2, ch. 3, doc. no. 168, The Papers of Dwight D. Eisenhower, Johns Hopkins University, Baltimore, Md., http://eisenhower.press.jhu.edu/index.html.

194 "broke out in violent objection": Ibid.

195 "There is no defense": Sherman Adams, *First Hand Report: The Inside Story of the Eisenhower Administration* (New York: Harper and Brothers, 1961), ch. 17, p. 360ff., in Paul Johnson, *A History of the American People* (New York: HarperCollins Publishers, 1998), p. 832.

195 "have plainly said that free people cannot preserve": Caro, *Master of the Senate*, p. 131.

195 "If economic stability goes down the drain": John Foster Dulles, Statement to the U.S.

Senate Foreign Relations and House Foreign Affairs Committees, May 5, 1953, cited in Gaddis, *Strategies of Containment*, p. 134.

195 "The relationship between military and economic strength": Charles C. Alexander, *Holding the Line: The Eisenhower Era* (Bloomington: Indiana University Press, 1976), p. 29.

195 "Regardless of the consequences": Eisenhower, *Mandate for a Change*, p. 130.

196 "Conservative Clique": Randall Bennett Woods, "The Cold War," in Zelizer, *American Congress*, pp. 507–9.

196 "spirit of true bipartisanship": Caro, *Master of the Senate*, p. 523.

196 "Any old jackass can kick a barn": Ibid.

196 "voted against more New Deal": Kennon and Rogers, *Committee on Ways and Means*, p. 313.

197 "emphatic in my opposition": Eisenhower, *Mandate for a Change*, p. 201.

197 "no matter what": Kennon and Rogers, *Committee on Ways and Means*, p. 313.

197 "could not agree that the country should have, or wanted": Eisenhower, *Mandate for a Change*, p. 130.

197 "Unhappily the danger": Dwight D. Eisenhower, Farewell Address to the Nation, January 17, 1961, http://mcadams.posc.mu.edu/ike.htm.

197 "the current problem in defense spending": Jeremy Isaacs and Taylor Downing, "Epilogue: What the Cold War Cost," *The Cold War*, CNN, episode 24, http://www.cnn.com/SPECIALS/cold.war/episodes/24epilogue/.

198 "for a long and indefinite": *Congressional Record*, 83rd Cong., 1st sess., vol. 94, May 20, 1953, p. 5180, in Ippolito, "Federal Budget Policy," Strategic Studies Institute, p. 3.

198 "Unbalanced budgets": Eisenhower, *Mandate for a Change*, p. 132.

198 "With this thief ": "The Presidency: Keeping the Peace," vol. 18, introduction, p. 5, The Papers of Dwight D. Eisenhower, Johns Hopkins University Press.

199 "a strong military posture": National Security Council Document 162/2, "Basic National Security Policy," October 30, 1953, http://www.jan.vandercrabben.name/nsc/index.php.

199 "members of Congress who so fearfully": Eisenhower, *Mandate for a Change*, p. 201.

199 "This country could choke itself": Adams, *First Hand Report*, p. 380ff, in Johnson, *History of the American People*, p. 832.

200 "He should know more": Sam Rayburn to Hall, April 2, 1953, in D. B. Hardeman and Donald C. Bacon, *Rayburn: A Biography* (Austin: Texas Monthly Press, 1987), p. 393.

200 "People grow weary of war": Gaddis, *Strategies of Containment*, p. 133.

200 greatly admired Andrew Mellon: Alexander, *Holding the Line*, pp. 38–39.

201 Air Force's enhanced role under the New Look: Ibid., pp. 69–70.

201 Army Chief of Staff Matthew B. Ridgway resigned: Ibid., p. 70.

201 "parochial": Matthew Bunker Ridgway obituary, Arlington National Cemetery Web site, March 1993, http://www.arlingtoncemetery.net/ridgway.htm.

201 "missile gap": Alexander, *Holding the Line*, p. 71.

201 "a private political relief bill": Eisenhower, *Mandate for a Change*, pp. 497–98.

201 "under conditions of high": Dwight D. Eisenhower, State of the Union, January 5, 1956, The American Presidency Project, http://www.presidency.ucsb.edu/ws/index.php?pid=10593.

202 "It is not under the authority": Dwight D. Eisenhower, news conference, April 25, 1956, http://www.presidency.ucsb.edu/ws/index.php?pid=10787.

202 "modern Republicanism": Alexander, *Holding the Line*, p. 191.

202 "which had exhibited": Ibid., p. 219.

203 "had been a casualty": Ibid., p. 220.

203 "to avoid the impulse": Eisenhower, Farewell Address.

204 "determination but also with patience": Jay Waltz, "U.S. Can Hit Back," *New York Times,* January 1, 1951.

205 "over the last 7 1/2 years": 1960 Democratic Platform, The American Presidency Project, http://www.presidency.ucsb.edu/showplatforms.php?platindex=D1960.

206 "In terms of total military strength": "Man of the Year: John F. Kennedy," *Time,* January 5, 1962, http://www.time.com/time/subscriber/personoftheyear/archieve/stories/1961. html.

7. "HARD AND INESCAPABLE FACTS"

208 "hard and inescapable facts": Lyndon B. Johnson, State of the Budget and Economy Message to the Congress, August 3, 1987, The American Presidency Project, www .presidency.ucsb.edu/ws/index.php?pid=28371.

209 "Eisenhower, they believed, had relied too heavily": John Lewis Gaddis, *Strategies of Containment: A Critical Appraisal of Postwar American National Security Policy* (New York: Oxford University Press, 1982), p. 202.

209 similar fate would befall the Great Society: Conversation with Joseph Califano, October 20, 2005.

210 "We can continue the Great Society": Lyndon B. Johnson, State of the Union, January 12, 1966, The American Presidency Project, http://www.presidency.ucsb.edu/ws/index .php?pid=28015.

210 "a sensible course": Lyndon B. Johnson, State of the Union, January 10, 1967, The American Presidency Project, http://www.presidency.ucsb.edu/ws/index.php?pid=28338.

210 "The economists in the administration watched with pain": Arthur M. Okun, *The Political Economy of Prosperity* (Washington, D.C.: Brookings Institution, 1970), pp. 71–72.

210 "Unless expenditures could be contained": Doris Kearns Goodwin, *Lyndon Johnson and the American Dream* (New York: St. Martin's Press, 1991), p. 296.

210 "cardinal rule": Ibid., p. 295.

211 "they refused to admit": Ibid., p. 297.

211 "When inflation set in": Ibid., p. 298.

211 "There was a complete lack": Jeffery W. Helsing, *Johnson's War/Johnson's Great Society: The Guns and Butter Trap* (Westport, Conn.: Praeger, 2000), p. 170.

211 "the National Security Council meetings were like sieves": Goodwin, *Lyndon Johnson,* p. 319.

212 "I had more information": William McChesney Martin, May 8, 1987, Martin Papers, Missouri Historical Society, St. Louis, Mo., in Allan Meltzer, "Origins of the Great Inflation," Federal Reserve Bank of St. Louis *Review* (March/April, 2005), pp. 1–2.

212 "president flatly refused my advice": Robert S. McNamara, *In Retrospect: The Tragedy and Lessons of Vietnam* (New York: Vintage Books, 1996), p. 205.

212 "firmly stated throughout . . . 1966": Robert P. Bremner, *Chairman of the Fed: William McChesney Martin and the Creation of the Modern Financial System* (New Haven, Conn.: Yale University Press, 2004), p. 220.

212 "Obviously you don't know": William Conrad Gibbons, *The U.S. Government and the Vietnam War, Part III, January–July 1965* (Princeton, N.J.: Princeton University Press, 1965), p. 389, in Helsing, *Johnson's War,* p. 172.

212 "all those conservatives in the Congress": Goodwin, *Lyndon Johnson,* p. 252.

213 "It would make more sense": Helsing, *Johnson's War,* p. 202.

213 "We are entitled": U.S. Department of Defense, Appropriations for 1966, Hearings before the Senate Finance Committee, Jan. 20, 1966, p. 875, in Helsing, *Johnson's War,* p. 204.

213 "to give the military": Helsing, *Johnson's War*, p. 224.

213 "to avoid the unnecessary": Anthony S. Campagna, *The Economic Consequences of the War in Vietnam* (New York: Praeger, 1991), p. 32.

213 "that the war would wind down": Helsing, *Johnson's War*, p. 224.

214 "The lack of accurate": "Economic Effect of Vietnam Spending," *Report of the Joint Economic Committee*, July 7, 1967, p. 3, in Helsing, *Johnson's War*, p. 204, http://www .vietnam.ttu.edu/star/images/227/2274104001o.pdf.

214 "ever since the Korean War": Helsing, *Johnson's War*, p. 170.

215 "the Vietnam conflict": Edwin C. Hargrove and Samuel A. Morley, eds., "Interview with Arthur Okun," in *The President and the Council of Economic Advisors: Interviews with CEA Chairmen* (Nashville, Tenn.: Vanderbilt University Press, 1964), p. 279.

215 "strong defensive posture": Helsing, *Johnson's War*, p. 179.

215 military spending increased: Ibid., p. 170.

215 Borrowing costs rose: Campagna, *Economic Consequences*, p. 39.

216 "sustain and stretch out": Bremner, *Chairman*, p. 206.

216 "a question whether the Federal Reserve": Minutes of the Federal Reserve Board of Governors, December 3, 1965, p. 28, in Allan H. Meltzer, "Origins of the Great Inflation," p. 164, http://research.stlouisfed.org/publications/review/05/03/part2/Meltzer.pdf.

216 "burning up the wires": Bremner, *Chairman*, p. 206.

216 "was very disagreeable": Meltzer, "Origins of the Great Inflation," p. 166.

217 "the intense pride": Bremner, *Chairman*, p. 211.

217 "Monetary policy has done": Ibid., p. 225.

217 "go-rounds with Johnson": Ibid., p. 220.

217 Vietnam deficits: Ibid., p. 224.

218 "candid presentation of the facts": Ibid., pp. 224–25.

218 LBJ held the line: Paul A. Volcker and Toyoo Ghoyten, *Changing Fortunes: The World's Money and the Threat to American Leadership* (New York: Times Books, 1992), p. 38.

218 "last for two years": Johnson, State of the Union, January 10, 1967, The American Presidency Project, www.presidency.ucsb.edu/ws/index.php?pid=28338.

218 "If Americans today still paid": Julian E. Zelizer, *Taxing America: Wilbur D. Mills, Congress and the State: 1945–1975* (Cambridge: Cambridge University Press, 1998), p. 262.

218 "You can't legislate on the basis of economic forecasts": Ibid., p. 227.

219 "the fact of the matter": Ibid., p. 262.

219 "What I wanted to do": Transcript, Wilbur Mills Oral History Interview 3, May 15, 1987, by Michael L. Gillette, LBJ Library, Austin, Tex, http://www.ssa.gov/history /pdf/mills3.pdf.

219 "The nation had an excellent chance": Hargrove and Morley, "Interview with Arthur Okun," in *President and the Council*, p. 279.

220 "I know it doesn't add to your polls": Joseph A. Califano Jr., *The Triumph and Tragedy of Lyndon Johnson: The White House Years* (New York: Simon and Schuster, 1991), p. 245.

220 "The overwhelming preponderance of economic opinion": Bremner, *Chairman*, p. 235.

220 "clear and present danger": Johnson, State of the Budget and Economy Message to the Congress, August 3, 1967.

221 "borrow it all": Lyndon B. Johnson, Transcript, President's News Conference on the Tax Message, Washington, D.C., August 3, 1967, The American Presidency Project, http:// www.presidency.ucsb.edu/ws/index.php?pid=28373.

221 "We cannot permit": "President's Message and an Analysis of the $196.2 Billion Federal Budget," *New York Times*, February 25, 1967.

221 "staying power": Max Frankel, "Plea by the President," *New York Times*, January 11,

1967, in Julian E. Zelizer, "Taxing the Homefront: Congress and Taxation in 1968 and 2003," conference paper, February 2005, Harvard University Business School, p. 5.

221 Harris poll numbers: Louis Harris, "The Public Favors Guns and Butter, But Would Give Priority to Guns," *Washington Post*, January 29, 1968, in Zelizer, "Taxing the Homefront," p. 7.

221 "American public opinion": Mead, *Special Providence*, p. 222.

221 "too many qualified targets": "The Vietnam War: The Jungle War, 1965–1968," The History Place Web site, http://www.historyplace.com/unitedstates/vietnam/index-1965.html.

221 "Mr. Ford and Mr. Mills have taken the position": Bremner, *Chairman*, p. 236.

222 "spirit and deed": Zelizer, *Taxing America*, p. 271.

222 "Failure to act—and to act promptly and decisively": Lyndon B. Johnson, "President's Address on the Vietnam War and his Political Plans," *New York Times*, April 1, 1968.

223 "any further confrontation": Zelizer, *Taxing America*, p. 276.

223 "This is a question of survival": Minutes of cabinet meeting, May 29, 1968, box 13, LBJ Cabinet Papers, Lyndon Baines Johnson Library and Museum, Austin, Tex.

223 Revenue and Expenditure Control Act: Zelizer, *Taxing America*, p. 277.

223 "I am certainly not talking about": Wilbur D. Mills, "Remarks at the Fifth Congressional District of Indians," January 26, 1968, Wilbur Mills Paper Collection, box 240, file 1, in Zelizer, *Taxing America*, p. 278.

224 "doom the millions": Henry Kissinger, *Years of Upheaval* (Boston: Little, Brown, 1982), p. 88.

224 "realized that for economic reasons": Stephen E. Ambrose and Douglas G. Brinkley, *Rise to Globalism: American Foreign Policy Since 1938* (New York: Penguin Books, 1985), pp. 242–43.

225 "idea has developed": Transcript, Mills Oral History Interview 3, May 15, 1987.

225 Congress was unwilling: Dennis S. Ippolito, "Budget Policy, Deficits and Defense: A Fiscal Framework for Defense Planning," Strategic Studies Institute, U.S. Army War College, June 2005, http://www.strategicstudiesinstitute.army.mil/pubs/display.cfm?pubID=604.

8. BANKRUPTING COMMUNISM

227 "during the course of the Cold War": Richard Reeves, *President Reagan: The Triumph of Imagination* (New York: Simon and Schuster, 2005), p. 9.

227 a great deal more defense spending: Interview with David Frum, in Lou Cannon, *President Reagan: The Role of a Lifetime* (New York: Public Affairs, 1982), p. 759.

228 A large majority: Ben J. Wattenberg, *The First Universal Nation: Leading Indicators and Ideas About the Surge of America in the 1990s* (New York: Free Press, 1991), p. 246.

228 "a consensus rare in American peacetime": Cannon, *President Reagan*, p. 132.

228 "In the last decade": Ronald Reagan, State of the Union, January 26, 1982, The American Presidency Project, http://www.presidency.ucsb.edu/ws/index.php?pid=42687.

228 "to contain, and reverse": National Security Decision Directive Number 32, doc. NSC-NSDD-32, May 20, 1982, http://www.fas.org/irp/offdocs/nsdd/nsdd-032.htm.

229 "the Soviets were too weak": Lou Cannon, "President Ronald Reagan," *Washington Post*, June 6, 2004, p. A1.

229 "all of the best studies have shown": Reeves, *President Reagan*, p. 198.

230 "A man of restless intellect": Cannon, *President Reagan*, p. 200.

230 a surrogate for John Anderson: Ibid., p. 63.

230 "military spending in a separate": Reeves, *President Reagan*, p. 20.

232 "government is not the solution": Cannon, *President Reagan*, p. 70.

232 "It is a myth": Reeves, *President Reagan*, p. 11.

233 "an odd mixture": Paul A. Volcker and Toyoo Ghoten, *Changing Fortunes: The World's Money and the Threat to American Leadership* (New York: Times Books, 1992).

233 "declared new guidelines for public policy": Reeves, *President Reagan*, p. 15.

233 "The Reagan economic program": Cannon, *President Reagan*, p. 199.

234 "wild assertion": Ibid., p. 758.

234 "you could have a big tax cut": David A. Stockman, *The Triumph of Politics: How the Reagan Revolution Failed* (New York: Harper and Row, 1986), p. 396.

234 "soggy economy": Ronald Reagan, "Remarks on Signing the Economic Recovery Act of 1981 and the Omnibus Budget Reconciliation Act of 1981," Question and answer session with the press, August 13, 1981, The American Presidency Project, www.presidency.ucsb .edu/ws/index.php?pid=44161.

234 "breezy optimism": Reeves, *President Reagan*, p. 20.

234 By 1982, 41 percent: Wattenberg, *First Universal Nation*, p. 248.

234 "if it comes down to": Interview with Caspar Weinberger, in Reeves, *President Reagan*, p. 92.

235 "They are in very bad shape": Ronald Reagan, *An American Life* (New York: Simon and Schuster, 1990), p. 316, in Reeves, *President Reagan*, p. 104.

235 "50 percent decline": Reeves, *President Reagan*, p. 104. Reeves cites a CIA memo dated June 1, 1982, that estimated that the USSR's growth rate had fallen from 5.5–5.9 percent in the 1950s to 2.7–3.7 percent in the 1970s.

235 "a policy of . . . forcing the USSR": National Security Decision Directive Number 32, May 20, 1982.

235 a long-term research and development program: Ronald Reagan, Address on Defense and National Security, March 23, 1984, http://www.thereaganlegacy.com/version2/ speechesdetails.asp?sID=33.

236 "cleaning up the CIA": Cannon, *President Reagan*, p. 61.

236 "We need to be backing": Peter Schweitzer, *Victory: The Reagan Administration's Secret Strategy that Hastened the Collapse of the Soviet Union* (New York: Atlantic Monthly Press, 1994), p. 23, in James M. Scott, "Reagan Doctrine? The Formulation of an American Foreign Policy Strategy," *Presidential Studies Quarterly* 26, no. 4 (Fall 1996), p. 1047.

236 "the United States was escalating": George Crile, *Charlie Wilson's War: The Extraordinary Story of the Largest Covert Operation in History* (New York: Atlantic Monthly Press, 2003), pp. 489–50.

237 "your problem is your witness": Interview with Robert McFarlane, September 6, 2006.

237 "the president's numbers": Reeves, *President Reagan*, p. 118.

237 Fiscal conservatives: Cannon, *President Reagan*, p. 198.

237 Robert Dole: Reeves, *President Reagan*, p. 119.

237 "warned the President": Lawrence Malkin, *The National Debt: How America Crashed into a Black Hole and How We Can Crawl Out* (New York: Henry Holt, 1987), p. 207.

238 "Extremely Confidential": Craig Fuller, Economic/Budget Policy, March 1982, White House Staff and Office Files, box 10972 (2 of 2), Ronald Reagan Presidential Library and Museum, in Reeves, *President Reagan*, pp. 100–101.

238 "believed inflation was 'a thief in the night' ": Interview with Peggy Noonan, September 22, 2006.

239 "I certainly want to see some more action": House Committee on Banking, Finance,

and Urban Development, Paul A. Volcker, Federal Reserve Board, *Hearing before the House Committee on Banking, Finance, and Urban Development*, 97th Cong., 2nd sess., July 21, 1982, serial no. 97–67t.

239 "revenue enhancers": Reeves, *President Reagan*, p. 122.

241 "We can't grow ourselves out": Ibid., p. 211.

241 "We are not going to let [the Republicans] tear asunder": Cannon, *President Reagan*, p. 203.

242 "The press is trying to paint me": Reagan, *An American Life*, p. 316.

242 "ruled out cuts in two": Cannon, *President Reagan*, pp. 103–4.

242 "the No. 1 special pleader in town": Dick Cheney, Opinion-Editorial, *Washington Post*, December 16, 1984.

242 In 1985, the deficit: Reeves, *President Reagan*, p. 243.

243 "force the president to choose": Editorial, *Baltimore Sun*, December 10, 1985, in Reeves, *President Reagan*, p. 303.

243 "in the eyes of the people": "For the Historical Record: Gorbachev: Reagan's Star Wars Did Not Force End of Soviet Union," *New Perspectives Quarterly*, 13, no. 1 (Winter 1996).

244 "telling me that we must pay for": Ronald Reagan, Remarks on Signing the Bill to Increase the Federal Debt Ceiling, September 29, 1987, http://www.reagan.utexas.edu/archives/speeches/1987/092987c.htm.

246 "broken all the rules": Malkin, *National Debt*, p. 209.

247 "the more starry-eyed Reaganauts": Volcker and Gyohten, *Changing Fortunes*, p. 177.

247 "Rather than increasing savings": Michael Mandel, "Lessons of the Reagan Years," *Business Week*, August 19, 1996.

249 "I feel very strongly": Deborah Hart Strober and Gerald Strober, *Reagan: The Man and His Presidency* (Boston: Houghton Mifflin, 1998), p. 371, in Reeves, *President Reagan*, p. xv.

9. NEW ENEMIES

251 "our allies and friends": 'tin cup' trip": George Bush and Brent Scowcroft, *A World Transformed* (New York: Alfred A. Knopf, 1998), p. 360.

254 "Congress demanded to know": Ibid., p. 354.

254 "no nation will be permitted": George H. W. Bush, Address Announcing War against Iraq, January 16, 1991, The History Place, http://historyplace.com/speeches/bush-war.htm.

255 "It was not initially planned that way": Conversation with President George H. W. Bush.

256 "now-now-ism": E. J. Dionne Jr., "Spending, Politics and Darman's Slap at the Profligate American," *New York Times*, July 30, 1989, section 4, p. 4.

256 Allowing the sequesters: Richard Darman, *Who's in Control? Polar Politics and the Sensible Center* (New York: Simon and Schuster, 1996), p. 277.

256 "did not believe that the political system": Ibid.

257 "would pursue tight": E-mail from Richard Darman, February 23, 2006.

257 "When push came to shove": Bush and Scowcroft, *World Transformed*, p. 390.

258 "I was very disappointed": Ibid., p. 380.

258 "were less than half the size": Darman, *Who's In Control?*, p. 272.

259 "had very much wished": Ibid., p. 277.

259 "had the virtue not only of contributing": Brownlee, *Federal Taxation on America*, p. 189.

260 "Americans should not expect": George W. Bush, Address to Joint Session of Congress, "War on Terrorism," 107th Cong., 1st sess., September 20, 2001.
260 "This will be a war": Donald Rumsfeld, Op-Ed, *New York Times*, September 27, 2001.
261 "terrorist attacks have created": Corey Robin, "Remembrance of Empires Past: 9/11 and the End of the Cold War," prepared for the "Cold War Triumphalism" Conference at New York University, April 19–20, 2002.
262 After 9/11: National Commission on Terrorist Attacks, *The 9/11 Commission Report* (Washington, D.C.: U.S. Government Printing Office, 2004), p. 362, http://www.9-11commission.gov/report/911Report.pdf.
263 "further diplomatic and other peaceful means": George W. Bush, Letter to the Speaker of the House and the President Pro-Temporary of the Senate, March 21, 2003, http://www.whitehouse.gov/news/releases/2003/03/20030321-5.html.
263 "very, very high": Richard Davis, "Bush Economic Aid Says Cost of Iraq War May Top $100 Billion," *Wall Street Journal*, September 16, 2002.
263 "baloney": Interview, Donald R. Rumsfeld, *This Week with George Stephanopoulos*, ABC News, January 19, 2003.
264 "The United States is committed to helping Iraq recover": *Washington Post*, April 21, 2003.
264 "I don't think he or she knows": Thomas E. Ricks, *Fiasco: The American Military Adventure in Iraq* (New York: Penguin Press, 2006), p. 198.
264 The head of the U.S. Agency for International Development: Ibid., p. 109.
264 Defense Department's budget totaled $290 billion: Budget Office, "Budget and Economic Outlook: An Update," August 17, 2006, http://www.cbo.gov/budget/budproj.shtml.
264 "oil revenues": Defense Subcommittee of the House Appropriations Committee, *Hearing on a Supplementary War Requisition before the Defense Subcommittee of the House Appropriations Committee*, March 27, 2003.
264 Pentagon task force warned: Jeff Gerth, "Report Offered Bleak Outlook About Iraq Oil," *New York Times*, October 5, 2003, p. A1.
264 L. Paul "Jerry" Bremer . . . submitted: *International Oil Daily*, September 22, 2003.
265 "We've got a huge coalition": Ricks, *Fiasco*, p. 346.
265 less than one-third had been disbursed: Jeremy M. Sharp and Christopher M. Blanchard, "Post-War Iraq: A Table and Chronology of Foreign Contributions, Updated" (Washington, D.C.: Congressional Research Service, March 2005).
266 "past Administrations have requested": Steve Daggett, "Military Operations: Precedents for Funding Contingency Operations in Regular or in Supplemental Appropriations Bills," June 13, 2006.
266 "The nature of the War on Terror": "GOP Leaders Work out Deal on Defense Spending," *Los Angeles Times*, September 22, 2006.
267 "The Bush administration has chosen": Jonathan Weisman and Shailagh Murray, "Emergency End-Run," *Washington Post*, May 12, 2005.
267 "really straightforward": Noam N. Levey, "GOP Leaders Work Out Deal on Defense Spending," *Los Angeles Times*, September 22, 2006.
267 "We're fighting a war on supplementals": "Congress Approves $82 Billion for Wars," *Washington Post*, May 11, 2005.
267 "because most of the costs": James A. Baker, Lee H. Hamilton, et al., *Iraq Study Group Report* (Washington, D.C.: U.S. Institute for Peace, 2006), p. 60, http://www.usip.org/isg/iraq_study_group_report/report/1206/index.html.
268 "the pace of the recovery": "President Bush Taking Action to Strengthen the American Economy," White House Press Office, fact sheet, January 7, 2003.
268 The congressional Joint Committee on Taxation: Joint Committee on Taxation Analysis of Bush 2004 Budget, Table JCX-15-03, March 4, 2003, in Joel Friedman, Richard

Kogan, and Denis Kadochnikov, "Administration's Tax Cutting Would Cost $2.7 Trillion Through 2013" (Washington, D.C.: Center on Budget and Policy Priorities, 2003).

268 "until Congress": David E. Rosenbaum, "Republicans Say They'll Cut Taxes Regardless of War," New York Times, March 19, 2003, p. A1.

268 "Nothing is more important": Tom DeLay, speech before America's Community Bankers meeting, March 12, 2003, as reported in "Congress Daily PM" (subscription only), National Journal, March 12, 2003, http://www.house.gov/georgemiller/lineoftheday31303.html.

268 "I heard somebody say": Jonathan Weisman, "The War and the Economy," Washington Post, September 16, 2003.

269 "international uncertainties": David E. Rosenbaum, "GOP Senators Oppose Size of Bush Tax Cut," New York Times, March 14, 2003.

269 "When you have a $300 billion deficit": David E. Rosenbaum, "Senate Votes to Reduce Bush's Tax Cut Plan," New York Times, March 26, 2003.

269 "unusually tense negotiation": David E. Rosenbaum and David Firestone, "$318 Billion Deal Set in Congress for Cutting Taxes," New York Times, May 22, 2003.

270 "Some in Washington say": Richard Kogan and Aviva Aron-Dine, "Claim that Tax Cuts 'Pay for Themselves' Is Too Good to Be True: Data Show There Is No Free Lunch," Center on Budget and Policy Priorities, July 11, 2006.

270 "When done right": Bill Frist, "Tax Cuts Make Money," Opinion-Editorial, USA Today, February 10, 2006.

271 Spending for discretionary programs: Stephen Slivinski, "The Grand Old Spending Party: How Republicans Became Big Spenders," The CATO Institute, Policy Analysis no. 543, May 3, 2005, p. 5, http://www.cato.org/pub_display.php?pub_id=3750.

272 The Congressional Research Service: Congressional Research Service Appropriations Team Memorandum, "Earmarks in FY 2006 Appropriations Acts," March 6, 2006, p. 10.

272 "The transportation, energy, information": Stephen Flynn, "The Neglected Home Front," Foreign Affairs 83, no. 5 (September/October 2004), p. 20.

272 "overall expenditures must be as much as tripled": Warren B. Rudman, chair, Richard A. Clarke, senior adviser, and Jamie F. Metzl, project director, Emergency Responders: Drastically Underfunded, Dangerously Unprepared (New York: Council on Foreign Relations Press, 2003), http://www.cfr.org/content/publications/attachments/Responders_TF.pdf.

273 "had not yet achieved its intended results": Eric Lipton, "Audit Faults U.S. for Its Spending on Port Defense," New York Times, February 20, 2005, p. A1.

273 "minimal progress": National Commission on Terrorist Attacks, "Report on the Status of 9/11 Commission Recommendations" (Washington, D.C.: U.S. Government Printing Office, September 14, 2005).

273 the largest such drop: James Horney and Richard Kogan, "Don't Pop the Corks: CBO Outlook for Federal Budget Is Still Bleak," Center on Budget and Policy Priorities, August 17, 2006.

273 "even with the spending for the wars": James Horney, "New CBO Deficit Estimate Indicates that Without Tax Cuts the Budget Would Be in Balance," Center on Budget and Policy Priorities, August 8, 2006.

274 If the recent tax cuts were to be made permanent: Congressional Budget Office, "Budget and Economic Outlook: An Update," August 17, 2006.

274 Concord Coalition: "Concord Coalition Warns that 10 Year Deficit Could Reach $5.7 Trillion," press release, August 15, 2005, Concord Coalition, Arlington, Va., http://www.concordcoalition.org/press/2005/050815release.htm.

274 "Although the economy grows": *Economic Report of the President* (Washington, D.C.: U.S. Government Printing Office, February 2003), pp. 57–58.

274 "supply side effect": Janet G. Gravelle, "Revenue Feedback from the 2001–2004 Tax Cuts" (Washington, D.C.: Congressional Research Service, September 27, 2006).

275 the CBO estimated: Congressional Budget Office, "The Budget and Economic Outlook: An Update," August 25, 2005, p. 17, http://www.cbo.gov/ftpdocs/66xx/doc6609/08-15-OutlookUpdate.pdf.

275 the Concord Coalition's scenario: Concord Coalition, press release, August 17, 2005.

278 "The cost of the war will be small": John Snow, U.S. Department of the Treasury, Testimony before the House Ways and Means Committee, *New York Times*, March 9, 2003.

279 "The danger, over the long term": R. W. Apple Jr., "Nature of Foe Is Obstacle in Appealing for Sacrifice," *New York Times*, October 15, 2001, p. B2.

CONCLUSION

280 "America's journey through international politics": Henry A. Kissinger, *Diplomacy* (New York: Simon and Schuster, 1994), p. 18.

283 "occur not because the government": Congressional Budget Office, "Budget and Economic Outlook: An Update," August 17, 2006.

285 "spent $500,000 on the event": Osama Bin Laden, Videotape, Al Jazeera TV, October 29, 2004.

285 "an acute awareness of where to hit": "Bin Laden's Target: U.S. Wallet," CBS News, November 2, 2004, http://www.cbsnews.com/stories/2004/10/29/terror/main652373.shtml.

286 "Panic selling of dollar assets": Gail Makinen, "Report for Congress: The Economic Effects of 9/11: A Retrospective Assessment" (Washington, D.C.: Congressional Research Service, September 27, 2002), http://www.fas.org/irp/crs/RL31617.pdf.

287 "international investors will adjust": Alan Greenspan, Remarks at the European Banking Congress, Frankfurt, Germany, November 19, 2004.

287 "It's hard to say to everybody": David Rosenbaum, "Afghanistan and Iraq Tab at $87 Billion in Subcommittee of the House of Representatives," *New York Times*, September 13, 2003, p. 1.

288 "Every gun that is made": Dwight D. Eisenhower, Speech to American Society of Newspaper Editors, April 16, 1953, Eisenhower Presidential Papers, 1953, p. 182, in John Lewis Gaddis, *Strategies of Containment: A Critical Appraisal of Postwar American National Security Policy* (New York: Oxford University Press, 1982), p. 133.

288 "unless Congress is willing to raise taxes considerably": "New Budget Outlook: A Little Good News and a Lot of Red Ink," Concord Coalition, press release, August 31, 2005, p. 8, http://www.concordcoalition.org/issues/fedbudget/issue-briefs/050831-cbo-issue-brief.pdf.

289 The CBO projected: Congressional Budget Office, "The Long-term Budget Outlook," December 2005, pp. 11–12.

289 "Continuing on this unsustainable path will gradually erode": Kathleen V. Shinasi, "DOD Acquisition Outcomes: A Case for Change," GAO-06-257T (Washington, D.C.: Government Accountability Office, November 15, 2005), p. 1, http://www.gao.gov/new.items/d06257t.pdf.

291 "tough choices will be required": Ibid.

292 "substantial reductions in the projected growth of spending": Congressional Budget Office, "Long-term Budget Outlook," December 2003, p. 17.

292 "Crucially, whatever size": Ben S. Bernanke, "Long-term Fiscal Challenges Facing the United States," testimony before the U.S. Senate Committee on the Budget, January 18, 2007, p. 3, http://www.federalreserve.gov/boarddocs/testimony/2007/20070118/default .htm.

292 "came to this office to confront problems directly and forcefully": George W. Bush, Remarks by the President on the Economy and the War on Terror, Radisson Hotel and Convention Center, San Bernardino California, October 16, 2003.

293 "No economic group except for the very needy": "Seven Signs of Fiscal Sense," Concord Coalition, December 19, 2005, p. 3, http://www.concordcoalition.org/issues/fedbudget/ doc/051219%20Seven_Signs_Cover.pdf.

293 Earmarks in the defense budget: Winslow T. Wheeler, "Congress, the Defense Budget and Pork: A Snout-to-tail Description of Congress's Foremost Concern in Security Legislation" (Washington, D.C.: The Independent Institute, August 21, 2006), http://www.independent.org/publications/policy_reports/detail.asp?type=full&id=21.

294 "running head-on": Shinasi, "DOD Acquisition Outcomes," p. 1.

294 "to rein in rapidly rising": Leslie Wayne, "White House Tries to Trim Military Cost," New York Times, December 6, 2005.

294 "requirements process generates": Shinasi, "DOD Acquisition Outcomes," p. 8.

295 "If [overall] deficits remain": Stephen Daggett, "Defense Budget: Long-Term Challenges for FY2006 and Beyond," RL32924 (Washington, D.C.: Congressional Research Service, April 20, 2005), p. 6, http://www.fas.org/sgp/crs/natsec/RL32924.pdf.

297 "The scientific evidence": "Stern Review: The Economics of Climate Change" (London: H.M. Treasury, October 30, 2006), http://www.hm-treasury.gov.uk./independent_ reviews/stern_review_economics_climate_change/stern_review_report.cfm.

297 "the moral equivalent of war": Jimmy Carter, "The President's Proposed Energy Policy," televised speech, April 18, 1977, http://www.mnforsustain.org/energy_speech_ president_carter.htm.

297 "Our oil dependence fuels the fundamentalism we're fighting": Joseph Biden, letter to the author, December 14, 2006.

297 "The global trend of foreign governments asserting greater control over oil and gas reserves": Richard Lugar, letter to the author, December, 14, 2006.

298 "could . . . scheme to wield weapons": National Commission on Terrorist Attacks, The 9/11 Commission Report (Washington, D.C.: U.S. Government Printing Office, 2004), p. 362, http://www.9-11commission.gov/report/911Report.pdf.

298 "bring merely short-term advantage but long-term disadvantage": Paul M. Kennedy, The Rise and Fall of the Great Powers: Economic Change and Military Conflict from 1500 to 2000 (New York: Random House, 1987), p. 534.

Selected Bibliography

Alexander, Charles C. *Holding the Line: The Eisenhower Era.* Bloomington: Indiana University Press, 1976.

Bender, Thomas. *A Nation Among Nations: America's Place in World History.* New York: Hill and Wang, 2006.

Blum, John Morton. *From the Morgenthau Diaries: The Years of War.* Boston: Houghton Mifflin, 1967.

———. *Roosevelt and Morgenthau: A Revision and Condensation from the Morgenthau Diaries.* Boston: Houghton Mifflin, 1970.

Brownlee, W. Elliot. *Federal Taxation on America: A Short History.* Cambridge: Cambridge University Press, 1996.

Buel, Richard, Jr. *America on the Brink: How the Political Struggle over the War of 1812 Almost Destroyed the Young Republic.* New York: Palgrave Macmillan, 2005.

Bush, George, and Brent Scowcroft. *A World Transformed.* New York: Alfred A. Knopf, 1998.

Califano, Joseph A., Jr. *The Triumph and Tragedy of Lyndon Johnson: The White House Years.* New York: Simon and Schuster, 1991.

Campagna, Anthony S. *The Economic Consequences of the War in Vietnam.* New York: Praeger, 1991.

Cannon, Lou. *President Reagan: The Role of a Lifetime.* New York: Public Affairs, 1982.

Caro, Robert A. *Master of the Senate: The Years of Lyndon Johnson.* New York: Alfred A. Knopf, 2002.

Chernow, Ron. *Alexander Hamilton.* New York: Penguin Press, 2004.

Darman, Richard. *Who's in Control? Polar Politics and the Sensible Center.* New York: Simon and Schuster, 1996.

Eisenhower, Dwight D. *Mandate for a Change.* Garden City, N.Y.: Doubleday, 1963.

Friedman, Benjamin M. *The Moral Consequences of Economic Growth.* New York: Alfred A. Knopf, 2005.

Friedman, Milton, and Anna Jacobsen Schwartz. *A Monetary History of the United States, 1867–1960.* Princeton, N.J.: Princeton University Press, 1963.

Gaddis, John Lewis. *The Origins of the Cold War, 1941–1947.* New York: Columbia University Press, 1972.

Gilbert, Charles. *American Financing.* Westport, Conn.: Greenwood Press, 1970.

Goodwin, Doris Kearns. *Lyndon Johnson and the American Dream*. New York: St. Martin's Press, 1991.

———. *Team of Rivals: The Political Genius of Abraham Lincoln*. New York: Simon and Schuster, 2005.

Gordon, John Steele. *An Empire of Wealth: The Epic History of American Economic Power*. New York: HarperCollins, 2004.

Helsing, Jeffery W. *Johnson's War/Johnson's Great Society: The Guns and Butter Trap*. Westport, Conn.: Praeger, 2000.

Isaacson, Walter, and Evan Thomas. *The Wise Men: Six Friends and the World They Made—Acheson, Bohlen, Harriman, Kennan, Lovett, McCloy*. New York: Simon and Schuster, 1986.

Janeway, Eliot. *The Economics of Crisis: War, Politics & the Dollar*. New York: Weybright and Talley, 1968.

Johnson, Paul. *A History of the American People*. New York: HarperCollins, 1998.

Kennedy, Paul. *The Rise and Fall of the Great Powers: Economic Change and Military Conflict from 1500 to 2000*. New York: Random House, 1988.

Kennon, Donald R., and Rebecca M. Rogers. *The Committee on Ways and Means: A Bicentennial History, 1789–1989*. Washington, D.C.: U.S. Government Printing Office, 1989.

Macdonald, James. *A Free Nation Deep in Debt: The Financial Roots of Democracy*. New York: Farrar, Straus, and Giroux, 2003.

Malkin, Lawrence. *The National Debt: How America Crashed into a Black Hole and How We Can Crawl Out*. New York: Henry Holt, 1987.

McAdoo, William G. *Crowded Years: The Reminiscences of William G. McAdoo*. Boston: Houghton Mifflin/Riverside Press, 1931.

McNamara, Robert S. *In Retrospect: The Tragedy and Lessons of Vietnam*. New York: Vintage Books, 1996.

McPherson, James M. *Battle Cry of Freedom: The Civil War Era*. New York: Ballantine Books, 1988.

Mead, Walter Russell. *Special Providence: American Foreign Policy and How It Changed the World*. New York: Alfred A. Knopf, 2001.

Mellon, Andrew. *Taxation: The People's Business*. New York: Macmillan, 1929.

National Commission on Terrorist Attacks. *The 9/11 Commission Report*. Washington, D.C.: U.S. Government Printing Office, 2004.

Okun, Arthur M. *The Political Economy of Prosperity*. Washington, D.C.: Brookings Institution, 1970.

Ratner, Sidney. *American Taxation: Its History as a Social Force in Democracy*. New York: W. W. Norton, 1942.

Reeves, Richard. *President Reagan: The Triumph of Imagination*. New York: Simon and Schuster, 2005.

Schlesinger, Arthur M., Jr. *War and the American Presidency*. New York: W. W. Norton, 2004.

Seligman, Edwin R. A. *The Income Tax: A Study of the History, Theory and Practice of Income Taxation at Home and Abroad*, 3rd edition. New York: Augustus M. Kelly, 1970.

Skidelsky, Robert. *John Maynard Keynes: Fighting for Freedom, 1937–1946*. New York: Penguin Books, 2000.

Smith, Adam. *An Inquiry into the Nature and Causes of the Wealth of Nations*. New York: Random House, 1937.

Stockman, David A. *The Triumph of Politics: How the Reagan Revolution Failed*. New York: Harper and Row, 1986.

Studenski, Paul, and Herman Edward Kroos. *The Financial History of the United States*. Washington, D.C.: Beard Books, 2003.

Summer, William G. *A History of American Currency.* New York: Henry Holt, 1876.

Thorndike, Joseph J. "An Army of Officials; The Civil War Bureau of Internal Revenue." Tax History Museum, December 21, 2001, http://www.tax.org/Museum/default.htm.

———. "The Price of Civilization: Taxation in Depression and War, 1933–1945." Tax History Museum, February 23, 2003, http://www.tax.org/Museum/default.htm.

U.S. Senate. *History of the Committee on Finance.* 97th Cong. 1st sess., 1981, Senate doc. 97–5, http://www.senate.finance.gov/history.pdf.

Volcker, Paul A., and Toyoo Ghoyten. *Changing Fortunes: The World's Money and the Threat to American Leadership.* New York: Times Books, 1992.

Wattenberg, Ben J. *The First Universal Nation: Leading Indicators and Ideas about the Surge of America in the 1990s.* New York: The Free Press, 1991.

Webber, Caroline, and Aaron Wildavasy. *A History of Taxation and Expenditure in the Western World.* New York: Simon and Schuster, 1966.

Weisman, Steven R. *The Great Tax Wars.* New York: Simon and Schuster, 2002.

Woolley, John, and Gerhard Peters. The American Presidency Project, University of California, Santa Barbara. http://www.presidency.ucsb.edu/.

Zelizer, Julian E., ed. *The American Congress: The Building of Democracy.* Boston: Houghton Mifflin, 2004.

———. *Taxing America: Wilbur D. Mills, Congress and the State: 1945–1975.* Cambridge: Cambridge University Press, 1998.

Acknowledgments

I wish to thank the many people who were so helpful to me in the various stages of writing this book.

I would especially like to thank Professor David M. Kennedy, Professor Richard Buel Jr., General John S. Brown, Professor John Lewis Gaddis, Paul A. Volcker, Robert Zoellick, Richard Reeves, Professor Charles Calomaris, Richard Darman, Douglas Holtz-Eakin, Jim Horney, Edward Lorenzen, Peggy Noonan, Robert McFarlane, Bill Janeway, Stephen Flynn, David Rothkopf, General David Melcher, R. Glenn Hubbard, Richard Greco, and Faryar Shirzad for taking the time to provide thoughtful and constructive comments, which added enormously to the quality and content of this book.

My old graduate school classmate Richard Weintraub deserves special credit for his intrepid reading of the text and for providing candid, thoughtful, and helpful comments. Nancy Nicholas and Loretta Sunnucks provided very skillful edits and highly useful suggestions. My assistant Kimberley D. Bentley showed great patience and thoughtfulness in helping to organize, produce, collate, and edit this book from start to finish. Daniel Hirsch, Saul Steinberg, Amanda McCaughey, Caroline McCaughey, and Diana McCaughey provided great encouragement and support during the process. The guidance of Paul Golob, the editorial director of Times Books, and the dedication of Chris O'Connell, the production editor, were of immeasurable help. Finally, I would like to thank my agent, Mort Janklow, for his wisdom and guidance in making this happen and my editor, Robin Dennis at Times Books, for her unflagging patience, persistence in pressing me to meet tight deadlines, tolerance of my poor handwriting, and sound advice during the months of producing this.

Index

ABOUT THE AUTHOR

ROBERT D. HORMATS is the vice chairman of Goldman Sachs (International) and a managing director of Goldman, Sachs & Co. He has served in numerous presidential administrations as a member of the National Security Council staff, deputy U.S. trade representative, and assistant secretary of state. A former member of the board of directors of the Council on Foreign Relations, he writes frequently for *The Wall Street Journal, Financial Times, The New York Times,* and *Foreign Affairs.* He lives in New York City.